Apache Solr 3 Enterprise Search Server

Enhance your search with faceted navigation, result highlighting, relevancy ranked sorting, and more

David Smiley

Eric Pugh

BIRMINGHAM - MUMBAI

Apache Solr 3 Enterprise Search Server

First published: August 2009

Second published: November 2011

Production Reference: 2071111

Published by Packt Publishing Ltd.
Livery Place
35 Livery Street
Birmingham B3 2PB, UK.

ISBN 978-1-84951-606-8

www.packtpub.com

Cover Image by Duraid Fatouhi (duraidfatouhi@yahoo.com)

Credits

Authors

David Smiley

Eric Pugh

Reviewers

Jerome Eteve

Mauricio Scheffer

Acquisition Editor

Sarah Cullington

Development Editors

Shreerang Deshpande

Gaurav Mehta

Technical Editor

Kavita Iyer

Project Coordinator

Joel Goveya

Proofreader

Steve Maguire

Indexers

Hemangini Bari

Rekha Nair

Production Coordinator

Alwin Roy

Cover Work

Alwin Roy

About the Authors

Born to code, **David Smiley** is a senior software engineer with a passion for programming and open source. He has written a book, taught a class, and presented at conferences on the subject of Solr. He has 12 years of experience in the defense industry at MITRE, using Java and various web technologies. Recently, David has been focusing his attention on the intersection of geospatial technologies with Lucene and Solr.

David first used Lucene in 2000 and was immediately struck by its speed and novelty. Years later he had the opportunity to work with Compass, a Lucene based library. In 2008, David built an enterprise people and project search service with Solr, with a focus on search relevancy tuning. David began to learn everything there is to know about Solr, culminating with the publishing of *Solr 1.4 Enterprise Search Server* in 2009 — the first book on Solr. He has since developed and taught a two-day Solr course for MITRE and he regularly offers technical advice to MITRE and its customers on the use of Solr. David also has experience using Endeca's competing product, which has broadened his experience in the search field.

On a technical level, David has solved challenging problems with Lucene and Solr including geospatial search, wildcard ngram query parsing, searching multiple multi-valued fields at coordinated positions, and part-of-speech search using Lucene payloads. In the area of geospatial search, David open sourced his geohash prefix/ grid based work to the Solr community tracked as SOLR-2155. This work has led to presentations at two conferences. Presently, David is collaborating with other Lucene and Solr committers on geospatial search.

Acknowledgement

Most, if not all authors seem to dedicate their book to someone. As simply a reader of books I have thought of this seeming prerequisite as customary tradition. That was my feeling before I embarked on writing about Solr, a project that has sapped my previously "free" time on nights and weekends for a year. I chose this sacrifice and want no pity for what was my decision, but my wife, family and friends did not choose it. I am married to my lovely wife Sylvie who has easily sacrificed as much as I have to work on this project. She has suffered through the first edition with an absentee husband while bearing our first child — Camille. The second edition was a similar circumstance with the birth of my second daughter — Adeline. I officially dedicate this book to my wife Sylvie and my daughters Camille and Adeline, who I both lovingly adore. I also pledge to read book dedications with new-found first-hand experience at what the dedication represents.

I would also like to thank others who helped bring this book to fruition. Namely, if it were not for Doug Cutting creating Lucene with an open source license, there would be no Solr. Furthermore, CNET's decision to open source what was an in-house project, Solr itself, in 2006, deserves praise. Many corporations do not understand that open source isn't just "free code" you get for free that others write: it is an opportunity to let your code flourish in the outside instead of it withering inside. Last, but not the least, this book would not have been completed in a reasonable time were it not for the assistance of my contributing author, Eric Pugh. His own perspectives and experiences have complemented mine so well that I am absolutely certain the quality of this book is much better than what I could have done alone.

Thank you all.

David Smiley

Eric Pugh has been fascinated by the "craft" of software development, and has been heavily involved in the open source world as a developer, committer, and user for the past five years. He is an emeritus member of the Apache Software Foundation and lately has been mulling over how we solve the problem of finding answers in datasets when we don't know the questions ahead of time to ask.

In biotech, financial services, and defense IT, he has helped European and American companies develop coherent strategies for embracing open source search software. As a speaker, he has advocated the advantages of Agile practices with a focus on testing in search engine implementation.

Eric became involved with Solr when he submitted the patch SOLR-284 for Parsing Rich Document types such as PDF and MS Office formats that became the single most popular patch as measured by votes! The patch was subsequently cleaned up and enhanced by three other individuals, demonstrating the power of the open source model to build great code collaboratively. SOLR-284 was eventually refactored into Solr Cell as part of Solr version 1.4.

He blogs at http://www.opensourceconnections.com/

Acknowledgement

When the topic of producing an update of this book for Solr 3 first came up, I thought it would be a matter of weeks to complete it. However, when David Smiley and I sat down to scope out what to change about the book, it was immediately apparent that we didn't want to just write an update for the latest Solr, we wanted to write a complete second edition of the book. We added a chapter, moved around content, rewrote whole sections of the book. David put in many more long nights than I over the past 9 months writing what I feel justifiable in calling the Second Edition of our book. So I must thank his wife Sylvie for being so supportive of him!

I also want to thank again Erik Hatcher for his continuing support and mentorship. Without his encouragement I wouldn't have spoken at Euro Lucene, or become involved in the Blacklight community.

I also want to thank all of my colleagues at OpenSource Connections. We've come a long way as a company in the last 18 months, and I look forward to the next 18 months. Our Friday afternoon hack sessions re-invigorate me every week!

My darling wife Kate, I know 2011 turned into a very busy year, but I couldn't be happier sharing my life with you, Morgan, and baby Asher. I love you.

Lastly I want to thank all the adopters of Solr and Lucene! Without you, I wouldn't have this wonderful open source project to be so incredibly proud to be a part of! I look forward to meeting more of you at the next LuceneRevolution or Euro Lucene conference.

About the Reviewers

Jerome Eteve holds a MSc in IT and Sciences from the University of Lille (France). After starting his career in the field of bioinformatics where he worked as a Biological Data Management and Analysis Consultant, he's now a Senior Application Developer with interests ranging from architecture to delivering a great user experience online. He's passionate about open source technologies, search engines, and web application architecture.

He now works for WCN Plc, a leading provider of recruitment software solutions.

He has worked on Packt's *Enterprise Solr* published in 2009.

Mauricio Scheffer is a software developer currently living in Buenos Aires, Argentina. He's worked in dot-coms on almost everything related to web application development, from architecture to user experience. He's very active in the open source community, having contributed to several projects and started many projects of his own. In 2007 he wrote SolrNet, a popular open source Solr interface for the .NET platform. Currently he's also researching the application of functional programming to web development as part of his Master's thesis.

He blogs at http://bugsquash.blogspot.com.

www.PacktPub.com

This book is published by Packt Publishing. You might want to visit Packt's website at www.PacktPub.com and take advantage of the following features and offers:

Discounts

Have you bought the print copy or Kindle version of this book? If so, you can get a massive 85% off the price of the eBook version, available in PDF, ePub, and MOBI.

Simply go to http://www.packtpub.com/apache-solr-3-enterprise-search-server/book, add it to your cart, and enter the following discount code:

as3esebk

Free eBooks

If you sign up to an account on www.PacktPub.com, you will have access to nine free eBooks.

Newsletters

Sign up for Packt's newsletters, which will keep you up to date with offers, discounts, books, and downloads.

You can set up your subscription at www.PacktPub.com/newsletters.

Code Downloads, Errata and Support

Packt supports all of its books with errata. While we work hard to eradicate errors from our books, some do creep in. Meanwhile, many Packt books have accompanying snippets of code to download.

You can find errata and code downloads at www.PacktPub.com/support.

 **PACKT**LiB

PacktLib.PacktPub.com

PacktLib offers instant solutions to your IT questions. It is Packt's fully searchable online digital book library, accessible from any device with a web browser.

- Contains every Packt book ever published. That's over 100,000 pages of content.
- Fully searchable. Find an immediate solution to your problem.
- Copy, paste, print, and bookmark content.
- Available on demand via your web browser.

If you have a Packt account, you might want to have a look at the nine free books which you can access now on PacktLib. Head to PacktLib.PacktPub.com and log in or register.

Table of Contents

Preface	**1**
Chapter 1: Quick Starting Solr	**7**
An introduction to Solr	**7**
Lucene, the underlying engine	8
Solr, a Lucene-based search server	9
Comparison to database technology	10
Getting started	**11**
Solr's installation directory structure	12
Solr's home directory and Solr cores	14
Running Solr	15
A quick tour of Solr	**16**
Loading sample data	18
A simple query	20
Some statistics	23
The sample browse interface	24
Configuration files	**25**
Resources outside this book	**27**
Summary	**28**
Chapter 2: Schema and Text Analysis	**29**
MusicBrainz.org	**30**
One combined index or separate indices	**31**
One combined index	32
Problems with using a single combined index	33
Separate indices	34
Schema design	**35**
Step 1: Determine which searches are going to be powered by Solr	36
Step 2: Determine the entities returned from each search	36
Step 3: Denormalize related data	37

Denormalizing—'one-to-one' associated data   37
Denormalizing—'one-to-many' associated data   38
Step 4: (Optional) Omit the inclusion of fields only used in search results   39
The schema.xml file   **40**
Defining field types   41
Built-in field type classes   42
Numbers and dates   42
Geospatial   43
Field options   43
Field definitions   44
Dynamic field definitions   45
Our MusicBrainz field definitions   46
Copying fields   48
The unique key   49
The default search field and query operator   49
Text analysis   **50**
Configuration   51
Experimenting with text analysis   54
Character filters   55
Tokenization   57
WordDelimiterFilter   59
Stemming   61
Correcting and augmenting stemming   62
Synonyms   63
Index-time versus query-time, and to expand or not   64
Stop words   65
Phonetic sounds-like analysis   66
Substring indexing and wildcards   67
ReversedWildcardFilter   68
N-grams   69
N-gram costs   70
Sorting Text   71
Miscellaneous token filters   72
Summary   **73**
Chapter 3: Indexing Data   **75**
Communicating with Solr   **76**
Direct HTTP or a convenient client API   76
Push data to Solr or have Solr pull it   76
Data formats   76
HTTP POSTing options to Solr   77
Remote streaming   79
Solr's Update-XML format   **80**

Deleting documents	81
Commit, optimize, and rollback	**82**
Sending CSV formatted data to Solr	**84**
Configuration options	86
The Data Import Handler Framework	**87**
Setup	88
The development console	89
Writing a DIH configuration file	90
Data Sources	90
Entity processors	91
Fields and transformers	92
Example DIH configurations	94
Importing from databases	94
Importing XML from a file with XSLT	96
Importing multiple rich document files (crawling)	97
Importing commands	98
Delta imports	99
Indexing documents with Solr Cell	**100**
Extracting text and metadata from files	100
Configuring Solr	101
Solr Cell parameters	102
Extracting karaoke lyrics	104
Indexing richer documents	106
Update request processors	**109**
Summary	**110**
Chapter 4: Searching	**111**
Your first search, a walk-through	**112**
Solr's generic XML structured data representation	**114**
Solr's XML response format	**115**
Parsing the URL	116
Request handlers	**117**
Query parameters	**119**
Search criteria related parameters	119
Result pagination related parameters	120
Output related parameters	121
Diagnostic related parameters	121
Query parsers and local-params	**122**
Query syntax (the lucene query parser)	**123**
Matching all the documents	125
Mandatory, prohibited, and optional clauses	125
Boolean operators	126
Sub-queries	127

Limitations of prohibited clauses in sub-queries	128
Field qualifier	128
Phrase queries and term proximity	129
Wildcard queries	129
Fuzzy queries	131
Range queries	131
Date math	132
Score boosting	133
Existence (and non-existence) queries	134
Escaping special characters	134
The Dismax query parser (part 1)	**135**
Searching multiple fields	137
Limited query syntax	137
Min-should-match	138
Basic rules	138
Multiple rules	139
What to choose	140
A default search	140
Filtering	**141**
Sorting	**142**
Geospatial search	**143**
Indexing locations	143
Filtering by distance	144
Sorting by distance	145
Summary	**146**
Chapter 5: Search Relevancy	**147**
Scoring	**148**
Query-time and index-time boosting	149
Troubleshooting queries and scoring	149
Dismax query parser (part 2)	**151**
Lucene's DisjunctionMaxQuery	152
Boosting: Automatic phrase boosting	153
Configuring automatic phrase boosting	153
Phrase slop configuration	154
Partial phrase boosting	154
Boosting: Boost queries	155
Boosting: Boost functions	156
Add or multiply boosts?	157
Function queries	**158**
Field references	159
Function reference	160
Mathematical primitives	161
Other math	161

ord and rord	162
Miscellaneous functions	162
Function query boosting	164
Formula: Logarithm	164
Formula: Inverse reciprocal	165
Formula: Reciprocal	167
Formula: Linear	168
How to boost based on an increasing numeric field	168
Step by step…	169
External field values	170
How to boost based on recent dates	170
Step by step…	170
Summary	**171**
Chapter 6: Faceting	**173**
A quick example: Faceting release types	**174**
MusicBrainz schema changes	176
Field requirements	**178**
Types of faceting	**178**
Faceting field values	**179**
Alphabetic range bucketing	181
Faceting numeric and date ranges	**182**
Range facet parameters	185
Facet queries	**187**
Building a filter query from a facet	**188**
Field value filter queries	189
Facet range filter queries	189
Excluding filters (multi-select faceting)	**190**
Hierarchical faceting	**194**
Summary	**196**
Chapter 7: Search Components	**197**
About components	**198**
The Highlight component	**200**
A highlighting example	200
Highlighting configuration	202
The regex fragmenter	205
The fast vector highlighter with multi-colored highlighting	205
The SpellCheck component	**207**
Schema configuration	208
Configuration in solrconfig.xml	209
Configuring spellcheckers (dictionaries)	211
Processing of the q parameter	213
Processing of the spellcheck.q parameter	213
Building the dictionary from its source	214

Issuing spellcheck requests	215
Example usage for a misspelled query	217
Query complete / suggest	**219**
Query term completion via facet.prefix	221
Query term completion via the Suggester	223
Query term completion via the Terms component	226
The QueryElevation component	**227**
Configuration	228
The MoreLikeThis component	**230**
Configuration parameters	231
Parameters specific to the MLT search component	231
Parameters specific to the MLT request handler	231
Common MLT parameters	232
MLT results example	234
The Stats component	**236**
Configuring the stats component	237
Statistics on track durations	237
The Clustering component	**238**
Result grouping/Field collapsing	**239**
Configuring result grouping	241
The TermVector component	**243**
Summary	**243**
Chapter 8: Deployment	**245**
Deployment methodology for Solr	**245**
Questions to ask	246
Installing Solr into a Servlet container	**247**
Differences between Servlet containers	248
Defining solr.home property	248
Logging	**249**
HTTP server request access logs	250
Solr application logging	251
Configuring logging output	252
Logging using Log4j	253
Jetty startup integration	253
Managing log levels at runtime	254
A SearchHandler per search interface?	**254**
Leveraging Solr cores	**256**
Configuring solr.xml	256
Property substitution	258
Include fragments of XML with XInclude	259
Managing cores	259
Why use multicore?	261

Monitoring Solr performance   **262**
  Stats.jsp   263
  JMX   264
    Starting Solr with JMX   265
Securing Solr from prying eyes   **270**
  Limiting server access   270
    Securing public searches   272
    Controlling JMX access   273
  Securing index data   273
    Controlling document access   273
    Other things to look at   274
Summary   **275**
Chapter 9: Integrating Solr   **277**
Working with included examples   **278**
  Inventory of examples   278
Solritas, the integrated search UI   **279**
  Pros and Cons of Solritas   281
SolrJ: Simple Java interface   **283**
  Using Heritrix to download artist pages   283
  SolrJ-based client for Indexing HTML   285
  SolrJ client API   287
    Embedding Solr   288
    Searching with SolrJ   289
    Indexing   290
  When should I use embedded Solr?   294
    In-process indexing   294
    Standalone desktop applications   295
    Upgrading from legacy Lucene   295
Using JavaScript with Solr   **296**
  Wait, what about security?   297
  Building a Solr powered artists autocomplete widget with jQuery and JSONP   298
  AJAX Solr   303
Using XSLT to expose Solr via OpenSearch   **305**
  OpenSearch based Browse plugin   306
    Installing the Search MBArtists plugin   306
Accessing Solr from PHP applications   **309**
  solr-php-client   310
  Drupal options   311
    Apache Solr Search integration module   312
    Hosted Solr by Acquia   312
Ruby on Rails integrations   **313**
  The Ruby query response writer   313

sunspot_rails gem	**314**
Setting up MyFaves project	315
Populating MyFaves relational database from Solr	316
Build Solr indexes from a relational database	318
Complete MyFaves website	320
Which Rails/Ruby library should I use?	**322**
Nutch for crawling web pages	**323**
Maintaining document security with ManifoldCF	**324**
Connectors	325
Putting ManifoldCF to use	325
Summary	**328**
Chapter 10: Scaling Solr	**329**
Tuning complex systems	**330**
Testing Solr performance with SolrMeter	**332**
Optimizing a single Solr server (Scale up)	**334**
Configuring JVM settings to improve memory usage	334
MMapDirectoryFactory to leverage additional virtual memory	335
Enabling downstream HTTP caching	335
Solr caching	338
Tuning caches	339
Indexing performance	340
Designing the schema	340
Sending data to Solr in bulk	341
Don't overlap commits	342
Disabling unique key checking	343
Index optimization factors	343
Enhancing faceting performance	345
Using term vectors	345
Improving phrase search performance	346
Moving to multiple Solr servers (Scale horizontally)	**348**
Replication	349
Starting multiple Solr servers	349
Configuring replication	351
Load balancing searches across slaves	352
Indexing into the master server	352
Configuring slaves	353
Configuring load balancing	354
Sharding indexes	356
Assigning documents to shards	357
Searching across shards (distributed search)	358
Combining replication and sharding (Scale deep)	**360**
Near real time search	362
Where next for scaling Solr?	**363**
Summary	**364**

Appendix: Search Quick Reference   365
Quick reference   366
Index   369

Preface

If you are a developer building an application today then you know how important a good search experience is. Apache Solr, built on Apache Lucene, is a wildly popular open source enterprise search server that easily delivers powerful search and faceted navigation features that are elusive with databases. Solr supports complex search criteria, faceting, result highlighting, query-completion, query spellcheck, relevancy tuning, and more.

Apache Solr 3 Enterprise Search Server is a comprehensive reference guide for every feature Solr has to offer. It serves the reader right from initiation to development to deployment. It also comes with complete running examples to demonstrate its use and show how to integrate Solr with other languages and frameworks.

Through using a large set of metadata about artists, releases, and tracks courtesy of the `MusicBrainz.org` project, you will have a testing ground for Solr, and will learn how to import this data in various ways. You will then learn how to search this data in different ways, including Solr's rich query syntax and "boosting" match scores based on record data. Finally, we'll cover various deployment considerations to include indexing strategies and performance-oriented configuration that will enable you to scale Solr to meet the needs of a high-volume site.

What this book covers

Chapter 1, Quick Starting Solr, will introduce Solr to you so that you understand its unique role in your application stack. You'll get started quickly by indexing example data and searching it with Solr's sample "/browse" UI.

Chapter 2, Schema and Text Analysis, explains that the first step in using Solr is writing a Solr schema for your data. You'll learn how to do this including telling Solr how to analyze the text for tokenization, synonyms, stemming, and more.

Chapter 3, Indexing Data, will explore all of the options Solr offers for importing data, such as XML, CSV, databases (SQL), and text extraction from common documents.

Chapter 4, Searching, you'll learn the basics of searching with Solr in this chapter. Primarily, this covers the query syntax, from the basics to boolean options to more advanced wildcard and fuzzy searches.

Chapter 5, Search Relevancy, in this advanced chapter you will learn how Solr scores documents for relevancy ranking. We'll review different options to influence the score, called boosting, and apply it to common examples like boosting recent documents and boosting by a user vote.

Chapter 6, Faceting, faceting is Solr's killer feature and this chapter will show you how to use it. You'll learn about the three types of facets and how to build filter queries for a faceted navigation interface.

Chapter 7, Search Components, you'll discover how to use a variety of valuable search features implemented as Solr search components. This includes result highlighting, query spell-check, query suggest/complete, result grouping, and more.

Chapter 8, Deployment, will guide you through deployment considerations in this chapter to include deploying Solr to Apache Tomcat, to logging, and to security.

Chapter 9, Integrating Solr, will explore some external integration options to interface with Solr. This includes some language specific frameworks for Java, Ruby, PHP, and JavaScript, as well as a web crawler, and more.

Chapter 10, Scaling Solr, you'll learn how to tune Solr to get the most out of it. Then we'll show you two mechanisms in Solr to scale out to multiple Solr instances when just one instance isn't sufficient.

Appendix, Search Quick Reference, is a convenient reference for common search related request parameters.

What you need for this book

In *Chapter 1*, the *Getting Started* section explains what you need in detail. In summary, you should obtain:

- Java 6, a JDK release. Do not use Java 7.
- Apache Solr 3.4.
- The code supplement to the book at:
  http://www.solrenterprisesearchserver.com/

Who this book is for

This book is for developers who want to learn how to use Apache Solr in their applications. Only basic programming skills are needed.

Conventions

In this book, you will find a number of styles of text that distinguish between different kinds of information. Here are some examples of these styles, and an explanation of their meaning.

Code words in text are shown as follows: "You should use LRUCache because the cache is evicting content frequently."

A block of code is set as follows:

```
<fieldType name="title_commonGrams" class="solr.TextField"
  positionIncrementGap="100"">
<analyzer type="index">
<tokenizer class="solr.StandardTokenizerFactory"/>
```

When we wish to draw your attention to a particular part of a code block, the relevant lines or items are set in bold:

```
<filter class="solr.EnglishMinimalStemFilterFactory"/>
<filter class="solr.CommonGramsQueryFilterFactory"
  words="commongrams.txt" ignoreCase="true""/>
</analyzer>
</fieldType>
```

Any command-line input or output is written as follows:

```
>>unzip mb_releases.csv.zip
```

New terms and **important words** are shown in bold. Words that you see on the screen, in menus or dialog boxes for example, appear in the text like this: "While you can use the Solr Admin **statistics** page to pull back these results".

 Warnings or important notes appear in a box like this.

 Tips and tricks appear like this.

Reader feedback

Feedback from our readers is always welcome. Let us know what you think about this book—what you liked or may have disliked. Reader feedback is important for us to develop titles that you really get the most out of.

To send us general feedback, simply send an e-mail to feedback@packtpub.com, and mention the book title via the subject of your message.

If there is a book that you need and would like to see us publish, please send us a note in the **SUGGEST A TITLE** form on www.packtpub.com or e-mail suggest@packtpub.com.

If there is a topic that you have expertise in and you are interested in either writing or contributing to a book, see our author guide on www.packtpub.com/authors.

Customer support

Now that you are the proud owner of a Packt book, we have a number of things to help you to get the most from your purchase.

Downloading the example code

You can download the example code files for all Packt books you have purchased from your account at http://www.PacktPub.com. If you purchased this book elsewhere, you can visit http://www.PacktPub.com/support and register to have the files e-mailed directly to you.

Errata

Although we have taken every care to ensure the accuracy of our content, mistakes do happen. If you find a mistake in one of our books—maybe a mistake in the text or the code—we would be grateful if you would report this to us. By doing so, you can save other readers from frustration and help us improve subsequent versions of this book. If you find any errata, please report them by visiting http://www.packtpub.com/support, selecting your book, clicking on the **errata submission form** link, and entering the details of your errata. Once your errata are verified, your submission will be accepted and the errata will be uploaded on our website, or added to any list of existing errata, under the Errata section of that title. Any existing errata can be viewed by selecting your title from http://www.packtpub.com/support. The authors are also publishing book errata to include the impact that upcoming Solr releases have on the book. You can find this on their website: http://www.solrenterprisesearchserver.com/

Piracy

Piracy of copyright material on the Internet is an ongoing problem across all media. At Packt, we take the protection of our copyright and licenses very seriously. If you come across any illegal copies of our works, in any form, on the Internet, please provide us with the location address or website name immediately so that we can pursue a remedy.

Please contact us at copyright@packtpub.com with a link to the suspected pirated material.

We appreciate your help in protecting our authors, and our ability to bring you valuable content.

Questions

You can contact us at questions@packtpub.com if you are having a problem with any aspect of the book, and we will do our best to address it.

Quick Starting Solr

1

Welcome to Solr! You've made an excellent choice in picking a technology to power your search needs. In this chapter, we're going to cover the following topics:

- An overview of what Solr and Lucene are all about
- What makes Solr different from databases
- How to get Solr, what's included, and what is where
- Running Solr and importing sample data
- A quick tour of the admin interface and key configuration files

An introduction to Solr

Solr is an open source enterprise search server. It is a mature product powering search for public sites such as CNET, Zappos, and Netflix, as well as countless other government and corporate intranet sites. It is written in Java, and that language is used to further extend and modify Solr through simple plugin interfaces. However, being a server that communicates using standards such as HTTP and XML and JSON, knowledge of Java is useful but not a requirement. In addition to the standard ability to return a list of search results for some query, Solr has numerous other features such as result highlighting, faceted navigation (as seen on most e-commerce sites), query spell correction, query completion, and a "more like this" feature for finding similar documents.

You will see many references in this book to the term **faceting**, also known as **faceted navigation**. It's a killer feature of Solr that most people have experienced at major e-commerce sites without realizing it. Faceting enhances search results with aggregated information over all of the documents found in the search. Faceting information is typically used as dynamic navigational filters, such as a product category, date and price groupings, and so on. *Chapter 6, Faceting* is dedicated to this technology.

Lucene, the underlying engine

Before describing Solr, it is best to start with Apache Lucene, the core technology underlying it. Lucene is an open source, high-performance text search engine library. Lucene was developed and open sourced by Doug Cutting in 2000 and has evolved and matured since then with a strong online community and is the most widely deployed search technology today. Being just a code library, Lucene is not a server and certainly isn't a web crawler either. This is an important fact. There aren't even any configuration files.

In order to use Lucene, you write your own search code using its API, starting with indexing documents: first you supply documents to it. A **document** in Lucene is merely a collection of **fields**, which are name-value pairs containing text or numbers. You configure Lucene with a text **analyzer** that will **tokenize** a field's text from a single string into a series of **tokens** (words) and further transform them by chopping off word stems, called **stemming**, substitute synonyms, and/or perform other processing. The final tokens are said to be the **terms**. The aforementioned process starting with the analyzer is referred to as **text analysis**. Lucene *indexes* each document into its so-called **index** stored on disk. The index is an **inverted index**, which means it stores a mapping of a field's terms to associated documents, along with the ordinal word position from the original text. Finally you search for documents with a user-provided query string that Lucene parses according to its syntax. Lucene assigns a numeric relevancy **score** to each matching document and only the top scoring documents are returned.

 The brief description just given of how to use Lucene is how Solr works at its core. It contains many important vocabulary words you will see throughout this book — they will be explained further at appropriate times.

The major features found in Lucene are:

- An inverted index for efficient retrieval of documents by indexed terms. The same technology supports numeric data with range queries too.

- A rich set of chainable text analysis components, such as tokenizers and language-specific stemmers that transform a text string into a series of terms (words).

- A query syntax with a parser and a variety of query types from a simple term lookup to exotic fuzzy matching.

- A good scoring algorithm based on sound **Information Retrieval (IR)** principles to produce the more likely candidates first, with flexible means to affect the scoring.

- Search enhancing features like:
    - A highlighter feature to show query words found in context.
    - A query spellchecker based on indexed content or a supplied dictionary.
    - A "more like this" feature to list documents that are statistically similar to provided text.

 To learn more about Lucene, read *Lucene In Action, 2nd Edition* by Michael McCandless, Erik Hatcher, and Otis Gospodnetić.

Solr, a Lucene-based search server

Apache Solr is an enterprise search server based on Lucene. Lucene is such a big part of what defines Solr that you'll see many references to Lucene directly throughout this book. Developing a high-performance, feature-rich application that uses Lucene directly is difficult and it's limited to Java applications. Solr solves this by exposing the wealth of power in Lucene via configuration files and HTTP parameters, while adding some features of its own. Some of Solr's most notable features beyond Lucene are:

- A server that communicates over HTTP via XML and JSON data formats.
- Configuration files, most notably for the index's schema, which defines the fields and configuration of their text analysis.
- Several caches for faster search responses.
- A web-based administrative interface including:
    - Runtime search and cache performance statistics.
    - A schema browser with index statistics on each field.
    - A diagnostic tool for debugging text analysis.
- Faceting of search results.
- A query parser called **dismax** that is more usable for parsing end user queries than Lucene's native query parser.
- Geospatial search for filtering and sorting by distance.
- Distributed-search support and index replication for scaling Solr.
- **Solritas**: A sample generic web search UI demonstrating many of Solr's search features.

Also, there are two *contrib* modules that ship with Solr that really stand out:

- The **DataImportHandler** (DIH): A database, e-mail, and file crawling data import capability. It includes a debugger tool.
- **Solr Cell**: An adapter to the Apache Tika open source project, which can extract text from numerous file types.

 As of the 3.1 release, there is a tight relationship between Solr and Lucene. The source code repository, committers, and developer mailing list are the same, and they release together using the same version number. This gives Solr an edge over other Lucene based competitors.

Comparison to database technology

There's a good chance you are unfamiliar with Lucene or Solr and you might be wondering what the fundamental differences are between it and a database. You might also wonder if you use Solr, whether you need a database.

The most important comparison to make is with respect to the data model—that is the organizational structure of the data. The most popular category of databases is a relational database—**RDBMS**. A defining characteristic of a relational database is a data model based on multiple tables with lookup keys between them and a *join* capability for querying across them. RDBMSs have a very flexible data model, but this makes it harder to scale them easily. Lucene instead has a more limiting *document oriented* data model, which is analogous to a single table without join possibilities. Document oriented databases, such as MongoDB are similar in this respect, but their documents can have a rich nested structure similar to XML or JSON, for example. Lucene's document structure is flat, but it does support multi-valued fields—that is a field with an array of values.

Taking a look at the Solr feature list naturally reveals plenty of search-oriented technology that databases generally either don't have, or don't do well. Notable features are relevancy score ordering, result highlighting, query spellcheck, and query-completion. These features are what drew you to Solr, no doubt.

Can Solr be a substitute for your database? You can add data to it and get it back out efficiently with indexes; so on the surface it seems plausible, provided the flat document-oriented data model suffices. The answer is that *you are almost always better off using Solr in addition to a database*. Databases, particularly RDBMSs, generally excel at *ACID* transactions, insert/update efficiency, in-place schema changes, multi-user access control, bulk data retrieval, and supporting rich ad-hoc query features. Solr falls short in all of these areas but I want to call attention to these:

- **No updates**: If any part of a document in Solr needs to be updated, the entire document must be replaced. Internally, this is a deletion and an addition.

- **Slow commits**: Solr's search performance and certain features are made possible due to extensive caches. When a commit operation is done to finalize recently added documents, the caches are rebuilt. This can take between seconds and a minute or even worse in extreme cases.

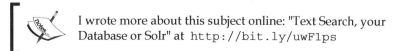 I wrote more about this subject online: "Text Search, your Database or Solr" at `http://bit.ly/uwF1ps`

Getting started

We're going to get started by downloading Solr, examine its directory structure, and then finally run it. This sets you up for the next section, which tours a running Solr server.

Get Solr: You can download Solr from its website: `http://lucene.apache.org/solr/`. The last Solr release this book was written for is version 3.4. Solr has had several relatively minor point-releases since 3.1 and it will continue. In general I recommend using the latest release since Solr and Lucene's code are extensively tested. For book errata describing how future Solr releases affect the book content, visit our website: `http://www.solrenterprisesearchserver.com/`. Lucid Imagination also provides a Solr distribution called "LucidWorks for Solr". As of this writing it is Solr 3.2 with some choice patches that came after to ensure its stability and performance. It's completely open source; previous LucidWorks releases were not as they included some extras with use limitations. LucidWorks for Solr is a good choice if maximum stability is your chief concern over newer features.

Get Java: The only prerequisite software needed to run Solr is Java 5 (a.k.a. java version 1.5) or later—ideally Java 6. Typing `java -version` at a command line will tell you exactly which version of Java you are using, if any.

Use latest version of Java!

The initial release of Java 7 included some serious bugs that were discovered shortly before its release that affect Lucene and Solr. The release of Java 7u1 on October 19th, 2011 resolves these issues. These same bugs occurred with Java 6 under certain JVM switches, and Java 6u29 resolves them. Therefore, I advise you to use the latest Java release.

Java is available on all major platforms including Windows, Solaris, Linux, and Apple. Visit http://www.java.com to download the distribution for your platform. Java always comes with the Java Runtime Environment (JRE) and that's all Solr requires. The Java Development Kit (JDK) includes the JRE plus the Java compiler and various diagnostic utility programs. One such useful program is jconsole, which we'll discuss in *Chapter 8, Deployment* and *Chapter 10, Scaling Solr* and so the JDK distribution is recommended.

Solr is a Java-based web application, but you don't need to be particularly familiar with Java in order to use it. This book assumes no such knowledge on your part.

Get the book supplement: This book includes a code supplement available at our website: http://www.solrenterprisesearchserver.com/. The software includes a Solr installation configured for data from MusicBrainz.org, a script to download and index that data into Solr—about 8 million documents in total, and of course various sample code and material organized by chapter. *This supplement is not required* to follow any of the material in the book. It will be useful if you want to experiment with searches using the same data used for the book's searches or if you want to see the code referenced in a chapter. The majority of code is for *Chapter 9, Integrating Solr*.

Solr's installation directory structure

When you unzip Solr after downloading it, you should find a relatively straightforward directory structure:

- client: Convenient language-specific client APIs for talking to Solr.

Ignore the client directory

Most client libraries are maintained by other organizations, except for the Java client SolrJ which lies in the dist/ directory. client/ only contains **solr-ruby**, which has fallen out of favor compared to **rsolr**—both of which are Ruby Solr clients. More information on using clients to communicate with Solr is in *Chapter 9*.

- contrib: Solr **contrib modules**. These are extensions to Solr. The final JAR file for each of these contrib modules is actually in dist/; so the actual files here are mainly the dependent JAR files.

    ○ analysis-extras: A few **text analysis** components that have large dependencies. There are some "ICU" Unicode classes for multilingual support, a Chinese stemmer, and a Polish stemmer. You'll learn more about text analysis in the next chapter.

    ○ clustering: A engine for clustering search results. There is a 1-page overview in *Chapter 7, Search Component,* referring you to Solr's wiki for further information: http://wiki.apache.org/solr/ClusteringComponent.

    ○ dataimporthandler: The **DataImportHandler** (DIH)—a very popular contrib module that imports data into Solr from a database and some other sources. See *Chapter 3, Indexing Data.*

    ○ extraction: Integration with Apache Tika– a framework for extracting text from common file formats. This module is also called **SolrCell** and Tika is also used by the DIH's TikaEntityProcessor— both are discussed in *Chapter 3, Indexing Data.*

    ○ uima: Integration with Apache UIMA—a framework for extracting metadata out of text. There are modules that identify proper names in text and identify the language, for example. To learn more, see Solr's wiki: http://wiki.apache.org/solr/SolrUIMA.

    ○ velocity: Simple Search UI framework based on the Velocity templating language. See *Chapter 9, Integrating Solr.*

- dist: Solr's WAR and contrib JAR files. The Solr WAR file is the main artifact that embodies Solr as a standalone file deployable to a Java web server. The WAR does not include any contrib JARs. You'll also find the core of Solr as a JAR file, which you might use if you are embedding Solr within an application, and Solr's test framework as a JAR file, which is to assist in testing Solr extensions. You'll also see SolrJ's dependent JAR files here.

- docs: Documentation—the HTML files and related assets for the public Solr website, to be precise. It includes a good quick tutorial, and of course Solr's API. Even if you don't plan on extending the API, some parts of it are useful as a reference to certain pluggable Solr configuration elements—see the listing for the Java package org.apache.solr.analysis in particular.

- `example`: A complete Solr server, serving as an example. It includes the Jetty servlet engine (a Java web server), Solr, some sample data and sample Solr configurations. The interesting child directories are:

   ◦ `example/etc`: Jetty's configuration. Among other things, here you can change the web port used from the pre-supplied 8983 to 80 (HTTP default).

   ◦ `exampledocs`: Sample documents to be indexed into the default Solr configuration, along with the `post.jar` program for sending the documents to Solr.

   ◦ `example/solr`: The default, sample Solr configuration. This should serve as a good starting point for new Solr applications. It is used in Solr's tutorial and we'll use it in this chapter too.

   ◦ `example/webapps`: Where Jetty expects to deploy Solr from. A copy of Solr's WAR file is here, which contains Solr's compiled code.

Solr's home directory and Solr cores

When Solr starts, the very first thing it does is determine where the **Solr home directory** is. *Chapter 8, Deployment* covers the various ways to tell Solr where it is, but by default it's the directory named simply `solr` relative to the current working directory where Solr is started. You will usually see a `solr.xml` file in the home directory, which is optional but recommended. It mainly lists **Solr cores**. For simpler configurations like `example/solr`, there is just one Solr core, which uses Solr's home directory as its **core instance directory**. A Solr core holds one Lucene index and the supporting Solr configuration for that index. Nearly all interactions with Solr are targeted at a specific core. If you want to index different types of data separately or shard a large index into multiple ones then Solr can host multiple Solr cores on the same Java server. *Chapter 8, Deployment* has further details on *multi-core* configuration.

A Solr core's instance directory is laid out like this:

- `conf`: Configuration files. The two I mention below are very important, but it will also contain some other `.txt` and `.xml` files which are referenced by these two.

- `conf/schema.xml`: The schema for the index including field type definitions with associated analyzer chains.

- `conf/solrconfig.xml`: The primary Solr configuration file.

- `conf/xslt`: Various XSLT files that can be used to transform Solr's XML query responses into formats such as Atom and RSS. See *Chapter 9, Integrating Solr*.

- `conf/velocity`: HTML templates and related web assets for rapid UI prototyping using Solritas, covered in *Chapter 9, Integrating Solr*. The soon to be discussed "browse" UI is implemented with these templates.
- `data`: Where Lucene's index data lives. It's binary data, so you won't be doing anything with it except perhaps deleting it occasionally to start anew.
- `lib`: Where extra Java JAR files can be placed that Solr will load on startup. This is a good place to put contrib JAR files, and their dependencies.

Running Solr

Now we're going to start up Jetty and finally see Solr running albeit without any data to query yet.

We're about to run Solr directly from the unzipped installation. This is great for exploring Solr and doing local development, but **it's not what you would seriously do in a production scenario**. In a production scenario you would have a script or other mechanism to start and stop the servlet engine with the operating system—Solr does not include this. And to keep your system organized, you should keep the example directly as exactly what its name implies—an example. So if you want to use the provided Jetty servlet engine in production, a fine choice then copy the example directory elsewhere and name it something else. *Chapter 8, Deployment,* covers how to deploy Solr to Apache Tomcat, the most popular Java servlet engine. It also covers other subjects like security, monitoring, and logging.

First go to the `example` directory, and then run Jetty's `start.jar` file by typing the following command:

```
>>cd example
```

```
>>java -jar start.jar
```

The `>>` notation is the command prompt. These commands will work across *nix and DOS shells. You'll see about a page of output, including references to Solr. When it is finished, you should see this output at the very end of the command prompt:

```
2008-08-07 14:10:50.516::INFO: Started SocketConnector @ 0.0.0.0:8983
```

Downloading the example code

You can download the example code files for all Packt books you have purchased from your account at http://www.PacktPub.com (url). If you purchased this book elsewhere, you can visit http://www.PacktPub.com/support (url) and register to have the files e-mailed directly to you.

The `0.0.0.0` means it's listening to connections from any host (not just localhost, notwithstanding potential firewalls) and 8983 is the port. If Jetty reports this, then it doesn't necessarily mean that Solr was deployed successfully. You might see an error such as a stack trace in the output if something went wrong. Even if it did go wrong, you should be able to access the web server: `http://localhost:8983`. Jetty will give you a 404 page but it will include a list of links to deployed web applications, which will just be Solr for this setup. Solr is accessible at: `http://localhost:8983/solr`, and if you browse to that page, then you should either see details about an error if Solr wasn't loaded correctly, or a simple page with a link to Solr's admin page, which should be `http://localhost:8983/solr/admin/`. You'll be visiting that link often.

 To quit Jetty (and many other command line programs for that matter), press *Ctrl+C* on the keyboard.

A quick tour of Solr

Start up Jetty if it isn't already running and point your browser to Solr's admin site at: `http://localhost:8983/solr/admin/`. This tour will help you get your bearings on this interface that is not yet familiar to you. We're not going to discuss it in any depth at this point.

 This part of Solr will get a dramatic face-lift for Solr 4. The current interface is functional, albeit crude.

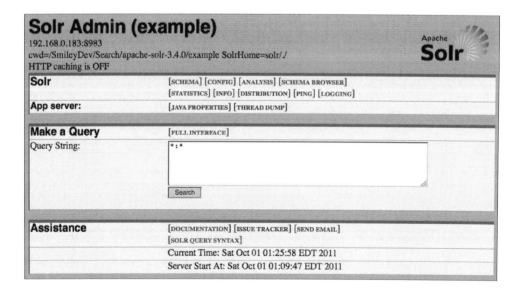

The top gray area in the preceding screenshot is a header that is on every page of the admin site. When you start dealing with multiple Solr instances—for example, development versus production, multicore, Solr clusters—it is important to know where you are. The IP and port are obvious. The **(example)** is a reference to the name of the schema—a simple label at the top of the schema file. If you have multiple schemas for different data sets, then this is a useful differentiator. Next is the current working directory `cwd`, and Solr's home. Arguably the name of the core and the location of the data directory should be on this overview page but they are not.

The block below this is a navigation menu to the different admin screens and configuration data. The navigation menu includes the following choices:

- **SCHEMA**: This retrieves the `schema.xml` configuration file directly to the browser. This is an important file which lists the fields in the index and defines their types.

> Most recent browsers show the XML color-coded and with controls to collapse sections. If you don't see readable results and won't upgrade or switch your browser, you can always use your browser's **View source** command.

- **CONFIG**: This downloads the `solrconfig.xml` configuration file directly to the browser. This is also an important file, which serves as the main configuration file.

- **ANALYSIS**: This is used for diagnosing query and indexing problems related to text analysis. This is an advanced screen and will be discussed later.

- **SCHEMA BROWSER**: This is an analytical view of the schema reflecting various heuristics of the actual data in the index. We'll return here later.

- **REPLICATION**: This contains index replication status information. *It is only shown when replication is enabled.* More information on this is in *Chapter 10, Scaling Solr*.

- **STATISTICS**: Here you will find stats such as timing and cache hit ratios. In *Chapter 10, Scaling Solr* we will visit this screen to evaluate Solr's performance.

- **INFO**: This lists static versioning information about internal components to Solr. Frankly, it's not very useful.

- **DISTRIBUTION**: This contains rsync-based index replication status information. This replication approach predates the internal Java based mechanism, and so *it is somewhat deprecated*. There is a mention in *Chapter 10, Scaling Solr* of it that ultimately refers you to Solr's wiki for how to use it.

- **PING**: This returns an XML formatted status document. It is designed to fail if Solr can't perform a search query you give it. If you are using a load balancer or some other infrastructure that can check if Solr is operational, configure it to request this URL.

- **LOGGING**: This allows you to adjust the logging levels for different parts of Solr at runtime. For Jetty as we're running it, this output goes to the console and nowhere else. See *Chapter 8, Deployment* for more information on configuring logging.

- **JAVA PROPERTIES**: This lists Java system properties, which are basically Java oriented global environment variables.

- **THREAD DUMP**: This displays a Java thread dump useful for experienced Java developers in diagnosing problems.

After the main menu is the **Make a Query** text box where you can type in a simple query. There's no data in Solr yet, so there's no point trying that right now.

- **FULL INTERFACE**: This brings you to a search form with more options. The form is still very limited, however, and only allows a fraction of the query options that you can submit to Solr. With or without this search form, you will soon wind up directly manipulating the URL using this book as a reference.

Finally, the bottom **Assistance** area contains useful information for Solr online. The last section of this chapter has more information on such resources.

Loading sample data

Solr comes with some sample data and a loader script, found in the `example/exampledocs` directory. We're going to use that for the remainder of this chapter so that we can explore Solr more without getting into schema design and deeper data loading options. For the rest of the book, we'll base the examples on the digital supplement to the book—more on that later.

We're going to invoke the `post.jar` Java program, officially called **SimplePostTool** with a list of Solr-formatted XML input files. Most JAR files aren't executable but this one is. This simple program iterates over each argument given, a file reference, and HTTP posts it to Solr running on the current machine at the example server's default configuration—`http://localhost:8983/solr/update`. Finally, it will send a **commit** command, which will cause documents that were posted prior to the last commit to be saved and visible. Obviously, Solr must be running for this to work, so ensure that it is first. Here is the command and its output:

```
>> cd example/exampledocs
>>java -jar post.jar *.xml
SimplePostTool: version 1.4
SimplePostTool: POSTing files to http://localhost:8983/solr/update..
SimplePostTool: POSTing file gb18030-example.xml
SimplePostTool: POSTing file hd.xml
SimplePostTool: POSTing file ipod_other.xml
… etc.
SimplePostTool: COMMITting Solr index changes..
```

If you are using a Unix-like environment, you have an alternate option of using the post.sh shell script, which behaves similarly by using curl. I recommend examining the contents of the post.sh bash shell script for illustrative purposes, even if you are on Windows—it's very short.

 The post.sh and post.jar programs could be used in a production scenario, but they are intended just for demonstration of the technology with the example data.

Let's take a look at one of these XML files we just posted to Solr, monitor.xml:

```xml
<add>
<doc>
  <field name="id">3007WFP</field>
  <field name="name">Dell Widescreen UltraSharp   3007WFP</field>
  <field name="manu">Dell, Inc.</field>
  <field name="cat">electronics</field>
  <field name="cat">monitor</field>
  <field name="features">30" TFT active matrix LCD, 2560 x 1600,
      .25mm dot pitch, 700:1 contrast</field>
  <field name="includes">USB cable</field>
  <field name="weight">401.6</field>
  <field name="price">2199</field>
  <field name="popularity">6</field>
  <field name="inStock">true</field>
  <!-- Buffalo store -->
  <field name="store">43.17614,-90.57341</field>
</doc>
</add>
```

The XML schema for XML files that can be posted to Solr is very simple. This file doesn't demonstrate all of the elements and attributes, but it shows most of what matters. Multiple documents, represented by the `<doc>` tag, can be present in series within the `<add>` tag, which is recommended in bulk data loading scenarios. The other essential tag, not seen here, is `<commit/>` which `post.jar` and `post.sh` send in a separate post. This syntax and command set may very well be all that you use. More about these options and other data loading choices will be discussed in *Chapter 3, Indexing Data*.

A simple query

On Solr's main admin page, run a simple query that searches for the word `monitor`. Simply type this word in and click on the **Search** button. The resulting URL will be:

```
http://localhost:8983/solr/select/?q=monitor&version=2.2&start=0&rows
=10&indent=on
```

Both this form and the **Full Interface** one are standard HTML forms; they are as simple as they come. The form inputs become URL parameters to another HTTP GET request which is a Solr search returning XML. The form only controls a basic subset of all possible parameters. The main benefit to the form is that it applies the URL escaping for special characters in the query, and for some basic options, you needn't remember what the parameter names are. It is convenient to use the form as a starting point for developing a search, and then subsequently refine the URL directly in the browser instead of returning to the form.

Solr's search results are by default in XML. Most modern browsers, such as Firefox, provide a good XML view with syntax coloring and hierarchical structure collapse controls. Solr can format responses in JSON and other formats but that's a topic for another time. They have the same basic structure as the XML you're about to see, by the way.

The XML response consists of a `<response/>` element, which wraps the entire message. The first child element contains request header metadata. Here is the beginning of the response:

```xml
<?xml version="1.0" encoding="UTF-8"?>
<response>
  <lst name="responseHeader">
    <int name="status">0</int>
    <int name="QTime">3</int>
    <lst name="params">
    <str name="indent">on</str>
    <str name="rows">10</str>
    <str name="start">0</str>
    <str name="q">monitor</str>
```

```
        <str name="version">2.2</str>
    </lst>
</lst>
...
```

Here we see:

- `status`: Is always zero unless there was a serious problem.

- `QTime`: Is the duration of time in milliseconds that Solr took to process the search. It does not include streaming back the response. Due to multiple layers of caching, you will find that your searches will often complete in a millisecond or less if you've run the query before.

- `params`: Lists the request parameters. By default, it only lists parameters explicitly in the URL; there are usually more specified in a `<requestHandler/>` in `solrconfig.xml`.

> More information on these parameters and many more are in *Chapter 4, Searching.*

Next up is the most important part, the results.

```
<result name="response" numFound="2" start="0">
```

The `numFound` number is the number of documents matching the query in the entire index. `start` is the index offset into those matching documents that are returned in the response below. Notice there is a search parameter by the same name as seen in the response header. There is also a parameter `rows` which specifies how many matching documents to return—just 10 in this example.

Often, you'll want to see the **score** of each matching document, which is a number assigned to it based on how relevant the document is to the search query. This search response doesn't refer to scores because it needs to be explicitly requested in the `fl` parameter—a comma separated field list. The **full interface** form includes the score by default. A search that requests the score will have a `maxScore` attribute in the `<result/>` element, which is the maximum score of all documents that matched the search. It's independent of the sort order or result paging parameters.

The content of the result tag is a list of documents that matched the query. The default sort is by descending score. Later, we'll do some sorting by specified fields.

```
<doc>
  <arrname="cat">
    <str>electronics</str>
    <str>monitor</str>
  </arr>
  <arr name="features">
    <str>30" TFT active matrix LCD, 2560 x 1600,.25mm dot pitch,
                                    700:1 contrast</str>
  </arr>
  <str name="id">3007WFP</str>
  <bool name="inStock">true</bool>
  <str name="includes">USB cable</str>
  <str name="manu">Dell, Inc.</str>
  <str name="name">Dell Widescreen UltraSharp 3007WFP</str>
  <int name="popularity">6</int>
  <float name="price">2199.0</float>
  <str name="store">43.17614,-90.57341</str>
  <float name="weight">401.6</float>
</doc>
<doc>
...
</doc>
</result>
</response>
```

The document list is pretty straightforward. By default, Solr will list all of the *stored* fields. Not all of the fields are necessarily stored—that is, you can query on them but not retrieve their value—an optimization choice. Notice that it uses the basic data types `str`, `bool`, `date`, `int`, and `float`. Also note that certain fields are multi-valued, as indicated by an `arr` tag.

This was a basic keyword search. As you start adding more options like faceting and highlighting, you will see additional XML following the `result` element.

Some statistics

Let's take a look at the statistics admin page: `http://localhost:8983/solr/admin/stats.jsp`. Before we loaded data into Solr, this page reported that `numDocs` was `0`, but now it should be `17`. If you are using a version of Solr other than 3.4, then this number may be different. The astute reader might observe we posted fewer XML files to Solr. The discrepancy is due to some XML files containing multiple Solr documents. `maxDocs` reports a number that is in some situations higher due to documents that have been deleted but not yet committed. That can happen either due to an explicit delete posted to Solr or by adding a document that replaces another in order to enforce a unique primary key. While you're at this page, notice that the **request handler** named `/update` has some stats too:

name	/update
class	org.apache.solr.handler.XmlUpdateRequestHandler
version	$Revision: 1165749 $
description	Add documents with XML
stats	handlerStart: 1317530339671
	requests: 15
	errors: 0
	timeouts: 0
	totalTime: 5276
	avgTimePerRequest: 351.73334
	avgRequestsPerSecond: 1.0589994E-4

Another request handler you'll want to examine is named `search`, which has been processing our search queries.

 These statistics are calculated only for the current running Solr, they are not stored to disk. As such, you cannot use them for long-term statistics.

The sample browse interface

The final destination of our quick Solr tour is to visit the so-called *browse interface* — available at `http://localhost:8983/solr/browse`. It's for demonstrating various Solr features:

- Standard keyword search. You can experiment with Solr's syntax.
- Query debugging: You can toggle display of the parsed query and document score explain information.
- Query-suggest: Start typing a word like "enco" and suddenly "encoded" will be suggested to you.
- Highlighting: The highlighting is in italics, which might not be obvious.
- More-Like-This: provides related products.
- Faceting: Field value facets, query facets, numeric range facets, and date range facets.
- Clustering: You must first start Solr as the on-screen instructions describe.
- Query boosting: By price.
- Query spellcheck: Using it requires building the spellcheck index and enabling spellcheck with a parameter. *Chapter 7, Search Component,* describes how to do this.
- Geospatial search: You can filter by distance. Click on the **spatial** link at the top-left to enable this.

This is also a demonstration of **Solritas**, which formats Solr requests using templates based on Apache Velocity. The templates are VM files in `example/solr/conf/velocity`. Solritas is primarily for search UI prototyping. It is not recommended for building anything substantial. See *Chapter 9, Integrating Solr* for more information.

 The browse UI as supplied assumes the default example Solr schema. It will not work out of the box against another schema without modification.

Here is a screenshot of the browse interface. Not all of it is captured in this image.

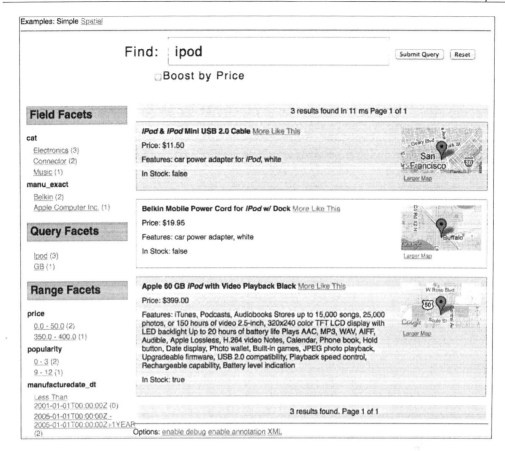

Configuration files

The configuration files in `example/solr/conf` are extremely well documented. We're not going to go over the details here but this should give you a sense of what is where.

> Unlike typical database software in which the configuration files don't need to be modified much if at all from their defaults, you will modify Solr's extensively—especially the schema. The as-provided state of these files is really just an example to both demonstrate features and document their configuration and should not be taken as the only way of configuring Solr.

Solr's schema for the index is defined in `schema.xml`. It contains field type definitions within the `<types>` element and then the index's fields within the `<fields>` element. You will observe that the names of the fields in the documents we added to Solr intuitively correspond to the sample schema. Aside from the fundamental parts of defining the fields, you may also notice `<copyField>` elements, which copy an input field as provided to another field. There are various reasons for doing this, but they boil down to needing to index data in different ways for specific search purposes. You'll learn all that you could want to know about the schema in the next chapter.

Solr's `solrconfig.xml` file contains lots of parameters that can be tweaked. At the moment, we're just going to take a peak at the **request handlers**, which are defined with `<requestHandler>` elements. They make up about half of the file. In our first query, we didn't specify any request handler, so we got the default one:

```
<requestHandler name="search" class="solr.SearchHandler
default="true">
  <!-- default values for query parameters can be specified, these
          will be overridden by parameters in the request
  -->
  <lst name="defaults">
    <str name="echoParams">explicit</str>
    <int name="rows">10</int>
  </lst>
  <!-- … many other comments … -->
</requestHandler>
```

Each HTTP request to Solr, including posting documents and searches, goes through a particular request handler. Handlers can be registered against certain URL paths by naming them with a leading "/". When we uploaded the documents earlier, it went to the handler defined like this, in which `/update` is a relative URL path:

```
<requestHandler name="/update" class="solr.XmlUpdateRequestHandler" />
```

The `qt` URL parameter can refer to a request handler by name as well.

Requests to Solr are nearly completely configurable through URL parameters or POST'ed form parameters. They can also be specified in the request handler definition within the `<lst name="defaults">`, element, such as how `rows` is set to `10` in the previously shown request handler. The well-documented file also explains how and when they can be added to `appends`, or `invariants` named `lst` blocks. This arrangement allows you to set up a request handler for a particular application that will be searching Solr without forcing the application to specify all of its query parameters. More information on request handlers is in *Chapter 4, Searching*.

Resources outside this book

The following are some Solr resources other than this book:

- *Apache Solr 3.1 Cookbook* is another Solr book published by Packt. It is a style of book that is comprised of a series of posed questions or problems followed by their solution. `http://www.packtpub.com/solr-3-1-enterprise-search-server-cookbook/book`

- Solr's Wiki: `http://wiki.apache.org/solr/` has a lot of great documentation and miscellaneous information. For a Wiki, it's fairly organized too. In particular, if you are going to use a particular app-server in production, then there is probably a Wiki page there on specific details.

- Within the Solr installation, you will also find that there are `README.txt` files in many directories within Solr and that the configuration files are very well documented. *Read them!*

- The `solr-user@lucene.apache.org` mailing list contains a wealth of information. If you have a few discriminating keywords then you can find nuggets of information in there with a search engine. The mailing lists of Solr and other Lucene sub-projects are best searched at: `http://www.lucidimagination.com/search/` or `http://search-lucene.com/solr` or `Nabble.com`.

 I highly recommend that you subscribe to the Solr-users mailing list. You'll learn a lot and potentially help others too.

- Solr's issue tracker contains information on enhancements and bugs. It's at `http://issues.apache.org/jira/browse/SOLR` and it uses Atlassian's **JIRA** software. Some of the comments attached to these issues can be extensive and enlightening.

 Notation convention: Solr's JIRA issues are referenced like this: SOLR-64. You'll see such references in this book and elsewhere. You can easily look these up at Solr's JIRA. You may also see issues for Lucene that follow the same convention, for example, LUCENE-1215.

There are of course resources for Lucene, like the *Lucene In Action* book. If you intend to dive into Solr's internals then you will find Lucene resources helpful, but that is not the focus of this book.

Summary

This completes a quick introduction to Solr. In the ensuing chapters, you're really going to get familiar with what Solr has to offer. I recommend that you proceed in order from the next chapter through *Chapter 7, Search Components*, because these build on each other and expose nearly all of the capabilities in Solr. These chapters are also useful as a reference to Solr's features. You can of course skip over sections that are not interesting to you. *Chapter 9, Integrating Solr*, is one you might peruse at any time, as it may have a section applicable to your Solr usage scenario. Finally, be sure that you don't miss the appendix for a search quick-reference cheat-sheet.

> The digital supplement to the book is available at http://www. solrenterprisesearchserver.com/ which includes both source code and a large multi-core Solr index. Our website should also include post-publication errata that should ideally be reviewed before continuing.

Schema and Text Analysis

2

The foundation of Solr is based on Lucene's index—the subject of this chapter. You will learn about:

- Schema design decisions in which you map your source data to Lucene's limited structure. In this book we'll consider the data from `MusicBrainz.org`.

- The structure of the `schema.xml` file where the schema definition is defined. Within this file are both the definition of field types and the fields of those types that store your data.

- Text analysis—the configuration of how text is processed (tokenized and so on) for indexing. This configuration affects whether or not a particular search is going to match a particular document.

The following diagram shows the big picture of how various aspects of working with Solr are related. In this chapter we are focusing on the foundational layer—the index:

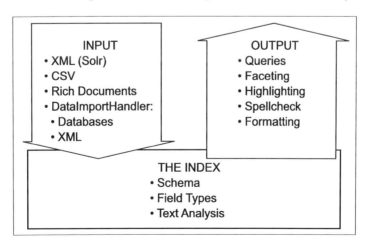

[

In a hurry?

This is a fairly important foundational chapter; that said, the subject of text analysis can be skimmed in lieu of using the predefined field types provided with Solr's example schema. Eventually, you will want to return to make adjustments.
]

MusicBrainz.org

Instead of continuing to work with the sample data that comes with Solr, we're going to use a large database of music metadata from the MusicBrainz project at `http://musicbrainz.org`. The data is free and is submitted by a large community of users. One way MusicBrainz offers this data is in the form of a large SQL file for import into a PostgreSQL database. In order to make it easier for you to play with this data, the online code supplement to this book includes the data in formats that can readily be imported into Solr. Alternatively, if you already have your own data then I recommend starting with that, using this book as a guide.

The `MusicBrainz.org` database is highly relational. Therefore, it will serve as an excellent instructional data set to discuss Solr schema choices. The MusicBrainz database schema is quite complex, and it would be a distraction to go over even half of it. I'm going to use a subset of it and express it in a way that has a straightforward mapping to the user interface seen on the MusicBrainz website. Each of these tables depicted in the following diagram can be easily constructed through SQL sub-queries or views from the actual MusicBrainz tables.

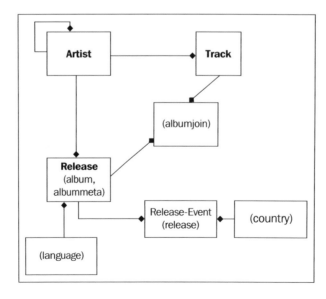

To describe the major tables above, I'll use some examples here from my favorite band, the *Smashing Pumpkins*.

- The Smashing Pumpkins is an **artist** with a type of "group" (a band). Some artists (groups in particular) have members who are also other artists of type "person". So this is a self-referential relationship. The *Smashing Pumpkins* has Billy Corgan, Jimmy Chamberline, and others as members.

- An artist is attributed as the creator of a **release**. The most common type of release is an "album" but there are also singles, EPs, compilations, and others. Furthermore, releases have a "status" property that is either official, promotional, or bootleg. A popular official album from the Smashing Pumpkins is titled "Siamese Dream".

- A release can be published at various times and places which MusicBrainz calls an "**event**" (a release-event). Each event contains the date, country, music label, and format (CD or tape).

- A release is composed of one or more **tracks**. Siamese Dream has 13 tracks starting with "Cherub Rock" and ending with "Luna". Note that a track is part of just one release and so it is not synonymous with a song. For example, the song "Cherub Rock" is not only a track on this release but also on a "Greatest Hits" release, as well as quite a few others in the database. A track has a **PUID (PortableUniqueIdentifier)**, an audio fingerprinting technology quasi-identifier based on the actual sound on a track. It's not foolproof as there are collisions, but these are rare. Another interesting bit of data MusicBrainz stores is the PUID "lookup count", which is how often it has been requested by their servers—a decent measure of popularity.

By the way, I'll be using the word "entity" occasionally here in the data modeling sense—it's basically a type of *thing* represented by the data. Artist, release, event, and track are all entity types with respect to MusicBrainz. In a relational database, most tables correspond to an entity type and the others serve to relate them or provide for multiple values. In Solr, each document will have a primary entity type, and it may contain other entities as a part of it too.

One combined index or separate indices

The following discussion concerns how to manage the searching of different types of data, such as artists and releases from MusicBrainz. In the example MusicBrainz configuration, each document of each type gets their own index but they all share the same configuration. Although I wouldn't generally recommend it, this approach was done for convenience and to reduce the complexity for this book at the expense of a one-size-fits-all schema and configuration.

A Solr server hosts one or more **Solr Cores**. A Solr Core is an instance of Solr to include the configuration and index, sometimes the word "core" is used synonymously with "index". Even if you have one type of data to search for in an application, you might still use multiple cores (with the same configuration) and *shard* the data for scaling. Managing Solr Cores is discussed further in the deployment chapter.

One combined index

A combined index might also be called an *aggregate index*. As mentioned in the first chapter, an index is conceptually like a single-table relational database schema, thus sharing similarities with some NoSQL (non-relational) databases. In spite of this limitation, there is nothing to stop you from putting different types of data (say, artists and releases from MusicBrainz) into a single index. All you have to do is use different fields for the different document types, and use a field to discriminate between the types. An identifier field would need to be unique across all documents in this index, no matter what the type is, so you could easily do this by concatenating the field type and the entity's identifier. This may appear ugly from a relational database design standpoint, *but this isn't a database!* More importantly, unlike a database, there is no overhead whatsoever for some documents to not populate some fields. This is where the spreadsheet metaphor can break down, because a blank cell in a spreadsheet takes up space, but not in an index.

Here's a sample `schema.xml` snippet of the fields for a single combined index approach:

```
<field name="id" ... /><!-- example: "artist:534445" -->
<field name="type" ... /><!-- example: "artist", "track", "release",
... -->
<field name="name" ... /><!-- (common to various types) -->

<!-- track fields: -->
<field name="PUID" ... />
<field name="num" ... /><!-- i.e. the track # on the release -->
<!-- ... -->
<!-- artist fields: -->
<field name="startDate" ... /><!-- date of first release -->
<field name="endDate" ... /><!-- date of last release -->
<field name="homeCountry" ... />
<!-- etc. -->
```

A combined index has the advantage of being easier to maintain, since it is just one configuration. It is also easier to do a search over multiple document types at once since this will naturally occur assuming you search on all relevant fields. For these reasons, it is a good approach to start off with. However, consider the shortcomings to be described shortly.

For the book, we've taken a hybrid approach in which there are separate Solr Cores (indices) for each MusicBrainz data type, but they all share the same configuration, including the schema.

Problems with using a single combined index

Although a combined index is more convenient to set up, there are some problems that you may face while using a single combined index:

- There may be namespace collision problems unless you prefix the field names by type such as: `artist_startDate` and `track_PUID`. In the example that we just saw, most entity types have a `name`. Therefore, it's straightforward for all of them to have this common field. If the type of the fields were different, then you would be forced to name them differently.

- If you share the same field for different entities like the `name` field in the example that we just saw, then there are some problems that can occur when using that field in a query and while filtering documents by document type. These caveats do not apply when searching across all documents.

  ° You will get scores that are of lesser quality due to sub-optimal **document frequency** values, a component of the IDF part of the score. The document frequency is simply the number of documents in which a queried term exists for a specific field. If you put different types of things into the same field, then what could be a rare word for a track name might not be for an artist name. Scoring is described further in *Chapter 5, Search Relevancy*.

  ° *Prefix*, *wildcard*, and *fuzzy* queries will take longer and will be more likely to reach internal scalability thresholds. If you share a field with different types of documents, then the total number of terms to search over is going to be larger, which takes longer for these query types. It will also match more terms than it would otherwise, while possibly generating a query that exceeds the `maxBooleanClauses` threshold (configurable in `solrconfig.xml`).

- The scores will be of lesser quality due to sub-optimal total document count figure, a component of the IDF part of the score. The total document count ends up being inflated instead of being limited to a specific document type (although the problem isn't as bad as the sub-optimal document frequency). Scoring is described further in *Chapter 5, Search Relevancy*.

- For a large number of documents, a strategy using multiple indices will prove to be more scalable. Only testing will indicate what "large" is for your data and your queries, but less than a million documents will not likely benefit from multiple indices. Ten million documents has been suggested as a reasonable maximum number for a single index. There are seven million tracks in MusicBrainz, so we'll definitely have to put tracks in its own index.

- Committing changes to a Solr index invalidates the caches used to speed up querying. If this happens often, and the changes are usually to one type of entity in the index, then you will get better query performance by using separate indices.

Separate indices

For separate indices, you simply develop your schemas independently. You can use a combined schema as previously described and use it for all of your cores so that you don't have to manage them separately; it's not an approach for the purists but it is convenient and it's what we've done for the book example code. The rest of the discussion here assumes the schemas are independent.

> To share the same schema field type definitions (described soon) across your schemas without having to keep them in sync, use the **XInclude** feature. XInclude is described in *Chapter 8, Deployment*.

If you do develop separate schemas and if you need to search across your indices in one search then you must perform a **distributed search**, described in the last chapter. A distributed search is usually a feature employed for a large corpus but it applies here too. Be sure to read more about it before using it since there are some limitations. As in the combined-schema, you will need a unique ID across all documents and you will want a field "type" to differentiate documents in your search results. You don't need commonly named fields to search on since the query will be processed at each core using the configuration there to determine, for example, what the default search field is.

You can't go wrong with multiple indices (Solr Cores); it's just a bit more to manage. And just because you have multiple indices doesn't preclude sharing as much of the configuration (including the schema) as you want to amongst the cores. The deployment chapter will discuss configuring the cores including sharing them and parameterizing them.

Schema design

A key thing to come to grips with is that the queries you need Solr to support *completely drive* your Solr schema design. Conversely, relational databases typically use standard third normal form decomposition of the data, largely because they have strong relational-join support. Since queries drive the Solr schema design, all the data needed to match a document, that is the criteria, must be in the document matched, not in a related one. To satisfy that requirement, data that would otherwise exist in one place is copied into related documents that need it to support a search. For example, an artist's name in MusicBrainz would not just exist on an artist document but also in a track document to support searching for tracks by artist. This may feel dirty because you're probably used to thinking in terms of relational databases.

Even if you're not working with a database as your source data, these concepts still apply. So pay close attention to this important subject in any case.

At this point I'm going to outline a series of steps to follow in order to arrive at one or more Solr schemas to power searches for an application of any sort. For specifics, we will consider the `MusicBrainz.org` website and hypothetically how it could work. It goes as far as listing the fields but not into text analysis or making changes for particular search features, like faceting. In truth, schema design is somewhat creative and it's always evolutionary—so *consider these steps a guide for your first time at it, not a foolproof process.*

Step 1: Determine which searches are going to be powered by Solr

Any text search capability is going to be Solr powered. At the risk of stating the obvious, I'm referring strictly to those places where a user types in a bit of text and subsequently gets some search results. On the MusicBrainz website, the main search function is accessed through the form that is always present on the left. There is also a more advanced form that adds a few options but is essentially the same capability, and I treat it as such from Solr's point of view. We can see the MusicBrainz search form in the following screenshot:

Once we look through the remaining steps, we may find that Solr should additionally power some faceted navigation in areas that are not accompanied by text search (that is, the facets are of the entire data set, not necessarily limited to the search results of a text query alongside it). An example of this at MusicBrainz is the "Top Voters" tally, which I'll address soon.

Step 2: Determine the entities returned from each search

For the MusicBrainz search form, this is easy. The entities are: Artists, Releases, Tracks, Labels, and Editors. It just so happens that in MusicBrainz, a search will only return one entity type. However, that needn't be the case. Note that internally, each result from a search corresponds to a distinct document in the Solr index and so each entity will have a corresponding document. This entity also probably corresponds to a particular row in a database table, assuming that's where it's coming from.

> The book examples and digital companion data only make use of MusicBrainz artists, releases, and tracks.

Step 3: Denormalize related data

For each entity type, find all of the data in the schema that will be needed across all searches of it. By "all searches of it," I mean that there might actually be multiple search forms, as identified in Step 1. Such data includes any data queried for (that is, criteria to determine whether a document matches or not) and any data that is displayed in the search results. The end result of denormalization is to have each document sufficiently self-contained, even if the data is duplicated across the index(es). Again, this is because Solr does not (*yet*) support relational joins.

> **Use Solr 4 to get join support**
>
> Solr 4 is not released yet as of this writing, but it includes many features already committed, including **join** support. A join allows a query to match a document based on data in another document related by some field in common. Without this feature, you need to denormalize data but that can be prohibitive in some circumstances. For more information, see:
> `http://wiki.apache.org/solr/Join`

Let's see an example. Consider a search for tracks matching **Cherub Rock**:

Score	Num	Track	Duration	Type	Artist	Album	Tracks
100	1	Cherub Rock	4:58	album	The Smashing Pumpkins	Siamese Dream	13
100	1	Cherub Rock	4:59	single	The Smashing Pumpkins	Cherub Rock	3
100	4	Cherub Rock	4:57	compilation	The Smashing Pumpkins	Greatest Hits (Rotten Apples)	18
100	14	Cherub Rock	4:29	live	The Smashing Pumpkins	Turpentine Kisses	14
100	11	Cherub Rock	5:55	live	The Smashing Pumpkins	Squashed Zucchini	13
100	2	Cherub	4:29	live	The Smashing	Unplugged: 100% Pure Acoustic Performances	15

Denormalizing—'one-to-one' associated data

A MusicBrainz track's name and duration are definitely in the track table, but the artist and album names are each in their own tables in the MusicBrainz schema. This is a relatively simple case, because each track has no more than one artist or album. Both the artist name and album name would get their own field in Solr's flat schema for a track. They also happen to be elsewhere in our Solr schema, because artists and albums were identified in Step 2. Since the artist and album names are not unambiguous references, it is useful to also add the IDs for these tables into the track schema to support linking in the user interface, among other things.

Denormalizing—'one-to-many' associated data

One-to-many associations can be easy to handle in the simple case of a field requiring multiple values. Unfortunately, databases usually make this harder than it should be if it's just a simple list. However, Solr's fields directly support the notion of multiple values. Remember in the MusicBrainz schema that an artist of type group can have some number of other artists as members. Although MusicBrainz's current search capability doesn't leverage this, we'll capture it anyway because it is useful for more interesting searches. The Solr schema to store this would simply have a member name field that is multi-valued. The `member_id` field alone would be insufficient, because denormalization requires that the member's name be copied into the artist. This example is a good segue to how things can get a little more complicated...

If we only record the member name, then it is problematic to do things like have links in the UI from a band member to that member's detail page. This is because we don't have that member's artist ID, only their name. So we'll add a multi-valued field for the member's ID. Multi-valued fields maintain ordering so that the two fields would have corresponding values at a given index. Beware, there can be a tricky case when one of the values can be blank, and you need to come up with a placeholder. The client code would have to know about this placeholder.

> What you should not do is try to shove different types of data into the same field by putting both the artist IDs and names into one field. It could introduce text analysis problems, as a field would have to satisfy both types, and it would require the client to parse out the pieces. The exception to this is when you are merely storing it for display, not searching it. Then you can store whatever you want in a field.

A problem with denormalizing one-to-many data comes into play when multiple fields from the other entity are brought in, and you need to search on more than one of those fields at once. For a hypothetical example, imagine a search for releases that contain a track with a particular word in the name and with a particular minimum duration. Both the track name and duration fields on a release would be multi-valued, and a search would have criteria for both. Unfortunately, Solr would erroneously return releases where one track's name satisfied the criteria and a separate track's duration satisfied the criteria but not necessarily for the same track. One work-around is searching the track index instead of the release one and using Solr's new **result grouping** feature to group by release. This solution of course depends on an additional index holding entity relationships going the other way. If you are faced with this challenge but can't create this additional index because the index would be prohibitively large for your data, then you may have to wait till Solr 4's join support.

Step 4: (Optional) Omit the inclusion of fields only used in search results

It's not likely that you will actually do this, but it's important to understand the concept. If there is any data shown on the search results that is not queryable, not sorted upon, not faceted on, nor are you using the highlighter feature for, and for that matter are not using any Solr feature that uses the field except to simply return it in search results, then it is not necessary to include it in the schema for this entity. Let's say, for the sake of argument, that the only information queryable, sortable, and so on is a track's name, when doing a query for tracks. You can opt not to inline the artist name, for example, into the track entity. When your application queries Solr for tracks and needs to render search results with the artist's name, the onus would be on your application to get this data from somewhere — it won't be in the search results from Solr. The application might look these up in a database, in some caching middleware, or perhaps even query our Solr artist index.

This clearly makes generating a search results screen more difficult, because you now have to get the data from more than one place. Moreover, to do it efficiently, you would need to take care to query the needed data in bulk, instead of each row individually. Additionally, it would be wise to consider a caching strategy to reduce the queries to the other data source. It will, in all likelihood, slow down the total render time too. However, the benefit is that you needn't get the data and store it into the index at indexing time. It might be a lot of data, which would grow your index, or it might be data that changes often, necessitating frequent index updates.

If you are using distributed search, as discussed in *Chapter 9, Integrating Solr* there is some performance gain in not sending too much data around in the requests. Let's say that you have song lyrics for each track, it is distributed on 20 machines, and you get 100 results. This could result in 2,000 records being sent around the network. Just sending the IDs around would be much more network efficient, but then this leaves you with the job of collecting the data elsewhere before display. The only way to know if this works for you is to test both scenarios. In general, if the data in question is not large then keep it in Solr.

At the other end of the extreme is storing all data in Solr. Why not? At least in the case of MusicBrainz, it wouldn't be appropriate. Take for example the **Top Voters** tally. The account names listed are actually editors in MusicBrainz terminology. This piece of the screen tallies an edit, grouped by the editor who performed the edit. It's the edit that is the entity in this case. The following screenshot shows the **Top Voters** (aka editors), which are tallied by the number of edits:

This data simply doesn't belong in an index, because there's no use case for searching edits, only lookup when we want to see the edits on some other entity like an artist. If you insisted on having the voter's tally (as seen above) powered by Solr, then you'd have to put all this data (of which there is a lot!) into an index, just because you wanted a simple statistical list of top voters. It's just not worth it!

One objective guide to help you decide on whether to put an entity in Solr or not is to ask yourself if users will ever be doing a text search on that entity—a feature where index technology stands out from databases. If not, then you probably don't want the entity in your Solr index.

The schema.xml file

Let's finally explore a Solr schema.

Before we continue, find a `schema.xml` file to follow along. This file belongs in the `conf` directory for a Solr instance configuration. For simple single-core Solr setups, this is the same as a Solr home directory. In the example code distributed with the book, available online, I suggest looking at `cores/mbtype/conf/schema.xml`. If you are working off of the Solr distribution, you'll find it in `example/solr/conf/schema.xml`. The example `schema.xml` is loaded with useful field types, documentation, and field definitions used for the sample data that comes with Solr.

I prefer to initialize a Solr configuration by copying the example Solr home directory and liberally modifying it as needed, ripping out or commenting what I don't need (which is often a lot). This is half way between starting with nothing, or starting with the example and making essential modifications. If you do start with Solr's example configuration, be sure to revisit your configuration at some point to clean out what you aren't using. In addition, it's tempting to keep the existing documentation comments, but you can always refer back to what comes with Solr as needed and keep your `config` file clean.

At the start of the file is the schema opening tag:

```
<schema name="musicbrainz" version="1.4">
```

We've set the name of this schema to `musicbrainz`, the name of our application. If we used different schema files, then we should name them differently to differentiate them.

Defining field types

The first section of the schema is the definition of the field types. In other words, these are the data types. This section is enclosed in the `<types/>` element and will consume lots of the file's content. The field types declare the types of fields, such as booleans, numbers, dates, and various text flavors. They are referenced later by the field definitions under the `<fields/>` element. Here is the field type for a boolean:

```
<fieldType name="boolean" class="solr.BoolField"
sortMissingLast="true" omitNorms="true"/>
```

A field type has a unique name and is implemented by a Java class specified by the `class` attribute.

 A fully qualified classname in Java looks like `org.apache.solr. schema.BoolField`. The last piece is the simple name of the class, and the part preceding it is called the package name. In order to make configuration files in Solr more concise, the package name can be abbreviated to just `solr` for most of Solr's packages.

Attributes other than the name and class represent configuration options; most are applicable to all types, like `omitNorms`, and some are specific to the implementing class. They can usually be overridden at the field declaration too. In addition to these attributes, there is also the text analysis configuration that is only applicable to text fields. That will be covered later in this chapter.

Built-in field type classes

There are a number of built-in field types and nearly all are present and documented to some extent in Solr's example schema. We're not going to enumerate them all here, but instead highlight some of them worthy of more explanation.

Numbers and dates

There are no less than five different field types to use to store an integer, perhaps six if you want to count string! It's about the same for float, double, long, and date. And to think that you probably initially thought this technology only did text! I'll explain when to use which, using Integer as an example. Most have an analogous name for the other numeric and date types. *The field types with names starting with "Trie" should serve 95% of your needs.* To clean up your schema, consider deleting the others.

- `TrieIntField` (with `precisionStep` = 0), commonly named "int". This is a good default field suitable for most uses.

- `TrieIntField` (with `precisionStep`> 0), commonly named "tint". If you expect to do numeric range queries (which include faceted ranges) over many values, then this field type has unbeatable performance at query time at the expense of a little more disk and indexing time cost. The default value configured in Solr's example schema is 8 for numeric and 6 for date; I recommend keeping these defaults. Smaller numbers (but > 0) will increase indexing space and time for query range performance; although the performance gains rapidly diminish with each step.

- `SortableIntField`, commonly named "sint". This is similar to Trie with `precisionStep` = 0 with the additional option of being able to specify `sortMissingFirst` and `sortMissingLast`, described shortly. `DateField` doesn't follow this naming convention but it also qualifies here.

- `IntField`, commonly named "pint". This is a legacy implementation; don't use it.

- `BCDIntField` (Binary Coded Decimal). Don't bother with it.

All of these numeric types sort in their natural numeric order instead of lexicographically.

Finally, there is a field type called `ExternalFileField`, which reads its float values from a plain text file instead of the index. It was designed for sorting or influencing scores of documents based on data that might change quickly (for example, a rating or click-through) without having to re-index a document. Remember that Lucene fundamentally cannot update just a single field; entire documents need to be re-indexed. This is a work-around for certain usecases. It is discussed further in *Chapter 5, Search Relevancy*.

Geospatial

Solr's geospatial support spans multiple parts of Solr from field types to query parsers, to function queries. Instead of having you read relevant parts of three chapters, I've consolidated it into *Chapter 4, Searching*.

Field options

The attributes listed here are common attributes applicable to most if not all field types.

> These options are assumed to be boolean (true/false) unless indicated, otherwise. Most default to false except for indexed and stored.
>
> Some of these options can be specified in the field type definition when applicable to any field of this type. The indented options defined below, underneath indexed (and stored) imply indexed (and stored) must be true.

- indexed: Indicates that this data can be searched and sorted. The only purpose a non-indexed field has is to be returned by Solr in search results.

    ◦ sortMissingLast, sortMissingFirst: Sorting on a field with one of these set to true indicates on which side of the search results to put documents that have no data for the specified field, regardless of the sort direction. The default behavior for such documents is to appear first for ascending and last for descending.

    ◦ omitNorms: (advanced) Basically, if you don't want the length of a field to affect its scoring (see *Chapter 5, Search Relevancy*) or it isn't used in the score any way (such as for faceting), and you aren't doing index-time document boosting (introduced in the next chapter), then enable this. Aside from its affect on scores, it saves a little memory too.

    ◦ omitPositions: (advanced, Solr 3.4) Omits term position information from the index to save a little space. Phrase queries won't work any more.

    ◦ omitTermFreqAndPositions: (advanced) Omits term frequency and term positions from the index to save a little space. Phrase queries won't work and scores will be less effective.

- ○ termVectors: (advanced) This will tell Lucene to store information that is used in a few cases to improve search performance. If a field is to be used by the MoreLikeThis feature, or for highlighting of a large text field, then try enabling this. It can substantially increase the index size and indexing time so do a before-and-after measurement. There are two more options which add more data to term vectors: termPositions and termOffsets. The FastVectorHighlighter requires these.

  - ○ positionIncrementGap: (advanced) For a multiValued field, this is the number of (virtual) non-existent words between each value to prevent inadvertent phrase queries matching across field values. For example, if A and B are given as two values for a field, a positionIncrementGap of more than 1 prevents the phrase query "A B" from matching.

- stored: Indicates that the field is eligible for inclusion in search results. Usually fields are stored, but sometimes the same data is copied into multiple fields that are indexed differently (which you'll begin to understand here), and so the redundant fields would not be marked as stored.

  - ○ compressed: **No longer supported.** This option was removed as of Solr v1.4.1 because the committers were unhappy with its implementation. It is expected to return: SOLR-752.

- multiValued: Enable this if a field can contain more than one value. Order is maintained from that supplied at index-time.

 There is a helpful table on Solr's wiki showing most of the options with some use cases that need them:
http://wiki.apache.org/solr/FieldOptionsByUseCase

Field definitions

The definitions of the fields in the schema are located within the <fields/> element. In addition to the field options defined above, a field has these attributes:

- name: Uniquely identifies the field. There aren't any restrictions on the characters used nor any words to avoid, except for score.

- type: A reference to one of the field types defined earlier in the schema.

- default: (optional) The default value, if an input document doesn't specify it. A common use of this is to timestamp documents: <field name="indexedAt" type="tdate" default="NOW/SECOND" />. For information on specifying dates, see **DateMath** in *Chapter 4, Searching*.

- `required`: (optional) Set this to `true` if you want Solr to fail to index a document that does not have a value for this field.

Dynamic field definitions

The very notion of a dynamic field definition highlights the flexibility of Lucene's index, as compared to typical relational database technology. Not only can you explicitly name fields in the schema, but you can also have some defined on the fly based on the name supplied for indexing. Solr's example schema contains some examples of this, such as:

```
<dynamicField name="*_dt" type="date" indexed="true"  stored="true"/>
```

If at index time a document contains a field that isn't matched by an explicit field definition, but does have a name matching this pattern (that is, ends with _dt such as `updated_dt`), then it gets processed according to that definition. A dynamic field is declared just like a regular field in the same section. However, the element is named `dynamicField`, and it has a name attribute that must either start or end with an asterisk (the wildcard). It can also be just `*`, which is the final fallback.

 The `*` fallback is most useful if you decide that all fields attempted to be stored in the index should succeed, even if you didn't know about the field when you designed the schema. It's also useful if you decide that instead of it being an error, such unknown fields should simply be ignored (that is, not `indexed` and not `stored`).

In the end, a field is a field, whether explicitly defined or defined dynamically according to a name pattern. Dynamic field definitions are just a convenience that makes defining schemas easier. There are no performance implications of using dynamic field definitions.

Our MusicBrainz field definitions

What follows is a first cut of our MusicBrainz schema definition. There are additional fields that will be added in other chapters to explore other search features. This is a *combined schema* defining all core entity types: artists, releases (AKA albums), and tracks. This approach was described earlier in the chapter. Notice that I chose to prefix field names by a character representing the entity type it is on (a_, r_, t_), to avoid overloading the use of any field across entity types. I also used this abbreviation when I denormalized relationships like in r_a_name (a release's artist's name).

```
<!-- COMMON TO ALL TYPES: -->
<field name="id" type="string" required="true" />
       <!-- Artist:11650 -->
<field name="type" type="string" required="true" />
       <!-- Artist | Release | Label -->
<field name="indexedAt" type="tdate" default="NOW/SECOND" />

<!-- ARTIST: -->
<field name="a_name" type="title" />
       <!-- The Smashing Pumpkins -->
<field name="a_name_sort" type="string" stored="false" />
  <!-- Smashing Pumpkins, The -->
<field name="a_alias" type="title" stored="false" multiValued="true"
/>
<field name="a_type" type="string" />
  <!-- group | person -->
<field name="a_begin_date" type="tdate" />
<field name="a_end_date" type="tdate" />
<field name="a_member_name" type="title" multiValued="true" />
       <!-- Billy Corgan -->
<field name="a_member_id" type="long" multiValued="true" />
       <!-- 102693 -->
<!-- RELEASE -->
<field name="r_name" type="title" />
  <!-- Siamese Dream -->
<field name="r_name_sort" type="string" stored="false" />
  <!-- Siamese Dream -->
<field name="r_a_name" type="title" />
  <!-- The Smashing Pumpkins -->
<field name="r_a_id" type="long" />
  <!-- 11650 -->
<field name="r_attributes" type="int" indexed="false"
multiValued="true" />
  <!-- ex: 0, 1, 100 -->
<field name="r_type" type="rType" stored="false" multiValued="true" />
  <!-- Album | Single | EP |... etc. -->
```

```
<field name="r_official" type="rOfficial" stored="false"multiValued="
true" />
  <!-- Official | Bootleg | Promotional -->
<field name="r_lang" type="string" indexed="false" />
  <!-- eng / latn -->
<field name="r_tracks" type="int" indexed="false" />
<field name="r_event_country" type="string" multiValued="true" />
        <!-- us -->
<field name="r_event_date" type="tdate" multiValued="true" />


  <!-- TRACK -->
<field name="t_name" type="title" />
  <!-- Cherub Rock -->
<field name="t_num" type="int" indexed="false" />
  <!-- 1 -->
<field name="t_duration" type="int"/>
        <!-- 298133 -->
<field name="t_a_id" type="long" />
        <!-- 11650 -->
<field name="t_a_name" type="title" />
  <!-- The Smashing Pumpkins -->
<field name="t_r_name" type="title" />
  <!-- Siamese Dream -->
<field name="t_r_tracks" type="int" indexed="false" />
  <!-- 13 -->
```

Put some sample data in your schema comments.

You'll find the sample data helpful and anyone else working
on your project will thank you for it! In the examples above, I
sometimes use actual values and on other occasions I list several
possible values separated by |, if there is a predefined list.

Also, note that the only fields that we can mark as required are those common to all,
which are ID and type, because we're doing a combined schema approach.

In our schema we're choosing to index most of the fields, even though MusicBrainz's
search doesn't require more than the name of each entity type. We're doing this
so that we can make the schema more interesting to demonstrate more of Solr's
capabilities. As it turns out, some of the other information in MusicBrainz's query
results actually are queryable if one uses the advanced form, checks **use advanced
query syntax,** and your query uses those fields (example: artist:"Smashing
Pumpkins").

At the time of writing this, MusicBrainz used Lucene for its text search and so it uses Lucene's query syntax. `http://wiki.musicbrainz.org/TextSearchSyntax`. You'll learn more about the syntax in *Chapter 4*.

Copying fields

Closely related to the field definitions are `copyField` directives. A `copyField` directive copies one or more input field values to another during indexing. A `copyField` directive looks like this:

```
<copyField source="r_name" dest="r_name_sort" maxChars="20" />
```

This directive is useful when a value needs to be copied to additional field(s) to be indexed differently. For example, sorting and faceting require a single indexed value. Another is a common technique in search systems in which many fields are copied to a common field that is indexed without norms and not stored. This permits searches, which would otherwise search many fields, to search one instead, thereby drastically improving performance at the expense of reducing score quality. This technique is usually complemented by searching some additional fields with higher boosts. The `dismax` query parser, which is described in a later chapter, makes this easy.

At index-time, each supplied field of input data has its name compared against the `source` attribute of all `copyField` directives. The source attribute might include a * wildcard so it's possible the input might match more than one `copyField`. If a wildcard is used in the destination, then it must refer to a dynamic field, and furthermore the source must include a wildcard too—otherwise a wildcard in the destination is an error. A match against a `copyField` has the effect of the input value being duplicated but using the field name of the `dest` attribute of the directive. If `maxChars` is optionally specified, the copy is truncated to this many characters. The duplicate does not replace any existing values that might be going to the field so be sure to mark the destination field as `multiValued` if needed.

 Finally, note that copying data to additional fields means longer indexing times and larger index file sizes.

The unique key

Near the bottom of the schema is the `<uniqueKey>` declaration specifying which field uniquely identifies each document, if any. This is what we have in our MusicBrainz schema:

```
<uniqueKey>id</uniqueKey>
```

Although it is technically not always required, you should define a unique ID field. In our MusicBrainz schema, the ID is a string that includes an entity type prefix type so that it's unique across the whole corpus, spanning multiple Solr Cores. Example: `Artist:11650`. If your source data does not have an ID field that you can propagate, then you may want to consider using a Universally Unique Identifier, a UUID, according to RFC-4122. Simply have a field with a field type for the class `solr.UUIDField` and either provide a UUID to Solr or supply the special value of "NEW", such as with setting `defaultField` and Solr will generate a UUID for you automatically. Solr's UUID support is based on `java.util.UUID`.

The default search field and query operator

Near the bottom of the schema file are a couple of configuration elements pertaining to search defaults when interpreting a query string:

```
<!-- <defaultSearchField>text</defaultSearchField>
<solrQueryParserdefaultOperator="AND"/> -->
```

The `defaultSearchField` declares the particular field that will be searched for queries that don't explicitly reference one. The `solrQueryParser` setting has a `defaultOperator` attribute which lets you specify the default search operator (that is AND, or OR) here in the schema. These are essentially defaults for searches that are processed by Solr request handlers defined in `solrconfig.xml`.

I strongly recommend that you ignore the `solrQueryParserdefaultOperator` attribute and not rely on the `defaultSearchField`. Instead, I configure the query parser in a request handler as desired in `solrconfig.xml` — documented in *Chapter 4, Searching*. These settings are optional here, and I've commented them out in the MusicBrainz schema.

Text analysis

Text analysis is a topic that covers text-processing steps such as tokenization, case normalization, stemming, synonyms, and other miscellaneous text processing. The analysis is applied to a text field at index time and as part of query string processing at search time. It's an important part of search engines since the details have an effect on getting good search results, especially to *recall*—a dimension of search result quality pertaining to whether all relevant documents are in the search results.

> This material is almost completely Lucene-centric and so also applies to any other software built on top of Lucene. For the most part, Solr merely offers XML configuration for the code in Lucene that provides this capability. For information beyond what is covered here, including writing your own analysis components, read the *Lucene In Action 2* book.

Text analysis converts text for a particular field into a sequence of terms. A **term** is the fundamental unit that Lucene actually indexes and searches. The analysis is used on the original incoming value at index time; the resulting terms are ultimately recorded onto disk in Lucene's index structure where it can be searched. The analysis is also performed on words and phrases parsed from the query string; the resulting terms are then searched in Lucene's index. An exception to this is prefix, wildcard and fuzzy queries which all skip text analysis. You'll read about them in *Chapter 4, Searching*.

> **In a hurry?**
> As a starting point, you should use the existing field types in Solr's default schema, which includes a variety of text field types for different situations. They will suffice for now and you can return to this chapter later. There will surely come a time when you are trying to figure out why a simple query isn't matching a document that you think it should, and it will quite often come down to your text analysis configuration.

Non-English text analysis

I try to cover Solr in a comprehensive fashion, but in the area of text analysis for non-English languages I'm going to refer you to this excellent Solr wiki page: `http://wiki.apache.org/solr/LanguageAnalysis`. There are 35 languages listed as of this writing. You'll notice that there is some variation in how to configure Solr for each of them, and that some languages have multiple options. Most language-specific elements are the stemmer and the stop word list, and for eastern languages, the tokenizer too. There is also a set of International Components for Unicode, ICU, related analysis components new to Solr 3.1, some of which you can use for mapping some non-Latin characters to Latin equivalents.

Configuration

Solr has various field types as we've previously explained, and the most important one is `solr.TextField`. This is the field type that has an analyzer configuration. Let's look at the configuration for the `text_en_splitting` field type definition that comes with Solr's example schema. It uses a diverse set of analysis components. I added in a character filter, albeit commented, to show what it looks like. As you read about text analysis in this chapter, you may want to flip back to see this configuration.

```
<fieldType name="text_en_splitting" class="solr.TextField"
        positionIncrementGap="100" autoGeneratePhraseQueries="true">
  <analyzer type="index">
<!--<charFilter class="solr.MappingCharFilterFactory"
    mapping="mapping-ISOLatin1Accent.txt"/>-->
    <tokenizer class="solr.WhitespaceTokenizerFactory"/>
    <filter class="solr.StopFilterFactory"
      ignoreCase="true"
      words="stopwords_en.txt"
      enablePositionIncrements="true"
    />
    <filter class="solr.WordDelimiterFilterFactory"
        generateWordParts="1" generateNumberParts="1"
        catenateWords="1" catenateNumbers="1"
        catenateAll="0" splitOnCaseChange="1"/>
    <filter class="solr.LowerCaseFilterFactory"/>
    <filter class="solr.KeywordMarkerFilterFactory"
        protected="protwords.txt"/>
    <filter class="solr.PorterStemFilterFactory"/>
  </analyzer>
  <analyzer type="query">
    <!--<charFilter class="solr.MappingCharFilterFactory"
        mapping="mapping-ISOLatin1Accent.txt"/>-->
    <tokenizer class="solr.WhitespaceTokenizerFactory"/>
```

```
          <filter class="solr.SynonymFilterFactory" synonyms="synonyms.
            txt" ignoreCase="true" expand="true"/>
          <filter class="solr.StopFilterFactory"
            ignoreCase="true"
            words="stopwords_en.txt"
            enablePositionIncrements="true"
          />
          <filter class="solr.WordDelimiterFilterFactory"
            generateWordParts="1" generateNumberParts="1"
            catenateWords="0" catenateNumbers="0" catenateAll="0"
            splitOnCaseChange="1"/>
          <filter class="solr.LowerCaseFilterFactory"/>
          <filter class="solr.KeywordMarkerFilterFactory"
            protected="protwords.txt"/>
          <filter class="solr.PorterStemFilterFactory"/>
      </analyzer>
  </fieldType>
```

The configuration example defines two **analyzers**, each of which specifies an ordered sequence of processing steps that convert text into a sequence of terms. The `type` attribute, which can hold a value of `index` or `query`, differentiates whether the analyzer is applied at index time or query time, respectively. If the same analysis is to be performed at both index and query times, then you can specify just one analyzer without a type. When both are specified as in the example above, they usually only differ a little.

Analyzers, Tokenizers, Filters, oh my!

The various components involved in text analysis go by various names, which are about to be defined. They are all conceptually the same: they take in text and spit out text, sometimes filtering, sometimes adding new terms, and sometimes modifying terms. The difference is in the specific flavor of input and output for them: either character based or token based. Also, **term**, **token**, and **word** are often used interchangeably.

An analyzer can optionally begin with one or more **character filters**, which operate at a streaming character level to perform manipulations on original input text. These are most commonly used to normalize characters, like remove accents, for example. Following any optional character filters is the **tokenizer**—the only mandatory piece of the chain. This analyzer takes a stream of characters and tokenizes it into a stream of tokens, usually with a simple algorithm such as splitting on whitespace. The remaining analysis steps, if any, are all **token filters** (often abbreviated to just **filters**), which perform a great variety of manipulations on tokens. The final tokens at the end, usually referred to as *terms* at this point, are what Lucene actually indexes or searches, depending on context. Note that some filters such as `WordDelimeterFilterFactory` actually perform a tokenization action, but they do it on a token whereas a bonafide tokenizer works from a character stream.

The class names all end with "Factory". This is a convention for the names of Solr's Java classes that accept the configuration and instantiate Lucene's analysis components that have the same simple name, less the "Factory" suffix. References to these analysis components in this book and elsewhere sometimes include the "Factory" suffix and sometimes not; no distinction is intended.

Finally, I want to point out the `autoGeneratePhraseQueries` boolean attribute—an option only applicable to text fields. If search-time query text analysis yields more than one token, such as `Wi-Fi` tokenizing to `Wi` and `Fi`, then by default these tokens are simply different search terms with no relation to their position. If this attribute is enabled, then the tokens become a phrase query, such as `"WiFi"` and consequently these tokens must be adjacent in the index. This automatic phrase query generation would always happen prior to Solr 3.1 but now it is configurable and defaults to false.

I recommend disabling autoGeneratePhraseQueries

There is conflicting opinion amongst experts on a suitable setting; setting it to false increases *recall* but decreases *precision*—two dimensions of search result quality. I favor that choice, since you'll learn in *Chapter 5, Search Relevancy* how to do automatic phrase boosting to get the most relevant documents (those that would match the phrase "Wi Fi") at the top of the results.

Experimenting with text analysis

Before we dive into the details of particular analysis components, it's important to become comfortable with Solr's analysis page, which is an experimentation and a troubleshooting tool that is absolutely indispensable. You'll use this to try out different configurations to verify whether you get the desired effect, and you'll use this when troubleshooting to find out why certain queries aren't matching certain text that you think they should. In Solr's admin pages, you'll see a link named **[ANALYSIS]** which takes you to this screen:

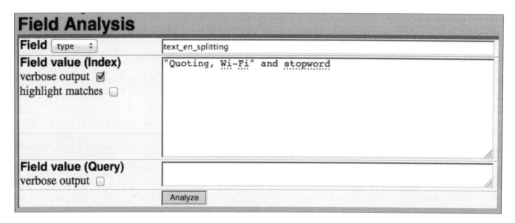

The first choice at the top of the page is required. You pick whether you want to choose a field type directly by its name, or if you want to indirectly choose one based on the name of a field. In this example, I'm choosing the `text_en_splitting` field type that has some interesting text analysis. This tool is mainly for the text oriented field types, not boolean, date, and numeric oriented types. You may get strange results if you try those.

At this point you can analyze index or query text or both at the same time. You activate that analysis by putting some text into the text box; otherwise it won't do that phase. If you are troubleshooting why a particular query isn't matching a particular document's field value, then you'd put the field value into the **Index** box and the query text into the **Query** box. Technically that might not be the same thing as the original query string, because the query string may use various operators to target specified fields, do fuzzy queries, and so on. You will want to check off **verbose output** to take full advantage of this tool. The **highlight matches** option is applicable when you are doing both query and index analysis together and want to see matches in the index part of the analysis corresponding with a query.

The output after clicking on the **Analyze** button is a bit verbose with verbose output checked and so I've disabled it for this upcoming screenshot. I encourage you to try it yourself.

Index Analyzer

"Quoting,	Wi-Fi"	and	stopword
"Quoting,	Wi-Fi"	stopword	
Quoting	Wi Fi		stopword
	WiFi		
quoting	wi fi		stopword
	wifi		
quoting	wi fi		stopword
	wifi		
quot	wi fi		stopword
	wifi		

Each row shown represents one step in the chain of processing as configured in the analyzer. For example, the third analysis component is WordDelimeterFilter and the results of its processing are shown in the third row. Columns separate the tokens, and if more than one token shares the same column, then they share the same **term position**. The distinction of the term position pertains to how phrase queries work. One interesting thing to notice about the analysis results is that **Quoting** ultimately became **quot** after stemming and lowercasing. Also, the word **and** was omitted by the StopFilter which is the second row.

Character filters

Character filters, declared with the <charFilter> element, process a stream of text prior to tokenization. There are only a few. This feature is not commonly used except for the first one described here which is configured to strip accents.

- `MappingCharFilterFactory`: This maps a character (or string) to another—potentially none. In other words, it's a find-replace capability. There is a `mapping` attribute in which you specify a configuration file. Solr's example configuration includes two such configuration files with useful mappings:

  - `mapping-FoldToASCII.txt`: A comprehensive mapping of non-ASCII characters to ASCII equivalents. For further details on the characters mapped, read the comments at the top of the file. This char filter has a token filter equivalent named `ASCIIFoldingFilterFactory` that should run faster and is recommended instead.

  - `mapping-ISOLatin1Accent.txt`: A smaller subset covering just the ISO Latin1 accent characters (like ñ to n). Given that FoldToASCII is more comprehensive, it's likely to be a better default than this one.

> This analysis component and quite a few others have an attribute in which you specify a configuration file. Usually you can specify more than one file, separated by comma but some components don't support that. They are always in the `conf` directory and UTF-8 encoded.

- `HTMLStripCharFilterFactory`: This is used for HTML or XML, and it need not be well formed. Essentially it removes all markup, leaving just the text content of elements. The text of script and style elements are removed. Entity references (for example: `&amp;`) are resolved.

> Instead of stripping markup at the analysis stage, which is very late, consider if this should be done at an earlier point with a `DataImportHandler` transformer, or some other pre-Solr stage. If you need to retain the markup in Solr's stored value, then you will indeed need to perform this step here.

- `PatternReplaceCharFilterFactory`: Performs a search based on a regular expression given as the `pattern` attribute, replacing it with the `replacement` attribute. The implementation involves a buffer window defaulting to 10,000 characters configurable with `maxBlockChars`. There is a regular expression based tokenizer and token filter too. Only use this char filter if the replacement should affect tokenization, such as by introducing a space.

The regular expression specification supported by Solr is the one that Java uses. It's handy to have this reference bookmarked: `http://download.oracle.com/javase/6/docs/api/java/util/regex/Pattern.html`

Tokenization

A tokenizer is an analysis component declared with the `<tokenizer>` element that takes text in the form of a character stream and splits it into so-called **tokens**, most of the time skipping insignificant bits like whitespace and joining punctuation. An analyzer has exactly one tokenizer. Your tokenizer choices are as follows:

- `KeywordTokenizerFactory`: This tokenizer doesn't actually do any tokenization! The entire character stream becomes a single token. The `string` field type has a similar effect but doesn't allow configuration of text analysis like lower-casing, for example. Any field used for sorting or most uses of faceting will require an indexed field with no more than one term per original value.

- `WhitespaceTokenizerFactory`: Text is tokenized by whitespace (that is, spaces, tabs, carriage returns).

- `StandardTokenizerFactory`: This is a general-purpose tokenizer for most Western languages. It tokenizes on whitespace and other points specified by the Unicode standard's annex on word boundaries. Whitespace and punctuation characters at these boundaries get removed. Hyphens are considered a word boundary, making this tokenizer less desirable for use with `WordDelimiterFilter`.

 As of Solr 3, the *former* `StandardTokenizer` was renamed to `ClassicTokenizer` and likewise `StandardFilter` was renamed to `ClassicFilter`. The current `StandardTokenizer` is new.

- `UAX29URLEmailTokenizer`: This behaves like `StandardTokenizer` with the additional property of recognizing e-mail addresses and URLs as single tokens.

- `ClassicTokenizerFactory`:(formerly the `StandardTokenizer`) This is a general-purpose tokenizer for English. On English text it does do a few things better than `StandardTokenizer`. Acronyms using periods are recognized, leaving the final period in place which would otherwise be removed – like `I.B.M.`; hyphens don't split words when the token contains a number; and e-mail addresses and Internet hostnames survive as one token.

Additionally, there is a `ClassicFilter` token filter that is usually configured to follow this tokenizer. It will strip the periods out of acronyms and remove any trailing apostrophes (English possessive). It will only work with `ClassicTokenizer`.

- `LetterTokenizerFactory`: This tokenizer considers each contiguous sequence of letters (as defined by Unicode) as a token and disregards other characters.

- `LowerCaseTokenizerFactory`: This tokenizer is functionally equivalent to `LetterTokenizer` followed by `LowerCaseFilter`, but faster.

- `PatternTokenizerFactory`: This regular expression based tokenizer can behave in one of two ways:

    ○ To split the text on some separator specified by a pattern, you can use it like this: `<tokenizer class="solr.PatternTokenizerFactory" pattern=";*" />`. This example would be good for a semi-colon separated list.

    ○ To match only particular patterns and possibly use only a subset of the pattern as the token. Example: `<tokenizer class="solr. PatternTokenizerFactory" pattern="\'([^\']+)\'" group="1" />`. The group attribute specifies which matching group will be the token. If you had input text like `aaa 'bbb' 'ccc'`, then this would result in tokens `bbb` and `ccc`.

- `PathHierarchyTokenizerFactory`: This is a configurable tokenizer that tokenizes strings that follow a simple character delimiter pattern, such as file paths or domain names. It's useful in implementing hierarchical faceting, as discussed in *Chapter 6, Faceting* or simply filtering documents by some root prefix of the hierarchy. As an example, the input string `/usr/local/apache` would be tokenized to these three tokens: `/usr`, `/usr/local`, `/usr/local/apache`. This tokenizer has four configuration options:

    ○ `delimiter`: The character delimiter—default: /

    ○ `replace`: A `replacement` character for `delimiter` (optional)

    ○ `reverse`: A boolean to indicate if the root of the hierarchy is on the right, such as with a host name—default: false

    ○ `skip`: The number of leading root tokens to skip—default: 0

- `WikipediaTokenizerFactory`: An experimental tokenizer for Mediawiki syntax, such as that used in Wikipedia.

There are some other tokenizers that exist for languages such as Chinese and Russian, as well as the ICUTokenizer which detects the language (or "script") used and tokenizes accordingly. And furthermore, NGramtokenizers will be discussed later. See http://wiki.apache.org/solr/AnalyzersTokenizersTokenFilters for more information on some of these tokenizers, or the API documentation.

WordDelimiterFilter

There may only be one official tokenizer in an analyzer, however the **token filter** named WordDelimiterFilter is essentially a tokenizer too:

```
<filter class="solr.WordDelimiterFilterFactory"
generateWordParts="1" generateNumberParts="1"
catenateWords="1" catenateNumbers="1"
catenateAll="0" splitOnCaseChange="1"/>
```

(not all options were just shown) The purpose of this analyzer is to both split and join compound words with various means of defining compound words. This one is typically used with WhitespaceTokenizer, not StandardTokenizer, which removes punctuation-based intra-word delimiters, thereby defeating some of this processing. The options to this analyzer have the values 1 to enable and 0 to disable.

 This analysis component is the most configurable of all and it can be a little confusing. Use Solr's **ANALYSIS** screen that is described in the *Experimenting with text analysis* section to validate your configuration.

The WordDelimiterFilter will first tokenize the input word, according to configured options. (Note: the commas on the right side of the following examples denote separate terms, and options are all true by default):

- split on intra-word delimiters: Wi-Fi to Wi, Fi
- split on letter-number transitions: SD500 to SD, 500 (if splitOnNumerics)
- omit any delimiters: /hello--there, dude to hello, there, dude
- remove trailing 's: David's to David (if stemEnglishPossessive)
- split on lower to upper case transitions: WiFi to Wi, Fi (if splitOnCaseChange)

At this point, the resulting terms are all filtered out unless some of the following options are enabled. Since they all default to false, you would always enable at least one of them.

- If generateWordParts or generateNumberParts is set, then all-alphabetic terms or all-number terms pass through (meaning, they are not filtered). Either way, they are still considered for the concatenation options.

- To concatenate a consecutive series of alphabetic terms, enable `catenateWords` (example: `wi-fi` to `wifi`). If `generateWordParts` is enabled, then this example would also generate `wi` and `fi` but not otherwise. This will work even if there is just one term in the series, thereby generating a term that disabling `generateWordParts` would have omitted. `catenateNumbers` works similarly but for numeric terms. `catenateAll` will concatenate all of the terms together. The concatenation process will take care to not emit duplicate terms.

- To preserve the original word, enable `preserveOriginal`.

Here is an example exercising all aforementioned options:

`WiFi-802.11b` to `Wi,Fi,WiFi,802,11,80211,b,WiFi80211b, WiFi-802.11b`

Internally, this filter assigns a type to each character (like letter, number) before looking for word boundaries. The types are determined by Unicode character categories. If you want to customize how the filter determines what the type of each character is, then you can provide one or more mapping files with the `types` option. An example use-case would be indexing Twitter tweets in which you want "#" and "@" treated as type ALPHA. For more details on this esoteric feature, see SOLR-2059.

Lastly, if there are a certain limited number of known input words that you want this filter to skip (that is pass through), then they can be listed in a file referred to with the `protected` option. Some other filters share this same feature.

Solr's out-of-the-box configuration for the `text_en_splitting` field type is a reasonable way to use the `WordDelimiterFilter`: generation of word and number parts at both index and query-time, but concatenating only at index time since doing so at query time too would be redundant.

Stemming

Stemming is the process for reducing inflected or sometimes derived words to their stem, base, or root form. For example, a stemming algorithm might reduce Riding and Rides, to just Ride. Stemming is done to improve search result *recall*, but at the expense of some *precision*. If you are processing general text, then you will improve your search results with stemming. However, if you have text that is mostly proper nouns, such as an artist's name in MusicBrainz, then anything more than light stemming will hurt the results. If you want to improve the *precision* of search results but retain the recall benefits, then you should consider indexing the data in two fields, one stemmed and one not, and then perform searches over both fields.

Many stemmers will generate stemmed tokens that are not correctly spelled words, like Bunnies becoming Bunni instead of Bunny or stemming Quote to Quot; you'll see this in Solr's analysis screen. This is harmless since stemming is applied at both index and search times; however, it does mean that a field that is stemmed like this also cannot be used for query spell-check, wildcard searches, or search term auto-complete—features described in later chapters. Those features directly use the indexed terms.

 A stemming algorithm is very language specific compared to other text analysis components; remember to visit http://wiki.apache.org/solr/LanguageAnalysis as advised earlier for non-English text. It includes information on a Solr token filter that performs *decompounding*, which is useful for certain languages (not English).

Here are stemmers suitable for the English language:

- `SnowballPorterFilterFactory`: This one lets you choose amongst many stemmers that were generated by the so-called *Snowball* program, hence the name. It has a `language` attribute in which you make the implementation choice from a list. Specifying `English` uses the "Porter2" algorithm — regarded as a slight improvement over the original. Specifying `Lovins` uses the Lovins algorithm for English — regarded as an improvement on Porter but too slow in its current form.

- `PorterStemFilterFactory`: This is the original English "Porter" algorithm. It is said to be twice as fast as using Snowball English.

- `KStemFilterFactory`: This English stemmer is *less aggressive* than Porter's algorithm. This means that it will not stem in as many cases as Porter will in an effort to reduce false-positives at the expense of missing stemming opportunities. **I recommend this as the default English stemmer**.

- `EnglishMinimalStemFilterFactory`: This is a simple stemmer that only stems on typical pluralization patterns. Unlike most other stemmers, the stemmed tokens that are generated are correctly spelled words; they are the singular form. A benefit of this is that a single Solr field with this stemmer is usable for both general search and for query term auto-complete simultaneously, thereby saving index size and making indexing faster.

Correcting and augmenting stemming

These stemmers are algorithmic instead of being based on a vetted thesaurus for the target language. Languages have so many spelling idiosyncrasies that algorithmic stemmers are imperfect—they sometimes stem incorrectly or don't stem when they should.

If there are particularly troublesome words that get stemmed, then you can prevent it by preceding the stemmer with a `KeywordMarkerFilter` with the `protected` attribute referring to a file of newline-separated tokens that should not be stemmed. An `ignoreCase` boolean option is available too. Some stemmers have or used to have a `protected` attribute that worked similarly, but that old approach isn't advised any more.

If you need to augment the stemming algorithm so you can tell it how to stem some specific words, then precede the stemmer with `StemmerOverrideFilter`. It takes a `dictionary` attribute referring to a UTF8-encoded file in the `conf` directory of token pairs, one pair per line, and a tab is used to separate the input token from the output token (the desired stemmed form of the input). An `ignoreCase` boolean option is available too. This filter will skip tokens already marked by `KeywordMarkerFilter` and it will keyword-mark all tokens it replaces itself, so that the stemmer will skip them.

Here is a sample excerpt of an analyzer chain showing three filters in support of stemming:

```
<filter class="solr.KeywordMarkerFilterFactory"
  protected="protwords.txt" />
<filter class="solr.StemmerOverrideFilterFactory"
  dictionary="stemdict.txt" />
<filter class="solr.PorterStemFilterFactory" />
```

Synonyms

The purpose of synonym processing is straightforward. Someone searches using a word that wasn't in the original document but is synonymous with a word that is indexed, so you want that document to match the query. Of course, the synonym need not be strictly those identified by a thesaurus, and they can be whatever you want including terminology specific to your application's domain.

> The most widely known free thesaurus is WordNet: `http://wordnet.princeton.edu/`. Solr 3.4 adds the ability to read WordNet's "prolog" formatted file via a `format="wordnet"` attribute on the synonym filter. However don't be surprised if you lose precision in the search results—it's not a clear win. For example, "Craftsman" in context might be a proper noun referring to a brand, but WordNet would make it synonymous with "artisan". Synonym processing doesn't know about context; it's simple and dumb.

Here is a sample analyzer configuration line for synonym processing:

```
<filter class="solr.SynonymFilterFactory" synonyms="synonyms.txt"
ignoreCase="true" expand="true"/>
```

The synonyms reference is to a file in the `conf` directory. Set `ignoreCase` to `true` for case-insensitive lookup of synonyms.

Before describing the `expand` option, let's consider an example. The synonyms file is processed line-by-line. Here is a sample line with an **explicit mapping** that uses the arrow `=>`:

```
i-pod, i pod =>ipod
```

This means that if either `i-pod` (one token) or `i` then `pod` (two tokens) are found in the incoming token stream to this filter, then they are replaced with `ipod`. There could have been multiple replacement synonyms, each of which might contain multiple tokens. Also notice that commas are what separates each synonym which is then split by whitespace for multiple tokens. To customize the tokenization to be something more sophisticated than whitespace, there is a `tokenizerFactory` attribute but it's rarely used.

Alternatively you may have lines that look like this:

```
ipod, i-pod, i pod
```

These lines don't have a `=>` and are interpreted differently according to the `expand` parameter. If `expand` is `true`, then it is translated to this explicit mapping:

```
ipod, i-pod, i pod =>ipod, i-pod, i pod
```

If `expand` is `false` then it becomes this explicit mapping, in which the first source synonym is the replacement synonym:

```
ipod, i-pod, i pod =>ipod
```

It's okay to have multiple lines that reference the same synonyms. If a source synonym in a new rule is already found to have replacement synonyms from another rule, then those replacements are merged.

Multi-word (aka Phrase) synonyms

For multi-word synonyms to work, the analysis must be applied at index-time and with expansion so that both the original words and the combined word get indexed. The next section elaborates on why this is so. Also, be aware that the tokenizer and previous filters can affect the tokens that the `SynonymFilter` sees. So, depending on the configuration, hyphens, other punctuations may or may not be stripped out.

Index-time versus query-time, and to expand or not

If you are doing synonym expansion (have any source synonyms that map to multiple replacement synonyms or tokens), then do synonym processing at either index-time or query-time, but not both. Doing it in both places would yield correct results but would perform slower. I recommend doing it at index-time because of these problems with doing it at query time:

- A source synonym containing multiple words (for example: i pod) isn't recognized at query-time because the query parser tokenizes on whitespace before the analyzer gets it.
- The IDF component of Lucene's scoring algorithm (discussed in *Chapter 5, Search Relevancy*) will be much higher for documents matching a synonym appearing rarely, as compared to its equivalents that are common. This reduces the scoring effectiveness.
- Prefix, wildcard, and fuzzy queries aren't analyzed, and thus won't match synonyms.

However, any analysis at index-time is less flexible, because any changes to the synonyms will require a complete re-index to take effect. Moreover, the index will get larger if you do index-time expansion—perhaps too large if you have a large set of synonyms such as with WordNet. It's plausible to imagine the issues above being rectified at some point. In spite of this, I usually recommend index-time.

Alternatively, you could choose not to do synonym expansion. This means that for a given synonym token, there is just one token that should replace it. This requires processing at both index-time and query-time to effectively normalize the synonymous tokens. However, since there is query-time processing, it suffers from the problems mentioned above (with the exception of poor scores, which isn't applicable). The benefit to this approach is that the index size would be smaller, because the number of indexed tokens is reduced.

You might also choose a blended approach to meet different goals. For example, if you have a huge index that you don't want to re-index often, but you need to respond rapidly to new synonyms, then you can put new synonyms into both a query-time synonym file and an index-time one. When a re-index finishes, you empty the query-time synonym file. You might also be fond of the query-time benefits, but due to the multiple word token issue, you decide to handle those particular synonyms at index-time.

Stop words

There is a simple filter called `StopFilterFactory` that filters out certain so-called **stop words** specified in a file in the `conf` directory, optionally ignoring case. Example usage:

```
<filter class="solr.StopFilterFactory" words="stopwords.txt"
ignoreCase="true"/>
```

When used, it is present in both index and query analyzer chains.

For indexes with lots of text, common uninteresting words like "the", "a", and so on, make the index large and slow down phrase queries that use them. A simple solution to this problem is to filter them out of fields where they show up often. Fields likely to contain more than a sentence are ideal candidates. Our MusicBrainz schema does *not* have content like this. The trade-off when omitting stop words from the index is that those words are no longer queryable. This is usually fine, but in some circumstances like searching for **To be or not to be**, it is obviously a problem.

The ideal solution to the common word problem is *not* to remove them. *Chapter 10* discusses an approach called **common-grams** implemented with `CommonGramsFilterFactory` that can be used to improve phrase search performance, while keeping these words. It is highly recommended.

Solr comes with a decent set of stop words for the English language. You may want to supplement it or use a different list altogether if you're indexing non-English text. In order to determine which words appear commonly in your index, access the **SCHEMA BROWSER** menu option in Solr's admin interface. A list of your fields will appear on the left. In case the list does not appear at once, be patient. For large indexes, there is a considerable delay before the field list appears because Solr is analyzing the data in your index. Now, choose a field that you know contains a lot of text. In the main viewing area, you'll see a variety of statistics about the field including the top-10 terms appearing most frequently.

Phonetic sounds-like analysis

Another useful text analysis option to enable searches that sound like a queried word is phonetic translation. A filter is used at both index and query-time that phonetically encodes each word into a **phoneme**. There are four phonetic encoding algorithms to choose from: `Caverphone`, `DoubleMetaphone`, `Metaphone`, `RefinedSoundex`, and `Soundex`. Anecdotally, `DoubleMetaphone` appears to be the best, even for non-English text. However, you might want to experiment in order to make your own choice. `RefinedSoundex` declares itself to be most suitable for spell check applications. However, Solr can't presently use phonetic analysis in its spell check component (described in a later chapter).

 Solr has three tools for more aggressive inexact searching: phonetic sounds-like, query spellchecking, and fuzzy searching. These are all employed a bit differently.

The following is a suggested configuration for phonetic analysis in the `schema.xml`:

```
<!-- for phonetic (sounds-like) indexing -->
<fieldType name="phonetic" class="solr.TextField"
    positionIncrementGap="100" stored="false" multiValued="true">
  <analyzer>
      <tokenizer class="solr.WhitespaceTokenizerFactory"/>
      <filter class="solr.WordDelimiterFilterFactory"
        generateWordParts="1" generateNumberParts="0"
        catenateWords="1" catenateNumbers="0" catenateAll="0"/>
      <filter class="solr.DoubleMetaphoneFilterFactory"
        inject="false" maxCodeLength="8"/>
  </analyzer>
</fieldType>
```

Note that the encoder options internally handle both upper and lower case.

In the MusicBrainz schema that is supplied with the book, a field named `a_phonetic` is declared to use this field type, and it has the artist name copied into it through a `copyField` directive. In *Chapter 4, Searching* you will read about the **dismax** query parser that can conveniently search across multiple fields with different scoring boosts. It could be configured to search not only the artist name (`a_name`) field, but also `a_phonetic` with a low boost, so that regular exact matches will come above those that match phonetically.

Using Solr's analysis admin page, it can be shown that this field type encodes `Smashing Pumpkins` as `SMXNK|XMXNK PMPKNS` (the use of a vertical bar | here indicates both sides are alternatives for the same position). This is not supposed to be meaningful, but it is useful for comparing similar spellings to detect its effectiveness.

The example above used the `DoubleMetaphoneFilterFactory` analysis filter, which has these two options:

- `inject`: A boolean defaulting to `true` that will cause the original words to pass through the filter. It might interfere with other filter options, querying, and potentially scoring. Therefore, it is preferred to disable this, and use a separate field dedicated to phonetic indexing.

- `maxCodeLength`: The maximum phoneme code (that is phonetic character, or syllable) length. It defaults to `4`. Longer codes are truncated. Only `DoubleMetaphone` supports this option.

In order to use one of the other three phonetic encoding algorithms, you must use this filter:

```
<filter class="solr.PhoneticFilterFactory" encoder="RefinedSoundex"
        inject="false"/>
```

The `encoder` attribute must be one of those algorithms listed in the first paragraph of this section.

Substring indexing and wildcards

Usually, text indexing technology is employed to search entire words. Occasionally however, there arises a need for a query to match an arbitrary substring of an indexed word or across them. Solr supports wildcards on queries (for example: `mus*ainz`) but there is some consideration needed in the way data is indexed.

It's useful to first get a sense of how Lucene handles a wildcard query at the index level. Lucene internally scans the sorted terms list on disk starting with the non-wildcard prefix (mus in the previous example). One thing to note about this is that the query takes exponentially longer for each fewer prefix character. In fact Solr configures Lucene to not accept a leading wildcard to ameliorate the problem. Another thing to note is that stemming, phonetic, and other non-trivial text analysis will interfere with these kinds of searches. For example, if running is stemmed to run, then runni* would not match.

Before employing these approaches, consider if what you really need is better tokenization for special codes. For example, if you have a long string code that internally has different parts that users might search on separately, then you can use a PatternReplaceFilterFactory with some other analyzers to split them up.

ReversedWildcardFilter

Solr doesn't permit a leading wildcard in a query unless you index the text in a reverse direction in addition to the forward direction. Doing this will also improve query performance when the wildcard is very close to the front. The following example configuration would appear at the end of the index analyzer chain:

```
<filter class="solr.ReversedWildcardFilterFactory" />
```

It has several performance-tuning options you can investigate further at its JavaDocs, but the defaults are reasonable. http://lucene.apache.org/solr/api/org/apache/solr/analysis/ReversedWildcardFilterFactory.html

Solr does not support a query with both a leading and trailing wildcard, for performance reasons. Given my explanation of the internals, I hope you understand why.

Wildcard queries can be slow, even if you use this reversing filter. If they are still too slow, consider looking at the next major release of Solr, v4.x (which is "trunk" in source control as of this writing) that contains some amazing performance improvements in this area. For still further ways to increase performance, read on to learn about n-grams.

N-grams

N-gram analysis slices text into many smaller substrings ranging between a minimum and maximum configured size. For example, consider the word **Tonight**. An NGramFilterFactory configured with minGramSize of 2 and maxGramSize of 5 would yield all of the following indexed terms: (2-grams:) To, on, ni, ig, gh, ht, (3-grams:) Ton, oni, nig, igh, ght, (4-grams:) Toni, onig, nigh, ight, (5-grams:) Tonig, onigh, night. Note that **Tonight** fully does not pass through because it has more characters than the maxGramSize. N-gram analysis can be used as a token filter, and it can also be used as a tokenizer with NGramTokenizerFactory, which will emit n-grams spanning across the words of the entire source text.

The following is a suggested analyzer configuration using n-grams to match substrings:

```
<fieldType name="nGram" class="solr.TextField"
        positionIncrementGap="100" stored="false" multiValued="true">
    <analyzer type="index">
        <tokenizer class="solr.StandardTokenizerFactory"/>
        <!-- potentially word delimiter, synonym filter, stop words,
            NOT stemming -->
        <filter class="solr.LowerCaseFilterFactory"/>
        <filter class="solr.NGramFilterFactory" minGramSize="2"
            maxGramSize="15"/>
    </analyzer>
    <analyzer type="query">
        <tokenizer class="solr.StandardTokenizerFactory"/>
        <!-- potentially word delimiter, synonym filter, stop words,
            NOT stemming -->
        <filter class="solr.LowerCaseFilterFactory"/>
    </analyzer>
</fieldType>
```

Notice that the n-gramming only happens at index-time. The range of gram sizes goes from the smallest number of characters you wish to enable substring searches on (2 in this example), to the maximum size permitted for substring searches (15 in this example).

This analysis would be applied to a field created solely for the purpose of matching substrings. Another field would exist for typical searches, and the dismaxquery parser, described in *Chapter 4, Searching* would be configured for searches to use both fields using a smaller boost for this field.

Another variation is `EdgeNGramTokenizerFactory` and `EdgeNGramFilterFactory`, which emit n-grams that are adjacent to either the start or end of the input text. For the filter-factory, this input-text is a term, and the tokenizer is the entire input. In addition to `minGramSize` and `maxGramSize`, these analyzers take a `side` argument that is either `front` or `back`. If only prefix or suffix matching is needed instead of both, then an `EdgeNGram` analyzer is for you.

N-gram costs

There is a high price to be paid for n-gramming. Recall that in the earlier example, **Tonight** was split into 15 substring terms, whereas typical analysis would probably leave only one. This translates to greater index sizes, and thus a longer time to index. Let's look at the effects of this in the MusicBrainz schema. The a_name field, which contains the artist name, is indexed in a typical fashion and is `stored`. The a_ngram field is fed by the artist name and is indexed with n-grams ranging from 2 to 15 characters in length. It is not a `stored` field because the artist's name is already stored in a_name.

	a_name	a_name + a_ngram	**Increase**
Indexing Time	46 seconds	479 seconds	> 10x
Disk Size	11.7 MB	59.7 MB	> 5x
Distinct Terms	203,431	1,288,720	> 6x

The preceding table shows a comparison of index statistics of an index with just a_name versus both a_name and a_ngram. Note the ten-fold increase in indexing time for the artist name, and a five-fold increase in disk space. Remember that this is just one field!

 Given these costs, n-gramming, if used at all, is generally only done on a field or two of small size where there is a clear requirement for substring matches.

The costs of n-gramming are lower if `minGramSize` is raised and to a lesser extent if `maxGramSize` is lowered. Edge n-gramming costs less too. This is because it is only based on one side. It definitely costs more to use the tokenizer-based n-grammers instead of the term-based filters used in the example before, because terms are generated that include and span whitespace. However, with such indexing, it is possible to match a substring spanning words.

Sorting Text

Usually, search results are sorted by relevancy via the magic `score` pseudo-field, but it is common to need to support conventional sorting by field values too. And in addition to sorting search results, there are ramifications to this discussion in doing a range query and when showing facet results in sorted order.

 Sorting limitations: A field needs to be indexed, not be multi-valued, and for text it should not have multiple tokens (either there is no text analysis or it yields just one token).

It just happens that MusicBrainz already supplies alternative artist and label names for sorting. When different from the original name, these sortable versions move words like "The" from the beginning to the end after a comma. We've marked the sort names as `indexed` but not `stored` since we're going to sort on it but not display it—deviating from what MusicBrainz does. Remember that `indexed` and `stored` are `true` by default. Because of the special text analysis restrictions of fields used for sorting, text fields in your schema that need to be sortable will usually be copied to another field and analyzed differently. The `copyField` directive in the schema facilitates this task. The `string` type is a type that has no text analysis and so it's perfect for our MusicBrainz case. As we're getting a sort-specific value from MusicBrainz, we don't need to derive something ourselves. However, note that in the MusicBrainz schema there are no sort-specific release names. We could opt to not support sorting by release name, but we're going to anyway. One option is to use the `string` type again. That's fine, but you may want to lowercase the text, remove punctuation, and collapse multiple spaces into one (if the data isn't clean). You could even use `PatternReplaceFilterFactory` to move words like "The" to the end. It's up to you. For the sake of variety in our example, we'll be taking the latter route; we're using a type `title_sort` that does these kinds of things.

By the way, Lucene sorts text by the internal Unicode code point. You probably won't notice any problem with the sort order. If you want sorting that is more accurate to the finer rules of various languages (English included), you should try the `CollationKeyFilterFactory`. Since it isn't commonly used and it's already well documented, I'll refer you to the wiki: `http://wiki.apache.org/solr/UnicodeCollation`

Miscellaneous token filters

Solr includes many other token filters:

- `ClassicFilterFactory`: (formerly named `StandardFilter` prior to Solr 3.1) Works in conjunction with `ClassicTokenizer`. It will remove periods in between acronyms and `s` at the end of terms:

  `"I.B.M. cat's" => "IBM", "cat"`

- `EnglishPossessiveFilterFactory`: Removes trailing `'s`.

- `TrimFilterFactory`: Removes leading and trailing whitespace. This is useful for text-analysis on a sort field given dirty input data.

- `LowerCaseFilterFactory`: Lowercases all text. Don't put this before `WordDelimeterFilterFactory` if you want to split on case transitions.

- `KeepWordFilterFactory`: Omits all of the words, except those in the specified file:

  `<filter class="solr.KeepWordFilterFactory" words="keepwords.txt" ignoreCase="true"/>`

  If you want to ensure a certain vocabulary of words in a special field, then you might enforce it with this.

- `LengthFilterFactory`: Filters out the terms that do not have a length within an inclusive range.

  `<filter class="solr.LengthFilterFactory" min="2" max="5" />`

- `LimitTokenCountFilterFactory`: Caps the number of tokens passing through to that specified in the `maxTokenCount` attribute. Solr also has a `<maxFieldLength/>` setting in `solrconfig.xml` that applies to all fields, which can be commented out to make the default unlimited. Even without any hard limits, you are effectively limited by the memory allocated to Java—reach that and Solr will throw an error.

- `RemoveDuplicatesTokenFilterFactory`: Ensures that no duplicate terms appear at the same position. This can happen, for example, when synonyms stem to a common root. It's a good idea to add this to your last analysis step if you are doing a fair amount of other analysis.

- `ASCIIFoldingFilterFactory`: See `MappingCharFilterFactory` in the earlier "Character filters" section.

- `CapitalizationFilterFactory`: Capitalizes each word according to the rules that you specify. For more information, see the Javadocs at http://lucene.apache.org/solr/api/org/apache/solr/analysis/CapitalizationFilterFactory.html.

- `PatternReplaceFilterFactory`: Takes a regular expression and replaces the matches. Example:

```
<filter class="solr.PatternReplaceFilterFactory" pattern=".*@(.*)"
        replacement="$1" replace="first" />
```

This example is for processing an e-mail address field to get only the domain of the address. This `replacement` happens to be a reference to a regular expression group, but it might be any old string. If the `replace` attribute is set to `first`, then only the first match is replaced; if `replace` is `all`, the default, then all matches are replaced.

- **Write your own**: Writing your own filter is an option if the existing ones don't suffice. Crack open the source code to Solr for one of these to get a handle on what's involved. Before you head down this path though, you'd be surprised at what a little creativity with `PatternReplaceFilterFactory` and some of the others can offer you. For starters, check out the `rType` field type in the `schema.xml` that is supplied online with this book.

There are some other miscellaneous Solr filters I didn't mention for various reasons. For common-grams or shingling, see *Chapter 10, Scaling Solr*. See the **all known implementing classes** section at the top of `http://lucene.apache.org/solr/api/org/apache/solr/analysis/TokenFilterFactory.html` for a complete list of token filter factories, including documentation.

Summary

At this point, you should have a schema that you believe will suit your needs—for now anyway. But do expect to revisit the schema. It is quite normal to start with something workable, and then subsequently make modifications to address issues, and implement features that require changes. The only irritant with changing the schema is that you probably need to re-index all of the data. The only exception to this would be an analysis step applied only at query-time. In the next chapter, you'll learn about the various ways to import data into the index.

3
Indexing Data

In this chapter we're going to explore ways to get data into Solr. The process of doing this is referred to as *indexing*, although *importing* is used too. This chapter is structured as follows:

- Communicating with Solr
- Sending data in Solr's Update-XML format
- Commit, optimize, rollback, and deleting
- Sending data in CSV format
- Direct database and XML import through Solr's **DataImportHandler** (the DIH)
- Extracting text from rich documents through Solr's **ExtractingRequestHandler** (also known as **Solr Cell**)
- Document post-processing with **UpdateRequestProcessors**

You will also find some related options in *Chapter 9, Integrating Solr* that have to do with language bindings and framework integration, including a web crawler. Most use Solr's Update-XML format.

In a hurry?

There are many approaches to get data into Solr and you don't need to be well versed in all of them. The section on commit and optimize is important for everyone because it is universal. If you plan to use a Solr integration framework that handles indexing data, such as Sunspot for Ruby on Rails, then you can follow the documentation for that framework and skip this chapter for now. Otherwise, the DataImportHandler will likely satisfy your needs.

Communicating with Solr

There are quite a few options in communicating with Solr to import data. In this section we'll look at a few choices to be made, and then follow up with interaction examples. Details on specific formats such as Solr's Update-XML comes later.

Direct HTTP or a convenient client API

Applications interact with Solr over HTTP. This can either be done directly using any HTTP client API of your choice, or indirectly via a Solr integration API such as SolrJ or Sunspot that will handle the HTTP interaction details. Such APIs are discussed in *Chapter 9, Integrating Solr*. This HTTP Solr interaction doesn't imply that the data to be indexed needs to move over this channel; you will learn soon that you can tell Solr to fetch the data.

 Another option is to *embed* Solr into your Java application instead of running it as a server. The SolrJ API is conveniently used for both remote and embedded use. More information about SolrJ and **Embedded Solr** can be found in *Chapter 9, Integrating Solr*.

Push data to Solr or have Solr pull it

Even though an application will be communicating with Solr over HTTP, it does not have to send Solr documents over this channel. Solr supports what it calls **remote streaming** in which it's given a URL to the data. It might be an HTTP URL, but more likely it is a file-system based URL, applicable when the data is already on Solr's machine or network drive. This option avoids the overhead of HTTP. Another way to ask Solr to pull data is to use the DataImportHandler (DIH) which can pull data from a database and other sources. The DIH offers an extensible framework that can be adapted to custom data sources.

Data formats

The following are various data formats for indexing data into Solr:

- **Solr's Update-XML**: Solr accepts documents expressed in XML conforming to a simple Solr-specific format. It has commands to delete documents and to perform optimizes and commits too.

    ◦ Other XML (Solr 3.4): Any arbitrary XML can be given to Solr along with an XSLT file that Solr will use to translate the XML to the Update-XML format for further processing. There is a short example of this in the DIH section, by way of comparison.

- **Solr's Update-JSON**: A JavaScript Object Notation variation of Solr's Update-XML. For more details, see: `http://wiki.apache.org/solr/UpdateJSON`

- **Java-Bin**: An efficient binary variation of Solr's Update-XML. Officially, only the SolrJ client API supports this, but there is a third-party Ruby port too.

- **CSV**: A comma (or other character) separated value format.

- **Rich documents**: Most user file formats such as PDF, XLS, DOC, PPT; text and metadata is extracted from these formats and put into various Solr fields. This is enabled via the Solr Cell contrib module.

 The DataImportHandler contrib module is a flexible data importing framework with out-of-the-box supports for importing arbitrary XML formats and e-mail, via the IMAP protocol. It is best known for pulling data from a relational database, though that isn't really a format, per-se.

We'll demonstrate Solr's capability to import MusicBrainz data in XML, CSV, and from a database. Other examples will include rich document import both via the DIH to crawl files and via Solr Cell. Most likely, an application would use just one format.

Before these approaches are described, we'll discuss **cURL** and **remote streaming**, which are foundational topics.

HTTP POSTing options to Solr

Solr receives commands and possibly document data through HTTP POST.

 Solr lets you use HTTP GET too, such as direct web browser access. However, this is an inappropriate HTTP verb for anything other than retrieving data. For more information on this concept, read about **REST** at `http://en.wikipedia.org/wiki/Representational_State_Transfer`

One way to send an HTTP POST is through the Unix command line program `curl` (also available on Windows through Cygwin: `http://www.cygwin.com`) and that's what we'll use here in the examples. An alternative cross-platform option that comes with Solr is `post.jar` located in Solr's `example/exampledocs` directory. To get some basic help on how to use it, run the following command:

```
>> java -jar example/exampledocs/post.jar -help
```

You'll see in a bit that you can post name-value pair options as HTML form data. However, `post.jar` doesn't support that, so you'll be forced to specify the URL and put the options in the query string.

There are several ways to tell Solr to index data, and all of them are through HTTP POST:

- Send the data as the entire POST payload. `curl` does this with `--data-binary` (or some similar options) and an appropriate content-type header for whatever the format is.

- Send some name-value pairs akin to an HTML form submission. With `curl`, such pairs are preceded by `-F`. If you're giving data to Solr to be indexed as opposed to it looking for it in a database, then there are a few ways to do that:

  ○ Put the data into the `stream.body` parameter. If it's small, perhaps less than a megabyte, then this approach is fine. The limit is configured with the `multipartUploadLimitInKB` setting in `solrconfig.xml`, defaulting to 2GB. If you're tempted to increase this limit, you should reconsider your approach.

  ○ Refer to the data through either a local file on the Solr server using the `stream.file` parameter or a URL that Solr will fetch through the `stream.url` parameter. These choices are a feature that Solr calls **remote streaming**.

Here is an example of the first choice. Let's say we have a Solr Update-XML file named `artists.xml` in the current directory. We can post it to Solr using the following command line:

```
>> curl http://localhost:8983/solr/mbartists/update -H 'Content-
type:text/xml; charset=utf-8' --data-binary @artists.xml
```

If it succeeds, then you'll have output that looks like this:

```
<?xml version="1.0" encoding="UTF-8"?>
<response>
<lst name="responseHeader">
    <int name="status">0</int><int name="QTime">128</int>
</lst>
</response>
```

To use the `stream.body` feature for the preceding example, you would do this:

```
curl http://localhost:8983/solr/mbartists/update -F stream.body=@artists.
xml
```

In both cases, the @ character instructs `curl` to get the data from the file instead of being `@artists.xml` literally. If the XML is short, then you can just as easily specify it literally on the command line:

```
curl http://localhost:8983/solr/mbartists/update -F stream.body=' <commit
/>'
```

Notice the leading space in the value. This was intentional. In this example, `curl` treats @ and < to mean things we don't want. In this case, it might be more appropriate to use `form-string` instead of `-F`. However, it's more typing, and I'm feeling lazy.

Remote streaming

In the preceding examples, we've given Solr the data to index in the HTTP message. Alternatively, the POST request can give Solr a pointer to the data in the form of either a file path accessible to Solr or an HTTP URL to it.

 The file path is accessed by the Solr server on its machine, not the client, and it must also have the necessary operating system file permissions too.

Just as before, the originating request does not return a response until Solr has finished processing it. If the file is of a decent size or is already at some known URL, then you may find remote streaming faster and/or more convenient, depending on your situation.

Here is an example of Solr accessing a local file:

```
curl http://localhost:8983/solr/mbartists/update -F stream.file=/tmp/
artists.xml
```

To use a URL, the parameter would change to `stream.url`, and we'd specify a URL. We're passing a name-value parameter (`stream.file` and the path), not the actual data.

 Security risk

Use of remote streaming (`stream.file` or `stream.url`), is enabled by default in `solrconfig.xml` (search for `enableRemoteStreaming`). This can be considered a security risk; so only turn it on if Solr is protected. See *Chapter 8, Deployment*, for more information.

Solr's Update-XML format

Using an XML formatted message, you can supply documents to be indexed, tell Solr to commit changes, to optimize the index, and to delete documents. Here is a sample XML file you can HTTP POST to Solr that adds (or replaces) a couple documents:

```
<add overwrite="true">
  <doc boost="2.0">
    <field name="id">5432a</field>
    <field name="type" ...</field>
    <field name="a_name" boost="0.5"></field>
    <!-- the date/time syntax MUST look just like this -->
    <field name="begin_date">2007-12-31T09:40:00Z</field>
  </doc>
  <doc>
    <field name="id">myid</field>
    <field name="type" ...
    <field name="begin_date">2007-12-31T09:40:00Z</field>
  </doc>
  <!-- more doc elements here as needed -->
</add>
```

A valid XML document has one root element. If you want to send multiple XML-based commands to Solr in the same message/file, then you can use an arbitrarily named root element to contain the XML elements Solr understands.

The `overwrite` attribute defaults to `true` to guarantee the uniqueness of values in the field that you have designated as the unique field in the schema, assuming you have such a field. If you were to add another document that has the same value for the unique field, then this document would overwrite the previous document. You will not get an error.

If you are sure that you will be adding a document that is not a duplicate, then you can set `overwrite` to `false` to get a small performance improvement since Solr won't check uniqueness of the unique key field.

The `boost` attribute affects the scores of matching documents in order to affect ranking in score-sorted search results. Providing a boost value, whether at the document or field level, is optional. The default value is `1.0`, which is effectively a non-boost. Technically, documents are not boosted, only fields are. The effective boost value of a field is that specified for the document multiplied by that specified for the field.

Specifying boosts here is called *index-time boosting*, which is rarely done as compared to the more flexible *query-time boosting*. Index-time boosting is less flexible because such boosting decisions must be decided at index-time and will apply to all of the queries. You'll learn more about boosting and scoring in *Chapter 5, Search Relevancy*.

Deleting documents

You can delete a document by its unique field. Here we delete two documents:

```
<delete><id>Artist:11604</id><id>Artist:11603</id></delete>
```

To more flexibly specify which documents to delete, you can alternatively use a Lucene/Solr query:

```
<delete><query>timestamp:[* TO NOW-12HOUR]</query></delete>
```

The contents of the `delete` tag can be any number of `id` and `query` tags if you want to batch many deletions into one message to Solr.

The query syntax is discussed in *Chapter 4, Searching*. Since we haven't gotten to that yet, I'll explain the preceding example. Let's suppose that all of your documents had a timestamp field with a value of the time it was indexed, and you have an update strategy that bulk loads all of the data on a daily basis. If the loading process results in documents that shouldn't be in the index anymore, then we can delete them immediately after a bulk load. This query would delete all of the documents not indexed within the last 12 hours. Twelve was chosen somewhat arbitrarily, but it needs to be less than 24 (the update process interval) and greater than the longest time it might conceivably take to bulk-load all the data.

 If you want to delete the entire index in the course of development (or perform major schema changes in production), then simply delete the `data` directory while Solr is shut down.

Commit, optimize, and rollback

Data sent to Solr is not immediately searchable, nor do deletions take immediate effect. Like a database, changes must be *committed* first. The easiest way to do this is to add a `commit=true` request parameter to a Solr update URL. The request to Solr could be the same request that contains data to be indexed then committed or an empty request—it doesn't matter. For example, you can visit this URL to issue a commit on our `mbreleases` core: `http://localhost:8983/solr/mbreleases/update?commit=true`. You can also commit changes using the XML syntax by simply sending this to Solr:

```
<commit />
```

There are three important things to know about commits that are unique to Solr:

- Commits are slow. Depending on the index size, Solr's auto-warming configuration, and Solr's cache state prior to committing, a commit can take a non-trivial amount of time. Typically, it takes a few seconds, but it can take some number of minutes in extreme cases. To learn how to decrease this time, read about realtime search in *Chapter 10, Scaling Solr.*

- There is no *transaction isolation*. This means that if more than one Solr client were to submit modifications and commit them at overlapping times, it is possible for part of one client's set of changes to be committed before that client told Solr to commit. This applies to *rollback* as well. If this is a problem for your architecture then consider using one client process responsible for updating Solr.

- Simultaneous commits should be avoided, particularly more than two. The problem actually pertains to simultaneous query warming which is the latter and lengthy part of a commit. Solr will use a lot of resources and it might even yield an error indicating there is too much simultaneous warming— though the commit will eventually still have its effect.

When you are bulk loading data, these concerns are not an issue since you're going to issue a final commit at the end. But if Solr is asynchronously updated by independent clients in response to changed data, commits could come too quickly and might overlap. To address this, Solr has two similar features, **autoCommit** and **commitWithin**. The first refers to a snippet of XML configuration commented in `solrconfig.xml` in which Solr will automatically commit at a document-count threshold or time-lapse threshold (time of oldest uncommitted document). In this case, Solr itself handles committing and so your application needn't send commits. `commitWithin` is a similar time-lapse option that is set by the client on either the `<add commitWithin="...">` element or the `<commit commitWithin="..."/>` element of an XML formatted update message or set a request parameter (as of Solr 3.4) in order to express another option available. It will ensure a commit occurs within the specified number of milliseconds. Here's an example of a 30 second commit window:

```
<commit commitWithin="30000"/>
```

commitWithin is preferred to autoCommit

The `commitWithin` attribute on an `add` or `commit` element is preferable to the `autoCommit` in `solrconfig.xml` because the latter is global and can't be disabled. Also, be careful not to pick a time window shorter than how long a commit takes since then commits will start to overlap, which is very bad!

Look for a future version of Solr to have what's called **near realtime search**—a much sought after feature. This will make commits cheap, thereby enabling Solr to be updated asynchronously when data changes and have it be searchable almost immediately.

Lucene's index is internally composed of one or more **segments**. When a buffer of indexed documents gets flushed to disk it creates a new segment. Deletes get recorded in another file, but they go to disk too. Sometimes, after a new segment is written, Lucene will merge some of them together. When Lucene has just one segment, it is in an **optimized** state. The more segments there are the more query performance degrades. Of course, optimizing an index comes at a cost; the larger your index is, the longer it will take to optimize. Finally, an optimize command implies commit semantics. You can specify an optimize command in all the places you specify a commit. So, to use it in a URL, try this: `http://localhost:8983/solr/mbreleases/update?optimize=true`. For the XML format, simply send this:

```
<optimize />
```

It is recommended to explicitly optimize the index at an opportune time like after a bulk load of data and/or a daily interval in off-peak hours, if there are sporadic updates to the index. The performance chapter has a tip on optimizing to more than one segment if the optimizes are taking too long.

Both commit and optimize commands take two additional boolean options that default to `true`:

```
<optimize waitFlush="true" waitSearcher="true"/>
```

If you were to set these to `false`, then commit and optimize commands return immediately, even though the operation hasn't actually finished yet. So if you wrote a script that committed with these at their false values and then executed a query against Solr, you may find that the search will not reflect the changes yet. By waiting for the data to flush to disk (`waitFlush`) and waiting for a new searcher to be ready to respond to changes (`waitSearcher`), this circumstance is avoided. These options are useful for executing an optimize command from a script that simply wants to optimize the index and otherwise doesn't care when newly added data is searchable.

 No matter how long a commit or optimize command takes, Solr still executes searches concurrently — there is no read lock.

There is one final indexing command to discuss — **rollback**. All uncommitted changes can be cancelled by sending Solr the rollback command either via a URL parameter such as: `http://localhost:8983/solr/mbreleases/update?rollback=true` or with this XML:

```
<rollback />
```

Sending CSV formatted data to Solr

If you have data in a CSV format or if it is more convenient for you to get CSV than XML or JSON, then you may prefer the CSV option. Solr's CSV support is fairly flexible. You won't be able to specify an index-time boost but that's an uncommon need.

 CSV is uniquely the only format that Solr supports for *round-tripping* data. As such, you can query for CSV formatted data that is suitable to be added right back into Solr (for stored fields only, of course). The XML and JSON query output formats are structured differently than their input formats so they don't count.

To get some CSV data out of a local PostgreSQL database for the MusicBrainz tracks, I ran this command:

```
psql -U postgres -d musicbrainz_db -c "COPY (\
select 'Track:' || t.id as id, 'Track' as type, t.name as t_name,
t.length/1000 as t_duration, a.id as t_a_id, a.name as t_a_name,
albumjoin.sequence as t_num, r.id as t_r_id, r.name as t_r_name, array_
to_string(r.attributes,' ') as t_r_attributes, albummeta.tracks as t_r_
tracks \
from (track t inner join albumjoin on t.id = albumjoin.track \
 inner join album r on albumjoin.album = r.id left join albummeta on
albumjoin.album = albummeta.id) inner join artist a on t.artist = a.id \
) to '/tmp/mb_tracks.csv' CSV HEADER"
```

And it generated about 7 million lines of output that looks like this (first three lines):

```
id,type,t_name,t_duration,t_a_id,t_a_name,t_num,t_r_id,t_r_name,t_r_
attributes,t_r_tracks

Track:183326,Track,In the Arms of Sleep,254,11650,The Smashing
Pumpkins,4,22471,Mellon Collie and the Infinite Sadness (disc 2: Twilight
to Starlight),0 1 100,14

Track:183328,Track,Tales of a Scorched Earth,228,11650,The Smashing
Pumpkins,6,22471,Mellon Collie and the Infinite Sadness (disc 2: Twilight
to Starlight),0 1 100,14

...
```

This CSV file is provided with the code supplement to the book. To get Solr to import the CSV file, type this at the command line:

```
curl http://localhost:8983/solr/update/csv -F f.t_r_attributes.split=true
-F f.t_r_attributes.separator=' ' -F overwrite=false -F commit=true -F
stream.file=/tmp/mb_tracks.csv
```

The CSV options were specified via form values (-F) here; you can alternatively encode them into the query portion of the URL—it doesn't matter.

Consider the Unix mkfifo command

When I actually did this I had PostgreSQL on one machine and Solr on another. I used the Unix `mkfifo` command to create an in-memory data pipe mounted at `/tmp/mb_tracks.csv`. This way, I didn't have to actually generate a huge CSV file. I could essentially stream it directly from PostgreSQL into Solr. Details on this approach and PostgreSQL are out of the scope of this book.

Configuration options

The following are the names of each configuration option with an explanation. For the MusicBrainz track CSV file, the defaults were used with the exception of specifying how to parse the multi-valued t_r_attributes field and disabling unique key processing for performance.

- separator: The character that separates each value on a line. Defaults to a comma.

 If you're using curl and need to specify a tab character or some other character that isn't visible other than a space, then the easiest way to do this is to specify this parameter on the URL as a query parameter instead of with -F. Remember to URL encode it. For example: .../update/csv?separator=%09 -F ... and so on.

- header: Is set to true if the first line lists the field names (the default).

- fieldnames: If the first line doesn't have the field names, then you'll have to use this instead to indicate what they are. They are comma separated. If no name is specified for a column, then its data is skipped.

- skip: The fields to not import in the CSV file.

- skipLines: The number of lines to skip in the input file. Defaults to 0.

- trim: If true, then removes leading and trailing whitespace as a final step, even if quoting is used to explicitly specify a space. Defaults to false. Solr already does an initial pass trim, but quoting may leave spaces.

- encapsulator: This character is used to encapsulate (that is surround, quote) values in order to preserve the field separator as a field value instead of mistakenly parsing it as the next field. This character itself is escaped by doubling it. It defaults to the double quote, unless escape is specified. Example:

  ```
  11604, foo, "The ""second"" word is quoted.", bar
  ```

- escape: If this character is found in the input text, then the next character is taken literally in place of this escape character, and it isn't otherwise treated specially by the file's syntax. Example:

  ```
  11604, foo, The second\, word is followed by a comma., bar
  ```

- keepEmpty: Specified whether blank (zero length) fields should be indexed as such or omitted. It defaults to false.

- overwrite: It indicates whether to enforce the unique key constraint of the schema by overwriting existing documents with the same ID. It defaults to true. Disable this to increase performance, if you are sure you are passing new documents.

- `split`: This is a field-specific option used to split what would normally be one value into multiple values. Another set of CSV configuration options (separator, and so on) can be specified for this field to instruct Solr on how to do that. See the previous tracks MusicBrainz example on how this is used.

- `map`: This is another field-specific option used to replace input values with another. It can be used to remove values too. The value should include a colon, which separates the left side which is replaced with the right side. If we were to use this feature on the tracks of the MusicBrainz data, then it could be used to map the numeric code in `t_r_attributes` to more meaningful values. Here's an example of such an attempt:

```
-F keepEmpty=false -F f.t_r_attributes.map=0:
  -F f.t_r_attributes.map=1:Album -F f.t_r_attributes.map=2:Single
```

This causes 0 to be removed, because it seems to be useless data, as nearly all tracks have it, and we map 1 to `Album` and 2 to `Single`.

The Data Import Handler Framework

Solr includes a very popular contrib module for importing data known as the `DataImportHandler` (DIH in short). It's a data processing pipeline built specifically for Solr. Here's a summary of notable capabilities:

- Imports data from databases through **JDBC (Java Database Connectivity)**
  - ° Supports importing only changed records, assuming a last-updated date
- Imports data from a URL (HTTP GET)
- Imports data from files (that is it *crawls* files)
- Imports e-mail from an IMAP server, including attachments
- Supports combining data from different sources
- Extracts text and metadata from rich document formats
- Applies XSLT transformations and XPath extraction on XML data
- Includes a diagnostic/development tool

Furthermore, you could write your own data source or transformation step once you learn how by seeing how the existing ones are coded.

Consider DIH alternatives

The DIH's capabilities really have little to do with Solr itself yet the DIH is tied to Solr (to a Solr core, to be precise). Consider alternative data *pipelines* such as those referenced here: http://wiki.apache.org/ solr/SolrEcosystem—this includes building your own. Alternatives can run on another machine to reduce the load on Solr when there is significant processing involved. And in being agnostic of where the data is delivered, your investment in them can be re-used for other purposes independent of Solr. With that said, the DIH is a strong choice because it is integrated with Solr and it has a lot of capabilities.

The complete reference documentation for the DIH is here: http://wiki.apache. org/solr/DataImportHandler. It's rather thorough. In this chapter I'll demonstrate some of its features but you'll need to turn to the wiki for further details.

Setup

The DIH is not considered a core part of Solr, even though it comes with the Solr download, and so you must add its Java JAR files to your Solr setup to use it. If this isn't done, you'll eventually see a ClassNotFoundException error. The DIH's JAR files are located in Solr's dist directory: apache-solr-dataimporthandler-3.4.0.jar and apache-solr-dataimporthandler-extras-3.4.0.jar. The easiest way to add JAR files to a Solr configuration is to copy them to the <solr_home>/ lib directory; you may need to create it. Another method is to reference them from solrconfig.xml via <lib/> tags—see Solr's example configuration for examples of that. *You will most likely need some additional JAR files as well.* If you'll be communicating with a database, then you'll need to get a JDBC driver for it. If you will be extracting text from various document formats then you'll need to add the JARs in /contrib/extraction/lib. Finally, if you'll be indexing e-mail then you'll need to add the JARs in /contrib/dataimporthandler/lib.

The DIH needs to be registered with Solr in solrconfig.xml like so:

```
<requestHandler name="/dih_artists_jdbc"
    class="org.apache.solr.handler.dataimport.DataImportHandler">
  <lst name="defaults">
    <str name="config">mb-dih-artists-jdbc.xml</str>
  </lst>
</requestHandler>
```

This reference mb-dih-artists-jdbc.xml is located in <solr-home>/conf, which specifies the details of a data importing process. We'll get to that file in a bit.

The development console

Before describing a DIH configuration file, we're going to take a look at the DIH development console. Visit this URL (modifications may be needed for your host, port, core, and so on):

```
http://localhost:8983/solr/mbartists/admin/dataimport.jsp
```

If there is more than one request handler registered, then you'll see a simple page listing them with links to continue to the development console for that handler. The development console looks like the following screenshot:

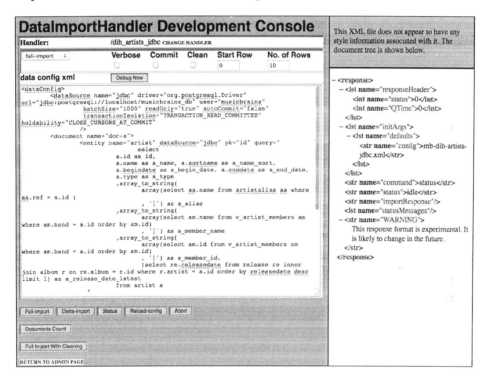

The screen is divided into two panes: on the left is the DIH control form and on the right is the command output as raw XML.

The control form is further subdivided into a development/debugging section to include *temporary* editing of the configuration file, and is followed by a master list of major DIH command buttons at the bottom.

The editable configuration is not saved to disk! It is purely for live trial-and-error debugging. Once you are satisfied with any changes, you'll need to save them back to the file yourself and then take some action to get Solr to reload the changes, such as by clicking on the **Reload Config** button, and then reload the page to pick up the changes on the screen. Furthermore, only the **Debug Now** button uses this text; not the buttons at the bottom.

The last section on DIH in this chapter goes into more detail on submitting a command to the DIH.

Writing a DIH configuration file

The key pieces of a DIH configuration file include a data source, an entity, some transformers, and a list of fields. There can be variable numbers of these things and sometimes they can be omitted. At first I'll list the various types of each of these DIH components with a simple description. Each has further details on usage that you'll need to see the wiki for. Then I'll show you a few sample configuration files to give you a sense of how it all comes together.

Data Sources

A `<dataSource/>` specifies, as you might guess, the source of data referenced by an entity. This is the simplest piece of the configuration. The `type` attribute specifies the type, which defaults to `JdbcDataSource`. Depending on the type, there are further configuration attributes (not listed here). There could be multiple data sources but not usually. Furthermore, with the exception of `JdbcDataSource`, each type handles either binary or text but not both. The following is a listing of available data source types. They all have a name ending with `DataSource`.

- `JdbcDataSource`: A reference to a database via JDBC; usually relational.
- `FieldStreamDataSource`, `FieldReaderDataSource`: For extracting binary or character data from a column from a `JdbcDataSource`.
- `BinFileDataSource`, `FileDataSource`: Specify a path to a binary or text file.
- `URLDataSource`: Specify a URL to a text resource.
- `BinContentStreamDataSource`, `ContentStreamDataSource`: Receives binary or text data posted to the DIH instead of the DIH pulling it from somewhere.

ContentStreamDataSource is very interesting because it lets you use the DIH to receive asynchronous on-demand data processing instead of the typical scheduled batch-process mode. It could be used for many things, even a Web Hook: http://www.webhooks.org/.

If you were looking for a MailDataSource, then there isn't any. The MailEntityProcessor was coded to fetch the mail itself instead of decoupling that function to a data source.

Entity processors

Following the data sources is a <document/> element, which contains one or more <entity/> elements referencing an Entity Processor via the processor attribute; the default is SqlEntityProcessor. An entity processor produces documents when it is executed. The data to produce the documents typically comes from a referenced data source. An entity that is an immediate child of <document> is by default a **root entity**, which means its documents are indexed by Solr. If the rootEntity attribute is explicitly set to false, then the DIH recursively traverses down until it finds one that doesn't have this marking. There can be sub-entities, which execute once for each parent document and which usually reference the parent document to narrow a query. Documents from a sub-entity are merged into its root entity's document, producing multi-valued fields when more than one document with the same field is produced by the sub-entity.

 This explanation is surely quite confusing without having seen several examples. You may want to read this again once you get to some examples.

The entity processors have some common configuration attributes and some that are unique to each one.

 There is a threads attribute, new to Solr 3. This allows you to specify how many concurrent Solr indexing threads are used, in order to index documents faster.

Entity processors all have a name ending with EntityProcessor. The following are a list of them:

- SqlEntityProcessor: References a JdbcDataSource and executes a specified SQL query. The columns in the result set, map to fields by the same name. This processor uniquely supports delta-import.

- `CachedSqlEntityProcessor`: Like `SqlEntityProcessor`, but caches every record in memory for future lookups instead of running the query each time. This is only an option for sub-entities of a root entity.

- `XPathEntityProcessor`: Processes XML from a text data source. It separates the XML into separate documents according to an XPath expression. Fields reference a part of the XML via an XPath expression.

- `PlainTextEntityProcessor`: Takes the text from a text data source putting it into a single field.

- `LineEntityProcessor`: Takes *each line* of text from a text data source, creating a document from each one. A suggested use is for an input file of URLs that are referenced by a sub-entity like Tika.

- `FileListEntityProcessor`: Finds all files meeting the specified criteria, creating a document from each one with the file path in a field. A sub-entity like Tika could then extract text from the file.

- `TikaEntityProcessor`: Extracts text from a binary data source, using Apache Tika. Tika supports many file types such as HTML, PDF, and Microsoft Office documents. This is an alternative approach to Solr Cell, described later.

- `MailEntityProcessor`: Fetches e-mail from an IMAP mail server, including attachments processed with Tika. It doesn't use a data source. You can specify a starting date but unfortunately it doesn't support DIH's delta-import.

Fields and transformers

Within an `<entity/>` are some `<field/>` elements that declare how the columns in the query map to Solr. The field element must have a `column` attribute that matches the corresponding named column in the SQL query. The `name` attribute is the Solr schema field name that the column is going into. If it is not specified, then it defaults to the column name. When a column in the result can be placed directly into Solr without further processing, there is no need to specify the field declaration, because it is implied.

When importing from a database, use the SQL **AS** keyword to use the same names as the Solr schema instead of the database schema. This reduces the number of `<field/>` elements and shortens existing ones.

An attribute of the entity declaration that we didn't mention yet is `transformer`. This declares a comma-separated list of **transformers** that create, modify, and delete fields and even entire documents. The transformers are evaluated in-order, which can be significant. Usually the transformers use attributes specific to them on a given field to trigger that it should take some action, whether it be splitting the field into multiple values or formatting it or whatever. The following is a list of transformers:

- `TemplateTransformer`: Overwrites or modifies a value based on a string template. The template can contain references to other fields and DIH variables.

- `RegexTransformer`: Either performs a string substitution, splits the field into multiple values, or splits the field into separately named fields. This transformer is very useful!

- `DateFormatTransformer`: Parses a date-time format according to a specified pattern. The output format is Solr's date format.

- `NumberFormatTransformer`: Parses a number according to a specified locale and "style" (that is number, percent, integer, currency). The output format is a plain number suitable for one of Solr's numeric fields.

- `HTMLStripTransformer`: Removes HTML markup according to `HTMLStripCharFilter` (documented in the previous chapter). By performing this step here instead of a text analysis component, the stored value will also be cleansed, not just the indexed (that is, searchable) data.

- `ClobTransformer`: Transforms a CLOB value from a database into a plain string.

- `LogTransformer`: Logs a string for diagnostic purposes, using a string template like `TemplateTransformer`. Unlike most transformers, this is configured at the entity since it is evaluated for each entity output document, not for each field.

- `ScriptTransformer`: Invokes user-defined code in-line defined in a `<script/>` element. This transformer is specified differently within the `transformers` attribute—use `...,script:myFunctionName,...` where `myFunctionName` is a named function in the provided code. The code is written in JavaScript by default but most other languages that run on the JVM languages can be used too.

The ScriptTransformer is powerful!

You should certainly use the other transformers as appropriate, but there is nearly nothing you can't do with this one. Your script function can emit multiple records by returning an array of them, and it can omit a record by returning null. You may want to consider testing your script by using a separate script file and writing unit tests for it.

By the way, DIH transformers are similar to Solr `UpdateRequestProcessors` described at the end of this chapter. The former operates strictly within the DIH framework whereas the latter is applicable to any importing mechanism.

Example DIH configurations

A DIH configuration file tends to look different depending on whether the source is a database, the content is XML, or if text is being extracted from documents.

It's important to understand that the various data sources, data formats, and transformers, are mostly independent. The next few examples pick combinations to demonstrate a variety of possibilities for illustrative purposes. You should pick the pieces that you need.

Importing from databases

The following is the `mb-dih-artists-jdbc.xml` file with a rather long SQL query:

```
<dataConfig>
  <dataSource name="jdbc" driver="org.postgresql.Driver"
    url="jdbc:postgresql://localhost/musicbrainz_db"
    user="musicbrainz" readOnly="true" autoCommit="false" />
  <document>
    <entity name="artist" dataSource="jdbc" pk="id" query="
      select
        a.id as id,
        a.name as a_name, a.sortname as a_name_sort,
        a.begindate as a_begin_date, a.enddate as a_end_date,
        a.type as a_type,
        array_to_string(
          array(select aa.name from artistalias aa
            where aa.ref = a.id ),
          '|') as a_alias,
        array_to_string(
          array(select am.name from v_artist_members am
            where am.band = a.id order by am.id),
          '|') as a_member_name,
```

```
              array_to_string(
                array(select am.id from v_artist_members am
                  where am.band = a.id order by am.id),
                '|') as a_member_id,
              (select re.releasedate from release re inner join
                album r on re.album = r.id where r.artist = a.id
                order by releasedate desc limit 1)
                as a_release_date_latest
          from artist a
              "
          transformer="RegexTransformer,DateFormatTransformer,
                  TemplateTransformer">
          <field column = "id" template="Artist:${artist.id}" />
          <field column = "type" template="Artist" />
          <field column = "a_begin_date"
            dateTimeFormat="yyyy-MM-dd" />
          <field column = "a_end_date"
            dateTimeFormat="yyyy-MM-dd" />
          <field column = "a_alias" splitBy="\|" />
          <field column = "a_member_name" splitBy="\|"/>
          <field column = "a_member_id" splitBy="\|" />
      </entity>
    </document>
  </dataConfig>
```

If the `type` attribute on `dataSource` is not specified (it isn't here) then it defaults to `JdbcDataSource`. Those familiar with JDBC should find the attributes in this example familiar, and there are others available. For a reference to all of them, see the wiki.

Efficient JDBC configuration

Many database drivers in the default configurations (including those for PostgreSQL and MySQL) fetch all of the query results into memory instead of on-demand or using a batch/fetch size! This may work well for typical database usage in which a relatively small amount of data needs to be fetched quickly, but is completely unworkable for ETL (**Extract Transform and Load**) usage such as this. Configuring the driver to stream the data will sometimes require driver-specific configuration settings. Settings for some specific databases are at `http://wiki.apache.org/solr/DataImportHandlerFaq`.

The main piece of an `<entity/>` used with a database is the `query` attribute, which is the SQL query to be evaluated. You'll notice that this query involves some sub-queries, which are made into arrays and then transformed into strings joined by spaces. The particular functions used to do these sorts of things are generally database specific. This is done to shoehorn multi-valued data into a single row in the results. It may create a more complicated query, but it does mean that the database does all of the heavy lifting so that all of the data Solr needs for an artist is in one row.

Sub-entities

There are numerous examples on the DIH wiki depicting entities within entities (assuming the parent entity is a *root entity*). This is an approach to the problem of getting multiple values for the same Solr field. It's also an approach for spanning different data sources. I advise caution against that approach because it will generate a separate query in response to each source record, which is very inefficient. It can be told to cache just one query to be used for future lookups but that is only applicable to data shared across records that can also fit in memory. If all required data is in your database, I recommend the approach illustrated above instead.

Importing XML from a file with XSLT

In this example, we're going to import an XML file from disk and use XSLT to do most of the work instead of DIH transformers.

Solr 3.4 added direct support for using XSLT to process input XML without requiring use of the DIH as we show in this simple example. The following command would have the same effect:

```
curl 'http://localhost:8983/solr/mbartists/update/
xslt?tr=artists.xsl&commit=true' -H 'Content-type:text/
xml' --data-binary @downloads/artists_veryshort.xml
```

```xml
<dataConfig>
 <dataSource name="artists" type="FileDataSource" encoding="UTF-8"/>
 <document name="artists">
   <entity name="artist" dataSource="artists"
     url="downloads/artists_veryshort.xml"
     processor="XPathEntityProcessor"
     xsl="cores/mbtype/conf/xslt/artists.xsl"
     useSolrAddSchema="true">
   </entity>
 </document>
</dataConfig>
```

This `dataSource` of type `FileDataSource` is for text files. The entity URL is relative to the `baseUrl` on the data source; since it's not specified then it defaults to the current working directory of the server. The referenced XSLT file is relative to the current working directory instead of the `conf` directory—a known bug: SOLR-1226. To see the referenced XSLT file, download the code supplement for the book.

An interesting thing about this example is not just the use of XSLT but `useSolrAddSchema` which signifies that the resulting XML structure follows Solr's XML `<add><doc><field name=...` structure. Our input file is an HTML table and the XSLT file transforms it. These two options are best used together.

 There are some other examples at the DIH wiki illustrating XML processing. One of them shows how to process a Wikipedia XML file dump, which is rather interesting.

Importing multiple rich document files (crawling)

In this example, we have a configuration that crawls all PDF files in a directory and then extracts text and metadata from them.

```
<dataConfig>
  <dataSource type="BinFileDataSource" />
  <document>
    <entity name="f" dataSource="null" rootEntity="false"
      processor="FileListEntityProcessor"
      baseDir="/my/file/path" fileName=".*pdf"
      recursive="true">
    <entity name="tika-test" processor="TikaEntityProcessor"
      url="${f.fileAbsolutePath}" format="text">
      <field column="Author" name="author" meta="true"/>
      <field column="title" name="title" meta="true"/>
      <field column="text" name="text"/>
    </entity>
    </entity>
  </document>
</dataConfig>
```

The `FileListEntityProcessor` is the piece that does the file crawling. It doesn't actually use a data source but it's required. Because this entity is not a *root entity*, thanks to `rootEntity="false"`, it's the sub-entity within it that is a root entity which corresponds to a Solr document. The entity is named `f` and the sub-entity `tika-test` refers to the path provided by `f` via `f.fileAbsolutePath` in its `url`. This example uses the variable substitution syntax `${...}`.

Speaking of which, there are a variety of variables that the DIH makes available for substitution, including those defined in `solr.xml` and `solrconfig.xml`. Again, see the DIH wiki for further details.

The `TikaEntityProcessor` part is relatively straightforward. Tika makes a variety of metadata available about documents; this example just used two.

Importing commands

The DIH is issued one of several different commands to do different things. Importing all data is called a **full import**, in contrast to a **delta import** that will be described shortly. Commands are given to the DIH request handler with the `command` attribute. We could tell the DIH to do a full import just by going to this URL: `http://localhost:8983/solr/mbartists/dataimport?command=full-import`. On the command line we would use:

```
curl http://localhost:8983/mbartists/solr/dataimport
   -F command=full-import
```

It uses HTTP POST, which is more appropriate than GET as discussed earlier.

Unlike the other importing mechanisms, the DIH returns an HTTP response immediately while the import continues asynchronously. To get the current status of the DIH, go to this URL `http://localhost:8983/solr/mbartists/dataimport`, and you'll get output like the following:

```
<response>
    <lst name="responseHeader">
        <int name="status">0</int>
        <int name="QTime">15</int>
    </lst>
    <lst name="initArgs">
        <lst name="defaults">
            <str name="config">mb-dih-artists-jdbc.xml</str>
        </lst>
    </lst>
    <str name="status">idle</str>
    <str name="importResponse"/>
    <lst name="statusMessages"/>
    <str name="WARNING">This response format is experimental. It is
likely to change in the future.</str>
</response>
```

The `command` attribute defaults to `status`, which is what this output shows. When an import is in progress, it shows statistics on that progress along with a status state of `busy`.

Other boolean parameters named `clean`, `commit`, and `optimize` may accompany the command, and they all default to `true`. `clean` is specific to DIH, and it means that before running the import, it will delete all documents first. To customize exactly which documents are deleted, you can specify a `preImportDeleteQuery` attribute on a root entity. You can even specify documents to be deleted *after* an import by using the `postImportDeleteQuery` attribute. The query syntax is documented in *Chapter 4, Searching*.

> Beware that these defaults are inconsistent with other Solr importing mechanisms. No other importing mechanism will delete all documents first, and none will commit or optimize by default.

Two other useful commands are `reload-config` and `abort`. The first will reload the DIH configuration file, which is useful for picking up changes without having to restart Solr. The second will cancel any existing imports in progress.

Delta imports

The DIH supports what it calls a **delta import**, which is a mode of operation in which only data that has changed since the last import is retrieved. A delta import is only supported by the `SqlEntityProcessor` and it assumes that your data is time-stamped. The official DIH approach to this is prominently documented on the wiki. It uses a `deltaImportQuery` and `deltaQuery` pair of attributes on the entity, and a `delta-import` command. That approach is verbose, hard to maintain, and it's slow compared to a novel alternative documented here: `http://wiki.apache.org/solr/DataImportHandlerDeltaQueryViaFullImport`.

Essentially, what you do is introduce a timestamp check in your SQL's WHERE clause using variable substitution, along with another check if the `clean` parameter was given to the DIH in order to control whether or not a delta or full import should happen. Here is a concise `<entity/>` definition on a fictitious schema and data set showing the relevant WHERE clause:

```
<entity name="item" pk="ID"
  query="SELECT * FROM item
    WHERE '${dataimporter.request.clean}' != 'false'
      OR last_modified > '${dataimporter.last_index_time}'">
```

Notice the `${...}` variable substitution syntax. To issue a full import, use the full-import command with `clean` enabled: `/dataimport?command=full-import&clean=true`. And for a delta import, we still use the `full-import` command but we set `clean` to `false`: `/dataimport?command=full-import&clean=false&optimize=false`. I also disabled the index optimization since it's not likely this is desired for a delta import.

Indexing documents with Solr Cell

While most of this book assumes that the content you want to index in Solr is in a neatly structured data format of some kind, such as in a database table, a selection of XML files, or CSV, the reality is that we also store information in the much messier world of binary formats such as PDF, Microsoft Office, or even images and music files.

Your author Eric Pugh first became involved with the Solr community when he needed to ingest the thousands of PDF and Microsoft Word documents that a client had produced over the years. The outgrowth of that early effort is **Solr Cell** providing a very powerful and simple framework for indexing rich document formats.

 Solr Cell is technically called the `ExtractingRequestHandler`. The current name came about as a derivation of "Content Extraction Library" which appeared more fitting to its author, Grant Ingersoll. Perhaps a name including Tika would have been most appropriate considering that this capability is a small adapter to Tika. You may have noticed that the DIH includes this capability via the appropriately named `TikaEntityProcessor`.

We'll look at how to leverage Solr Cell for extracting karaoke song lyrics from MIDI files. Just think you can build a Solr powered index of all your favorite karaoke songs! The complete reference material for Solr Cell is available at `http://wiki.apache.org/solr/ExtractingRequestHandler`.

Extracting text and metadata from files

Every file format is different, and all of them provide different types of metadata, as well as different methods of extracting content. The heavy lifting of providing a single API to an ever expanding list of formats is delegated to **Apache Tika**:

> *Apache Tika is a toolkit for detecting and extracting metadata and structured text content from various documents using existing parser libraries.*

Tika supports a wide variety of formats, from the predictable to the unexpected. Some of the most commonly used formats supported are Adobe PDF, Microsoft Office including Word, Excel, PowerPoint, Visio, and Outlook. Other formats that are supported include extracting metadata from images such as JPG, GIF, and PNG, as well as from various audio formats such as MP3, MIDI, and Wave audio. Tika itself does not attempt to parse the individual document formats. Instead, it delegates the parsing to various third-party libraries, while providing a high level stream of XML SAX events as the documents are parsed. A full list of the supported document formats supported by the 0.8 version used by Solr 3.4 is available at `http://tika.apache.org/0.8/formats.html`.

Solr Cell is a fairly thin adapter to Tika consisting of a SAX `ContentHandler` that consumes the SAX events and builds the input document from the fields that are specified for extraction.

Some not so obvious things to keep in mind when indexing binary documents are:

- You can supply any kind of supported document to Tika, and Tika will attempt to discover the correct MIME type of the document in order to use the correct parser. If you know the correct MIME type then you can specify it via the `stream.type` parameter.

- The default `SolrContentHandler` that is used by Solr Cell is fairly simplistic. You may find that you need to perform extra massaging of the data being indexed beyond what Solr Cell offers to reduce the junk data being indexed. One approach is to implement a custom Solr `UpdateRequestProcessor`, described later in this chapter. Another is to subclass `ExtractingRequestHandler` and override `createFactory()` to provide a custom `SolrContentHandler`.

- Remember that during indexing you are potentially sending large binary files over the wire that must then be parsed by Solr, which can be very slow. If you are looking to only index metadata, then it may make sense to write your own parser using Tika directly, extract the metadata, and post that across to the server. See the *SolrJ: Indexing* section in *Chapter 9, Integrating Solr* for an example of parsing out metadata from an archive of a website and posting the data through SolrJ.

You can learn more about the Tika project at `http://tika.apache.org/`.

Configuring Solr

In `/examples/cores/karaoke/conf/solrconfig.xml` lies the request handler for parsing binary documents:

```
<requestHandler name="/update/extract"
  class="org.apache.solr.handler.extraction.ExtractingRequestHandler">
    <lst name="defaults">
      <str name="map.Last-Modified">last_modified</str>
      <str name="uprefix">metadata_</str>
    </lst>
</requestHandler>
```

Here we can see that the Tika metadata attribute `Last-Modified` is being mapped to the Solr field `last_modified`, assuming we are provided that Tika attribute. The parameter `uprefix` is specifying the prefix to use when storing any Tika fields that don't have a corresponding matching Solr field.

Solr Cell is distributed as a **contrib** module and is made up of the `apache-solr-cell-3.4.0.jar` and roughly 25 more JARs that support parsing individual document formats. In order to use Solr Cell, we placed the Solr Cell JAR and supporting JARs in the lib directory for the karaoke core, `./examples/cores/karaoke/lib/`, as it is not included by default in `solr.war` and none of the other cores need those JARs. The JAR files placed in this `lib` directory are available only to the karaoke core. To share these libs across multiple cores you would add them to `./examples/cores/lib/` and specifying the directory as a shared lib in `solr.xml`:

```
<solr persistent="false" sharedLib="lib">
```

For this example, we are parsing karaoke files that are recorded in the MIDI format using the standard Java package `javax.audio.midi`. If you know which specific document types you are parsing you can pick and choose which JARs you want, which would make your deployment smaller; however, for completeness we put all of the supporting JARs such as `pdfbox`, `poi`, and `icu4j` in `./cores/karaoke/lib`.

Solr Cell parameters

Before jumping into examples, we'll review Solr Cell's configuration parameters, all of which are optional. They are organized below and ordered roughly by when they are used.

At first, Solr Cell (or more specifically Tika) determines the format of the document. It generally makes good guesses, but it can be assisted with these parameters:

- `resource.name`: This is an optional parameter for specifying the name of the file. This assists Tika in determining the correct MIME type.

- `stream.type`: This optional parameter allows you to explicitly specify the MIME type of the document being extracted to Tika, taking precedence over Tika guessing.

Tika converts all input documents into a basic XHTML document, including metadata in the head section. The metadata becomes fields and all text within the body goes into the `content` field. These parameters further refine this:

- `capture`: XHTML element name (for example, "p") to be copied into its own field; can be set multiple times.

- `captureAttr`: Set to `true` to capture XHTML attributes into fields named after the attribute. A common example is for Tika to extract `href` attributes from all the `<a/>` anchor tags for indexing into a separate field.

- `xpath`: Allows you to specify an XPath query to filter which element's text is put into the `content` field. To return only the metadata, and discard all the body content of the XHMTL you would use `xpath=/xhtml:html/xhtml:head/descendant:node()`. Notice the use of the `xhtml:` namespace prefix for each element. Note that only a limited subset of the XPath specification is supported. See `http://tika.apache.org/0.8/api/org/apache/tika/sax/xpath/XPathParser.html`. The API fails to mention that it also supports `/descendant:node()`

- `literal.[fieldname]`: Allows you to supply the specified value for this field, for example, for the ID field.

At this point each resulting field name is potentially renamed in order to map into the schema. These parameters control this process:

- `lowernames`: Set to true to lower-case the field names and convert non-alphanumeric characters to an underscore. For example `Last-Updated` becomes `last_updated`.

- `fmap.[tikaFieldName]`: Maps a source field name to a target field name. For example, `fmap.last_modified=timestamp` maps the metadata field *last_modified* generated by Tika to be recorded in the *timestamp* field defined in the Solr schema.

- `uprefix`: This prefix is applied to the field name, **if** the unprefixed name doesn't match an existing field. Used in conjunction with a dynamic field for mapping individual metadata fields separately:

```
uprefix=meta_

<dynamicField name="meta_*" type="text_general" indexed="true"
stored="true" multiValued="true"/>
```

- `defaultField`: Field to use if `uprefix` isn't specified, and no existing field matches. Can be used to map all the metadata fields into one multi-valued field:

```
defaultField=meta

<field name="meta" type="text_general" indexed="true"
stored="true" multiValued="true"/>
```

Ignoring metadata fields

If you don't want to index the metadata fields, then you can throw them away by mapping them to the `ignored_` dynamic field by setting `uprefix="ignore_"` and using the ignored field type:

```
<dynamicField name="ignored_*" type="ignored"
multiValued="true"/>
```

Other miscellaneous parameters:

- `boost.[fieldname]`: Boost the specified field by this factor to affect scoring.

- `extractOnly`: Set to true to return the XHTML structure of the document as parsed by Tika *without indexing the document*. Typically done in conjunction with `wt=json&indent=true` to make the XHTML easier to read. The purpose of this option is to aid in debugging.

- `extractFormat`: (when `extractOnly=true`) Defaults to `xml` to produce the XHMTL structure. Can be set to `text` to return the raw text extracted from the document.

Extracting karaoke lyrics

We are now ready to extract karaoke lyrics by posting MIDI files to our Solr / `update/extract` request handler. Some classic ABBA tunes for your enjoyment are available in the `./examples/3/karaoke/` directory, gratefully sourced from FreeKaraoke at `http://www.freekaraoke.com/`.

In order to index the song *Angel Eyes* from the command line using `curl`, the simplest command to run is:

```
>> curl 'http://localhost:8983/solr/karaoke/update/extract?fmap.
content=text' -F "file=@angeleyes.kar"
```

Don't forget to commit your changes:

```
>> curl http://localhost:8983/solr/karaoke/update?commit=true
```

You could trigger a commit in the same request that submits the document with the commit=true query parameter; however, this is very inefficient if you are indexing many documents!

We have a single `fmap.content=text` parameter that specifies the default field for content extracted from the source. In this case, the lyrics from `angeleyes.kar` should be stored in the Solr field `text`. Now go look for the results at `http://localhost:8983/solr/karaoke/select/?q=*:*`. You should see:

```
<result name="response" numFound="1" start="0">
  <doc>
    <arr name="text">
      <str>
```

```
     Angel Eyes by Abba sequenced by Michael Boyce
     tinker@worldnet.att.netSoft karaoke@KMIDI KARAOKE
     FILEWords@LENGL@TAngel Eyes@TABBA\Last night I was taking a walk
     along the river/And I saw him together with a young girl/And the
     look that he gave made me shiver/'Cause he always used ...
        </str>
       </arr>
      </doc>
    </result>
```

You've now indexed information about the song and the lyrics in the text field that forms the textual content of the MIDI file. However, what about the metadata, for the MIDI file that Tika also exposes? Well, this is where dynamic fields come in very handy. Every binary format has a set of metadata that to a varying extent overlaps with other formats. Fortunately, it is very easy to specify to Solr Cell how you would want to map metadata fields by using the uprefix property. We specify that all of the metadata_* fields should be created using dynamic fields in schema.xml:

```
<dynamicField name="metadata_*"  type="string"  indexed="true"
             stored="true" multiValued="true"/>
```

Since handling metadata properly is something we want to standardize on, we add to the configuration element in solrconfig.xml:

```
<str name="uprefix">metadata_</str>
```

If you know ahead of time some of the metadata fields and have a named field for them, then you can just map them:

```
<str name="fmap.content_type">content_type</str>
```

When you search for all documents, you should see indexed metadata for *Angel Eyes*, prefixed with metadata_ except for the content_type:

```
<str name="content_type">audio/midi</str>
<arr name="metadata_patches"><str>0</str></arr>
<arr name="metadata_stream_content_type"><str>application/octet-
stream</str></arr>
<arr name="metadata_stream_size"><str>55677</str></arr>
<arr name="metadata_stream_source_info"><str>file</str></arr>
<arr name="metadata_tracks"><str>16</str></arr>
```

Obviously, in most use cases, every time you index the same file you don't want to index a separate Solr document. If your schema has a `uniqueKey` field defined such as `id`, then you can provide a specific ID by passing a literal value using `literal.id=34`. Each time you index the file using the same ID it will delete and insert that document. However, that implies that you have the ability to manage IDs through some third-party system like a database. If you want to use the metadata, such as the `stream_name` provided by Tika to provide the key, then you just need to map that field using `fmap.stream_name=id`. To make the example work, update `./examples/cores/karaoke/schema.xml` to specify `<uniqueKey>id</uniqueKey>`.

```
>> curl 'http://localhost:8983/solr/karaoke/update/extract?fmap.
content=text&fmap.stream_name=id'  -F "file=@angeleyes.kar"
```

This assumes that you've defined `<uniqueKey>id</uniqueKey>` to be of type string, not a number!

Indexing richer documents

Indexing karaoke lyrics from MIDI files is a fairly trivial example. We basically just stripped out all of the contents, and stored them in the Solr text field without trying to make any sense of the structure of the document.

However, the structure of other documents, such as PDFs, can be much more complicated, and just grabbing all the text may not lead to great searchable content. Let's look at *Take a Chance on Me*, a complex PDF file that explains what a Monte Carlo simulation is, while making lots of puns about the lyrics and titles of various songs by ABBA!

Open `./examples/3/karaoke/mccm.pdf`, and you will see a complex PDF document with multiple fonts, background images, complex mathematical equations, Greek symbols, and charts. Despite the complexity of the PDF document, indexing is as simple as the prior karaoke example:

```
>> curl 'http://localhost:8983/solr/karaoke/update/extract?map.
content=text&commit=true'  -F "file=@mccm.pdf"
```

If you do a search for the document using the filename as the `stream_name` via `http://localhost:8983/solr/karaoke/select/?q=stream_name:mccm.pdf`, then you'll also see that the `last_modified` field that we mapped in `solrconfig.xml` is being populated by the Tika extracted metadata property `Last-Modified`.

The `lowercase=true` property that was set as a default translates `Last-Modified` to `last_modified` to make field names consistent with typical conventions:

```
<doc>
  <arr name="id">
```

```
        <str>mccm.pdf</str>
    </arr>
    <arr name="last_modified">
        <str>Sun Mar 03 15:55:09 EST 2002</str>
    </arr>
    <arr name="text">
        <str>
            Take A Chance On Me
```

So with these richer documents, how can we get a handle on the metadata and content that is available? Passing `extractOnly=true` on the URL will output what Solr Cell has extracted as an XML document, including metadata fields, without actually indexing them.

Appending `wt=json` makes it easier to parse out the embedded XML content:

```
>> curl 'http://localhost:8983/solr/karaoke/update/extract?extractOnly=tr
ue&wt=json&indent=true'  -F "file=@mccm.pdf"
```

Copy and paste the XML embedded in the JSON output and use your favorite HTML tidy tool to clean up the output. I used TextMate's HTML plugin; another great option is the free formatter service at `http://xmlindent.com/`:

```
<html>
  <head>
    <meta name="stream_source_info" content="file">
    <meta name="subject" content="Monte carlo condensed">
    <meta name="Last-Modified" content="2002-03-03T20:55:09Z">
    <meta name="Author" content="Andrew" n.="">
    <meta name="xmpTPg:NPages" content="11">
    <meta name="Creation-Date" content="2002-03-03T20:53:14Z">
    <meta name="Keywords" content="ABBA">
    <title>
      Take A Chance On Me
    </title>
  </head>
  <body>
    <p>
      "\n\n \n \n \n \n \n \n \n \n \n \n \n \n \n \n \n \n \n
    </p>
    <div class="page">
      \n\n
      <p>
        Take A Chance On MeMonte Carlo Condensed MatterA very brief
guide to Monte Carlo simulation.An explanation of what I do.A chance
for far too many ABBA puns.
```

```
        </p>\n
   </div>
   <p>
      \n
   </p>
   <div class="page">
      \n\n
      <p>
         What's The Name Of The Game?Simulation:'I have a dream,
a fantasy,to help me through reality'Given some model many-body
system.Simulate the evolution of the system.We can then measure
various observables.Attempt to predict properties of real systems.
Eg Equilibrium Properties All about knowing free-energies, phase
behavior, compressibility, specific heat,knowing M(E), knowing m.
      </p>\n
   </div>
```

This returns an XHMTL document that contains the metadata extracted from the document in the `<head/>` stanza, as well as the basic structure of the contents expressed as XHTML.

Binary file size

Take a Chance on Me is a 372 KB file located at `./examples/3/karaoke/mccm.pdf`, and highlights one of the challenges of using Solr Cell. If you are indexing a thousand PDF documents that each average 372 KB, then you are shipping 372 megabytes over the wire, assuming the data is not already on a file system accessible by Solr. However, if you extract the contents of the PDF on the client side and only send that over the Web, then what is sent to the Solr text field is just 5.1 KB. Look at `./examples/3/karaoke/mccm.xml` to see the actual text extracted from `mccm.pdf`. Generously assuming that the metadata adds an extra 1 KB of information, then you have a total content sent over the wire of 6.1 megabytes ((5.1 KB + 1.0 KB) * 1000).

Solr Cell offers a quick way to start indexing the vast amount of information stored in previously inaccessible binary formats without the overhead of resorting to custom code development per binary format. However, depending on the files, you may be needlessly transmitting a lot of raw data, only to extract a small portion of that data. Moreover, you may find that the tools provided by Solr Cell for parsing and selecting just the data you want to index may not be rich enough. In that case you may be better off building a dedicated client-side tool that does all of the parsing and munging you require.

Update request processors

No matter how you choose to import data, there is a final configuration point within Solr that allows manipulation of the imported data before it gets indexed. The Solr request handlers that update data put documents on an **update request processor chain**. If you search `solrconfig.xml` for `updateRequestProcessorChain` then you'll see an example.

You can specify which chain to use on the update request with the `update.chain` parameter (formerly `update.processor` prior to Solr 3.2). It could be useful, but you'll probably always use one chain. If no chain is specified, you get a default chain of `LogUpdateProcessorFactory` and `RunUpdateProcessorFactory`. The following are the possible update request processors to choose from. Their names all end in `UpdateProcessorFactory`.

- `SignatureUpdateProcessorFactory`: This generates a hash ID value based off of other field values you specify. If you want to de-duplicate your data (that is you don't want to add the same data twice accidentally) then this will do that for you. For further information see `http://wiki.apache.org/solr/Deduplication`.

- `UIMAUpdateProcessorFactory`: This hands the document off to the Unstructured Information Management Architecture (UIMA), a Solr contrib module that enhances the document through natural language processing (NLP) techniques. For further information see `http://wiki.apache.org/solr/SolrUIMA`.

> Although it's nice to see an NLP integration option in Solr, beware that NLP processing tends to be computationally expensive. Instead of using UIMA in this way, consider performing this processing external to Solr and cache the results to avoid re-computation as you adjust your indexing process.

- `LogUpdateProcessorFactory`: This is the one responsible for writing the log messages you see when an update occurs.

- `RunUpdateProcessorFactory`: This is the one that actually indexes the document; don't forget it or the document will vanish! To decompose this last step further, it hands the document to Lucene, which will then process each field according to the analysis configuration in the schema.

More processors are expected in the future that do interesting tasks, including a scriptable one similar to the DIH's `ScriptTransformer`; see SOLR-1725. You can of course write your own. It's a recognized extensibility point in Solr that consequently doesn't require modifying Solr itself.

Summary

At this point, you should have a schema that you believe will suit your needs, and you should know how to get your data into it. From Solr's native XML to JSON to CSV to databases to rich documents, Solr offers a variety of possibilities to ingest data into the index. *Chapter 9, Integrating Solr* will discuss some additional language and framework integration choices for importing data. In the end, usually one or two mechanisms will be used. In addition, you can usually expect the need to write a little code, perhaps just a simple bash or ant script to implement the automation of getting data from your source system into Solr.

Now that we've got data in Solr, we can finally start searching it. The next chapter will describe Solr's query syntax in detail, which includes phrase queries, range queries, wildcards, boosting, as well as the description of Solr's **DateMath** syntax. The chapters after that will get to more interesting searching topics that of course depend on having data to search on!

4
Searching

At this point, you have Solr running and some data indexed, and you're finally ready to put Solr to the test. Searching with Solr is arguably the most fun aspect of working with it, because it's quick and easy to do. While searching your data, you will learn more about its nature than before. It is also a source of interesting puzzles to solve when you troubleshoot why a search didn't find a document or conversely why it did, or similarly why a document wasn't scored sufficiently high.

In this chapter, you are going to learn about:

- Request handlers
- Query parameters
- Solr's "lucene" query syntax
- The "dismax" query parser (part 1)
- Filtering
- Sorting
- Geospatial

The subject of searching will progress into the next chapter for debugging queries, relevancy (that is, scoring) matters, function queries—an advanced capability used commonly in relevancy but also in sorting and filtering, and geospatial search.

In a hurry?

This chapter has a lot of key information on searching that is important. That said, if you're in a hurry you can skim/skip query parsers, local-params, and the query syntax—you'll use dismax instead. And you can skip dismax's "min-should-match" too. Read about geospatial if it's applicable.

Your first search, a walk-through

We've got a lot of data indexed, and now it's time to actually use Solr for what it is intended—searching, also known as querying. When your application interacts with Solr, it will use HTTP, either directly via common APIs or indirectly through one of Solr's client APIs. However, as we demonstrate Solr's capabilities in this chapter, we'll use Solr's web-based admin interface. Surely you've noticed the search box on the first screen of Solr's admin interface. It's a bit too basic; so instead click on the **[FULL INTERFACE]** link to take you to a query form with more options.

The following screenshot is seen after clicking on the **[FULL INTERFACE]** link:

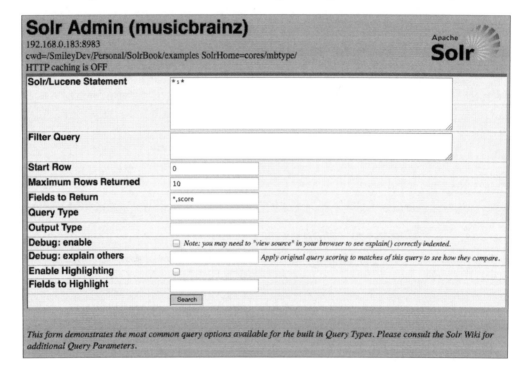

The URL is `http://localhost:8983/solr/mbartists/admin/form.jsp`. Contrary to what the label **FULL INTERFACE** might suggest, this form only has a fraction of the options you might possibly specify to run a search. Let's do a quick search. In the **Solr/Lucene Statement** box, we'll leave the default of: *:* (an asterisk, colon, and then another asterisk). That is admittedly cryptic if you've never seen it before, but it basically means "match anything in any field", which is to say, it matches all documents. Much more about the query syntax will be discussed soon enough. Click on the **Search** button, and you'll get output like this:

```xml
<?xml version="1.0" encoding="UTF-8"?>
<response>
<lst name="responseHeader">
  <int name="status">0</int>
  <int name="QTime">392</int>
  <lst name="params">
    <str name="explainOther"/>
    <str name="fl">*,score</str>
    <str name="indent">on</str>
    <str name="start">0</str>
    <str name="q">*:*</str>
    <str name="hl.fl"/>
    <str name="qt"/>
    <str name="wt"/>
    <str name="fq"/>
    <str name="version">2.2</str>
    <str name="rows">10</str>
  </lst>
</lst>
<result name="response" numFound="399182" start="0" maxScore="1.0">
  <doc>
    <float name="score">1.0</float>
    <arr name="a_member_id">
      <long>123122</long><long>346621</long>
    </arr>
    <arr name="a_member_name">
      <str>Backslash</str><str>Thomas Woznik</str>
    </arr>
    <str name="a_name">Plasticmen</str>
    <str name="a_type">group</str>
    <str name="id">Artist:309843</str>
    <date name="indexedAt">2011-07-15T05:20:06Z</date>
    <str name="type">Artist</str>
  </doc>
  <doc>
    <float name="score">1.0</float>
    <str name="a_name">Gnawa Njoum Experience</str>
    <str name="id">Artist:215841</str>
    <date name="indexedAt">2011-07-15T05:20:06Z</date>
    <str name="type">Artist</str>
  </doc>
  <doc>
    <float name="score">1.0</float>
    <str name="a_name">Ultravoice vs. Rizo</str>
```

```
        <str name="a_type">group</str>
        <str name="id">Artist:482488</str>
        <date name="indexedAt">2011-07-15T05:20:06Z</date>
        <str name="type">Artist</str>
    </doc>
  <!-- ** 7 other docs omitted for brevity ** -->
  </result>
  </response>
```

Browser note

Use Firefox for best results when searching Solr. Solr's search results return XML, and Firefox renders XML color coded and pretty-printed. Safari on Mac OS X Lion finally gained this feature too. For other browsers (notably an older Safari or Chrome), you may find yourself having to use the **View Source** feature or using a response format other than XML to see the results. Even in Firefox, however, there are cases where you will use **View Source** in order to look at the XML with the original indentation, which is relevant when diagnosing the scoring debug output.

Solr's generic XML structured data representation

Solr has its own generic XML representation of typed and named data structures. This XML is used for most of the response XML and it is also used in parts of `solconfig.xml` too. The XML elements involved in this partial XML schema are:

- `<lst>`: A named list. Each of its child nodes should have a name attribute. This generic XML is often stored within an element that is not part of this schema, like `<doc>`, but is in effect equivalent to `lst`.

- `<arr>`: An array of values. Each of its child nodes is a member of this array.

The following elements represent simple values with the text of the element storing the value. The numeric ranges match that of the Java language. They will have a `name` attribute if they are underneath `lst` (or an equivalent element like `doc`), but not otherwise.

- `<str>`: A string of text
- `<int>`: An integer in the range -2^{31} to $2^{31}-1$
- `<long>`: An integer in the range -2^{63} to $2^{63}-1$
- `<float>`: A floating point number in the range 1.4e-45 to about 3.4e38
- `<double>`: A floating point number in the range 4.9e-324 to about 1.8e308

- `<bool>`: A boolean value represented as `true` or `false`. When supplying values in a configuration file: `on`, `off`, `yes`, and `no` are also supported.

- `<date>`: A date in the ISO-8601 format like so: `1965-11-30T05:00:00Z`, which is always in the UTC time zone represented by `z`. Even if your data isn't actually in this time zone, when working with Solr you might pretend that it is because Solr doesn't support anything else.

Solr's XML response format

The `<response/>` element wraps the entire response.

The first child element is `<lst name="responseHeader">`, which is intuitively the response header that captures some basic metadata about the response.

- `status`: Always `0`. If a Solr error occurs, then the HTTP response status code will reflect it and a plain HTML page will display the error.

- `QTime`: The number of milliseconds Solr takes to process the entire request on the server. Due to internal caching, you should see this number drop to a couple of milliseconds or so for subsequent requests of the same query. If subsequent identical searches are much faster, yet you see the same `QTime`, then your web browser (or intermediate HTTP Proxy) cached the response. Solr's HTTP caching configuration is discussed in *Chapter 10*.

- Other data may be present depending on query parameters.

The main body of the response is the search result listing enclosed by this: `<result name="response" numFound="1002272" start="0" maxScore="1.0">`, and it contains a `<doc>` child node for each returned document. Some of the fields are explained below:

- `numFound`: The total number of documents matched by the query. This is not impacted by the `rows` parameter and as such may be larger (but not smaller) than the number of child `<doc>` elements.

- `start`: The same as the `start` request parameter, described shortly, which is the offset of the returned results into the query's result set.

- `maxScore`: Of all documents matched by the query (`numFound`), this is the highest score. If you didn't explicitly ask for the score in the field list using the `fl` request parameter, described shortly, then this won't be here. Scoring is described in the next chapter.

The contents of the resultant element are a list of doc elements. Each of these elements represent a document in the index. The child elements of a doc element represent fields in the index and are named correspondingly. The types of these elements use Solr's generic data representation, which was described earlier. They are simple values if they are not multi-valued in the schema. For multi-valued values, the field would be represented by an ordered array of simple values.

There was no data following the results element in our demonstration query. However, there can be, depending on the query parameters enabling features such as faceting and highlighting. When we cover those features, the corresponding XML will be explained.

Parsing the URL

The search form is as basic as they come. It submits the form using HTTP GET, essentially resulting in the browser loading a new URL with the form elements becoming part of the URL's query string. Take a good look at the URL in the browser page showing the XML response. Understanding the URL's structure is very important for grasping how searching Solr works:

```
http://localhost:8983/solr/mbartists/select?indent=on&version=2.2&q=*
%3A*&fq=&start=0&rows=10&fl=*%2Cscore&qt=&wt=&explainOther=&hl.fl=
```

- The /solr/ is the web application context where Solr is installed on the Java servlet engine. If you have a dedicated server for Solr, then you might opt to install it at the root. This would make it just /. How to do this is out of scope of this book, but letting it remain at /solr/ is fine.

- After the web application context is a reference to the Solr core named mbartists. If you are experimenting with Solr's example setup then you won't see a core name because it has a default one. We'll learn more about configuring Solr cores in *Chapter 8, Deployment*.

- The /select in combination with the qt= parameter is a reference to the Solr **request handler**. More on this is covered next.

- Following the ?, is a set of unordered URL parameters, also known as **query parameters** in the context of searching. The format of this part of the URL is an & separating set of unordered name=value pairs. As the form doesn't have an option for all query parameters, you will manually modify the URL in your browser to add query parameters as needed.

Text in the URL must be UTF-8 encoded then URL-escaped so that the URL complies with its specification. This concept should be familiar to anyone who has done web development. Depending on the context in which the URL is actually constructed, there are API calls you should use to ensure this escaping happens properly. For example, in JavaScript, you would use `encodeURIComponent()`. In the URL above, Solr interpreted the `%3A` as a colon and `%2C` as a comma. The most common escaped character in URLs is a space, which is escaped as either + or `%20`. Fortunately, when experimenting with the URL, browsers are lenient and will permit some characters that should be escaped. For more information on URL encoding see `http://en.wikipedia.org/wiki/Percent-encoding`.

Request handlers

Searching Solr and most other interactions with Solr, including indexing for that matter, is processed by what Solr calls a **request handler**. Request handlers are configured in the `solrconfig.xml` file and are clearly labeled as such. Most of them exist for special purposes like handling a CSV import, for example. Our searches in this chapter have been directed to the default request handler because we didn't specify one in the URL. Here is how the default request handler is configured:

```
<requestHandler name="standard" class="solr.SearchHandler"
            default="true">
  <!-- default values for query parameters -->
  <lst name="defaults">
  <str name="echoParams">explicit</str>
  <int name="rows">10</int>
  <str name="fl">*</str>
  <str name="version">2.1</str>
  </lst>
</requestHandler>
```

The request handlers that perform searches allow configuration of two things:

- Establishing default parameters and making some unchangeable
- Registering Solr search components such as faceting and highlighting

Create a request handler configuration for your application.

Instead of using the default request handler for use by the application you are building, I recommend that you create a request handler for each type of search that your application does. In doing so, you can change various search options more easily in Solr through re-configuration, instead of having your application hard-wired more than it has to be. This centralizes the search configuration a bit more too. Finally, this gives you better granularity of search statistics on Solr's **STATISTICS** screen.

Let's say that in the MusicBrainz search interface we have a search form that searches for bands. We have a Solr core just for artists named `mbartists` but this contains not only bands but also individual band members. When the field named `a_type` is "group", we have a band. To start, copy the default configuration, removing the attribute `default="true"`, and give it a name such as `bands`. We can now use this request handler with `qt=bands` in the URL as shown below:

```
/solr/mbartists/select?qt=bands&q=Smashing&.....
```

An alternative to this is to precede the name with /. Now this handler is invoked like this:

```
/solr/mbartists/bands&q=Smashing&.....
```

Let's now configure this request handler to filter searches to find only the bands, without the searching application having to specify this. We'll also set a few other options.

```
<requestHandler name="bands" class="solr.SearchHandler">
    <lst name="defaults">
      <str name="echoParams">none</str>
      <int name="rows">20</int>
    </lst>
    <lst name="appends">
      <str name="fq">a_type:group</str>
    </lst>
    <lst name="invariants">
      <str name="facet">false</str>
    </lst>
</requestHandler>
```

Request handlers have several lists to configure. These use Solr's generic XML data structure, which was described earlier.

- `defaults`: These simply establish default values for various request parameters. Parameters in the request will override them.

- `appends`: For parameters that can be set multiple times, like `fq`, this section specifies values that will be set in addition to any that may be specified by the request.

- `invariants`: This sets defaults that cannot be overridden. This is useful for security purposes — a topic for *Chapter 8, Deployment*.

- `first-components`, `components`, `last-components`: These list the Solr **search components** to be registered for possible use with this request handler. By default, a set of search components are already registered to enable functionality such as querying and faceting. Setting `first-components` or `last-components` would prepend or append to this list respectively, whereas setting `components` would override the list completely. For more information about search components, read *Chapter 7, Search Components*.

Query parameters

There are a great number of request parameters for configuring Solr searches, especially when considering all of the components like faceting and highlighting. Only the core search parameters not specific to any query parser are listed here. Furthermore, in-depth explanations for some lie further in the chapter.

For the boolean parameters, a true value can be any one of `true`, `on`, or `yes`. False values can be any of `false`, `off`, and `no`.

Search criteria related parameters

The parameters affecting the query are as follows:

- `q`: The *user query* or just "query" for short. This typically originates directly from user input. The query syntax is determined by the `defType` parameter.

- `defType`: A reference to the query parser for the user query in `q`. The default is `lucene` with the syntax to be described shortly. You'll most likely use `dismax` or `edismax` discussed later in the chapter.

Prefer dismax for user queries

For processing queries from users, I highly recommend using `dismax` or `edismax`, which is described later in the chapter. It supports several features that enhance relevancy, and more limited syntax options that prevent a user from getting unexpected results or an error if they inadvertently use the `lucene` native syntax.

- `fq`: A filter query that limits the scope of the user query, similar to a *WHERE* clause in SQL. Unlike the `q` parameter, this has no effect on scoring. This parameter can be repeated as desired. Filtering is described later in the chapter.

- `qt`: A reference to the query type, more commonly known as the request handler, described earlier. An alternative is to name the request handler with a leading / such as `/artists` and then use `/artists` in your URL path instead of `/select?....`

Result pagination related parameters

A query could match any number of the documents in the index, perhaps even all of them, such as in our first example of `*:*`. Solr doesn't generally return all the documents. Instead, you indicate to Solr with the `start` and `rows` parameters to return a contiguous series of them. The `start` and `rows` parameters are explained below:

- `start`: (default: `0`) This is the zero-based index of the first document to be returned from the result set. In other words, this is the number of documents to skip from the beginning of the search results. If this number exceeds the result count, then it will simply return no documents, but it's not considered an error.

- `rows`: (default: `10`) This is the number of documents to be returned in the response XML starting at index `start`. Fewer rows will be returned if there aren't enough matching documents. This number is basically the number of results displayed at a time on your search user interface.

> Solr is not yet optimized to do "deep paging" or return a large number of results. This issue is tracked as SOLR-1726. Until this is addressed, the further from the beginning you need results (the greater `start+rows` is), Solr will respond exponentially slower. At least for the first thousand documents or so, it shouldn't be noticeable. As a consequence, consider preventing users and web crawlers from paging far into the results.

Output related parameters

The output related parameters are explained below:

- `fl`: This is the field list, separated by commas and/or spaces. These fields are to be returned in the response. Use `*` to refer to all of the fields but not the score. In order to get the score, you must specify the pseudo-field `score`.

- `sort`: A comma-separated field listing to sort on, with a directionality specifier of `asc` or `desc` after each field. Example: `r_name asc, score desc`. The default is `score desc`. You can also sort by functions, which is a more advanced subject for the next chapter. *There is more to sorting than meets the eye; read more about it later in this chapter.*

- `wt`: The response format, also known as **writer type** or **query response writer**, defined in `solrconfig.xml`. Since the subject of picking a response format has to do with how you will integrate with Solr, further recommendations and details are left to *Chapter 9, Integrating Solr*. For now, here is the list of options by name: `xml` (the default and aliased to `standard`), `json`, `python`, `php`, `phps`, `ruby`, `javabin`, `csv`, `xslt`, `velocity`.

- `version`: The requested version of Solr's response structure, if different than the default. This is not particularly useful at the time of writing. However, if Solr's response structure changes, then it will do so under a new version. By using this in the request, a best-practice for your automated searches, you reduce the chances of your client code breaking if Solr is updated.

Diagnostic related parameters

These diagnostic parameters are helpful during development with Solr. Obviously, you'll want to be sure NOT to use these, particularly `debugQuery`, in a production setting because of performance concerns.

- `indent`: A boolean option that will indent the output to make it easier to read. It works for most of the response formats.

- debugQuery: If `true`, then following the search results is `<lst name="debug">` with diagnostic information. It contains voluminous information about the parsed query string, how the scores were computed, and millisecond timings for all of the Solr components to perform their part of the processing such as faceting. You may need to use the `View Source` function of your browser to preserve the formatting used in the score computation section. *Debugging queries and enhancing relevancy is documented further in the next chapter.*

  - explainOther: If you want to determine why a particular document wasn't matched by the query or why it wasn't scored high enough, then you can put a query for this value, such as `id:"Release:12345"`, and debugQuery's output will be sure to include the first document matching this query in its output.

- echoHandler: If `true`, then this emits the Java class name identifying the Solr request handler.

- echoParams: Controls if any query parameters are returned in the response header, as seen verbatim earlier. This is for debugging URL encoding issues or for verifying the complete set of parameters in effect, taking into consideration those defined in the request handler. Specifying `none` disables this, which is appropriate for production real-world use. The standard request handler is configured for this to be `explicit` by default, which means to list those parameters explicitly mentioned in the URL. Finally, you can use `all` to include those parameters configured in the request handler in addition to those in the URL.

Finally, there is another parameter not easily categorized above called `timeAllowed` in which you specify a time limit in milliseconds for a query to take before it is interrupted and intermediate results are returned. Long-running queries should be very rare and this allows you to cap them so that they don't over-burden your production server.

Query parsers and local-params

A **query parser** parses a string into an internal Lucene query object, potentially considering request parameters and so-called **local-params**—parameters local to the query string. Only a few parsers actually do real parsing and some parsers like those for geospatial don't even use the query string. The default query parser throughout Solr is named `lucene` and it has a special leading syntax to switch the parser to another and/or to specify some parameters. Here's an example choosing the `dismax` parser along with two local-params and a query string of "billy corgan":

```
{!dismax qf="a_name^2 a_alias" tie=0.1}billy corgan
```

It's not common to see this syntax in the user query, q, since its parser is conveniently set via defType.

There are a few things to know about the local-params syntax:

- The leading query parser name (for example, dismax) is optional. Without it, the parser remains as lucene. Furthermore, this syntax is a shortcut for putting the query parser name in the type local-param.

- *Usually*, a query parser treats local-params as an override to request parameters in the URL.

- A parameter value can refer to a request parameter via a leading $, for example v=$qq.

- The special parameter v can be used to hold the query string as an alternative to it following the }. Some advanced scenarios require this approach.

- A parameter value doesn't have to be quoted if there are no spaces. There wasn't any for the tie parameter in the example above.

For an interesting example, see the sub-query syntax later.

Solr includes quite a few different query parsers. In the next section you'll learn all about lucene. For processing user queries, you should typically use dismax or edismax (short for extended-dismax), which are described afterwards. The other query parsers are for special things like geospatial search, also described at the end of this chapter. This book only explores the most useful parsers; for further information, see: http://wiki.apache.org/solr/SolrQuerySyntax.

Query syntax (the lucene query parser)

Solr's native / full query syntax is implemented by the query parser named lucene. It is based on Lucene's old syntax with a few additions that will be pointed out explicitly. In fact, you've already seen the first addition which is local-params.

 The best practice for the user query (the q parameter) is to use the dismax or edismax query parsers, not the default lucene query parser described here. dismax only supports a basic essential subset of the full syntax that is unlikely to cause unintended behavior by a general user, whereas edismax supports the syntax here but is *safer* and has many bonus features. You'll read more about these query parsers in the next section.

The lucene query parser does have a couple query parameters that can be set. Usually these aren't specified as Lucene is rarely used for the user query and because Lucene's query syntax is easily made explicit to not need these options.

- `q.op`: The default query operator, either AND or OR to signify if all of the search terms or just one of the search terms need to match. If this isn't present, then the default is specified in `schema.xml` near the bottom in the `defaultOperator` attribute. If that isn't specified, then the default is OR.

- `df`: The default field that will be searched by the user query. If this isn't specified, then the default is specified in `schema.xml` near the bottom in the `<defaultSearchField>` element. If that isn't specified, then a query that does not explicitly specify a field to search will be an error.

In the following examples:

- If you are using the example data with the book, you could use the search form here: `http://localhost:8983/solr/mbartists/admin/`. No changes are needed.

- `q.op` is set to OR (which is the default choice, if it isn't specified anywhere).

- The default search field was set to `a_name` in the schema. Had it been something else, we'd use the `df` parameter.

- You may find it easier to scan the resulting XML if you set `fl` (the field list) to `a_name, score`.

Use `debugQuery=on`

To see a normalized string representation of the parsed query tree, enable query debugging. Then look for `parsedquery` in the debug output. See how it changes depending on the query.

A final point to be made is that there are query capabilities within Lucene that are not exposed in query parsers that come with Solr. Notably, there is a family of so-called "span queries" which allow for some advanced phrase queries that can be composed together by their relative position. To learn more about that, I advise reading the *Lucene In Action* book. There is also the ability to search for a term matching a regular expression.

Matching all the documents

Lucene doesn't natively have a query syntax to match all documents. Solr enhanced Lucene's query syntax to support it with the following syntax:

```
*:*
```

When using `dismax`, it's common to set `q.alt` to this match-everything query so that a blank query returns all results.

Mandatory, prohibited, and optional clauses

Lucene has a unique way of combining multiple clauses in a query string. It is tempting to think of this as a mundane detail common to boolean operations in programming languages, but Lucene doesn't quite work that way.

A query expression is decomposed into a set of unordered clauses of three types:

- A clause can be **mandatory**: `+Smashing`

  This matches only artists containing the word `Smashing`.

- A clause can be **prohibited**: `-Smashing`

  This matches all artists except those with `Smashing`. You can also use an exclamation mark as in `!Smashing` but that's rarely used.

- A clause can be **optional**: `Smashing`

 It's okay for spaces to come between + or - and the search word. However, when Solr 4 arrives, this will no longer be the case.

The term "optional" deserves further explanation. If the query expression contains at least one mandatory clause, then any optional clause is just that—optional. This notion may seem pointless, but it serves a useful function in scoring documents that match more of them higher. If the query expression does not contain any mandatory clauses, then *at least one* of the optional clauses must match. The next two examples illustrate optional clauses.

Here, `Pumpkins` is optional, and my favorite band will surely be at the top of the list, ahead of bands with names like `Smashing Atoms`:

```
+Smashing Pumpkins
```

In this example there are no mandatory clauses and so documents with `Smashing` or `Pumpkins` are matched, but not `Atoms`. My favorite band is at the top because it matched both, followed by other bands containing only one of those words:

```
Smashing Pumpkins -Atoms
```

If you would like to specify that a certain number or percentage of optional clauses should match or should not match, then you can instead use the dismax query parser with the min-should-match feature, described later in the chapter.

Boolean operators

The boolean operators `AND`, `OR`, and `NOT` can be used as an alternative syntax to arrive at the same set of mandatory, optional, and prohibited clauses that were mentioned previously. Use the `debugQuery` feature, and observe that the `parsedquery` string normalizes-away this syntax into the previous (clauses being optional by default such as `OR`).

 Case matters! At least this means that it is harder to accidentally specify a boolean operator.

When the `AND` or `&&` operator is used between clauses, then both the left and right sides of the operand become mandatory if not already marked as prohibited. So:

```
Smashing AND Pumpkins
```

is equivalent to:

```
+Smashing +Pumpkins
```

Similarly, if the `OR` or `||` operator is used between clauses, then both the left and right sides of the operand become optional, unless they are marked mandatory or prohibited. If the default operator is already `OR` then this syntax is redundant. If the default operator is `AND`, then this is the only way to mark a clause as optional.

To match artist names that contain `Smashing` **or** `Pumpkins` try:

```
Smashing || Pumpkins
```

The `NOT` operator is equivalent to the - syntax. So to find artists with `Smashing` but not `Atoms` in the name, you can do this:

```
Smashing NOT Atoms
```

We didn't need to specify a + on `Smashing`. This is because it is the only optional clause and there are no explicit mandatory clauses. Likewise, using an AND or OR would have no effect in this example.

It may be tempting to try to combine AND with OR such as:

~~Smashing AND Pumpkins OR Green AND Day~~

However, this doesn't work as you might expect. Remember that AND is equivalent to both sides of the operand being mandatory, and thus each of the four clauses becomes mandatory. Our data set returned no results for this query. In order to combine query clauses in some ways, you will need to use *sub-queries*.

Sub-queries

You can use parenthesis to compose a query of smaller queries, referred to as sub-queries or nested queries. The following example satisfies the intent of the previous example:

```
(Smashing AND Pumpkins) OR (Green AND Day)
```

Using what we know previously, this could also be written as:

```
(+Smashing +Pumpkins) (+Green +Day)
```

But this is *not* the same as:

```
+(Smashing Pumpkins) +(Green Day)
```

The preceding sub-query is interpreted as documents that must have a name with either `Smashing` or `Pumpkins` and either `Green` or `Day` in its name. So *if* there was a band named `Green Pumpkins`, then it would match.

Solr added another syntax for sub-queries to Lucene's old syntax that allows the sub-query to use a different query parser including local-params. This is an advanced technique so don't worry if you don't understand it at first. The syntax is a bit of a hack using a magic field named `_query_` with its value being the sub-query, which practically speaking, needs to be quoted. As an example, suppose you have a search interface with multiple query boxes, whereas each box is for searching a different field. You could compose the query string yourself but you would have some query escaping issues to deal with. And if you wanted to take advantage of the `dismax` parser then with what you know so far, that isn't possible. Here's an approach using this new syntax:

```
+_query_:"{!dismax qf=a_name v=$q.a_name}" +_query_:"{!dismax qf=a_
alias v=$q.a_alias}"
```

This example assumes that request parameters of `q.a_name` and `q.a_alias` are supplied for the user input for these fields in the schema. Recall from the local-params definition that the parameter `v` can hold the query and that the `$` refers to another named request parameter.

Limitations of prohibited clauses in sub-queries

Lucene doesn't actually support a *pure negative query*, for example:

```
-Smashing -Pumpkins
```

Solr enhances Lucene to support this, but only at the top level query such as in the preceding example. Consider the following admittedly strange query:

```
Smashing (-Pumpkins)
```

This query attempts to ask the question: Which artist names contain either `Smashing` or do not contain `Pumpkins`? However, it doesn't work and only matches the first clause—(4 documents). The second clause should essentially match most documents resulting in a total for the query that is nearly every document. The artist named `Wild Pumpkins at Midnight` is the only one in my index that does not contain `Smashing` but does contain `Pumpkins`, and so this query should match every document *except* that one. To make this work, you have to take the sub-expression containing only negative clauses, and add the all-documents query clause: `*:*`, as shown below:

```
Smashing (-Pumpkins *:*)
```

Interestingly, this limitation is fixed in the `edismax` query parser. Hopefully a future version of Solr will fix it universally, thereby making this work-around unnecessary.

Field qualifier

To have a clause explicitly search a particular field, you need to precede the relevant clause with the field's name, and then add a colon. Spaces may be used in-between, but that is generally not done.

```
a_member_name:Corgan
```

This matches bands containing a member with the name `Corgan`. To match, `Billy` and `Corgan`:

```
+a_member_name:Billy +a_member_name:Corgan
```

Or use this shortcut to match multiple words:

```
a_member_name:(+Billy +Corgan)
```

The content of the parenthesis is a sub-query, but with the default field being overridden to be a_member_name, instead of what the default field would be otherwise. By the way, we could have used AND instead of + of course. Moreover, in these examples, all of the searches were targeting the same field, but you can certainly match any combination of fields needed.

Phrase queries and term proximity

A clause may be a phrase query: a contiguous series of words to be matched in that order. In the previous examples, we've searched for text containing multiple words like Billy and Corgan, but let's say we wanted to match Billy Corgan (that is, the two words adjacent to each other in that order). This further constrains the query. Double quotes are used to indicate a phrase query, as shown in the following code:

```
"Billy Corgan"
```

Related to phrase queries is the notion of the **term proximity**, aka the **slop factor** or a **near query**. In our previous example, if we wanted to permit these words to be separated by no more than say three words in–between, then we could do this:

```
"Billy Corgan"~3
```

For the MusicBrainz data set, this is probably of little use. For larger text fields, this can be useful in improving search relevance. The dismax query parser, which is described in the next chapter, can automatically turn a user's query into a phrase query with a configured slop.

Wildcard queries

A plain keyword search will look in the index for an exact match, subsequent to text analysis processing on both the query and input document text (for example, tokenization, lowercasing). But sometimes you need to express a query for a partial match expressed using wildcards.

 There is a highly relevant section in the text analysis chapter on partial/substring indexing. In particular, read about ReversedWildcardFilterFactory. N-Grams is a different approach that does not work with wildcard queries.

There are a few points to understand about wildcard queries:

- No text analysis is performed on the search word containing the wildcard, not even lowercasing. So if you want to find a word starting with sma, then sma* is required instead of Sma*, assuming the index side of the field's type includes lowercasing. This shortcoming is tracked on SOLR-219. Moreover, if the field that you want to use the wildcard query on is stemmed in the analysis, then smashing* would not find the original text Smashing because the stemming process transforms this to smash. Consequently, don't stem.

- Wildcard queries are one of the slowest types you can run. Use of ReversedWildcardFilterFactory helps with this a lot. But if you have an asterisk wildcard on both ends of the word, then this is the worst-case scenario.

- Leading wildcards will result in an error in Solr unless ReversedWildcardFilterFactory is used.

To find artists containing words starting with Smash, you can do:

```
smash*
```

Or perhaps those starting with sma and ending with ing:

```
sma*ing
```

The asterisk matches any number of characters (perhaps none). You can also use ? to force a match of any character at that position:

```
sma??*
```

That would match words that start with sma and that have at least two more characters but potentially more.

As far as scoring is concerned, each matching term gets the same score regardless of how close it is to the query pattern. Lucene can support a variable score at the expense of performance but you would need to do some hacking to get Solr to do that.

> Here's a trick question: What would this query do: * (just an asterisk)? Based on intuition, it appears it should match all documents that have at least one indexed value for a_name. What will actually happen depends on whether there is *any* field type in the schema, even an unused one that has ReversedWildcardFilterFactory in its index chain. If so, the * works intuitively on any field, if not then you get an error about leading wildcards not being supported. See SOLR-1982 for the bug report. The official way to find all documents with at least a value will be explained shortly.

Fuzzy queries

Fuzzy queries are useful when your search term needn't be an exact match, but the closer the better. The fewer the number of character insertions, deletions, or exchanges relative to the search term length, the better the score. The algorithm used is known as **the Levenshtein Distance** algorithm, also known as **the edit distance**. Fuzzy queries have the same need to lowercase and to avoid stemming just as wildcard queries do. For example:

```
Smashing~
```

Notice the tilde character at the end. Without this notation, simply `Smashing` would match only four documents because only that many artist names contain that word. `Smashing~` matched 578 words and it took my computer 359 milliseconds. You can modify the proximity threshold, which is a number between `0` and `1`, defaulting to `0.5`. For instance, changing the proximity to a more stringent `0.7`:

```
Smashing~0.7
```

25 matched documents resulted and it took 174 milliseconds. If you want to use fuzzy queries, then you should consider experimenting with different thresholds.

To illustrate how text analysis can still pose a problem, consider the search for:

```
SMASH~
```

There is an artist named `S.M.A.S.H.`, and our analysis configuration emits `smash` as a term. So `SMASH` would be a perfect match, but adding the tilde results in a search term in which every character is different due to the case difference and so this search returns nothing. As with wildcard searches, if you intend on using fuzzy searches then you should lowercase the query string.

Range queries

Lucene lets you query for numeric, date, and even text ranges. The following query matches all of the bands formed in the 1990s:

```
a_type:2 AND a_begin_date:[1990-01-01T00:00:00.000Z TO
1999-12-31T24:59:99.999Z]
```

Observe that the date format is the full ISO-8601 date-time in UTC, which Solr mandates (the same format used by Solr to index dates and that which is emitted in search results). The `.999` milliseconds part is optional. The `[` and `]` brackets signify an inclusive range, and therefore it includes the dates on both ends. To specify an exclusive range, use `{` and `}`. In Solr 3, both sides must be inclusive or both exclusive; Solr 4 allows both. The workaround in Solr 3 is to introduce an extra clause to include or exclude a side of the range. There is an example of this below.

Use the right field type

To get the fastest numerical/date range query performance, particularly when there are many indexed values, use a `trie` field (for example, `tdate`) with a `precisionStep`. It was discussed in *Chapter 2, Schema and Text Analysis*.

For most numbers in the MusicBrainz schema, we only have identifiers, and so it made sense to use the plain `long` field type, but there are some other fields. For the track duration in the tracks data, we could do a query such as this to find all of the tracks that are longer than 5 minutes (300 seconds, 300,000 milliseconds):

```
t_duration:[300000 TO *]
```

In this example, we can see Solr's support for *open-ended* range queries by using `*`. This feature is not available in Lucene.

Although uncommon, you can also use range queries with text fields. For this to have any use, the field should have only one term indexed. You can control this either by using the `string` field type, or by using the `KeywordTokenizer`. You may want to do some experimentation. The following example finds all documents where `somefield` has a term starting with B. We effectively make the right side of the range exclusive by excluding it with another query clause.

```
somefield:([B TO C] -C)
```

Both sides of the range, B and C, are not processed with text analysis that could exist in the field type definition. If there is any text analysis like lowercasing, you will need to do the same to the query or you will get no results.

Date math

Solr extended Lucene's old query parser to add date literals as well as some simple math that is especially useful in specifying date ranges. In addition, there is a way to specify the current date-time using NOW. The syntax offers addition, subtraction, and rounding at various levels of date granularity, like years, seconds, and so on down to milliseconds. The operations can be chained together as needed, in which case they are executed from left to right. Spaces aren't allowed. For example:

```
r_event_date:[* TO NOW-2YEAR]
```

In the preceding example, we searched for documents where an album was released over two years ago. NOW has millisecond precision. Let's say what we really wanted was precision to the day. By using / we can round down (it never rounds up):

```
r_event_date:[* TO NOW/DAY-2YEAR]
```

The units to choose from are: YEAR, MONTH, DAY, DATE (synonymous with DAY), HOUR, MINUTE, SECOND, MILLISECOND, and MILLI (synonymous with MILLISECOND). Furthermore, they can be pluralized by adding an S as in YEARS.

> This so-called **DateMath** syntax is not just for querying dates; it is for supplying dates to be indexed by Solr too! When supplying dates to Solr for indexing, consider concatenating a rounding operation to coursen the time granularity sufficient for your needs. There is an example below on how to use it. Solr will evaluate the math and index the result. Full millisecond precision time takes up more disk space and is slower to query than a courser granularity. Another index-time common usage is to timestamp added data. Using the NOW syntax as the `default` attribute of a timestamp field definition makes this easy. Here's how to do that:
> `<field name="indexedAt" type="tdate" default="NOW/SECOND" />`

Score boosting

You can easily modify the degree to which a clause in the query string contributes to the ultimate relevancy score by adding a multiplier. This is called **boosting**. A value between 0 and 1 reduces the score, and numbers greater than 1 increase it. You'll learn more about scoring in the next chapter. In the following example, we search for artists that either have a member named Billy, or have a name containing the word Smashing:

```
a_member_name:Billy^2 OR Smashing
```

Here we search for an artist name containing Billy, and optionally Bob or Corgan, but we're less interested in those that are also named Corgan:

```
+Billy Bob Corgan^0.7
```

Existence (and non-existence) queries

This is actually not a new syntax case, but an application of range queries. Suppose you wanted to match all of the documents that have an indexed value in a field. Here we find all of the documents that have something in a_name:

```
a_name:[* TO *]
```

As a_name is the default field, just [* TO *] will do.

This can be negated to find documents that *do not* have a value for a_name, as shown in the following code:

```
-a_name:[* TO *]
```

> Due to an unintended side effect of having
> ReversedWildcardFilterFactory somewhere in the schema, just *
> is equivalent. Similarly, -* for negation. Even though it's more intuitive
> than a range query, do not rely on this working until (and if) a future Solr
> officially supports this. See SOLR-1982.

Like wildcard and fuzzy queries, these are expensive, slowing down as the number of distinct terms in the field increases.

> **Performance tip**
>
> If you need to perform these frequently, perhaps because you
> want to do dynamic faceting, consider adding this to your schema:
> `<field name="fields" type="string" stored="false"`
> `multiValued="true" />` and at index time add the name of fields
> that have a value to it. There is a patch in SOLR-1280 providing an
> UpdateRequestProcessor to do this automatically. Alternatively,
> you could do this yourself somewhere like a DIH transformer or in
> your client code. The query would then simply be `fields:a_name`
> which is as fast as it gets.

Escaping special characters

The following characters are used by the query syntax, as described in this chapter:

```
+ - && || ! ( ) { } [ ] ^ " ~ * ? : \
```

In order to use any of these without their syntactical meaning, you need to escape them by a preceding \ such as seen here:

```
id:Artist\:11650
```

This also applies to the field name part. In some cases such as this one where the character is part of the text that is indexed, the double-quotes phrase query will also work, even though there is only one term:

```
id:"Artist:11650"
```

 If you're using SolrJ to interface with Solr, the `ClientUtils.`
`escapeQueryChars()` method will do the escaping for you.

A common situation in which a query needs to be generated, and thus escaped properly, is when generating a simple filter query in response to choosing a field-value facet when faceting. This syntax and suggested situation is getting ahead of us but I'll show it anyway since it relates to escaping. The query uses the `term` query parser as follows: `{!term f=a_type}group`. What follows } is not escaped at all, even a \ is interpreted literally, and so with this trick you needn't worry about escaping rules at all.

The Dismax query parser (part 1)

The `lucene` query parser we've been using so far for searching offers a rich syntax, but it doesn't do anything more. A notable problem with using this parser is that the query must be well formed according to the aforementioned syntax rules, such as having balanced quotes and parenthesis. Users might type just about anything for a query, not knowing anything about this syntax, possibly resulting in an error or unexpected results. The `dismax` query parser, named after Lucene's `DisjunctionMaxQuery`, addresses this problem and adds many features to enhance search relevancy (that is good scoring). The features of this query parser that have a more direct relationship to scoring are described in part 2, in the next chapter. Use of this parser is so important that we introduce it here.

You'll see references here to **edismax** whereby the "e" stands for "extended". This is an evolution of dismax new to Solr 3.1 that adds features. In a future Solr version, perhaps as soon as the next release, I expect `dismax` to refer to the enhanced version while the older one will likely exist under another name.

 Almost always use defType=dismax

The `dismax` (or `edismax`) query parser should almost always be chosen for parsing user queries – q. Set it in the request handler definition for your app. Furthermore, I recommend use of `edismax` which has seen plenty of production use. The only consideration to consider against this is whether it's a problem for users to be able to use Solr's full syntax, whether inadvertently or maliciously. This is explained shortly.

Here is a summary of the features that the `dismax` query parser has over the `lucene` query parser:

- Searches across multiple fields with different score boosts through Lucene's `DisjunctionMaxQuery`.
- Limits the query syntax to an essential subset. `edismax` permits Solr's full syntax assuming it parses correctly.
- Automatic phrase boosting of the entire search query. `edismax` boosts contiguous portions of the query too.
- Convenient query boosting parameters, generally for use with function queries.
- Can specify the minimum number of words to match, depending on the number of words in a query string.
- Can specify a default query to use when no user query is specified.

`edismax` was only mentioned a couple of times in this list but it improves on the details of how some of these features work.

Use debugQuery=on

Enable query debugging to see a normalized string representation of the parsed query tree, considering all value-add options that `dismax` performs. Then, look for `parsedquery` in the debug output. See how it changes depending on the query.

These features will subsequently be described in greater detail. But first, let's take a look at a request handler I've set up for searching artists. Solr configuration that is not related to the schema is located in `solrconfig.xml`. The following definition is a simplified version of the one in this book's code supplement:

```
<requestHandler name="mb_artists" class="solr.SearchHandler">
    <lst name="defaults">
        <str name="defType">edismax</str>
        <str name="qf">a_name a_alias^0.8 a_member_name^0.4</str>
        <str name="q.alt">*:*</str>
    </lst>
</requestHandler>
```

In Solr's full search interface screen, we can refer to this with a **Query Type** of `mb_artists`. This value aligns with the `qt` parameter, which you will observe in the URL when you submit the form. It wasn't necessary to set up such a request handler, because Solr is fully configurable from a URL, but it's a good practice and it's convenient for Solr's search form.

Searching multiple fields

You use the `qf` parameter to tell the `dismax` query parser which fields you want to search and their corresponding score boosts. As explained in the section on request handlers, the query parameters can be specified in the URL or in the request handler configuration in `solrconfig.xml`—you'll probably choose the latter for this one. Here is the relevant configuration line from our `dismax` based handler configuration earlier:

```
<str name="qf">a_name a_alias^0.8 a_member_name^0.4</str>
```

This syntax is a space-separated list of field names that can have optional boosts applied to them using the same syntax for boosting that is used in the query syntax. This request handler is intended to find artists from a user's query. Such a query would ideally match the artist's name, but we'll also search aliases, and bands that the artist is a member of. Perhaps the user didn't recall the band name but knew the artist's name. This configuration would give them the band in the search results, most likely towards the end.

> The score boosts do not strictly order the results in a cascading fashion. An exact match in `a_alias` that matched only part of `a_name` will probably appear on top. If in your application you are matching identifiers of some sort, then you may want to give a boost to that field that is very high, such as 1000, to virtually assure it will be on top.

One detail involved in searching multiple fields is the effect of stop words (for example, "the", "a", …) in the schema definition. If `qf` refers to some fields using stop words and others that don't, then a search involving stop words will usually return no results. `edismax` fixes this by making them all optional in the query unless the query is entirely stop words. With `dismax`, you can ensure the query analyzer chain in queried fields filter out the same set of stop words.

Limited query syntax

The `edismax` query parser will first try to parse the user query with the full syntax supported by the `lucene` query parser, with a couple tweaks. If it fails to parse, it will fall back to the limited syntax of the original `dismax` in the next paragraph. Some day, this should be configurable but it is not at this time. The aforementioned "tweaks" to the full syntax is that, `or` and `and` boolean operators can be used in a lower-case form, and pure-negative sub-queries are supported.

When using `dismax` (or `edismax`, the user query failed to parse with the `lucene` query parser), the parser will restrict the syntax permitted to terms, phrases, and use of + and - (but not AND, OR, &&, ||) to make a clause mandatory or prohibited. Anything else is escaped if needed to ensure that the underlying query is valid. The intention is to never trigger an error but unless you're using `edismax`, you'll have to code for this possibility due to outstanding bugs (SOLR-422, SOLR-874).

The following query example uses all of the supported features of this limited syntax:

```
"a phrase query" plus +mandatory without -prohibited
```

Min-should-match

With the `lucene` query parser, you have a choice of the default operator being OR, thereby requiring just one query clause (that is word) to match, or choosing AND to make all clauses required. This of course only applies to clauses not otherwise explicitly marked required or prohibited in the query using + and -. But these are two extremes, and it would be useful to pick some middle ground. The `dismax` parser uses a method called **min-should-match**, a feature which describes how many clauses should match, depending on how many there are in the query—required and prohibited clauses are not included in the numbers. This allows you to quantify the number of clauses as either a percentage or a fixed number. The configuration of this setting is entirely contained within the mm query parameter using a concise syntax specification that I'll describe in a moment.

This feature is more useful if users use many words in their queries—at least three. This in turn suggests a text field that has some substantial text in it but that is not the case for our MusicBrainz data set. Nevertheless, we will put this feature to good use.

Basic rules

The following are the four basic mm specification formats expressed as examples:

3	3 clauses are *required*, the rest are optional.
-2	2 clauses are *optional*, the rest are required.
66%	66% of the clauses (rounded down) are *required*, the rest are optional.
-25%	25% of the clauses (rounded down) are *optional*, the rest are required.

Notice that - inverses the required/optional definition. It does not make any number negative from the standpoint of any definitions herein.

 Note that 75% and -25% may seem the same but are not due to rounding. Given five queried clauses, the first requires three, whereas the second requires four. This shows that if you desire a round-up calculation, then you can invert the sign and subtract it from 100.

Two additional points about these rules are as follows:

- If the mm rule is a fixed number n, but there are fewer queried clauses, then n is reduced to the queried clause count so that the rule will make sense. For example: if mm is -5 and only two clauses are in the query, then all are optional. Sort of!
- Remember that in all circumstances across Lucene (and thus Solr); at least one clause in a query must match, even if every clause is optional. So in the example above and for 0 or 0%, one clause must still match, assuming that there are no required clauses present in the query.

Multiple rules

Now that you understand the basic mm specification format, which is for one simple rule, I'll describe the final format, which allows for multiple rules. This format is composed of an ordered space-separated series of the following: number<basicmm— which can be read as "If the clause count is greater than number, then apply rule basicmm". Only the right-most rule that meets the clause count threshold is evaluated. As they are ordered in an ascending order, the chosen rule is the one that requires the greatest number of clauses. If none match because there are fewer clauses, then all clauses are required—that is a basic specification of 100%.

An example of the mm specification is given in the following example:

```
2<75% 9<-3
```

This reads: If there are over nine clauses, then all but three are required (three are optional, and the rest are required). If there are over two clauses, then 75% are required (rounded down). Otherwise (one or two clauses) all clauses are required, which is the default rule.

 I find it easier to interpret these rules if they are read right to left.

What to choose

A simple configuration for min-should-match is making all of the search terms optional. This is effectively equivalent to a default OR operator in the Lucene query parser. This is configured as shown in the following example:

```
0%
```

Conversely, the other extreme is requiring all of the terms, and this is equivalent to a default AND operator. This is configured as shown in the following example:

```
100%
```

For MusicBrainz searches, I do not expect users to be using many terms, but I expect most of them to match. If a user searches for three or more terms, then I'll let one be optional. Here is the mm spec:

```
2<-1
```

> You may be inclined to require all of the search terms; and that's a good common approach—it's the default in fact. However, if just one word isn't found then there will be no search results—an occurrence that most search software tries to minimize. Even if you make some of the words optional, the matching documents that have more of the search words will be towards the top of the search results assuming score-sorted order (you'll learn why in the next chapter). There are other ways to approach this problem like performing a secondary search if the first returns none or too few. Solr doesn't do this for you but it's easy for the client to do. This approach could even tell the user that this was done which would yield a better search experience.

A default search

The dismax query parser supports a *default search*, which is used in the event the user query, q, is not specified. This parameter is q.alt and it is not subject to the limited syntax of dismax. Here's an example of it used for matching all documents, from within the request handler defaults in solrconfig.xml:

```
<str name="q.alt">*:*</str>
```

This parameter is usually set to *:* to match all documents and is often specified in the request handler configuration in solrconfig.xml. You'll see with faceting in the next section, that there will not necessarily even be a user query, and so you'll want to display facets over all of the data. If you'd rather it not match any documents (0 results), simply use -*:*.

Filtering

Separate from the q parameter (that is the user query), you can specify additional so-called **filter queries** that will filter the search results. Arguably the user query is also a filter but you instead see the word "search" used for that. Filter queries don't affect scoring, unlike the user query. To add a filter, simply use the fq parameter. This parameter can be added multiple times for additional filters. A document must match *all* filter queries and the user query for it to be in the results.

As an example, let's say we wanted to make a search form for MusicBrainz that lets the user search for bands, not individual artists, and those that released an album in the last 10 years. Let's also say that the user's query string is Green. In the index, a_type is either person for an individual or group for a band, or 0 if unknown. Therefore, a query that would find non-individuals would be this, combined with the user's query:

```
+Green -a_type:person +a_release_date_latest:[NOW/YEAR-10YEARS TO *]
```

However, you should **not** use this approach. Instead, use multiple fq query parameters:

```
q=Green&fq=-a_type%3Aperson&fq=a_release_date_latest%3A%5BNOW/YEAR-
10YEARS+TO+*%5D
```

Remember that in the URL snippet above we needed to URL Encode special characters like the colons.

Filter queries have some tangential benefits. They:

- Improve performance, because each filter query is cached in Solr's **filter cache** and can be applied extremely quickly.
- Clarify the logs, which show what the user searched for without it being confused with the filters.

In general, raw user input doesn't wind up being part of a filter-query. Instead, the filters are either known by your application in advance or are generated based on your data, for example, in faceted navigation. Although it wouldn't necessarily be a problem for user query text to become a filter, there may be scalability issues if many unique filter queries end up being performed that don't get re-used and so consume needless memory.

Solr 3.4 added the ability to disable caching of a filter by setting the `cache` local-param to `false`. This is useful for avoiding pollution of the filter cache when you know the query is not likely to be used again. And if the query is a function query (discussed in *Chapter 5, Search Relevancy*), there is a potential performance benefit because non-cached function queries are evaluated on a fraction of the total documents instead of all of them. For further details on this advanced technique, see the wiki: `http://wiki.apache.org/solr/CommonQueryParameters#Caching_of_filters`

Sorting

The sorting specification is specified with the `sort` query parameter. The default is `score desc`. `score` is not a field but a special reference to a relevancy number, described in detail in the next chapter. `desc` means descending order, use `asc` for ascending order. In the following example, suppose we searched for artists that are not individuals (a previous example in the chapter), and then we might want to ensure that those that are surely bands, get top placement ahead of those that are unknown. Secondly, we want the typical descending score search. This would simply be:

```
sort=a_type desc,score desc
```

Pay attention to the field types and text analysis you're using in your schema for fields that you sort on. Basically, fields need to be single valued, indexed, and not-tokenized. Some but not all support `sortMissingFirst` and `sortMissingLast` options. See the section on sorting in *Chapter 2, Schema and Text Analysis* for further information.

In addition to sorting on field values and the score, Solr supports sorting on a function query. Function queries are usually mathematical in nature and used for things like computing a geospatial distance or a time difference between now and some field value. Function queries are discussed in detail in the next chapter, but here's a simple example sorting by the difference between the artist begin and end date:

```
sort=sub(a_end_date,a_begin_date) desc
```

An interesting use-case that has nothing to do with math is a trick to sort based on multi-valued field data in limited circumstances. For example, what if we wanted to sort on MusicBrainz releases which are declared to be of type `Album` (`r_type` is a multi-valued field remember):

```
sort=query({!v="r_type:Album"}) desc
```

To understand how to parse and understand this admittedly complicated expression, read the earlier section on query parsers and local-params, and read the definition of the `query()` function query in the next chapter. We had to use the local-params `v` parameter to specify the query string instead of simply using the query because of syntax restrictions in the context of the how the `sort` parameter value is parsed.

Sorting and memory usage

When you ask Solr to sort on a field, every indexed value is put into an array in memory in the "field cache". This is more of a problem with text than other fields. Not only does this use a lot of memory, but the first time this happens, it takes time to bring in all the values from disk. You should add a query that sorts on the fields your app might sort on into `newSearcher` in `solrconfig.xml`.

Geospatial search

Geospatial search broadly refers to a search that in some way uses geospatially-indexed locations. A common specific need is filtering search results by distance from a center point and also to sort the results by that distance. Other uses are influencing relevancy order and faceting by distance ranges. **Spatial search** is similar but based on a 2-dimensional Cartesian plane instead of geospatial's sphere / planetary orientation. For documentation on the less useful spatial search, go to Solr's wiki.

The geospatial support about to be described is entirely new to Solr 3.1. This is just the beginning; expect much more in future releases. It may very well work quite differently in the future.

Indexing locations

You need raw location data in the form of a latitude and longitude to take advantage of Solr's geospatial capabilities.

If you have named locations (for example, "Boston, MA") then the data needs to be resolved to latitudes and longitudes using a **gazetteer** like Geonames—http://www.geonames.org. If all you have is free-form natural language text without the locations identified, then you'll have to perform a more difficult task that uses Natural Language Processing techniques to find the named locations. These approaches are out of scope of this book.

The principle field type in Solr for geospatial is `LatLonType`, which stores a single latitude-longitude pair. Under the hood, this field type copies the latitude and longitude into a pair of indexed fields using the provided field name suffix. In the following excerpt taken from Solr's example schema, given the field name `store`, there will be two additional fields named `store_0_coordinate` and `store_1_coordinate`, which you'll see in Solr's schema browser.

```
<fieldType name="location" class="solr.LatLonType"
  subFieldSuffix="_coordinate"/>
<!-- … -->
<field name="store" type="location" indexed="true"
  stored="true"/>
<!-- … -->
<dynamicField name="*_coordinate" type="tdouble"
  indexed="true" stored="false"/>
```

When providing data to this field, it is formatted as a string with the latitude and longitude separated by a comma like this:

```
<field name="store">43.17614,-90.57341</field>
```

Geohashes

Another geospatial field type to be aware of is `GeoHashField`, but there is no point in using it at this time. Geohashes have the *opportunity* for multi-valued data, indexed shape data other than points, and very fast filtering. However the implementation presently in Solr doesn't leverage any of this—for one that does, take a look at SOLR-2155—a patch of mine. There is a good chance this will make it into Solr 4 in some form.

Filtering by distance

Perhaps the most common geospatial need is to filter search results to those documents within a distance radius from a center point. If you are building an application in which the user is presented with a map, perhaps using Google Maps, then the center point is the center of the map the user is looking at and the distance radius is the distance from the center to the nearest map edge. Such a query is generally specified using a Solr filter query (`fq` parameter) leaving q open for the possibility of a combined keyword search if desired. Both the `geofilt` and `bbox` query parsers perform geospatial filtering. `geofilt` implements a point-distance based filter, a circle shape, whereas `bbox` uses the minimum bounding latitude-longitude box surrounding that circle.

bbox is preferred

The bbox query parser is faster than geofilt because it is able to make simple latitude and longitude numeric range searches whereas geofilt must compute every distance using the Haversine algorithm, which is more expensive. Furthermore, as the user is probably looking at a latitude-longitude box, having the query shape be a box makes sense too.

Here is a quick example based on Solr's example schema and data set, showing the URL parameters needed to do the search:

```
q=*:*&fq={!bbox}&sfield=store&pt=45.15,-93.85&d=5
```

The parameters that geofilt and bbox require can be specified as either local-params (between the parser name and closing bracket) or standard request parameters as shown above. The advantage to the latter is that a subsequent distance sort can re-use the same parameters, as you'll see in a bit. Here are geofilt and bbox's parameters:

- sfield: The name of the location field.
- pt: A latitude-comma-longitude pair for the center point of the query.
- d: The query distance from pt as measured in kilometers.

Sorting by distance

Geospatial distance sorting is implemented using a Solr function query that calculates the distance. There are a few such functions but the primary one you should use is geodist() which is the only one I'll document here. It returns the Earth geospatial distance using the Haversine formula between a pair of points. The points are each taken from the first available of: an argument, the parameter pt, or the parameter sfield. Any of these might be absent but at least two must be specified. When a point is specified as an argument, it can simply be a geospatial field or a pair of typical arguments (a field name or constant) to the latitude and longitude. Here's an example of both: geodist(store,42.4,-71.1)

By design, these parameter names align with those for the geofilt and bbox query parsers, which pairs well with geodist(). Consequently it is rare to supply arguments.

To apply a distance sort to the earlier example filtering by distance, simply add `&sort=geodist()+asc` to the URL parameter list.

Returning the distance in search results

A future version of Solr (certainly 4.0) will support returning the results of a function query in the search results. In the meantime, the only way this is possible is by using the `func` query parser to process q in which the document score is the result of the function. A keyword search, if needed, would then be displaced to a filter query in which it will not be able to influence relevancy (although use of the `query()` function query in the sort could be a way around that). Here's an example URL snippet:

```
q={!func}geodist()&fl=*,score
&fq={!bbox}&sfield=store&pt=45.15,-93.85&d=5
```

Summary

At this point, you've learned the essentials of searching in Solr, from request handlers, to the full query syntax, to dismax, and more. We spent a lot of time on the query syntax because you'll see the syntax pop-up in several places across Solr, not just the user's query. Such places include filter queries, delete queries, boost queries, facet queries, embedded within certain function queries, and query warming (discussed in later chapters). Even if you don't wish to expose the syntax to your users, you will probably be using it for various things. Finally, you got a taste of geospatial search. The subject of searching continues in the next chapter with a focus on relevancy / scoring matters. This starts with an explanation of Lucene/Solr's scoring model, and then various tools Solr gives you to influence the score such as function queries—also useful in sorting and filtering.

5
Search Relevancy

At this point you know how to search, filter, and sort. You've undoubtedly been sorting by score in descending order, the default, but have no understanding as to where those scores came from. This chapter is all about search relevancy, which basically means it's about scoring but it's also about other non-trivial methods of sorting to produce relevant results. A core Solr feature enabling these more advanced techniques called "function queries" will be introduced. The major topics covered in this chapter are:

- Factors influencing the score
- Troubleshooting queries, to include scoring
- Dismax part 2: features that enhance relevancy
- Function queries

In a hurry?

Use the edismax query parser for user queries by setting the defType parameter. Configure the qf (query fields) as explained in the previous chapter, set pf (phrase fields) considering the call-out tip in this chapter, and set tie to 0.1. If at some point you need help troubleshooting a query (and you will!) then return to read *Troubleshooting queries and scoring*.

Scoring

Scoring in Lucene is an advanced subject, but in spite of this it is important to at least have a basic understanding of it. Instead of presenting the algorithm, comprehension of which is a bit of an advanced subject not suitable for this book, we will discuss the factors influencing the score and where to look for diagnostic scoring information. If this overview is insufficient for your interest, then you can get the full details here at `http://lucene.apache.org/java/3_3_0/api/core/org/apache/lucene/search/Similarity.html`

An important thing to understand about scores is not to attribute much meaning to a score by itself; it's *almost* meaningless. The relative value of an individual score to the max score is more relevant. A document scored as 0.25 might be a great match or not, there's no telling. But if you compare this score to another from the very same search and find it to be twice as large, then it is fair to say that the document matched the query twice as well. This being said, you will usually find that scores in the vicinity of 0.5 or better are decent matches. The factors influencing the score are as follows:

- **Term frequency**—`tf`: The more times a term is found in a document's field, the higher the score it gets. This concept is most intuitive. Obviously, it doesn't matter how many times the term may appear in some other field, it's the searched field that is relevant (whether explicit in the query or the default).

- **Inverse document frequency**—`idf`: The rarer a term is in the index, the higher its score is. The document frequency is the number of documents in which the term appears, on a per-field basis, of course. It is the *inverse* of the document frequency that is positively correlated with the score.

- **Co-ordination factor**—`coord`: The greater the number of query clauses that match a document, the greater the score will be. Any mandatory clauses must match and the prohibited ones must not match, leaving the relevance of this piece of the score to situations where there are optional clauses.

- **Field length**—`fieldNorm`: The shorter the matching field is, measured in number of indexed terms, the greater the matching document's score will be. For example, if there was a band named just `Smashing`, and another named `Smashing Pumpkins`, then this factor in the scoring would be higher for the first band upon a search for just `Smashing`, as it has one word, while the other has two. Norms for a field can be marked as omitted in the schema with the `omitNorms` attribute, effectively neutralizing this component of the score.

These factors are the *intrinsic* components contributing to the score of a document in the results. If you introduce other components of the score then that is referred to as **boosting**. Usually, boosting is a simple multiplier to a field's score, either at index or query time, but it's not limited to that.

Query-time and index-time boosting

At index-time, you have the option to boost a particular document specified at the document level or at a specific field. The document level boost is the same as boosting each field by that value. This is internally stored as part of the norms number. Norms must not be omitted in the relevant fields in the schema. It's uncommon to perform index-time boosting because it is not as flexible as query-time. That said, I do find index-time boosting to have a more predictable and controllable influence on the final score.

At query-time, we described in the previous chapter how to explicitly boost a particular clause of a query higher or lower if needed using the trailing ^ syntax. We also showed how the dismax query parser's qf parameter not only lists the fields to search but allows a boost for them as well. There are a few more ways dismax can boost queries that you'll read about shortly.

Troubleshooting queries and scoring

An invaluable tool in diagnosing scoring behavior (or why a document isn't in the result or is but shouldn't be) is enabling query debugging with the debugQuery query parameter. There is no better way to describe it than with an example. Consider the fuzzy query:

```
a_name:Smashing~
```

We would intuitively expect that documents with fields containing Smashing would get the top scores, but that didn't happen. Execute the preceding query mentioned with debugQuery=on, and ensure that you're looking at the original indentation by using the **View Source** feature in your browser. Try right-clicking the XML to see the option.

The top score is 2.664175, and there were two documents matching, neither with Smashing. One had Mashina, and the other had Smashin'.

```
<doc>
  <float name="score">2.664175</float>
  <str name="a_name">Mashina</str>
</doc>
<doc>
  <float name="score">2.664175</float>
  <str name="a_name">Smashin'</str>
</doc>
<doc>
  <float name="score">2.5235493</float>
  <str name="a_name">Smashing Atoms</str>
</doc>
```

The first two documents have words that differ from smashing by only two characters (remember the case difference). The third document finally matched Smashing. Its score was a little less, but not enough to overtake the top two. What's going on here? Let's look at the following debug output, showing the first and the third document. We'll skip the second, as it has the same score as the first:

```
<lst name="explain">
  <str name="Artist:227132">
2.664175 = (MATCH) sum of:
  2.664175 = (MATCH) weight(a_name:mashina^0.42857146 in 286945),
  product of:
    0.20176922 = queryWeight(a_name:mashina^0.42857146),
    product of:
      0.42857146 = boost
      13.204025 = idf(docFreq=1, numDocs=399182)
      0.035655525 = queryNorm
    13.204025 = (MATCH) fieldWeight(a_name:mashina in 286945),
    product of:
      1.0 = tf(termFreq(a_name:mashina)=1)
      13.204025 = idf(docFreq=1, numDocs=399182)
      1.0 = fieldNorm(field=a_name, doc=286945)
  </str>
<!-- skip 2nd doc ...-->
  <str name="Artist:93855">
2.5235493 = (MATCH) sum of:
  2.5235493 = (MATCH) weight(a_name:smashing^0.75 in 9796),
  product of:
    0.32859424 = queryWeight(a_name:smashing^0.75),
    product of:
      0.75 = boost
      12.287735 = idf(docFreq=4, numDocs=399182)
      0.035655525 = queryNorm
    7.6798344 = (MATCH) fieldWeight(a_name:smashing in 9796),
    product of:
      1.0 = tf(termFreq(a_name:smashing)=1)
      12.287735 = idf(docFreq=4, numDocs=1002272)
      0.625 = fieldNorm(field=a_name, doc=9796)
  </str>
```

What we see here is the mathematical breakdown of the various components of the score. We see that mashina (the term actually in the index) was given a query-time boost of 0.43, whereas smashing was given a query-time boost of 0.75. We expected this because the fuzzy matching was going to give higher weights to stronger matches, and it did. However, other factors pulled the final score in the other direction. Notice that the fieldNorm for mashina was 1.0 whereas smashing had a fieldNorm of 0.625. This is because the document we wanted to score higher had a field with more indexed terms (Smashing Atoms) versus just the one that Mashina had. So arguably, Mashina is a closer match than Smashing Atoms to the fuzzy query Smashing~.

How might we "fix" this? Well it's not broken, and the number three spot in the search results isn't bad. This is also a fuzzy query which is fairly unusual and arguably isn't a circumstance to optimize for. The first thing to do is to try and lowercase a fuzzy query so that there isn't a case difference. If that is insufficient then try enabling omitNorms in the schema, at the expense of no score differentiation on matches in shorter versus longer fields. There are other things to try for more experienced developers like experimenting with something called SweetSpotSimilarity—Google it for more information.

Dismax query parser (part 2) ·

In the previous chapter you were introduced to the dismax query parser as the preferred choice for user queries, the q parameter. The parser for user queries is set with the defType parameter. The syntax, the fields that are queried (with boosts)—qf, the min-should-match syntax—mm, and the default query—q.alt, were already described. We're now going to complete your education on this parser by discussing the remaining features which are most closely related to scoring.

Any mention herein to dismax applies to the edismax query parser too, unless specified otherwise. As explained in the previous chapter, edismax is the extended dismax parser that is expected to replace dismax in a future release. edismax is generally superior to dismax as you'll see in this section.

Lucene's DisjunctionMaxQuery

The ability to search across multiple fields with different boosts in this query parser is a feature powered by Lucene's **DisjunctionMaxQuery** query type. Let's start with an example. If the query string is simply rock, then dismax might be configured to turn this into a DisjunctionMaxQuery *similar* to this:

```
fieldA:rock^2 OR fieldB:rock^1.2 OR fieldC:rock^0.5
```

Advanced topic warning

The following discussion is advanced, and you needn't understand it. Just know that a dismax query is ideal for searching multiple fields and to set the tie parameter to 0.1, which is a reasonable choice.

The boolean query mentioned above is not quite equivalent to what the dismax query actually does; the difference is in the scoring. A boolean query, such as this, will have a score based on the *sum* of each of the three clauses whereas a DisjunctionMaxQuery takes the *maximum* of each (this is a simplification). The dismax behavior should produce better scores for this use case, which is where you are looking in multiple fields for the same term, where some fields are deemed to be more significant than others. An example from the API docs of this feature explains that if a user searched for albino elephant, then dismax ensures that albino matching one field and elephant matching another gets a higher score than albino matching both fields but elephant neither.

Another wrinkle on this description of dismax scoring is the tie parameter, which is between zero (the default) and one. By raising this value above zero, the scoring begins to favor documents that matched multiple terms over those that were boosted higher. This can be moved to the extreme by using 1—resulting in scoring that is closer to that of a boolean query. In practice, a small value like 0.1 is effective.

Boosting: Automatic phrase boosting

Suppose a user searches for `Billy Joel`. This is interpreted as two terms to search for, and depending on how the request handler is configured, either both must be found in the document or just one. Perhaps for one of the matching documents, `Billy` is the sole name of a band, and it has a member named `Joel`. Great, Solr found this document and perhaps it is of interest to the user, after all, it contained both words the user typed. However, it's a fairly intuitive observation that a document field containing the entirety of what the user typed, `Billy Joel`, represents a closer match to what the user is looking for. Solr would certainly find such a document too, without question, but it's hard to predict what the relative scoring might be. To improve the scoring, you might be tempted to automatically quote the user's query, but that would omit documents that don't have the adjacent words. What the dismax handler can do is add a phrased version of the user's query onto the original query as an *optional* clause. So, in a nutshell, it rewrites this query:

```
Billy Joel
```

into

```
+(Billy Joel) "Billy Joel"
```

 The queries here illustrate phrase boosting in its most basic form. It doesn't depict the `DisjunctionMaxQuery` that dismax uses.

The rewritten query depicts that the original query is mandatory by using +, and it shows that we've added an *optional* phrase. A document containing the phrase `Billy Joel` not only matches that clause of the rewritten query, but it also matches `Billy` and `Joel` — three clauses in total. If in another document the phrase didn't match, but it had both words, then only two clauses would match. Lucene's scoring algorithm would give a higher **coordination factor** to the first document, and would score it higher, all other factors being equal.

Configuring automatic phrase boosting

Automatic phrase boosting is not enabled by default. In order to use this feature, you must use the `pf` parameter, which is an abbreviation of "phrase fields". The syntax is identical to `qf`. You should start with the same value and then make adjustments. Common reasons to vary `pf` from `qf`:

- To use different (typically lower) boost factors so that the impact of phrase boosting isn't overpowering. Some experimentation may guide you to make such adjustments.

- To omit fields that are always one term, such as an identifier because there's no point in searching the field for phrases.

- To omit some of the fields that have lots of text since that might slow down search performance too much.

- To substitute a field for another that has the same data but analyzed differently. For example, you might choose to perform **shingling** (a text analysis technique described in *Chapter 10, Scaling Solr*) into a separate field instead of shingling the original field. Such a shingling configuration would be a little different than described in that chapter; you would set `outputUnigrams` to `false`.

> **pf Tips**
>
> Start with the same value used as `qf`, but with boosts cut in half. Remove fields that are always one term, such as an identifier. Also, use of **common-grams** or **shingling**, as described in *Chapter 10, Scaling Solr*, is highly recommended to increase performance.

Phrase slop configuration

In the previous chapter, we had mentioned the phrase **slop**, aka term proximity, by following a phrase with a tilde and a number, as shown below:

```
"Billy Joel"~1
```

`dismax` adds two parameters to automatically set the slop: `qs` for any explicit phrase queries that the user entered and `ps` for the phrase boosting mentioned previously. If slop is not specified, then there is no slop, which is equivalent to a value of zero. For more information about slop, see the corresponding discussion in the previous chapter. Here is a sample configuration of both slop settings:

```
<str name="qs">1</str>
<str name="ps">0</str>
```

Partial phrase boosting

In addition to boosting the entire query as a phrase, `edismax` supports boosting consecutive word pairs if there are more than two queried words and consecutive triples if there are more than three queried words. These are configured by setting `pf2` and `pf3`, respectively, in the same manner that the `pf` parameter is defined. For example, this query:

```
how now brown cow
```

Would become:

```
+(how now brown cow) "how now brown cow" "how now" "now brown" "brown
cow" "how now brown" "now brown cow"
```

This feature is not affected by the `ps` (phrase slop) parameter, which only applies to the entire phrase boost.

> You can certainly expect the relevancy to improve for longer queries, but of course these queries are going to be even slower now. To speed up such queries, use common-grams or shingling, described *Chapter 10, Scaling Solr.* If you are using `pf2` or `pf3`, consider a `maxShingleSize` of 3 (but monitor its impact on index size!), and consider omitting the larger text fields from `pf2` or `pf3`.

Boosting: Boost queries

Continuing with the boosting theme is another way to affect the score of documents: boost queries. The dismax parser lets you specify multiple additional queries using `bq` parameter(s), which, like the automatic phrase boost, get added onto the user's query in a similar manner. Remember that boosting only serves to affect the scoring of documents that already matched the user's query in the `q` parameter. If a matched document also matches a `bq` query, then it will be scored higher.

For a realistic example of using a boost query, we're going to look at MusicBrainz releases data. Releases have an `r_type` field containing values like Album, Single, Compilation, and others, and an `r_official` field containing values like Official, Promotion, Bootleg, and Pseudo-Release. We don't want to sort search results based on these since we want the natural scoring algorithm to consider the user's query in the relevancy; however, we might want to influence the score based on these. For example, let's say albums are the most relevant release type whereas a **compilation** is the least relevant. And let's say that an official release is more relevant than bootleg or promotional or pseudo-releases. We might express this using a boost query like this (defined in the request handler):

```
<str name="bq">r_type:Album^2 (*:* -r_type:Compilation)^2 r_
official:Official^2</str>
```

Searching releases for "airplane flies" showed that this boost query did what it should by breaking a score tie in which the release names were the same but these attributes varied. *In reality the boosting on each term, all three in this example, would be tweaked to have the relevancy boost desired* by carefully examining the debugQuery output. One oddity in this query is (*:* -r_type:Compilation)^2 which boosts all documents except compilations. Using r_type:Compilation^0.5 would not work since it would still be added to the score. To understand why *:* is needed, read the previous chapter on the limitations of pure negative queries.

> Boost queries are not as useful as boost functions, described in the next section—especially since edismax supports a multiplied boost, which is generally more desirable than addition. Even in the preceding example, it's awkward to tune the boost of each query clause because of the inverse document frequency (IDF) that varies for each term. For example, you might want the effect of r_type being Album and r_official being Official to have an equivalent boost. You would need to perform a query with debugQuery enabled to look at what the score is for each of these terms, which will be different, and then use disproportionate boosts (not both as in the example) so that when multiplied by their intrinsic score, they wind up being the same. This is a pain and it's brittle.

Boosting: Boost functions

Boost functions offer a powerful way to either add or multiply the result of a user-specified formula to a document's score. By *formula* I refer to a composition of Solr **function queries**, which are described in detail next in this chapter. To add to the score, specify the function query with the bf parameter. edismax adds support for multiplying the result to the score in which you specify the function query with the boost parameter. You can specify bf and boost each as many times as you wish.

> For a thorough explanation of function queries including useful MusicBrainz examples, see the next section.

An example of boosting MusicBrainz tracks by how recently they were released is:

```
<str name="boost">recip(map(rord(r_event_date_earliest),0,0,99000)
        ,1,95000,95000)</str>
```

There cannot be any spaces within the function. The bf and boost parameters are actually not parsed in the same way. The bf parameter allows multiple boost functions within the same parameter, separated by space, as an alternative to using additional bf parameters. You can also apply a multiplied boost factor to the function in bf by appending ^100 (or another number) to the end of the function query. This is just a convenience for using the mul() function query, described later.

Finally, ensure `newSearcher` in `solrconfig.xml` has a sample query using the boost functions you're using. In doing so you ensure that any referenced fields are in Lucene's field cache instead of penalizing the first query with this cost. *Chapter 10, Scaling Solr* has more information on performance tuning.

Add or multiply boosts?

In a nutshell, if you can tame the difficulty in additive boosting (`bf` param) then you'll probably be more satisfied with the scoring. Multiplicative boosting (`boost` param) is easier to use, especially if the intended boost query is considered less than or equal to the user query, which is usually true.

If you describe how you'd like the scoring to work as: "I'd like 2/3 of the document score to come from the user query and the remainder 1/3 to be from my formula" (or whatever ratios) then additive scores are for you. The trick is that you need to know the top score for an excellent match on the user query in order to balance out the proportions right. Try an exact match on a title (a highly boosted field in the query) and see what the top score is. Do this a bunch of times for a variety of documents, looking for reasonable consistency. So if, for example, the top end of the user query ends up being 1.5, and you want the function query to make up about half as much as the user query does in the final score, then adjust the function query so its upper bound is 0.75. Simply multiply by that if you already have the function query in the 0-1 nominal range. Even if these instructions don't seem too bad, in practice tuning additive scores is tricky since Lucene will react to every change you do by changing the `queryNorm` part of the score out from under you, which you have no control over. As it does this, keep your eye on the overall ratios that you want between the added boost part and the user query part, not the particular score values. Another bigger problem is that your experiments in gauging the maximum score of the user query will change as your data changes, which will mean some ongoing monitoring of whatever values you choose.

The other way of thinking about your boost function is as a user query score multiplier (a *factor*). With multiplication you don't need to concern yourself with whatever a "good" user query score is—it has no bearing here. The tricky part of multiplicative boosts is weighting your boost, so it has the relative impact you want. If you simply supply your nominal range (0-1) function directly as the boost then it has the same weight as the user query. As you shift the function's values above 0 then you reduce the influence it has relative to the user query. For example, if you add 1 to your nominal 0-1 range so that it goes from 1-2, then it is weighted roughly half as much (formula: $(2-1)/2 = 0.5$).

It's possible to use multiplicative boosts that are weighted as more relevant than the user query but I haven't fully worked out the details. A place to start experimenting with this is boosting the boost function by a power, say 1.7, which appeared to about double the weight.

Function queries

A function query is a user-specified composition of Solr-provided functions, most of which are mathematical in nature. It is evaluated on each matching document, taking constants and references to single-valued fields as input and returning a floating-point number via its score. Because they are technically queries, albeit strange ones, they can be used in any place you see queries in Solr (search, filtering, and so on.) and since Solr 3 they can be used to sort on too.

There are quite a few ways in which you can incorporate a function query into your searches in Solr:

 Despite the multitude of options here, you'll most likely just use them in boosting with the dismax parser. It's good to know about other possibilities, though.

- **Dismax query parser using the** bf **or** boost **parameters:**

  These two parameters add or multiply the function query to the user query score for boosting. They were previously described in the chapter but you'll see in-depth examples on deriving a function query coming up.

- **Boost query parser:**

  Like dismax's boost parameter, this query parser lets you specify a function query that is multiplied to the main query. Unlike dismax, the query string is parsed by the lucene query parser. Here is an example query:

  ```
  {!boost b=log(t_trm_lookups)}t_name:Daydreaming
  ```

- **Lucene query parser using the _val_ pseudo-field hack:**

  Here is an example:

  ```
  t_name:Daydreaming && _val_:"log(t_trm_lookups)"^0.01
  ```

  There is no field named _val_; this just triggers the query parser to treat the quoted part as a function query instead of as a field value to search. It'll match all documents, so combine it with other required clauses to actually limit the results. The score is added to the other parts of the query.

- **Func query parser:**

    The func query parser is particularly useful in debugging a function query, and as of Solr 3 it is the only way to get the computed result of a function query in the search results. Solr 4 will support returning function query results without requiring this parser, but Solr 4 isn't released yet. Here is an example URL snippet:

    ```
    q=log(t_trm_lookups)&defType=func&fl=t_trm_lookups,score
    ```

    The score of each document in the results is the evaluation of the function query.

- **Frange (function range) query parser:**

    This query parser is similar to the func query parser but it also *filters* documents based on the resulting score being in a specified range, instead of returning all documents. It takes an l parameter for the lower bound, a u parameter for the upper bound, and incl and incu boolean parameters to specify whether the lower or upper bounds are inclusive—which they are by default. The parameters are optional but you will specify at least one of u or l for meaningful effect. Here's an example URL snippet from its documentation:

    ```
    fq={!frange l=0 u=2.2}sum(user_ranking,editor_ranking)
    ```

- **Sorting:**

    In addition to sorting on field values, as mentioned in the previous chapter, Solr 3 adds sorting on function queries too. Here's an example URL snippet sorting by geospatial distance. It assumes use of the geofilt query parser— partially omitted here:

    ```
    sort=geodist(pt=… sfield=… d=…) asc
    ```

Field references

For fields used in a function query, the constraints are the same as sorting. Essentially this means the field must be indexed, not multi-valued, and if text fields are used then they must analyze down to no more than one token. And like sorting, all values get stored in the field cache. The implication of the field cache is that you should have enough memory and also that you should have a suitable query in newSearcher in solrconfig.xml so that the first search after a commit isn't penalized with the initialization cost.

> If you have a multi-valued field you hoped to use, you'll instead have to put a suitable value into another field during indexing. This might be a simple minimum, maximum, or average calculation. If you are using the Data Import Handler (DIH, see *Chapter 3, Indexing Data*), you should consider a DIH transformer, or you could simply do this on the client before sending the data to Solr.

If there is no value in the field for the document then the result is zero, otherwise, numeric fields result in the corresponding numeric value. But what about other field types? For `TrieDateField` you get the `ms()` value, explained shortly. Note that `0` ambiguously means the date might be 1970 or blank. For older date fields, you get the `ord()` value, also explained shortly. For boolean fields, true is 2 and false is 1 — rather unexpected but it is immaterial. For text fields, you get the `ord()` value. Some functions can work with the text value — in such cases you'll need to explicitly use the `literal()` function.

Function reference

This section contains a reference of the majority of function queries in Solr.

An argument to a function can be a literal constant such as a number, a field reference, or an embedded function. String constants are quoted. One interesting thing you can do is pull out any argument into a separate named request parameter (in the URL) of your choosing and then refer to it with a leading $:

```
&defType=func&q=max(t_trm_lookups,$min)&min=50
```

The parameter might be in the request or configured into the request handler configuration. If this parameter dereferencing syntax is familiar to you, then that's because it works the same way in **local-params** too, as explained in *Chapter 4, Searching*.

> Not all arguments can be of any type. For the function definitions below, any argument named x, y, or z can be any expression: constants, field references, or functions. Other arguments like a, or `min` *require* a literal constant. If you attempt to do otherwise, then you will get an unhelpful parsing error.

Mathematical primitives

These functions cover basic math operations and constants:

- `sum(x,y,z,...)` aliased to `add`: Sums, that is adds, all of the arguments.
- `sub(x,y)`: Subtracts y from x as in the expression x-y.
- `product(x,y,z,...)`, aliased to `mul`: Multiplies the arguments together.
- `div(x,y)`: Divides x by y as in the expression x/y.
- `log(x)`, `ln(x)`: The base-10 logarithm and the natural logarithm.
- `sqrt(x)`, `cbrt(x)`, `ceil(x)`, `floor(x)`, `rint(x)`, `pow(x,y)`, `exp(x)`, `e()`: See the `java.lang.Math` API http://download.oracle.com/javase/6/docs/api/java/lang/Math.html

Geometric/Trigonometric:

- `rad(x)`, `deg(x)`: Converts degrees to radians, and radians to degrees.
- `sin(x)`, `cos(x)`, `tan(x)`, `asin(x)`, `acos(x)`, `atan(x)`, `sinh(x)`, `cosh(x)`, `tanh(x)`, `hypot(x,y)`, `atan2(y,x)`, `pi()`: See the `java.lang.Math` API
- Geospatial functions are covered later.

Other math

These are useful and straightforward mathematical functions:

- `map(x,min,max,target,def?)`: If x is found to be between `min` and `max` inclusive, then `target` is returned. Otherwise if `def` (an optional parameter) is supplied then that is returned. Otherwise x is returned. This is useful for dealing with default values or to limit x, to ensure that it isn't above or below some threshold.
- `max(x,c)`: Returns the greater value of x and c.
- `scale(x,minTarget,maxTarget)`: Returns x scaled to be between `minTarget` and `maxTarget`. For example, if the value of x is found to be one-third from the smallest and largest values of x across all documents, then x is returned as one-third of the distance between `minTarget` and `maxTarget`.

 `scale()` will traverse the entire document set and evaluate the function to determine the smallest and largest values for each query invocation, and it is not cached. This makes it impractical for many uses, as it is too slow.

- `linear(x,m,c)`: A macro for `sum(product(m,x),c)` for convenience and speed.
- `recip(x,m,a,c)`: A macro for `div(a,linear(x,m,c))` for convenience and speed.

ord and rord

Before `ms()` was introduced in Solr 1.4, `ord()` and `rord()` were mediocre substitutes. You probably won't use them. `ms()` is described next.

As mentioned earlier, `ord(fieldReference)` is implied for references to text fields in the function query.

- `ord(fieldReference)`: Given a hypothetical ascending sorted array of all unique indexed values for `fieldReference`, this returns the array position, in other words, the ordinal of a document's indexed value. `fieldReference` is of course a reference to a field. Unlike most other functions it cannot be any other kind of expression. The order of the values is in an ascending order and the first position is 1. A non-existent value results in 0.
- `rord(fieldReference)`: The same as `ord()`, but with the ordering reversed.

A definition of `ord` is not sufficient to fully convey its ramification. Suppose five documents are added to an index with the following values in a field x: 70, 70, 90, 95, 98. Even though there are five documents, `ord(x)` is going to return values ranging from 1 to 4, because there are only four distinct values; one of them, 70, is repeated. There is another difference that is subtler. The original values are not distributed in a linear fashion. They are more clumped together towards the higher values (do not consider duplicates). `ord` and `rord` in-effect linearizes the data so that the distribution of the original value is lost, assuming it was non-linear.

To determine how high `ord`/`rord` can get, you can use Solr's web admin interface. Go to the **Schema Browser**. Click on an indexed field, and observe the **distinct** number.

Miscellaneous functions

There are multiple ways to use the `ms()` function to get a date-time value since its arguments are all optional. Times are in milliseconds since the commonly used time epoch of 1970-01-01T00:00:00Z which is zero. Times before then are negative. Note that any field reference to a time will be ambiguous to a blank value, which is zero.

- `ms(date1?,date2?)`: If no arguments are supplied you get the current time. If one argument is supplied, its value is returned; if two are supplied, the second is subtracted from the first. The date reference might be the name of a field or Solr's *date math*. For example: `ms(NOW/DAY,a_end_date)`

Interestingly, there are a couple function queries which return the score results of *another query*. It's a fairly esoteric feature but it has its uses. One such use is to sort by whether a field has a value. See the previous chapter for an example.

- `query(q,def?)`: Returns the document's score as applied to the query given in the first argument. If it doesn't match then the optional second parameter is returned if supplied, otherwise 0 is. Due to the awkward location of the query during function query parsing, it can't be entered plainly. The query can be put in another parameter and referenced, like this:
  `query($param)&param=t_trm_attributes:4`
  or it can be specified using local-params with the query in v, like this:
  `query({!v="t_trm_attributes:4"})`.
- `boost(q,boost)`: Similar to `query(q)` but with the score multiplied by the `boost` constant.

Another interesting function query is one that calculates the *string distance* between two strings based on a specified algorithm. The values are between 0 and 1.

- `strdist(x,y,alg)`: The first two arguments are strings to compute the string distance on. Next is one of `jw` (Jaro Winkler), `edit` (Levenshtein), or `ngram` in quotes. The default ngram size is 2 but you can supply an additional argument for something else.

There are a few ways to calculate geospatial distance. The primary one you should use is `geodist()` which is the only one I'll document here:

- `geodist(...)`: Returns the Earth geospatial distance using the Haversine formula between a pair of points. The points are each taken from the first available of: an argument, the parameter `pt`, or the parameter `sfield`. Any of these might be blank but at least two must be specified. When a point is specified as an argument, it can be simply a `LatLonType` based field or a pair of typical arguments (a field name or constant) to the latitude and longitude. Here's an example of both: `geodist(store,42.4,-71.1)`

 By design these parameter names align with those for the `geofilt` query parser, which pairs well with `geodist()`. Consequently it is rare to supply arguments.

There are some function queries I chose to omit for various reasons. Solr's wiki `http://wiki.apache.org/solr/FunctionQuery` has the full list with some descriptions. I omitted `vector()`, `dist()`, `sqedist()`, `ghhsin()`, `geohash()`, `top()`, and `literal()`. The vector calculations look interesting but a real use-case is not clear.

Function query boosting

The overall process to function query boosting is as follows:

1. Pick a formula that has the desired plotted shape.

2. Plug in values specific to your data.

3. Decide the relative weighting of the boost relative to the user query (for example, 1/3).

4. Choose additive or multiplicative boosting and then apply the relative weighting according to the approach you chose (see *Add or multiply boosts?*).

The upcoming examples address common scenarios with ready-made formulas for you.

If you want to work on formulas instead of taking one provided here as is, I recommend a tool such as a graphing calculator or other software to plot the functions. If you are using Mac OS X as I am, then your computer already includes `Grapher`, which generated the charts in this chapter. I highly recommend it. You might be inclined to use a spreadsheet like Microsoft Excel, but that's really not the right tool. With luck, you may find some websites that will suffice, perhaps `http://www.wolframapha.com`.

If your data changes in ways causing you to alter the constants in your function queries, then consider implementing a periodic automated test of your Solr data to ensure that the data fits within expected bounds. A **Continuous Integration (CI)** server might be configured to do this task. An approach is to run a search simply sorting by the data field in question to get the highest or lowest value.

Formula: Logarithm

The logarithm is a popular formula for inputs that grow without bounds, but the output is also unbounded. However, the growth of the curve is stunted for larger numbers. This in practice is usually fine even when you ideally want the output to be capped. The logarithm cannot be inverted without the risk of a negative score, which should be avoided.

Here is a graph of our formula, given inputs from a future example.

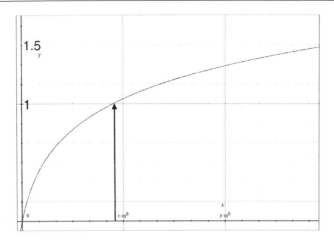

And here is the formula:

$$\log_c\big((c-1)\,m\cdot x +1\big)$$

c is a number greater than 1 and is a value of your choosing that will alter how the curve bends. I recommend `10` as seen in the preceding graph. Smaller values make it too linear and greater values put a knee bend in the curve that seems too early. m is the inverse of what I'll call the *horizon*. At this value, the result is 1. With the logarithm, further values advance the output steadily but at a shallow slope that slowly gets shallower. Here is the Solr function query to use, simplified for when c is 10: `log(linear(x,m,1))`

- x: The input; typically a field reference. It must **not** be negative.
- m: *9/horizon* where *horizon* is as described above.

Verify your formula by supplying 0 which should result in 0, and then supply *horizon* (as defined above) which should result in 1. Now that you have your formula, you are ready to proceed with the other function query boosting steps.

Formula: Inverse reciprocal

In general, the reciprocal of a linear function is favorable because it gives results that are bounded as the input grows without bounds.

Here is a sample graph to show the curve. The inputs are from a later how-to. The arrow in the following graph shows where the "horizon" (*1/m*) lies:

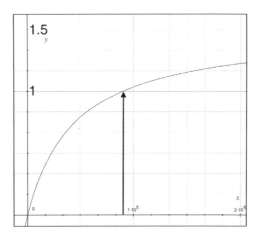

Here is the formula:

$$\frac{-max^2 + max}{m \cdot x + max - 1} + max$$

Here, max is the value that this function approaches, but never quite reaches. It should be greater than 1 and less than 2; 1.5 works well. You can experiment with this to see how it changes the bend in the curve below. m is the inverse of what I'll call the *horizon*. At this value, the result is 1, and larger inputs only increase it negligibly.

Here is the Solr function query to use: `sum(recip(x,m,a,c),max)`

- x: The input; typically a field reference. It must **not** be negative.
- m: *1/horizon* where *horizon* is as described above.
- a: *max-max*max*
- c: *max – 1*
- max: *1.5* or otherwise as defined above.

Verify your formula by supplying 0 which should result in 0, to *horizon* (as defined above) which should result in 1. Now that you have your formula, you are ready to proceed with the other function query boosting steps.

Formula: Reciprocal

The reciprocal is an excellent formula to use when you want to maximally boost at input 0 and boost decreasingly less as the input increases. It is often used to boost newly added content by looking at how old a document is.

Here is a sample graph to show the curve. The inputs are from a later how-to. The arrow roughly shows where the *horizon* input value is.

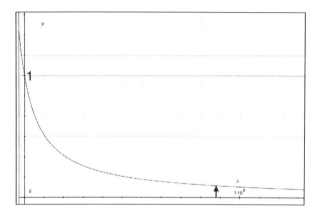

The formula is simply:

$$\frac{c}{x+c}$$

Which translates easily to a Solr function query as `recip(x,1,c,c)`.

- *x*: The input—a field or another function referencing a field. It should **not** be negative.
- *c*: Roughly 1/10 the *horizon* input value. As larger values are supplied, the boost effect is negligible.

Verify your formula by supplying 0 which should result in 1, and then *horizon* (as defined above) which should result in a number very close to 0.09. Now that you have your formula, you are ready to proceed with the other function query boosting steps.

Formula: Linear

If you have a value in your schema (or a computed formula) that you are certain will stay within a fixed range, then the formula to scale and shift this to the 0-1 nominal range is easy. We're also assuming that there is a linear relationship between the desired boost effect and the input.

Simply use the `linear(x,m,c)` function with appropriate values. Below, *a* refers to the end of the range that will have the least significant boost. So if your input ranges from 5 to 10 and if 5 is least relevant compared to 10, then *a* is 5. *b* takes the other side of the input range:

- x: The input, typically a field.
- m: Compute *1/(b – a)* and plug in.
- c: Compute *a/(a - b)* and plug in.

Verify your formula by supplying a value from each end of the range and verifying its 0 or 1 with 1 being the biggest boost. Now that you have your formula, you are ready to proceed with the other function query boosting steps.

How to boost based on an increasing numeric field

In this section I'm going to describe a few ways to boost a document based on one of its numeric fields. The greater this number is for a document, the greater boost this document should receive. This number might be a count of "Like" or "Thumbs-Up" votes by users, or the number of times a user accessed (for example, clicked) the referenced document, or something else.

In the MusicBrainz database, there are TRM and PUID lookup counts. TRM and PUID are MusicBrainz's audio fingerprint technologies. These identifiers roughly correspond to a song, which in MusicBrainz appears as multiple tracks due to various releases that occur as singles, compilations, and so on. By the way, audio fingerprints aren't perfect, and so a very small percentage of TRM IDs and PUIDs refer to songs that are completely different. Since we're only using this to influence scoring, imperfection is not a problem.

MusicBrainz records the number of times one of these IDs are looked up from its servers, which is a good measure of popularity. A track that contains a higher lookup count should score higher than one with a smaller value, with all other factors being equal. This scheme could easily be aggregated to releases and artists, if desired. In the data loading I've arranged for the sum of TRM and PUID lookup counts to be stored into our track data as t_trm_lookups with the following field specification in the schema:

```
<field name="t_trm_lookups" type="tint" />
```

About 25% of the tracks have a non-zero value. The maximum value is nearly 300,000 but further inspection shows that only a handful of records exceed a value of 90,000.

Step by step…

The first step is to pick a formula. Since this is a classic case of an increasing number without bound in which the greater the number is, the greater the boost should be, the **inverse reciprocal** is a very good choice. Next, we plug in our data into the formula specified earlier and we end up with this function query:

```
sum(recip(t_trm_lookups,0.0000111,-0.75,0.5),1.5)
```

We verify the formula by plugging in 0 and 90,000, which maps to 0 and 1.

The next step is to choose between additive boosts versus multiplicative. Multiplicative with edismax is easier so we'll choose that. And let's say this function query should weigh 1/3 of the user query. According to earlier instructions, adding to our function query will reduce its weight. Adding 2 shifts the 0-1 range to 2-3 and (3-2)/3 results in the 1/3 boost we're looking for. Since our function query conveniently has sum() as its outer function, we can simply add another argument of 2. Here is a URL snippet showing relevant parameters:

```
q=cherub+rock&defType=edismax&qf=t_name
&boost=sum(recip(t_trm_lookups,0.0000111,-0.75,0.5),1.5,2)
```

This boost absolutely had the desired effect, altering the score order as we wanted. One unintended outcome is that the top document scores used to be ~8.6 and now they are ~21.1, but **don't worry about it**! The actual scores are irrelevant—a point made in the beginning of the chapter. The goal is to change the relative order of score sorted documents.

External field values

As you may recall from *Chapter 3, Indexing Data*, Solr does not support updating a document; instead the entire document must be added again. If you were to consider doing this just to increase a number every time a user clicked on a document or clicked some "Thumbs-Up" button, and so on, then there is quite a bit of work Solr is doing just to ultimately increase a number. For this specific use-case, Solr has a specialized field type called `ExternalFileField` which gets its data from a text file containing the field's values. This field type is very limited–the values are limited to floating point numbers and the field can only be referenced within Solr in a function query. You do still need to issue a commit to Solr for any changes to be picked up. As already explained in *Chapter 3, Indexing Data*, don't commit too frequently since commits are slow and resource-intensive. An application using this feature would generate this file on a periodic basis on par with the commit frequency. For more information on how to use this advanced feature, consult the API docs: `http://lucene.apache.org/solr/api/org/apache/solr/schema/ExternalFileField.html` and search Solr's mailing list.

How to boost based on recent dates

Using dates in scores presents some different issues. Suppose when we search for releases, we want to include a boost that is larger for more recent releases. At first glance, this problem may seem just like the previous one, because dates increase as the scores are expected to, but it is different in practice. Instead of the data ranging from zero to some value that changes occasionally, we now have data ranging from a non-zero value that might change rarely to a value that we always know, but changes continuously — the current date. Instead, approach this from the other side, that is, by considering how much time there is between the current date and the document's date. So at x=0 in the graph (x representing time delta), we want 1 for the greatest boost, and we want it to slope downward towards 0, but not below it.

Step by step…

The first step is to pick a formula. The **reciprocal** is perfect for this scenario. The function query form as detailed earlier is `recip(x,1,c,c)`.

Based on this scenario, x is the age — a time duration from the present. Our MusicBrainz schema has `r_event_date`, which is a promising candidate; however, multi-valued fields are not supported by function queries. I made a simple addition to the schema and index to record the earliest release event date: `r_event_date_earliest`. With that done, now we can calculate the age with the two-argument variant of `ms()`. As a reminder to show how to run these function queries while debugging, here's a URL snippet:

```
q={!func}ms(NOW,r_event_date_earliest)
&fl=id,r_name,r_event_date_earliest,score&sort=score+asc
```

The book's data set has been constant but at the time I received it, I observed some releases were in the future! What I would have seen then is reproducible by substituting NOW-4YEARS instead of NOW in the function, as I write this. The first documents (score ascending) have negative values which means they are from the future. We can't have negative inputs, so instead we'll wrap this function with the absolute value using abs(). Another thing to fine-tune is the cache-ability of the function query. Instead of using NOW, using NOW/DAY makes this query re-usable by subsequent requests for a 24 hour period.

The other aspect of the inputs to the reciprocal function is finding out what the *horizon* is. This should be a duration of time such that any longer durations have a negligible boost impact. Without too much thought, 20 years seems good. Here's a query to have Solr do the math so we can get our millisecond-count: q={!func} ms(NOW,NOW-20YEARS) which is about 6.3E11. In the documentation for the reciprocal formula, we take 1/10 of that for c. Here is our function query:

```
recip(abs(ms(NOW/DAY,r_event_date_earliest)),1,6.3E10,6.3E10)
```

At this point you can follow the final steps in the previous how-to.

Summary

In this chapter, we've covered the most advanced topics the book has to offer — scoring and function queries. We began with a fundamental background on Lucene scoring. Next, we saw a real-world example of using the debugQuery parameter to diagnose a scoring issue. That exercise might be the most important exercise in the chapter, since it gives you the tools to diagnose why a document matched or didn't match a query. Next, we concluded the coverage of the dismax query parser. Even if you aren't inclined to use fancy boosting function queries, you can improve your search relevancy simply by configuring phrase boosting. dismax's boost function parameters was the segue to the second half of the chapter: function queries. Even if you aren't a math whiz, you should be able to use formulas provided to you here, especially if you worked through the how-to's.

You might say this is the last of the foundational chapters. The next two cover specific search value-adds that are each fairly compartmentalized. The stand-out feature that contributes to much of Solr's popularity is faceting, covered next in its own chapter.

6
Faceting

Faceting is Solr's killer-feature. It's a must-have feature for most search implementations, especially those with structured data like in e-commerce, yet there are few products that have this capability, especially in open source. Of course search fundamentals, including highlighting, are critical too but they tend to be taken for granted. **Faceting** enhances search results with aggregated information over all the documents found in the search, not the entire index. It can answer questions about the MusicBrainz data such as:

- How many releases are official, bootleg, or promotional?
- What were the top five most common countries in which the releases occurred?
- Over the past ten years, how many were released in each year?
- How many releases have names in these ranges: A-C, D-F, G-I, and so on?
- How many tracks are < 2 minutes long, 2-3, 3-4, or longer?

In a hurry?

Faceting is a key feature. Look through the upcoming example, which demonstrates the most common type of faceting, and review the faceting types.

Faceting in the context of the user experience is often referred to as **faceted navigation**, but also faceted search, faceted browsing, guided navigation, or parametric search. The facets are typically displayed with clickable links that apply Solr filter queries to a subsequent search. Now might be a good time for a screenshot but instead I'll direct you to a collection of them at Endeca's excellent UX Design Pattern Library: `http://patterns.endeca.com/` and click on "Faceted Navigation"

If we revisit the comparison of search technology to databases, then faceting is more or less analogous to SQL's GROUP BY feature on a column with count(*). However, in Solr, facet processing is performed subsequent to an existing search as part of a single request-response with both the primary search results and the faceting results coming back together. In SQL, you would need to perform a series of separate queries to get the same information. Furthermore, faceting works so fast that its search response time overhead is almost always negligible. For more information on why implementing faceting with relational databases is hard and doesn't scale, visit this old article: http://web.archive.org/web/20090321120327/http://www.kimbly.com/blog/000239.html

A quick example: Faceting release types

Observe the following search results. echoParams is set to explicit (defined in solrconfig.xml) so that the search parameters are seen here. This example is using the default lucene query parser. dismax is more typical but it plays no bearing on these examples. The query parameter q is *:*, which matches all documents. In this case, the index I'm using only has releases. *If there were non-releases in the index,* then I would add a filter fq=type:Release to the URL or put this in the request handler configuration, as that is the data set we'll be using for most of this chapter. Filter queries are used in conjunction with faceting a fair amount so be sure you are already familiar with them from *Chapter 4, Searching*. I wanted to keep this example brief so I set rows to 2. Sometimes when using faceting, you only want the facet information and not the main search, so you would set rows to 0.

> It's **critical** to understand that the faceting numbers are computed over the entire *search result* — 603,090 releases, which is all of the releases in this example, and not just the two rows being returned.

```xml
<?xml version="1.0" encoding="UTF-8"?>
<response>
<lst name="responseHeader">
  <int name="status">0</int>
  <int name="QTime">160</int>
  <lst name="params">
    <str name="wt">standard</str>
    <str name="rows">2</str>
    <str name="facet">true</str>
    <str name="q">*:*</str>
    <str name="fl">*,score</str>
    <str name="qt">standard</str>
    <str name="facet.field">r_official</str>
```

```
      <str name="f.r_official.facet.missing">true</str>
      <str name="f.r_official.facet.method">enum</str>
      <str name="indent">on</str>
   </lst>
</lst>
<result name="response" numFound="603090" start="0" maxScore="1.0">
   <doc>
      <float name="score">1.0</float>
      <str name="id">Release:136192</str>
      <str name="r_a_id">3143</str>
      <str name="r_a_name">Janis Joplin</str>
      <arr name="r_attributes"><int>0</int><int>9</int>
                              <int>100</int></arr>
      <str name="r_name">Texas International Pop Festival
            11-30-69</str>
      <int name="r_tracks">7</int>
      <str name="type">Release</str>
   </doc>
   <doc>
      <float name="score">1.0</float>
      <str name="id">Release:133202</str>
      <str name="r_a_id">6774</str>
      <str name="r_a_name">The Dubliners</str>
      <arr name="r_attributes"><int>0</int></arr>
      <str name="r_lang">English</str>
      <str name="r_name">40 Jahre</str>
      <int name="r_tracks">20</int>
      <str name="type">Release</str>
   </doc>
</result>
<lst name="facet_counts">
   <lst name="facet_queries"/>
   <lst name="facet_fields">
      <lst name="r_official">
         <int name="Official">519168</int>
         <int name="Bootleg">19559</int>
         <int name="Promotion">16562</int>
         <int name="Pseudo-Release">2819</int>
         <int>44982</int>
      </lst>
   </lst>
   <lst name="facet_dates"/>
   <lst name="facet_ranges"/>
</lst>
</response>
```

The facet related search parameters are highlighted at the top. The `facet.missing` parameter was set using the field-specific syntax, which will be explained shortly.

Notice that the facet results (highlighted) follow the main search result and are given the name `facet_counts`. In this example, we only faceted on one field, `r_official`, but you'll learn in a bit that you can facet on as many fields as you desire. Within `<lst name="r_official">` lie the facet counts for this field. The `name` attribute, like "Official", holds a **facet value**, which is simply an indexed term, and the integer following it is the number of documents in the search results containing that term — the **facet count**. The last facet has the count but no corresponding name. It is a special facet to indicate how many documents in the results don't have any indexed terms. The next section gives us an explanation of where `r_official` and `r_type` came from.

MusicBrainz schema changes

In order to get better self-explanatory faceting results out of the `r_attributes` field and to split its dual-meaning, I modified the schema. `r_attributes` is an array of numeric constants, which signify various types of releases and it's *official-ness*, for lack of a better word. As it represents two different things, I created two new fields: `r_type` and `r_official`. It isn't truly necessary to map the numbers to their names, as the user interface, which is going to present the data, could very well map it on the fly.

At this point there are two paths to take, with similar results. *The recommended path is to modify the import process* to map specific constants to their named values into these two new fields. For example, if you were using the Data Import Handler from *Chapter 3, Indexing Data* this would occur in a DIH transformer. We'll take another path here to illustrate what can be done with a little text analysis. The stored value, if we chose to mark the fields as stored, would hold the original set of constants, which is less than ideal. And in this scenario, we're forced to mark both fields as multi-valued even though one of them isn't.

Let's continue with the text analysis based approach. I used `copyField` directives to copy `r_attributes` into both new fields:

```
<field name="r_attributes" type="int" multiValued="true"
   indexed="false" /><!-- ex: 0, 1, 100 -->
<field name="r_type" type="rType" multiValued="true"
   stored="false" /><!-- Album | Single | EP |... etc. -->
<field name="r_official" type="rOfficial" multiValued="true"
   stored="false" /><!-- Official | Bootleg | Promotional -->
```

And:

```
<copyField source="r_attributes" dest="r_type" />
<copyField source="r_attributes" dest="r_official" />
```

In order to map the constants to human-readable definitions, I created two field types: rType and rOfficial that use a regular expression to pull out the desired numbers and a synonym list to map from the constant to the human-readable definition. Conveniently, the constants for r_type are in the range1-11, whereas r_official are 100-103. I removed the constant 0, as it seemed to be bogus.

```
<fieldType name="rType" class="solr.TextField"
  sortMissingLast="true" omitNorms="true">
  <analyzer>
    <tokenizer class="solr.KeywordTokenizerFactory"/>
    <filter class="solr.PatternReplaceFilterFactory"
            pattern="^(0|1\d\d)$" replacement="" replace="first" />
    <filter class="solr.LengthFilterFactory" min="1" max="100" />
    <filter class="solr.SynonymFilterFactory"
            synonyms="mb_attributes.txt"
            ignoreCase="false" expand="false"/>
  </analyzer>
</fieldType>
```

The definition of the type rOfficial is the same as rType, except it has this regular expression: ^(0|\d\d?)$.

The presence of LengthFilterFactory is to ensure that no zero-length (empty-string) terms get indexed. Otherwise, this would happen because the previous regular expression reduces text fitting unwanted patterns to empty strings.

The content of mb_attributes.txt is as follows:

```
# from: http://bugs.musicbrainz.org/browser/mb_server/trunk/
# cgi-bin/MusicBrainz/Server/Release.pm#L48
#note: non-album track seems bogus; almost everything has it
0=>Non-Album\ Track
1=>Album
2=>Single
3=>EP
4=>Compilation
5=>Soundtrack
6=>Spokenword
7=>Interview
8=>Audiobook
9=>Live
```

```
10=>Remix
11=>Other

100=>Official
101=>Promotion
102=>Bootleg
103=>Pseudo-Release
```

> It does not matter if the user interface uses the name (for example, Official) or constant (for example, 100) when applying filter queries when implementing faceted navigation, as the text analysis will let the names through and will map the constants to the names. This is not necessarily true in a general case, but it is for the text analysis as I've configured it above.

Field requirements

The principal requirement of a field that will be faceted on is that it must be indexed; it does *not* have to be stored. And for text fields, tokenization is *usually* undesirable. For example, `Non-Album\ Track` appears in `mb_attributes.txt` with the space escaped with a `\`. Otherwise, faceting on `r_type` would show tallies for `Non-Album` and `Track` separately. On the other hand, tag-clouds, hierarchical faceting, and term-suggest are faceting use-cases that handle tokenization just fine. Keep in mind that with faceting, the facet values returned in search results are the actual indexed terms, and not the stored value, which isn't used.

> If you have conflicting indexing needs for a field, which is not uncommon, you will find it necessary to have a copy of a field just for faceting.

Types of faceting

Solr's faceting is broken down into three types. They are as follows:

- **field values**: This is the most common type of faceting which counts the number of occurrences of each indexed term in a field. The facet counts are grouped in the output under the name `facet_fields`.

> Solr 4 includes a new variation for field values called Pivot Faceting (that is Decision Tree). Essentially, it performs recursive faceting for a series of fields.

- **ranges**: Given a numeric or date field, this creates facets for a set of ranges. The facet counts are grouped in the output under the name `facet_ranges`.

> Solr 3 deprecated "date faceting" with the introduction of the generic range faceting. I won't document it further.

- **queries**: This is a very flexible type of faceting which counts the number of documents matching each specified query. The facet counts are grouped in the output under `facet_queries`.

In the rest of this chapter, we will describe how to do these different types of facets. But before that, there is one common parameter to enable faceting:

- `facet`: It defaults to blank. In order to enable faceting, you must set this to `true` or `on`. If this is not done, then the faceting parameters will be ignored.

In all of the examples here, we've obviously set `facet=true`.

Faceting field values

Field value faceting is the most common type of faceting. The first example in this chapter demonstrated it in action. Solr, in essence, iterates over all of the indexed terms for the field and tallies a count for the number of searched documents that have the term. Sophisticated algorithms and caching makes this so fast that its overhead is usually negligible. The following are the request parameters for using it:

- `facet.field`: You **must** set this parameter to a field's name in order to facet on that field. Repeat this parameter for each field to be faceted on. See the previous Field requirements section.

> The remaining faceting parameters can be set on a per-field basis, otherwise they apply to all faceted fields that don't have a field-specific setting. **You will usually specify them per-field**, especially if you are faceting on more than one field so that you don't get your faceting configuration mixed up. For example: `f.r_type.facet.sort=lex` (`r_type` is a field name, `facet.sort` is a facet parameter).

- `facet.sort`: It is set to either `count` to sort the facet values by descending totals or to `index` to sort lexicographically, as if you sorted on the field. If `facet.limit` is greater than zero (it's `100` by default), then Solr picks `count` as the default, otherwise `index` is chosen.

- `facet.limit`: It defaults to `100`. It limits the number of facet values returned in the search results of a field. As these are usually going to be displayed to the user, it doesn't make sense to have a large number of these in the response. If you need all of them then disable the limit with a value of `-1`.

- `facet.offset`: It defaults to `0`. It is the index into the facet value list from which the values are returned. This enables paging of facet values when used with `facet.limit`.

- `facet.mincount`: This defaults to `0`. It filters out facet values that have facet counts less than this. This is applied before `limit` and `offset` so that paging works as expected. **It is common to set this to 1 since 0 is almost useless.**

- `facet.missing`: It defaults to blank and is set to `true` or `on` for the facet value listing to include an unnamed count at the end, which is the number of searched documents that have no indexed terms. The first facet example in the chapter demonstrates this.

- `facet.prefix`: It filters the facet values to those starting with this value. This is applied before `limit` and `offset` so that paging works as expected. At the end of this chapter you'll see how this can be used for hierarchical faceting. In the next chapter you'll see how faceting with this prefix can be used to power query term-suggest.

- `facet.method`: (advanced) Tells Solr which of its 3 different field value faceting algorithms to use, in order to influence memory use, query performance, and commit speed. Solr makes good choices by default. You can specify one of: `enum` or `fc`; or neither and Solr will under the right circumstances choose the third, known as `UnInvertedField`. `fc` refers to the *field cache* which is only for single-valued fields that are not tokenized. Trie based fields that are configured for fast range queries (for example, `tint`, *not* `int`) are only facetable with `UnInvertedField`. If you set `facet.method` incorrectly then Solr will ignore it.

When to specify facet.method

Normally you should not specify `facet.method`, thereby letting Solr's internal logic choose an appropriate algorithm. However, if you are faceting on a multi-valued field that only has a small number of distinct values (less than 100, but ideally perhaps 10), then it is advisable to explicitly set this to `enum`. Solr will use a *filter cache* entry for each value, so keep that in mind when optimizing that cache's size. Solr uses `enum` by default for boolean fields only, as it knows there can only be two values. Another parameter I'll mention for completeness is `facet.enum.cache.minDf`, which is the minimum document frequency for filter cache entries (0—no minimum by default). If the field contains rarely used values occurring less than ~30 times, then setting this threshold to `30` makes sense.

Alphabetic range bucketing

Solr does not directly support alphabetic range bucketing (A-C, D-F, and so on). However, with a creative application of text analysis and a dedicated field, we can achieve this with little effort. Let's say we want to have these range buckets on the release names. We need to extract the first character of r_name, and store this into a field that will be used for this purpose. We'll call it r_name_facetLetter. Here is our field definition:

```
<field name="r_name_facetLetter" type="bucketFirstLetter"
    stored="false" />
```

And here is the copyField:

```
<copyField source="r_name" dest="r_name_facetLetter" />
```

The definition of the type bucketFirstLetter is the following:

```
<fieldType name="bucketFirstLetter" class="solr.TextField"
        sortMissingLast="true" omitNorms="true">
  <analyzer type="index">
    <tokenizer class="solr.PatternTokenizerFactory"
            pattern="^([a-zA-Z]).*" group="1" />
    <filter class="solr.SynonymFilterFactory"
            synonyms="mb_letterBuckets.txt"
            ignoreCase="true"
            expand="false"/>
  </analyzer>
  <analyzer type="query">
    <tokenizer class="solr.KeywordTokenizerFactory"/>
  </analyzer>
</fieldType>
```

The PatternTokenizerFactory, as configured, plucks out the first character, and the SynonymFilterFactory maps each letter of the alphabet to a range like A-C. The mapping is in conf/mb_letterBuckets.txt. The field types used for faceting generally have a KeywordTokenizerFactory for the query analysis to satisfy a possible filter query on a given facet value returned from a previous faceted search. After validating these changes with Solr's analysis admin screen, we then re-index the data. For the facet query, we're going to advise Solr to use the enum method, because there aren't many facet values in total. Here's the URL to search Solr:

```
http://localhost:8983/solr/mbreleases/select?indent=on&q=*%3A*
&facet=on&facet.field=r_name_facetLetter&facet.sort=lex&facet.
missing=on&facet.method=enum
```

The URL produced results containing the following facet data:

```
<lst name="facet_counts">
  <lst name="facet_queries"/>
  <lst name="facet_fields">
    <lst name="r_name_facetLetter">
      <int name="A-C">99005</int>
      <int name="D-F">68376</int>
      <int name="G-I">60569</int>
      <int name="J-L">49871</int>
      <int name="M-O">59006</int>
      <int name="P-R">47032</int>
      <int name="S-U">143376</int>
      <int name="V-Z">33233</int>
      <int>42622</int>
    </lst>
  </lst>
<lst name="facet_dates"/>
</lst>
<lst name="facet_ranges"/>
</lst>
```

Faceting numeric and date ranges

Solr has built-in support for faceting numeric and date fields by a range and a divided interval. You can think of this as a convenience-feature that calculates the ranges for you with succinct input parameters and output versus you calculating and submitting a series of *facet queries*. Facet queries are described after this section. Range faceting is particularly useful for dates. I'll demonstrate an example against MusicBrainz release dates and another against MusicBrainz track durations, and then describe the parameters and their options.

> *Date faceting* is the date-specific predecessor of range faceting and it's deprecated as of Solr 3. Date faceting uses similar parameters starting with `facet.date` and it has similar output under `facet_dates`.
>
> Range faceting doesn't support **distributed search** (that is sharding); you may have to resort to generating your own facet queries instead. This has been fixed in SOLR-1709—committed for Solr 4.

```
<response>
<lst name="responseHeader">
  <int name="status">0</int>
  <int name="QTime">298</int>
```

```
    <lst name="params">
      <str name="facet.range.other">all</str>
      <str name="facet">on</str>
      <str name="echoParams">explicit</str>
      <str name="f.r_event_date_earliest.facet.range.start">
              NOW/YEAR-5YEARS</str>
      <str name="indent">on</str>
      <str name="q">smashing</str>
      <str name="facet.range">r_event_date_earliest</str>
      <str name="facet.range.end">NOW/YEAR</str>
      <str name="facet.range.gap">+1YEAR</str>
      <str name="qt">mb_releases</str>
      <str name="rows">0</str>
    </lst>
  </lst>
  <result name="response" numFound="248" start="0"/>
  <lst name="facet_counts">
    <lst name="facet_queries"/>
    <lst name="facet_fields"/>
    <lst name="facet_dates"/>
    <lst name="facet_ranges">
      <lst name="r_event_date_earliest">
        <lst name="counts">
          <int name="2006-01-01T00:00:00Z">3</int>
          <int name="2007-01-01T00:00:00Z">11</int>
          <int name="2008-01-01T00:00:00Z">0</int>
          <int name="2009-01-01T00:00:00Z">0</int>
          <int name="2010-01-01T00:00:00Z">0</int>
        </lst>
        <str name="gap">+1YEAR</str>
        <date name="start">2006-01-01T00:00:00Z</date>
        <date name="end">2011-01-01T00:00:00Z</date>
        <int name="before">97</int>
        <int name="after">0</int>
        <int name="between">14</int>
      </lst>
    </lst>
  </lst>
</response>
```

This example demonstrates a few things, not only range faceting:

- qt=mb_releases is a request handler using dismax to query appropriate release fields.

- q=smashing indicates that we're faceting on a keyword search instead of all the documents. We kept the rows at zero, which is unrealistic, but not pertinent.

- The facet start date was specified using the field specific syntax for demonstration purposes. *You would do this with every parameter or none depending on if you need to do a range facet on other fields.*

- The <date name="end"> part below the facet counts indicates the upper bound of the last facet count. It may or may not be the same as facet. range.end (see facet.range.hardend explained in the next section).

- The before, after, and between counts are for specifying facet.range. other. We'll see shortly what this means.

The results of our facet range query shows that there were three releases released in 2006, and eleven in 2007. There is no data after that, since the data is out of date at this point.

Here is another example, this time using range faceting on a number—MusicBrainz track durations (in seconds):

```
<response>
<lst name="responseHeader">
  <int name="status">0</int>
  <int name="QTime">5</int>
  <lst name="params">
    <str name="facet.range.other">after</str>
    <str name="facet">on</str>
    <str name="echoParams">explicit</str>
    <str name="indent">on</str>
    <str name="q">Geek</str>
    <str name="facet.range.start">0</str>
    <str name="facet.range">t_duration</str>
    <str name="facet.range.end">240</str>
    <str name="facet.range.gap">60</str>
    <str name="qt">mb_tracks</str>
    <str name="rows">0</str>
  </lst>
</lst>
<result name="response" numFound="552" start="0"/>
<lst name="facet_counts">
  <lst name="facet_queries"/>
```

```
<lst name="facet_fields"/>
<lst name="facet_dates"/>
<lst name="facet_ranges">
  <lst name="t_duration">
    <lst name="counts">
      <int name="0">128</int>
      <int name="60">64</int>
      <int name="120">111</int>
      <int name="180">132</int>
    </lst>
    <int name="gap">60</int>
    <int name="start">0</int>
    <int name="end">240</int>
    <int name="after">117</int>
  </lst>
</lst>
</lst>
</response>
```

Taking the first facet, we see that there are 128 tracks that are 0-59 seconds long, given the keyword search "Geek".

Range facet parameters

All of the range faceting parameters start with `facet.range`. As with most other faceting parameters, they can be made field specific in the same way. The parameters are explained as follows:

- `facet.range`: You must set this parameter to a field's name to range-facet on that field. The trie based numeric and date field types (those starting with "t" as in `tlong` and `tdate`) perform best, but others will work. Repeat this parameter for each field to be faceted on.

 The remainder of these range faceting parameters can be specified on a per-field basis in the same fashion that the field-value faceting parameters can. For example: `f.r_event_date_earliest.facet.range.start`.

- `facet.range.start`: Mandatory, this is a number or date to specify the start of the range to facet on. For dates, see the *Date math* section in *Chapter 4, Searching*. Using NOW with some Solr date math is quite effective as in this example: NOW/YEAR-5YEARS, which is interpreted as five years ago, starting at the beginning of the year.

- facet.range.end: Mandatory, this is a number or date to specify the end of the range. It has the same syntax as facet.range.start. Note that the actual end of the range may be different (see facet.range.hardend).

- facet.range.gap: Mandatory, this specifies the interval to divide the range. For dates, it uses a subset of Solr's *Date Math* syntax, as it's a time *duration* and not a particular time. It should always start with a +. Examples: +1YEAR or +1MINUTE+30SECONDS. Note that after URL encoding, + becomes %2B.

 Note that for dates, the facet.range.gap is not necessarily a fixed length of time. For example +1MONTH is different depending on the month.

- facet.range.hardend: It defaults to false. This parameter instructs Solr on what to do when facet.range.gap does not divide evenly into the facet range (start | end). If this is true, then the last range will be shortened. Moreover, you will observe that the end value in the facet results is the same as facet.range.end. Otherwise, by default, the end is essentially increased sufficiently so that the ranges are all equal according to the gap value.

- facet.range.other: It defaults to none. This parameter adds more faceting counts depending on its value. It can be specified multiple times. See the example using this at the start of this section.

    ○ before: Count of documents before the faceted range

    ○ after: Count of documents following the faceted range

    ○ between: Documents within the faceted range

    ○ none: (disabled) The default

    ○ all: Shortcut for all three (before, between, and after)

- facet.range.include: It defaults to lower. Specifies which range boundaries are inclusive. The choices are lower, upper, edge, outer, and all (all being equivalent to all the others). This parameter can be set multiple times to combine choices. Instead of defining each value, I will describe when a given boundary is inclusive:

    ○ The lower boundary of a gap-based range is included if lower is specified. It is also included if it's the first gap range and edge is specified.

    ○ The upper boundary of a gap-based range is included if upper is specified. It is also included if it's the last gap range and edge is specified.

- ○ The upper boundary of the `before` range is included if the boundary is not already included by the first gap-based range. It's also included if `outer` is specified.

- ○ The lower boundary of the `after` range is included if the boundary is not already included by the last gap-based range. It's also included if `outer` is specified.

Avoid double-counting

The default `facet.range.include` of `lower` ensures that an indexed value occurring at a range boundary is counted in exactly one of the adjacent ranges. This is usually desirable, but your requirements may differ. To ensure you don't double-count, don't choose both `lower` and `upper` together and don't choose `outer`.

Facet queries

This is the final type of faceting, and it offers a lot of flexibility. Instead of choosing a field to facet its values on or faceting a specified range of values, we specify some number of Solr queries that each itself becomes a facet. For each facet query specified, the number of documents matching the facet query that also match the main search is counted. Each facet query with its facet count is returned in the results under the `facet_queries` section. Facet queries are each cached in the *filter cache*.

There is only one parameter for configuring facet queries:

- `facet.query`: A Solr query to be evaluated over the search results. The number of matching documents (the facet count) is returned as an entry in the results next to this query. Specify this multiple times to have Solr evaluate multiple facet queries.

In general, if field value faceting or range faceting don't do what you want, you can probably turn to facet queries. For example, if range faceting is too limiting because `facet.range.gap` is fixed, then you could specify a facet query for each particular range you need. Let's use that scenario for our example. Here are search results showing a few facet queries on MusicBrainz release dates. I've used `echoParams` to make the search parameters clear instead of showing a lengthy URL.

```
<lst name="responseHeader">
  <int name="status">0</int>
  <int name="QTime">8</int>
  <lst name="params">
    <str name="facet">on</str>
```

```
        <str name="echoParams">explicit</str>
        <str name="indent">on</str>
        <arr name="facet.query">
          <str>a_release_date_latest:[NOW/DAY-1YEAR TO *]</str>
          <str>a_release_date_latest:[NOW/DAY-5YEAR TO *]</str>
          <str>a_release_date_latest:[NOW/DAY-20YEAR TO *]</str>
        </arr>
        <str name="qt">mb_artists</str>
        <str name="rows">0</str>
      </lst>
  </lst>
  <result name="response" numFound="399182" start="0"/>
  <lst name="facet_counts">
    <lst name="facet_queries">
      <int name="a_release_date_latest:[NOW/DAY-1YEAR TO *]">0</int>
      <int name="a_release_date_latest:[NOW/DAY-5YEAR TO *]">25501</int>
      <int name="a_release_date_latest:[NOW/DAY-20YEAR TO *]">82181</int>
    </lst>
    <lst name="facet_fields"/>
    <lst name="facet_dates"/>
    <lst name="facet_ranges"/>
  </lst>
</response>
```

In this example, the `facet.query` parameter was specified three times showing releases released in the past 1 year, 5 years, and 20 years. An interesting thing to note about the facet query response is that the name of each of these facets is the query itself.

Building a filter query from a facet

When faceting is used, it is usually used in the context of faceted navigation in which a facet value becomes a navigation choice for the user to filter on. In Solr that becomes an additional filter query in a subsequent search. The total matching documents of that search should be equal to the facet value count. In this section we'll review how to build the filter queries. I won't show an example for facet query faceting because there's nothing to do—the facet query is a query and can be supplied directly as an `fq` parameter.

 To keep the filter queries easier to read I won't show them URL encoded.

Field value filter queries

For the case of field value faceting, consider the first example in the chapter where `r_official` has a value like `Bootleg`. Generating a filter query for this couldn't be simpler: `fq=r_official:Bootleg`. But what if the value contained a space or some other problematic character? You'd have to escape it using quoting or backslash escaping as explained in *Chapter 4, Searching*. This is a separate issue from URL encoding, which I'm omitting here for clarity; this pertains to the query syntax. Another potential problem relates to the fact that the value, even if escaped, still might have to go through text analysis in the field type configuration, which could modify the value resulting in a failed match. This is a rare circumstance and it's impossible with the `string` field type, but nonetheless it's something to watch out for, particularly for tag-cloud like use-cases. A solution to both problems is to use the `term` query parser, introduced in Solr 3.2, like so: `fq={!term f=r_official}` `Bootleg` in which there is no escaping needed of the value as it sidesteps text analysis.

 Consider using the `term` query parser for all text field value faceting as it avoids escaping problems.

You might be wondering how to generate a filter query for the `facet.missing` facet, as there is no value to filter on. *Chapter 4, Searching* covered a little known trick to query for a field with no indexed data involving a range query. Here it is for `r_official`, without URL encoding: `fq=-r_official:[* TO *]`

Facet range filter queries

Range faceting is the most complicated to generate filter queries for. Consider the first date range example. The first facet returned is:

```
<int name="2006-01-01T00:00:00Z">3</int>
```

The gap is `+1YEAR`. The facet's `name` attribute is the start of the range. The end of the range is the next facet value. If there are no more, then the final range's end point depends on `facet.range.hardend`—if it is `false`, the default, then you add `facet.range.gap`. For numbers you calculate this math yourself but for dates you can conveniently concatenate the string like so: `2006-01-01T00:00:00Z+1YEAR`. On the other hand if there is a hard end, then the last range end point is simply `facet.range.end`.

At this point, you might think the filter query for the first range is `fq=r_event_date_earliest:[2006-01-01T00:00:00Z TO 2007-01-01T00:00:00Z]`. *However, that is incorrect!* You must now consider the implications of `facet.range.include`. If you set this parameter to both `lower` and `upper` then the aforementioned filter query would be correct, but by default it's just `lower` (which is generally a good default that doesn't double-count). If a date falls on precisely New Year's Eve of the new 2007 year then we don't want to count that date.

> Solr 4 allows mixed use of [ ] and { } bracket styles to vary inclusivity and exclusivity but until then you must use the same type on both ends.

The solution I favor is the following: `fq=r_event_date_earliest:([2006-01-01T00:00:00Z TO 2007-01-01T00:00:00Z] NOT "2007-01-01T00:00:00Z")` It is verbose, but the approach works universally for both date and numeric types. Another approach is to simply append `-1MILLI` to the end date range or for numeric range faceting on integers you would actually perform the math of subtracting 1. But this approach might have problems for floating point numbers. Again, adding the NOT clause and the end point is universal, if perhaps verbose.

Generating filter queries for the `before` and `after` ranges isn't too hard. Here is the filter query for the `before` range which is exclusive of the `facet.range.start` point: `fq=r_event_date_earliest:{* TO 2006-01-01T00:00:00Z}`

Excluding filters (multi-select faceting)

Consider a scenario where you are implementing faceted navigation and you want to let the user pick several values of a field to filter on instead of just one. Typically, when an individual facet value is chosen, this becomes a filter. The filter makes subsequent faceting on that field almost pointless because the filter filters out the possibility of seeing other facet choices—assuming a single-valued field. In this scenario, we'd like to exclude this filter for this facet field.

The preceding screenshot is from `http://search-lucene.com` in which you can search across the mailing lists, API documentation, and other places that have information about Lucene, Solr, and other related projects. This screenshot shows that it lets users choose more than one type of information to filter results on at the same time, by letting users pick as many check boxes as they like.

I'll demonstrate the problem that multi-select faceting solves with a MusicBrainz example and then show how to solve it.

Here is a search for releases containing `smashing`, faceting on `r_type`. We'll leave `rows` at `0` for brevity, but observe the `numFound` value nonetheless. At this point, the user has not chosen a filter (therefore no `fq`).

```
http://localhost:8983/solr/mbreleases/select?indent=on&qt=mb_re
leases&rows=0&q=smashing&facet=on&facet.field=r_type&facet.
mincount=1&facet.sort=index
```

And the output of the previous URL is:

```
<?xml version="1.0" encoding="UTF-8"?>
<response>
<lst name="responseHeader">
  <int name="status">0</int>
  <int name="QTime">24</int>
</lst>
<result name="response" numFound="248" start="0"/>
<lst name="facet_counts">
  <lst name="facet_queries"/>
  <lst name="facet_fields">
  <lst name="r_type">
    <int name="Album">29</int>
    <int name="Compilation">41</int>
    int name="EP">7</int>
```

```
      <int name="Interview">3</int>
      <int name="Live">95</int>
      <int name="Other">19</int>
      <int name="Remix">1</int>
      <int name="Single">45</int>
      <int name="Soundtrack">1</int>
    </lst>
    </lst>
    <lst name="facet_dates"/>
    <lst name="facet_ranges"/>
  </lst>
</response>
```

Now the user chooses the `Album` facet value. This adds a filter query. As a result, now the URL is as before but has `&fq=r_type%3AAlbum` at the end and has this output:

```
<response>
<lst name="responseHeader">
  <int name="status">0</int>
  <int name="QTime">17</int>
</lst>
<result name="response" numFound="29" start="0"/>
<lst name="facet_counts">
  <lst name="facet_queries"/>
  <lst name="facet_fields">
    <lst name="r_type">
      <int name="Album">29</int>
    </lst>
  </lst>
  <lst name="facet_dates"/>
</lst>
</response>
```

Notice that the other `r_type` facet counts are gone because of the filter, yet in this scenario we want these to show the user what their counts would be if the filter wasn't there. The reduced `numFound` of `29` is good though, because at this moment the user did indeed filter on a value so far.

Solr can solve this problem with some additional metadata on both the filter query and the facet field reference using *Local-Params*. The local-params syntax was described in *Chapter 4, Searching* where it appears at the beginning of a query to switch the query parser and to supply parameters to it. As you're about to see, it can also be supplied at the start of `facet.field`—a bit of a hack, perhaps, to implement this feature. The previous example would change as follows:

- `fq` would now be `{!tag=foo}r_type:Album`
- `facet.field` would now be `{!ex=foo}r_type`

 Remember to URL Encode this added syntax when used in the URL. The only problem character is =, which becomes %3D.

Explanation:

- `tag` is a local parameter to give an arbitrary label to this filter query.
- The tag name `foo` was an arbitrarily chosen name to illustrate that it doesn't matter what it's named. If multiple fields and filter queries are to be tagged correspondingly, then you would probably use the field name as the tag name to differentiate them consistently.
- `ex` is a local parameter on a facet field that refers to tagged filter queries to be *excluded* in the facet count. Multiple tags can be referenced with commas separating them. For example, `{!ex=t1,t2,t3}r_type`.
- Advanced usage: Not shown here is an optional facet field local-param called `key` that provides an alternative label to the field name in the response. By providing an alternative name, the field can be faceted on multiple times with varying names and filter query exclusions.

The new complete URL is:

```
http://localhost:8983/solr/mbreleases/select?indent=on&qt=mb_relea
ses&rows=0&q=smashing&facet=on&facet.field={!ex%3Dfoo}r_type&facet.
mincount=1&facet.sort=index&fq={!tag%3Dfoo}r_type%3AAlbum.
```

And here is the output. The facet counts are back, but `numFound` remains at the filtered `29`:

```
<response>
<lst name="responseHeader">
  <int name="status">0</int>
  <int name="QTime">4</int>
</lst>
```

```
<result name="response" numFound="29" start="0"/>
<lst name="facet_counts">
  <lst name="facet_queries"/>
  <lst name="facet_fields">
    <lst name="r_type">
      <int name="Album">29</int>
      <int name="Compilation">41</int>
      <int name="EP">7</int>
      <int name="Interview">3</int>
      <int name="Live">95</int>
      <int name="Other">19</int>
      <int name="Remix">1</int>
      <int name="Single">45</int>
      <int name="Soundtrack">1</int>
    </lst>
  </lst>
  <lst name="facet_dates"/>
  <lst name="facet_ranges"/>
</lst>
</response>
```

At this point, if the user chooses additional values from this facet, then the filter query would be modified to allow for more possibilities, such as: `fq={!tag=foo}` `r_type:Album r_type:Other` (not URL escaped for clarity) which filters for releases that are *either* of type `Album` or `Other` as the default query parser boolean logic is OR.

Hierarchical faceting

Imagine if your documents have some sort of taxonomy or other hierarchical label. This might be a file path or URL path. It could be a geographic location organized by continent, country, state/province, and then city. Or it might be a large company's organizational hierarchy for employees. A faceted navigation experience for such data might be a tree browser common in file navigation with an added facet count at each node.

```
Department
‹ Any Department
  ‹ Books
    Computers & Internet
      Web Development (12,132)
      Software (10,362)
      Networking (12,286)
      Home Computing (11,729)
      Hardware (3,449)
      Certification Central (3,357)
```

The preceding screenshot is from Amazon, which has a simple hierarchical interface easily implemented with Solr.

 Solr does not *directly* feature hierarchical faceting but it has the underlying capabilities for you to achieve it without modifying Solr, as you're about to see. Solr's wiki on this subject: `http://wiki.apache.org/solr/HierarchicalFaceting` contains information on a couple patches in Solr's JIRA that add direct support for this.

There are a number of ways to go about implementing hierarchical faceting; no best-practice approach has emerged yet. A big cause of the variation is that applications have different requirements. The requirement that has the biggest impact on the ultimate approach, in my opinion, is the answer to this question: Will the user navigate the tree incrementally, one level at a time? Or will the application expand the tree automatically, possibly with a threshold like a depth or facet count for large trees?

If the tree is *only* going to be navigated incrementally by the user, then the solution set is quite simple. Simply specify a `string` field for each level that exists in the hierarchy and index the data directly into them without doing anything special. At query time, you use the field value faceting skills you've learned in this chapter without need for any special tricks. The details are left as an exercise to the reader. If the data is multi-valued, then the solution is mildly more complicated. For each field you need to prefix the value with an ancestor path to disambiguate it. For example, if you have a country field with USA and a province field with MA and a city field with Boston, then these fields would instead hold USA, USA/MA, USA/MA/Boston, respectively. You'll strip these prefixes out for display purposes, and you will need to use the `facet.prefix` parameter in your facet queries.

If the tree is going to be automatically expanded by depth, then the simplest approach I can suggest is to use Solr 4's new *Pivot faceting* feature, which was committed a long time ago. You would still need to index the data as I just described for incremental navigation. There are more complicated solutions involving a single tokenized field, which scales better to arbitrary hierarchy depths. In pursuing such a strategy, you would likely use `PathHierarchyTokenizer`. I haven't found a complete approach using this technique that doesn't require a Solr patch.

Another hierarchical faceting requirement to consider is whether you want to expand each ancestor node from the current selected node. Amazon does *not* do this, so you won't see it in the screenshot. To implement this, facet on each ancestor level field above the current level with `facet.prefix`. You will need to use the `{!ex ...}` filter query exclusion to reveal facet filtered away by the current navigation filter.

Summary

Faceting is possibly the most valuable and popular Solr search component. We've covered the three types of faceting, how to build filter queries from them, and some interesting use cases such as alphabetic range bucketing and hierarchical faceting. Now you have the essential knowledge to put it to use in faceted navigation based user interfaces and other uses.

In the next chapter, we'll cover **Solr Search Components**. You've actually been using them already because performing a query, enabling debug output, and faceting are each actually implemented as search components. But there's also search result highlighting, spelling correction, term-suggest, suggesting similar documents, collapsing/rolling up search results, editorially elevating or evicting results, and more!

7
Search Components

Solr's primary extension mechanism is called a **Search Component**. You've actually been using several of them already: QueryComponent performs the actual searches (notably the q parameter), DebugComponent outputs the invaluable query debugging information when setting debugQuery, and FacetComponent performs the faceting we used in *Chapter 6, Faceting*. In addition, there are many more that do all sorts of useful things that can really enhance your search experience:

- **Highlighting**: For returning highlighted text snippets of matching text in the original data

- **Spell checking**: For suggesting alternative queries; often called "Did you mean?"

- **Suggester***: For suggesting complete queries based on partially typed input; often called *query autocomplete*

- **Query elevation**: For manually modifying search results for certain queries

- **More-like-this**: For finding documents similar to another document or provided text

- **Stats**: For mathematical statistics of indexed numbers

- **Clustering**: For organizing search results into statistically similar clusters

- **Result grouping***: For grouping search results by a field and limiting the number of results per group

- **Terms** and **TermVector**: For retrieving raw indexed data

[*] These aren't really search components but they similarly add value to the search experience.

In a hurry?

Search features like search result highlighting, query spell-checking, and query autocomplete suggestions are high-value for most search applications; don't miss them. Take a peak at the others to see if they are applicable to you.

About components

At this point you should be familiar with the `<requestHandler/>` definitions defined in `solrconfig.xml` — this was explained in *Chapter 4, Searching*. Any request handlers with `class="solr.SearchRequestHandler"` are intuitively related to searching. The Java code implementing `org.apache.solr.SearchRequestHandler` doesn't actually do any searching! Instead, it maintains a list of `SearchComponents` that are invoked in sequence for a request. The search components used and their order are of course configurable.

What follows is our request handler for MusicBrainz releases but modified to explicitly configure the components:

```
<requestHandler name="mb_releases" class="solr.SearchHandler">
  <!-- default values for query parameters -->
  <lst name="defaults">
    <str name="defType">edismax</str>
    <str name="qf">r_name r_a_name^0.4</str>
    <str name="pf">r_name^0.5 r_a_name^0.2</str>
    <str name="qs">1</str>
    <str name="ps">0</str>
    <str name="tie">0.1</str>
    <str name="q.alt">*:*</str>
  </lst>
  <!-- note: these components are the default ones -->
  <arr name="components">
    <str>query</str>
    <str>facet</str>
    <str>mlt</str>
    <str>highlight</str>
    <str>stats</str>
    <str>debug</str>
  </arr>
  <!-- INSTEAD, "first-components" and/or
    "last-components" may be specified. -->
</requestHandler>
```

The named search components in the above XML comment are the default ones that are automatically registered if you do not specify the `components` section. This named list is also known as the **standard component list**. To specify additional components, you can either re-specify `components` with changes, or you can add it to the `first-components` or `last-components` lists, which are prepended and appended respectively to the standard component list.

> Many components depend on other components being executed first, especially the query component, so you will usually add components to `last-components`.

Search components must be registered with Solr to be activated so that they can then be referred to in a components list. All of the standard components are pre-registered. Here's an example of how a search component named `elevator` is registered in `solrconfig.xml`:

```
<searchComponent name="elevator" class="solr.QueryElevationComponent">
  <str name="queryFieldType">string</str>
  <str name="config-file">elevate.xml</str>
</searchComponent>
```

The functionality in `QueryComponent`, `FacetComponent`, and `DebugComponent` has been described in previous chapters. The rest of this chapter describes other search components that come with Solr.

Doing a distributed-search?

A Solr **Distributed-search** is having Solr search across multiple Solr cores/servers (*shards* in distributed-search lingo) as if it were one logical index. It is discussed in *Chapter 10, Scaling Solr*. One thing to be aware of is that a sharded request will by default go to the default request handler, even if your client issued a request to another handler. To ensure that the relevant search components are still activated on a sharded request, you can use the `shards.qt` parameter just as you would `qt`.

The Highlight component

You are probably most familiar with search highlighting when you use an Internet search engine like Google. Most search results come back with a snippet of text from the site containing the word(s) you search for, highlighted. Solr can do the same thing. In the following screenshot we see Google highlighting a search including **Solr** and **search** (in bold):

Introduction to The **Solr** Enterprise **Search** Server ⬆ ✕
Solr is a standalone enterprise **search** server with a web-services like API. You put documents in it (called "indexing") via XML over HTTP. ...
lucene.apache.org/**solr**/features.html - 13k - Cached - Similar pages - ⬯

A non-obvious way to make use of the highlighting feature is to not actually do any highlighting. Instead Solr's highlighter can be used to inform the user which fields in the document satisfied their search, not to actually highlight the matched values. In this scenario, there would be a search that searches across many fields or a catch-all field and then hl.fl (the highlighted field list) is set to *. Solr will generate a snippet, but you ignore it aside from recognizing which field matched.

A highlighting example

Admittedly the MusicBrainz data set does not make an ideal example to show off highlighting because there's no substantial text, but it can be useful nonetheless.

The following is a sample use of highlighting on a search for Corgan in the artist MusicBrainz data set. Recall that the mb_artists request handler is configured to search against the artist name, alias, and members fields.

```
http://localhost:8983/solr/mbartists/select?indent=on&q=corgan&rows=3
&qt=mb_artists&hl=true
```

And here is the output of the above URL:

```
<?xml version="1.0" encoding="UTF-8"?>
<response>
<lst name="responseHeader">
    <int name="status">0</int>
    <int name="QTime">89</int>
</lst>
<result name="response" numFound="5" start="0">
    <doc>
        <date name="a_begin_date">1967-03-17T05:00:00Z</date>
        <str name="a_name">Billy Corgan</str>
```

```
            <date name="a_release_date_latest">
                     2005-06-21T04:00:00Z</date>
        <str name="a_type">1</str>
        <str name="id">Artist:102693</str>
        <str name="type">Artist</str>
    </doc>
    <doc>
        <str name="a_name">Billy Corgan &amp; Mike Garson</str>
        <str name="a_type">2</str>
        <str name="id">Artist:84909</str>
        <str name="type">Artist</str>
    </doc>
    <doc>
        <arr name="a_member_id"><str>102693</str></arr>
        <arr name="a_member_name"><str>Billy Corgan</str></arr>
        <str name="a_name">Starchildren</str>
        <str name="id">Artist:35656</str>
        <str name="type">Artist</str>
    </doc>
</result>
<lst name="highlighting">
    <lst name="Artist:102693">
        <arr name="a_name">
        <str>Billy &lt;em&gt;Corgan&lt;/em&gt;</str>
        </arr>
    </lst>
    <lst name="Artist:84909">
        <arr name="a_name">
        <str>Billy &lt;em&gt;Corgan&lt;/em&gt; &amp; Mike Garson</str>
        </arr>
    </lst>
    <lst name="Artist:35656">
        <arr name="a_member_name">
        <str>Billy &lt;em&gt;Corgan&lt;/em&gt;</str>
        </arr>
    </lst>
</lst>
</response>
```

What should be noted in this example is the manner in which the highlighting results are in the response data. Also note that not all of the result highlighting was against the same field.

> It is possible to enable highlighting and discover that some of the results are not highlighted. Sometimes this can be due to complex text analysis; although more likely it could simply be that there is a mismatch between the fields searched and those highlighted.

Highlighting configuration

Highlighting, like most parts of Solr searching, is configured through request parameters. You can specify them in the URL, but it is more appropriate to specify the majority of these in your application's request handler in `solrconfig.xml` because they are unlikely to change between requests. Some parts of the highlighting configuration have defaults configured within the `<highlighting/>` element if you wish to change them there.

Understand that like faceting, nearly all of these parameters can be overridden on a per-field basis. The syntax looks like `f.fieldName.paramName=value` for example: `f.allText.snippets=0`

> **So many configuration options!**
>
> There are more highlighting configuration parameters than any other part of Solr! However, it's the simplest to use, so don't let all these options overwhelm you. Like most things in Solr, the defaults are quite reasonable. The only parameter required is `hl`, which enables highlighting. You'll probably set `hl.fl`, and enable `hl.usePhraseHighlighter` and `hl.highlightMultiTerm` and a couple others that suit your fancy.

The following are the parameters observed by the highlighter search component:

- `hl`: Set to `true` to enable search highlighting. Without this, the other parameters are ignored, and highlighting is effectively disabled.

- `hl.fl`: A comma or space separated list of fields that will be highlighted. It is important for a field to be marked as stored in the schema in order to highlight on it. If this parameter is omitted, then it defaults to the default field(s) used by the query parser: the `df` parameter for the `lucene` query parser or the `qf` parameter for the `dismax` query parser. You may use an asterisk wildcard to conveniently highlight on all of the text fields, such as `*` or `r_*`. If you use a wildcard, then consider enabling the `hl.requireFieldMatch` option.

- `hl.requireFieldMatch`: If set to `true`, then a field will not be highlighted for a result unless the query also matched against that field. This is set to `false` by default, meaning that it's possible to query one field and highlight another and get highlights back as long as the terms searched for are found within the highlighted field. If you use a wildcard in `hl.fl`, then you will probably enable this. However, if you query against an all-text catch-all field (probably using copy-field directives), then leave this as `false` so that the search results can indicate from which field the query text was found in.

- `hl.usePhraseHighlighter`: If the query contained a phrase (it was quoted), then this will ensure that only the phrase is highlighted and not the words out of context of the queried phrase. So, if "a b c" is the query with quotes, then the "b" in the stored text "x b z" will not be highlighted if this option is enabled. This is strangely set to `false` by default. *You should probably always enable this.*

  - `hl.highlightMultiTerm`: If any wildcard or fuzzy queries are used, then this will ensure that the highlighting matches such terms correctly. This defaults to `false` and it requires `hl.usePhraseHighlighter`. *You should probably enable this.*

- `hl.snippets`: This is the maximum number of highlighted snippets (aka fragments) that will be generated per field. It defaults to `1`, which you will probably not change. By setting this to `0` for a particular field (example: `f.allText.hl.snippets=0`), you can effectively disable highlighting for that field. You might do that if you used a wildcard for `hl.fl` and want to make an exception.

- `hl.fragsize`: The maximum number of characters returned in each snippet (aka fragment), measured in characters. The default is `100`. If `0` is specified, then the field is not fragmented and whole field values are returned. Obviously, be wary of doing this for large text fields.

- `hl.mergeContiguous`: If set to `true`, then overlapping snippets are merged. The merged fragment size is not limited by `hl.fragsize`. The default is `false`, but you will probably set this to `true` when `hl.snippets` is greater than zero and `fragsize` is non-zero.

- `hl.maxAnalyzedChars`: The maximum number of characters in a field that will be sought for highlighting. If you want to disable the limit, then set this to `-1`. The default is `51200` characters. If your Solr instance has documents of substantial size then you should consider raising this, at the expense of some performance loss.

- `hl.alternateField`: If a snippet couldn't be generated (no terms matched) for a field, then this parameter refers to a field that will be returned as the snippet. You might use some sort of summary field for a document or potentially the searched field itself. There is none by default. If you always want to ensure there is some data from the document to show in the event highlighting fails, then enable this.

  - `hl.maxAlternateFieldLength`: The maximum number of characters to return for `hl.alternateField`. It's 0 by default, which means unlimited. Set this to something reasonably close to `hl.snippets` * `hl.fragsize` to maintain consistent sizing in the results.

- `hl.fragmenter`: Choose the snippet fragmenting algorithm. This parameter refers to a named `<fragmenter/>` element in `<highlighting/>` in `solconfig.xml`. `gap` is the default typical choice based on a fragment size. `regex` is an alternative in which the highlighted fragment boundaries can be defined with a regular expression. See below for regex-specific options.

- `hl.formatter`: Choose how to format the highlighting. This parameter refers to a named `<formatter/>` element in `<highlighting/>` in `solconfig.xml`. The default implementation (and only option) named `html` further specifies two more parameters:

  - `hl.simple.pre` and `hl.simple.post`: (for the html formatter) This is the text that will be inserted immediately before and after matched terms in the snippet in order to demarcate them from the surrounding text. The default is `<em>` and `</em>` (HTML emphasis tags). Note that the circumstantial presence of whatever values are chosen in the original text, such as HTML with pre-existing emphasis tags, are not escaped, and in rare circumstances may lead to a false highlight.

- `hl.encoder`: Choose the escaping/encoding algorithm to be applied to the final snippet response. It isn't applied to the surrounding markup that is introduced (for example, `<em></em>`). This is a reference to a named `<encoder/>` element in `<highlighting/>` in `solconfig.xml`. The default configuration uses an HTML escaping algorithm. There is another choice with the class `solr.highlight.DefaultEncoder` that doesn't do any escaping.

 The formatter and encoder options have web centric defaults. If the output is not going to be rendered on a web page, then consider changing them.

The regex fragmenter

The various options available for the `regex` fragmenter are as follows:

- `hl.regex.pattern`: This is a regular expression matching a block of text that will serve as the snippet/fragment to subsequently be highlighted. The default is `[-\w ,/\n\"']{20,200}`, which roughly looks for sentences. If you are using the `regex` fragmenter, then you will most likely tune a regular expression to your needs. The regular expression language definition used by Java and thus Solr is here at `http://download.oracle.com/javase/1.5.0/docs/api/java/util/regex/Pattern.html`.

- `hl.regex.slop`: This is the factor to which `hl.fragsize` can vary to accommodate the regular expression. The default is `0.6`, which means that fragment sizes may vary between `40` and `160` if `hl.fragsize` is `100`.

- `hl.increment`: Sets the minimum Lucene *position increment gap* from one term to the next to trigger a new fragment. There is no `regex` in the parameter name, but it is indeed only for the `regex` fragmenter. It defaults to `50`, which is fine.

- `hl.regex.maxAnalyzedChars`: For performance reasons, this puts a limit on the number of leading characters of the field that are fragmented based on the regular expression. After this limit is exceeded, the remaining characters up to `hl.maxAnalyzedChars` are fragmented in a fashion consistent with the `gap` fragmenter, which is faster. The default is `10000` characters.

The fast vector highlighter with multi-colored highlighting

New in Solr 3.1 is the **fast vector highlighter (FVH)**, which is an alternative underlying algorithm with additional schema field requirements. When in use for a field, highlighting on that field is faster, especially for long text common in indexing full documents. As an added bonus, it has the option of highlighting each query term with different markup such as a distinct color. The field requirements are: `indexed="true" stored="true" termVectors="true" termPositions="true" termOffsets="true"`.

Use the fast vector highlighter for web or document indexing

If your use of Solr involves large text fields, as is common in web or document crawling, then use the FVH for that text field. You needn't index all fields this way, just the big ones—probably just one. Instructing Lucene to store term vectors with positions and offsets will increase disk requirements. A very rough estimate is 20% of the stored field value size.

Some previously mentioned parameters are ignored or unsupported:
`hl.highlightMultiTerm`, `hl.mergeContiguous`, `hl.maxAnalyzedChars`,
`hl.fragmenter`, and `hl.formatter` (the FVH has its own variants of these last two).
The following are additional configuration parameters specific to the fast vector
highlighter:

- `hl.useFastVectorHighligher`: This must be set to true to enable the
  fast vector highlighter, as it defaults to false. Additionally, the field to be
  highlighted must meet the aforementioned schema requirements. If the
  requirements are not met then the default (non-FVH) algorithm is used; it is
  not an error condition. *This is evaluated on a field-by-field basis* as listed in `hl.fl`.

- `hl.fragListBuilder`: Choose the snippet fragmenting algorithm.
  This parameter refers to a named `<fragListBuilder/>` element in
  `<highlighting/>` in `solconfig.xml`. The default is named `simple`. Another
  is named `single` which returns the entire field contents as one snippet.

> The `simple` one does **not** take care to create snippets at word
> boundaries—see LUCENE-1824. As a quick fix, you could manually
> trim the start and end of the snippet to the nearest whitespace
> character before displaying it to the user.

- `hl.fragmentsBuilder`: Choose how to format the highlighting.
  This parameter refers to a named `<fragmentsBuilder/>` element in
  `<highlighting/>` in `solconfig.xml`. The default, named `default`, uses
  `<em></em>` HTML markup to highlight the text. The other pre-configured
  choice is named `colored` which uses HTML markup that looks like this: `<b
  style="background:yellow"></b>` where the color varies over ten different
  ones.

  - `hl.tag.pre` and `hl.tag.post`: This is the text that will be inserted
    immediately before and after matched terms in the snippet in order
    to demarcate them from the surrounding text. If commas are present,
    it is treated as a list. The fragments builder will use a consistent index
    into the list for a queried term. If there are more queried terms than
    pre or post tags then it loops back to the front of the array recursively.

> Notice that `hl.tag.pre` and `hl.tag.post` is a different pair of
> parameters than `hl.simple.pre` and `hl.simple.post` for the
> non-FVH. Since the FVH is typically used on a subset of highlighted
> fields, you should configure both pairs of parameters consistently to get
> consistent highlighting tags. It is this way by default.

- ○ `hl.multiValuedSeparatorChar`: This is the character that separates one value from the next in a snippet that spans more than one value for a multi-valued field. It's a space character by default. Arguably the snippet shouldn't span values in the first place—the non-FVH will not.

- `hl.phraseLimit`: This performance optimization limits the number of phrases examined to find the highest-scoring phrase. It defaults to -1, which means no limit.

> Set `hl.phraseLimit` to `5000` to protect against pathologically bad cases on large documents. You might even consider a value like 1 if it is sufficient to simply highlight the first possible phrase in the document instead of the highest scoring one, in exchange for a substantial improvement in highlighting performance.

The SpellCheck component

One of the better ways to enhance the search experience is by offering spelling corrections. This is sometimes presented at the top of search results with such text as "Did you mean ...". Solr supports this with the `SpellCheckComponent`.

> A related technique is to use fuzzy queries using the tilde syntax. However, fuzzy queries don't tell you what alternative spellings were used, are not as scalable for large indexes, and might require more programming than using this search component.

For spelling corrections to work, Solr must clearly have a corpus of words (a dictionary) to suggest alternatives to those in the user's query. "Dictionary" is meant loosely as the collection of correctly known spelled words, and not their definitions. Solr can be configured in either of the following two ways:

- **A text file of words**: For a freely available English word list, check out **SCOWL (Spell Checker Oriented Word Lists)** at `http://wordlist.sourceforge.net`. In addition, see the dictionary files for OpenOffice which supports many languages: `http://wiki.services.openoffice.org/wiki/Dictionaries`

- **Indexed content**: This is generally preferred, principally because your data contains proper nouns and other words not in a dictionary.

Before reading on about configuring spell checking in `solrconfig.xml`, you may want to jump ahead and take a quick peek at an example towards the end of this section, and then come back.

Schema configuration

If your dictionary is going to be based on indexed content as is recommended, then a field should be set aside exclusively for this purpose. This is so that it can be analyzed appropriately and so that other fields can be copied into it as the index-based dictionary uses just one field. Most Solr setups would have one field; our MusicBrainz searches, on the other hand, are segmented by the data type (artists, releases, tracks), and so one for each would be best. For the purposes of demonstrating this feature, we will only do it for artists.

In `schema.xml`, we need to define the field type for spellchecking. This particular configuration is one I recommend for most scenarios:

```
<!--
SpellCheck analysis config based off of http://wiki.apache.org/solr/
SpellCheckingAnalysis
-->
<fieldType name="textSpell" class="solr.TextField"
      positionIncrementGap="100" stored="false" multiValued="true">
  <analyzer type="index">
    <tokenizer class="solr.StandardTokenizerFactory"/>
    <filter class="solr.LowerCaseFilterFactory"/>
    <filter class="solr.SynonymFilterFactory"
            synonyms="synonyms.txt" ignoreCase="true"
            expand="true"/>
    <filter class="solr.StopFilterFactory" ignoreCase="true"
            words="stopwords.txt"/>
    <filter class="solr.StandardFilterFactory"/>
    <filter class="solr.RemoveDuplicatesTokenFilterFactory"/>
  </analyzer>
  <analyzer type="query">
    <tokenizer class="solr.StandardTokenizerFactory"/>
    <filter class="solr.LowerCaseFilterFactory"/>
    <filter class="solr.StopFilterFactory" ignoreCase="true"
            words="stopwords.txt"/>
    <filter class="solr.StandardFilterFactory"/>
    <filter class="solr.RemoveDuplicatesTokenFilterFactory"/>
  </analyzer>
</fieldType>
```

A field type for spellchecking is not marked as stored because the spellcheck component only uses the indexed terms. The important thing is to ensure that the text analysis does *not* do stemming as the corrections presented would suggest the stems, which would look very odd to the user for most stemmer algorithms. It's also hard to imagine a use-case that doesn't apply lowercasing.

Now we need to create a field for this data:

```
<field name="a_spell" type="textSpell" />
```

And we need to get data into it with some `copyField` directives:

```
<copyField source="a_name" dest="a_spell" />
<copyField source="a_alias" dest="a_spell" />
```

Arguably, `a_member_name` may be an additional choice to copy as well, as the `dismax` search we configured (seen in the following code) searches it too, albeit at a reduced score. This, as well as many decisions with search configuration, is subjective.

Configuration in solrconfig.xml

To use any search component, it needs to be in the components list of a request handler. The spellcheck component is not in the standard list so it needs to be added.

```
<requestHandler name="mb_artists" class="solr.SearchHandler">
  <!-- default values for query parameters -->
  <lst name="defaults">
    <str name="defType">dismax</str>
    <str name="qf">a_name a_alias^0.8 a_member_name^0.4</str>
    <!-- etc. -->
  </lst>
  <arr name="last-components">
    <str>spellcheck</str>
  </arr>
</requestHandler>
```

This component should already be defined in `solrconfig.xml`. Within the spellchecker search component, there are one or more XML blocks named `spellchecker` so that different dictionaries and other options can be configured. These might also be loosely referred to as the dictionaries, because the parameter that refers to this choice is named that way (more on that later). We have three spellcheckers configured as follows:

- `a_spell`: An index-based spellchecker that is a typical recommended configuration.

- `jarowinkler`: This uses the same built dictionary, `spellcheckIndexDir`, as `a_spell`, but contains an alternative configuration setting for experimentation.
- `file`: A sample configuration where the input dictionary comes from a file (not included).

A complete MusicBrainz implementation would have a different spellchecker for each MB data type, with all of them configured similarly.

Following the excerpt below is a description of all options available:

```
<!-- The spell check component can return a list of
  alternative spelling suggestions.  -->
<searchComponent name="spellcheck"
    class="solr.SpellCheckComponent">
  <str name="queryAnalyzerFieldType">textSpell</str><!-- 'q'
    only -->

  <lst name="spellchecker">
    <str name="name">a_spell</str>
    <str name="field">a_spell</str>
    <str name="buildOnOptimize">true</str>
    <str name="spellcheckIndexDir">./spellchecker_a_spell</str>
  </lst>
  <lst name="spellchecker">
    <!-- Use previous spellchecker index with different
         distance measure -->
    <str name="name">jarowinkler</str>
    <str name="field">a_spell</str>
    <str name="distanceMeasure">
        org.apache.lucene.search.spell.JaroWinklerDistance</str>
    <str name="spellcheckIndexDir">./spellchecker_a_spell</str>
  </lst>
  <!-- just an example -->
  <lst name="spellchecker">
    <str name="name">file</str>
    <str name="classname">solr.FileBasedSpellChecker</str>
    <str name="sourceLocation">spellings.txt</str>
    <str name="characterEncoding">UTF-8</str>
    <str name="spellcheckIndexDir">./spellcheckerFile</str>
  </lst>
</searchComponent>
```

Configuring spellcheckers (dictionaries)

The double layer of spellchecker configuration is perhaps a little confusing. The outer one just names the search component—it's just a container for configuration(s). The inner ones are distinct configurations to choose at search time.

The following options are common to both index and file based spellcheckers:

- name: The name of the spellcheck configuration. It defaults to default. Be sure not to have more than one configuration with the same name.

- classname: The implementation of the spellchecker. It defaults to solr. IndexBasedSpellChecker; the other is solr.FileBasedSpellChecker. Further information on these is just ahead.

- spellcheckIndexDir: This is a reference to the directory location where the spellchecker's internal dictionary is *built*, not its source. It is relative to Solr's data directory, which in turn defaults to being within the Solr home directory. This is actually optional, which results in an in-memory dictionary.

> In our spellchecker named jarowinkler, we're actually referring to another spellchecker's index so that we can try other configuration options without having to duplicate the data or building time. If this is done, be sure to use the spellcheck.reload command for this dictionary if it changes, as described later.

> For a high load Solr server, an in-memory index is appealing. Until SOLR-780 is addressed, you'll have to take care to tell Solr to build the dictionary whenever the Solr core gets loaded. This happens at startup or if you tell Solr to reload a core.

- buildOnCommit and buildOnOptimize: These boolean options (defaulting to false) enable the spellchecker's internal index to be built automatically when either Solr performs a commit or optimize. Most likely you'll set one of these.

- accuracy: Sets the minimum spelling correction accuracy to act as a threshold. It falls between 0 and 1 with a default of 0.5. The higher this number is, the simpler the corrections are.

- distanceMeasure: This is a Java class name implementing the algorithm to gauge similarity between a possible misspelling and a candidate correction. By the way, it defaults to org.apache.lucene.search. spell.LevensteinDistance which is the same algorithm used in fuzzy query matching,. Alternatively, org.apache.lucene.search.spell. JaroWinklerDistance works quite well.

- `fieldType`: This is a reference to a field type in `schema.xml` for performing text-analysis on words to be spellchecked by the `spellcheck.q` parameter (not q). If this isn't specified, then it defaults to the field type of the `field` parameter (used only by the index-based spellchecker) and if not specified, then defaults to a simple whitespace delimiter, which most likely would be a misconfiguration. When using the file-based spellchecker with `spellcheck.q`, be sure to specify this.

IndexBasedSpellChecker options

The `IndexBasedSpellChecker` gets the dictionary from the indexed content of a field in a Lucene/Solr index, and the options are explained as follows:

- `sourceLocation`: If specified, then it refers to an external Lucene/Solr index path. This is an unusual choice, but shows that the source dictionary does not need to come from Solr's main index; it could be from another location, perhaps from another Solr core. This is an advanced option. If you are doing this, then you'll probably also need to use the `spellcheck.reload` command mentioned later.

 Warning: This option name is actually common to both types of spellcheckers but is defined differently.

- `field`: It is mandatory and refers to the name of the field within the index that contains the dictionary. Furthermore, it must be indexed as the data is taken from there, and not from the stored content, which is ignored. Generally, this field exists expressly for spell correction purposes and other fields are copied into it.

- `thresholdTokenFrequency`: Specifies a document frequency threshold, which will exclude words that don't occur often. This is expressed as a fraction in the range 0-1, defaulting to 0, which effectively disables the threshold, letting all words through.

 If there is a lot of data and lots of common words, as opposed to proper nouns, then this threshold should be effective. If testing shows spelling candidates including strange fluke words found in the index, then introduce a threshold that is high enough to weed out such outliers. The threshold will probably be less than $0.01 - 1$ percent of documents.

FileBasedSpellChecker options

The `FileBasedSpellChecker` gets the dictionary from a plain text file.

- `sourceLocation`: This is mandatory and references a plain text file with each word on its own line. Note that an option by the same name but different meaning exists for the index-based spellchecker.

- `characterEncoding`: This is optional but should be set. It is the character encoding of `sourceLocation`, defaulting to that of your operating system, which is probably not suitable. Examples: US-ASCII or UTF-8 or ISO-8859-1.

We've not yet discussed the parameters to a search with the spellchecker component enabled. But at this point of the configuration discussion, understand that you have a choice of just letting the user query, q get processed or you can use `spellcheck.q`.

Processing of the q parameter

When a user query (q parameter) is processed by the `spellcheck` component to look for spelling errors, Solr needs to determine what words are to be examined. This is a two-step process. The first step is to pull out the queried words from the query string, ignoring any syntax such as AND. The next step is to process the words with an analyzer so that, among other things, lowercasing is performed. The analyzer chosen is through a field type specified directly within the search component configuration with `queryAnalyzerFieldType`. It really should be specified, but it's actually optional. If left unspecified, there would be no text-analysis, which would in all likelihood be a misconfiguration.

 This algorithm is implemented by a spellcheck **query converter**—a Solr extension point. The default query converter, known as `SpellingQueryConverter`, is probably fine.

Processing of the spellcheck.q parameter

If the `spellcheck.q` parameter is given (which really isn't a query per se), then the string is processed with the text analysis referenced by the `fieldType` option of the spellchecker being used. If a file-based spellchecker is being used, then you should set this explicitly. Index-based spellcheckers will sensibly use the field type of the referenced indexed spelling field.

 The dichotomy of the ways in which the analyzer is configured between both q and `spellcheck.q`, arguably needs improvement.

Building the dictionary from its source

Each spellchecker requires it to be *built*, which is the process in which the dictionary is read and is built into the `spellcheckIndexDir`. If it isn't built, then no corrections will be offered, and you'll probably be very confused. You'll be even more confused troubleshooting the results if it was built once but is far out of date and needs to be built again.

> The `DirectSolrSpellChecker` feature has already been completed for the upcoming Solr 4, which uses the Solr index directly without requiring a separate spellchecker index that needs building.

Generally, building is required if it has never been built before, and it should be built periodically when the dictionary changes. It need not necessarily be built for every change, but it obviously won't benefit from any such modifications.

> Using `buildOnOptimize` or `buildOnCommit` is a low-hassle way to keep the spellcheck index up to date. If you rarely optimize or if you commit too frequently then you'll instead have to issue build commands manually on a suitable time period. Furthermore, setting `spellcheckIndexDir` will ensure the built spellcheck index is persisted between Solr restarts.

In order to perform a build of a spellchecker, simply enable the component with `spellcheck=true`, add a special parameter called `spellcheck.build`, and set it to true:

```
http://localhost:8983/solr/mbartists/select?&qt=mb_
artists&rows=0&spellcheck=
true&spellcheck.build=true&spellcheck.dictionary=jarowinkler
```

The other spellcheck parameters will be explained shortly. It is important to note that only one spellchecker (dictionary) was built. To build more than one, separate requests must be issued. Anecdotally, the time it took to build this dictionary of nearly 400K documents, each of which were very small, was 25 seconds on a mediocre machine.

There is an additional related option similar to `spellcheck.build` called `spellcheck.reload`. This doesn't rebuild the index, but it basically re-establishes connections with the index (both `sourceLocation` for index-based spellcheckers and `spellcheckIndexDir` for all types). If you've decided to have some external process build the dictionary or simply share built indexes between spellcheckers as we've done, then Solr needs to know to reload it to see the changes—a quick operation.

Issuing spellcheck requests

At this point, we've covered how to configure the spellchecker and dictionaries but not how to issue requests that actually use it. Let's finally do it! Fortunately, there aren't many search parameters governing this end of the component. The parameters are as follows:

- `spellcheck`: A boolean switch that must be set to `true` to enable the component in order to see suggested spelling corrections.

- `spellcheck.dictionary`: The named reference to a dictionary (spellchecker) to use configured in `solrconfig.xml`. It defaults to `default`.

- `spellcheck.q` or `q`: The string containing words to be processed by this component can be specified as the `spellcheck.q` parameter, and if not present, then the `q` parameter. Please look for the information presented earlier on how these are processed.

Which should you use?: `spellcheck.q` or `q`

Assuming you're handling user queries to Solr that might contain some query syntax, then the default `q` is right, as Solr will then know to filter out possible uses of Lucene/Solr's syntax such as AND, OR, `fieldname:word`, and so on.). If not, then `spellcheck.q` is preferred, as it won't go through that unnecessary processing. It also allows its parsing to be different on a spellchecker-by-spellchecker basis, which we'll leverage in our example.

- `spellcheck.count`: The maximum number of corrections to offer per word. The default is `1`. Corrections are ordered by those closest to the original, as determined by the `distanceMeasure` algorithm.

Although counter-intuitive, raising this number affects the suggestion ordering—the results get better! The internal algorithm sees ~10 times as many as this number and then it orders them by closest match. Consequently, use a number between 5 and `10` or so to get quality results.

- `spellcheck.onlyMorePopular`: A boolean switch that will offer spelling suggestions for queried words that *were* found in the index, provided that the suggestions occur more often. This is in addition to the normal behavior of only offering suggestions for queried words *not* found in the index. If `extendedResults` is also enabled, then looking for `origFreq` being greater than `0` will indicate when this happens. This is disabled by default.

This parameter is good for situations where the user's query returns very few results, or when no results and no spellcheck suggestion was offered due to the query being correctly spelled (`correctlySpelled` is `true` in extended output). When this happens, consider automatically issuing a *secondary* search with this parameter enabled and with `spellcheck.collateExtendedResults` enabled to check if there is a collated query result that has more hits than the user's original query did. This shouldn't be enabled in the first search.

- `spellcheck.extendedResults`: A boolean switch that adds frequency information, both for the original word and for the suggestions. It's helpful when debugging.

- `spellcheck.collate`: A boolean switch that adds a revised query string to the output that alters the original query (from `spellcheck.q` or `q`) to use the top recommendation for each suggested word. It's smart enough to leave any other query syntax in place. The following are some additional options for use when collation is enabled, (added in Solr 3):

  - `spellcheck.maxCollations`: The maximum number of collations to return, defaulting to 1.

  - `spellcheck.maxCollationTries`: The maximum number of collations to *try* (verify it yields results), defaulting to 0. If this is non-zero, then the spellchecker will not return collations that yield no results.

  - `spellcheck.maxCollationEvaluations`: The maximum number of word correction combinations to rank before the top candidates are tried (verified). Without this limit, queries with many misspelled words could yield a combinatoric explosion of possibilities. The default is `10000`, which should be fine.

  - `spellcheck.collateExtendedResults`: A boolean switch that adds more details to the collation response. It adds the collation hits (number of documents found) and a mapping of misspelled words to corrected words.

Enable `spellcheck.collate` as a user interface will most likely want to present a convenient link to use the spelling suggestions. Furthermore, ensure the collation is verified to return results by setting `spellcheck.maxCollationTries` to a small non-zero number—perhaps 5.

Example usage for a misspelled query

We'll try out a typical spellcheck configuration that we've named a_spell. jarowinkler is almost the same but has slightly different results (bettor or worse is subjective), so we won't bother showing it here. I've disabled showing the query results with rows=0 because the actual query results aren't the point of these examples. In this example, it is imagined that the user is searching for the band Smashing Pumpkins, but with a misspelling.

Here are the search results for Smashg Pumpkins using the a_spell dictionary:

```xml
<?xml version="1.0"?>
<response>
<lst name="responseHeader">
    <int name="status">0</int>
    <int name="QTime">124</int>
    <lst name="params">
    <str name="spellcheck">true</str>
    <str name="indent">on</str>
    <str name="spellcheck.extendedResults">true</str>
    <str name="spellcheck.collateExtendedResults">true</str>
    <str name="spellcheck.maxCollationTries">5</str>
    <str name="spellcheck.collate">true</str>
    <str name="rows">0</str>
    <str name="echoParams">explicit</str>
    <str name="q">Smashg Pumpkins</str>
    <str name="spellcheck.dictionary">a_spell</str>
    <str name="spellcheck.count">5</str>
    <str name="qt">mb_artists</str>
  </lst>
</lst>
<result name="response" numFound="0" start="0"/>
<lst name="spellcheck">
  <lst name="suggestions">
    <lst name="smashg">
      <int name="numFound">5</int>
      <int name="startOffset">0</int>
      <int name="endOffset">6</int>
      <int name="origFreq">0</int>
      <arr name="suggestion">
        <lst>
          <str name="word">smash</str>
          <int name="freq">36</int>
```

```
      </lst>
      <lst>
        <str name="word">smashing</str>
        <int name="freq">4</int>
      </lst>
      <lst>
        <str name="word">smashign</str>
        <int name="freq">1</int>
      </lst>
      <lst>
        <str name="word">smashed</str>
        <int name="freq">5</int>
      </lst>
      <lst>
        <str name="word">smasher</str>
        <int name="freq">2</int>
      </lst>
    </arr>
  </lst>
  <bool name="correctlySpelled">false</bool>
  <lst name="collation">
    <str name="collationQuery">smashing Pumpkins</str>
    <int name="hits">1</int>
    <lst name="misspellingsAndCorrections">
      <str name="smashg">smashing</str>
    </lst>
  </lst>
</lst>
</lst>
</response>
```

In this scenario, I intentionally chose a misspelling that is closer to another word: "smash". Were it not for `maxCollationTries`, the suggested collation would be "smash Pumpkins" which would return no results. There are a few things I want to point out regarding the spellchecker response:

- Applications consuming this data will probably only use the collation query, despite the presence of a lot of other information.

- The suggestions are ordered by the so-called *edit-distance* score (closest match), which is not displayed. It may seem here that it is ordered by frequency, which is a coincidence.

There is an extension point to the spellchecker to customize the ordering—search Solr's wiki for `comparatorClass` for further information. You could write one that orders results based on a formula fusing both the suggestion score and document frequency.

- `startOffset` and `endOffset` are the index into the query of the spellchecked word. This information can be used by the client to display the query differently, perhaps displaying the corrected words in bold.

- `numFound` is always the number of suggested words returned, not the total number available if `spellcheck.count` were raised.

- `correctlySpelled` is intuitively `true` or `false`, depending on whether all of the query words were found in the dictionary or not.

Query complete / suggest

One of the most effective features of a search user interface is automatic/instant-search or completion of query input in a search input box. It is typically displayed as a drop-down menu that appears automatically after typing. There are several ways this can work:

- **Instant-search**: Here, the menu is populated with search results. Each row is a document, just like the regular search results are. At your discretion, you might opt to consider the last word partially typed. Examples of this are the URL bar in web browsers and various person search services. This is particularly effective for quick lookup scenarios against identifying information like a name / title / identifier. It's less effective for broader searches. One way to implement the search with the last word as a prefix is to put the last word into a filter query as a prefix query (that is with a trailing "*"). This word could be added as a dismax boost query too, to get an exact match at the top of the results. This is the gist of it; there are many details I am omitting.

- **Query log completion**: If your application has sufficient query volume, then you should perform the query completion against previously executed queries that returned results. The pop-up menu is then populated with queries others have typed. This is what Google does. It's a bit of work to set this up. To get the query string and other information, you could write a custom search component, or parse Solr's log files, or hook into the logging system and parse it there. The query strings could be appended to a plain query log file, or inserted into a database, or added directly to a Solr index. Putting the data into a database before it winds up in a Solr index affords more flexibility on how to ultimately index it in Solr.

Finally, at this point you could index the field with an `EdgeNGramTokenizer` and perform searches against it, or use a `KeywordTokenizer` and then use one of the approaches listed for query term completion below. I recommend reading this excellent article by Jay Hill on doing this with `EdgeNGrams`: `http://www.lucidimagination.com/blog/2009/09/08/auto-suggest-from-popular-queries-using-edgengrams/`.

Monitor your user's queries!

Even if you don't plan to do query log completion, you should capture useful information about each request for ancillary usage analysis, especially to monitor which searches return no results. Capture the request parameters, the response time, the result count, and add a timestamp.

- **Query term completion**: The last word of the user's query is searched within the index as a prefix, and other indexed words starting with that prefix are provided. This type is an alternative to query log completion and it's easy to implement. There are several implementation approaches: Facet the word using `facet.prefix`, use Solr's new **Suggester** feature, or use the Terms component. You should consider these choices in that order.

- **Facet / field value completion**: This is similar to query term completion but it is done on data that you would facet or filter on. The pop-up menu of choices will give suggestions across multiple fields with a label telling you which field it is filtering on, and the value will be the exact field value, not the subset of it that the user typed. This is particularly useful when there are many possible filter choices. I've seen it used at `Mint.com` and elsewhere to great effect, but it is under-utilized in my opinion. My recommended implementation approach is to build a search index dedicated to this information. For each value, a document would be created containing a field referencing the field in the main index and another for the value using typical tokenized text analysis.

There are other interesting query completion concepts I've seen on sites too, and some of these can be combined effectively. I'll now describe the three approaches to implementing Query term completion. It's a popular type of query completion, and the three approaches highlight different technologies within Solr.

Query term completion via facet.prefix

Most people don't realize that faceting can be used to implement query term completion, but it can. This approach has the unique and valuable benefit of returning completions filtered by filter queries (that is faceted navigation state), and by query words prior to the last one being completed. This means the completion suggestions that, if chosen, will result in a search that has results, which is *not* the case for the other techniques. However, there are limits to its scalability in terms of memory use and inappropriateness for real-time search applications...

Faceting on a tokenized field is going to use an entry in the **field value cache** (based on UnInvertedField) to hold all words in memory. It will use a hefty chunk of memory for many words and it's going to take a non-trivial amount of time to build this cache on every commit during the auto-warming phase. For a data point, consider MusicBrainz' largest field: t_name (track name). It has nearly 700K words in it. It consumes nearly 100 MB of memory and it took 33 seconds to initialize on my machine. The mandatory initialization per-commit makes this approach unsuitable for real-time-search applications (See *Chapter 10, Scaling Solr* for more information).

Measure this for yourself. Perform a trivial query to trigger its initialization and measure how long it takes. Then search Solr's statistics page for **fieldValueCache**. The size is given in bytes next to **memSize**. This statistic is also logged quite clearly.

For this example, we have a search box searching track names and it contains:

```
michael ja
```

All of the words here except the last one become the main query for the term-suggest. For our example, this is just michael. If there isn't anything, then we'd want to ensure that the request handler used would search for all documents. The faceted field is a_spell, and we want to sort by occurrence. We also want there to be at least one occurrence, and we don't want more than five suggestions. We don't need the actual search results either. This leaves the facet.prefix faceting parameter to make this work. This parameter filters the facet values to those starting with this value.

Remember that facet values are the final result of text analysis, and therefore are probably lowercased for fields you might want to do term completion on. You'll need to pre-process the prefix value similarly, or else nothing will be found.

We're going to set this to `ja`, the last word that the user has partially typed. Here is a URL for such a search:

```
http://localhost:8983/solr/mbartists/select?q=michael&qt=mb_artists
&wt=json&indent=on&facet=on&rows=0&facet.limit=5&facet.mincount=1
&facet.field=a_spell&facet.prefix=ja
```

 When setting this up for real, I recommend creating a request handler just for term completion with many of these parameters defined there, so that they can be configured separately from your application.

In this example, we're going to use Solr's JSON response format. Here is the result:

```
{
  "responseHeader":{
  "status":0,
  "QTime":5},
  "response":{"numFound":2498,"start":0,"docs":[]
},
  "facet_counts":{
  "facet_queries":{},
  "facet_fields":{
    "a_spell":[
    "jackson",18,
    "james",16,
    "jason",4,
    "jay",4,
    "jane",3]},
  "facet_dates":{},
  "facet_ranges":{}}}
```

This is exactly the information needed to populate a pop-up menu of choices that the user can conveniently choose.

However, there are some issues to be aware of with this feature:

- You may want to retain the case information of what the user is typing so that it can then be re-applied to the Solr results. Remember that `facet.prefix` will probably need to be lowercased depending on text analysis.

- If stemming text analysis is performed on the field at the time of indexing, then the user might get completion choices that are clearly wrong. Most stemmers, namely Porter-based ones, stem off the suffix to an invalid word. Consider using a minimal stemmer if any, but ideally none at all. For stemming and other text analysis reasons, you might want to create a separate field with suitable text analysis just for this feature. In our example here we used `a_spell` on purpose because spelling suggestions and term completion have the same text analysis requirements.

- If you would like to do term-completion of multiple fields, then you'll be disappointed that you can't do that directly. The easiest way is to combine several fields at index-time. Alternatively, a query searching multiple fields with faceting configured for multiple fields can be done. It would be up to you to merge the faceting results based on ordered counts.

Query term completion via the Suggester

New in Solr 3 is a high-speed approach to implement term completion, called the **Suggester**. The Suggester is not its own search component; it's an extension of the spell-check component. This means that it's not necessarily as up-to-date as your index and it needs to be *built*, but the Suggester only takes a couple seconds or so for this, and you are not forced to do this per-commit, unlike with faceting. The Suggester principally features the fastest search performance—a handful of milliseconds per search at most. The performance characteristics are largely determined by a configuration choice, shown later, called `lookupImpl`, in which I recommend `org.apache.solr.suggest.fst.FSTLookup` (new in Solr 3.3) almost always. The FST uses ~1/20th the memory of faceting's `UnInvertedField` data structure. Additionally, the Suggester uniquely includes a method of loading its dictionary from a file that optionally includes a sorting weight.

Solr does not include a sample configuration of how to use the Suggester, so I'll provide one here. We're going to use it for MusicBrainz artist name completion. The following goes in `solrconfig.xml`:

```
<requestHandler name="/suggest" class="solr.SearchHandler">
  <lst name="defaults">
    <str name="spellcheck">true</str>
    <str name="spellcheck.dictionary">a_suggest</str>
    <str name="spellcheck.onlyMorePopular">true</str>
    <str name="spellcheck.count">5</str>
    <str name="spellcheck.collate">true</str>
  </lst>
  <arr name="components">
    <str>suggest</str>
```

```
    </arr>
  </requestHandler>

  <searchComponent name="suggest" class="solr.SpellCheckComponent">
    <lst name="spellchecker">
      <str name="name">a_suggest</str>
      <str name="classname">
  org.apache.solr.spelling.suggest.Suggester</str>
      <str name="lookupImpl">
  org.apache.solr.spelling.suggest.fst.FSTLookup</str>
      <str name="field">a_spell</str>
      <!-- <float name="threshold">0.005</float> -->
      <str name="buildOnOptimize">true</str>
      <int name="weightBuckets">100</int><!-- an FST option -->
    </lst>
  </searchComponent>
```

The first part of this is a request handler definition just for using the Suggester. Note that `spellcheck.onlyMorePopular` was an atypical option for spell-check suggestions, but in the Suggester, this parameter means that the results should be sorted by frequency (versus alphabetically)—almost certainly what is desired. The `weightBuckets` option is specific to FSTLookup. The FST approximates the frequency of the terms it stores into a discrete set of buckets, defaulting to 10. It can range between 1 and 255.

Increase weightBuckets

In my experience, increasing `weightBuckets` to 100 or more improves the fidelity of the weights, resulting in more relevant suggestions. It will come at some performance cost, though. It is unclear at what value it is negligible or not.

The second part of this is an instantiation of the spell-check search component but named `suggest`. What makes this use the Suggester is the `classname` setting referencing the implementation code. The dictionary here is loaded from the `a_spell` field in the main index, but if a file is desired, then you can provide the `sourceLocation` parameter. The document frequency threshold for suggestions is commented here because MusicBrainz has unique names that we don't want filtered out. However, in common scenarios this threshold is advised.

As the Suggester is based on the spell-check component, it needs to be *built*, which is the process of loading the dictionary into memory. If you try to get suggestions beforehand, there will be no results. Suggestions only take a couple seconds or so to build and so I recommend building it automatically on startup via a firstSearcher warming query in solrconfig.xml:

```
<query>
...
    <listener event="firstSearcher" class="solr.QuerySenderListener">
      <arr name="queries">
        <lst>
          <str name="qt">/suggest</str>
          <str name="spellcheck.build">true</str>
        </lst>
        ...
      </arr>
    </listener>
...
</query>
```

To be kept up-to-date, it needs to be re-built from time to time. If commits are infrequent, you should use the buildOnCommit setting. We've chosen the buildOnOptimize setting.

Now let's issue a request to the Suggester. Here's a completion for the incomplete query string sma:

```
http://localhost:8983/solr/mbartists/suggest?q=sma&wt=json
```

And the output, indented:

```
{
  "responseHeader":{
    "status":0,
    "QTime":1},
  "spellcheck":{
    "suggestions":[
      "sma",{
        "numFound":4,
        "startOffset":0,
        "endOffset":3,
        "suggestion":["sma",
          "small",
          "smaak",
          "smack"]},
        "collation","sma"]}}
```

For more information about the Suggester, see the wiki: `http://wiki. apache.org/solr/Suggester`. You'll find information on alternatives to the FST implementation, and other details. However, some secrets of the Suggester are still undocumented, buried in the code.

Query term completion via the Terms component

The Terms component is used to expose raw indexed term information, including term frequency, for an indexed field. It has a lot of options for paging into this voluminous data and filtering out terms by term frequency.

For implementing suggestion functionality, the terms component has the benefit of using no Java heap memory and consequently there is no initialization penalty. It's always up to date with the indexed data, like faceting but unlike the Suggester. The performance is typically good but for high query load on large indexes, it will suffer compared to the other approaches. An interesting feature unique to this approach is a regular expression term match option. This can be used for case-insensitive matching, but it probably doesn't scale too many terms.

Here is how to set it up in `solrconfig.xml` for suggestions of MusicBrainz artist names:

```
<searchComponent name="terms" class="solr.TermsComponent"/>

<!-- A request handler for demonstrating the terms component for query
term-complete/suggest-->
<requestHandler name="/termsSuggest" class="solr.SearchHandler">
  <lst name="defaults">
    <bool name="terms">true</bool>
    <str name="terms.fl">a_spell</str>
    <str name="terms.sort">count</str>
    <int name="terms.limit">5</int>
    <!-- <int name="terms.mincount">2</int> -->
  </lst>
  <arr name="components">
    <str>terms</str>
  </arr>
</requestHandler>
```

And here is a request to complete the word `sma`:

```
http://localhost:8983/solr/mbartists/termsSuggest?terms.prefix=sma&wt=
json&omitHeader=true
```

And here's the response, indented:

```
{
  "terms":{
    "a_spell":[
      "small",110,
      "smart",50,
      "smash",36,
      "smalley",9,
      "smallwood",9]}}
```

For more information about this component, visit Solr's wiki:

```
http://wiki.apache.org/solr/TermsComponent
```

The QueryElevation component

At times, it may be desired to make editorial / manual modifications to the search results of particular user queries. This might be done as a solution to a popular user query that doesn't score an expected document sufficiently high—if it even matched at all. The query might have found nothing at all, perhaps due to a common misspelling. The opposite may also be true: the top result for a popular user query might yield a document that technically matched according to your search configuration, but certainly isn't what you were looking for. Another usage scenario is implementing a system akin to paid keywords for certain documents to be on top for certain user queries.

This feature isn't a general approach to fix queries not yielding effective search results; it is a band-aid for that problem. If a query isn't returning an expected document scored sufficiently high enough (if at all), then use Solr's query debugging to observe the score computation. You may end up troubleshooting text analysis issues too, if a search query doesn't match an expected document—perhaps by adding a synonym. The end result may be tuning the boosts or applying function queries to incorporate other relevant fields into the scoring. When you are satisfied with the scoring and just need to make an occasional editorial decision, then this component is for you.

Configuration

This search component is not in the standard component list and so it must be registered with a handler in `solrconfig.xml`. Here we'll add it to the `mb_artists` request handler definition, just for this example, anyway.

```
<requestHandler name="mb_artists" class="solr.SearchHandler">
  <lst name="defaults">
...
  </lst>
  <arr name="last-components">
    <str>elevateArtists</str>
  </arr>
</requestHandler>

<searchComponent name="elevateArtists"
    class="solr.QueryElevationComponent">
  <str name="queryFieldType">text</str>
  <str name="config-file">elevateArtists.xml</str>
  <str name="forceElevation">false</str>
</searchComponent>
```

This excerpt also reveals the registration of the search component using the same name as that referenced in `last-components`. A name was chosen reflecting the fact that this elevation configuration is only for artists. There are three named configuration parameters for a query elevation component, and they are explained as follows:

- `config-file`: This is a reference to the configuration file containing the editorial adjustments. As most other configuration files, it can be located in Solr's `conf` directory.

> `config-file` can also be placed within the `data` directory (usually a sibling to `conf`) where it will be reloaded, when Solr's internal `IndexReaders` get reloaded which occurs for commits of new data, Solr core reloads, and some other events. This presents an interesting option if the elevation choices need to be loaded more often.

- `queryFieldType`: This is a reference to a field type in `schema.xml`. It is used to normalize both a query (the `q` parameter) and the query text attribute found in the configuration file for comparison purposes. A field type might be crafted just for this purpose, but it should suffice to simply choose one that at least performs lowercasing. By default, there is no normalization.

- forceElevation: The query elevation component fools Solr into thinking the specified documents matched the user's query and scored the highest. However, by default, it will not violate the desired sort as specified by the sort parameter. In order to force the elevated documents to the top no matter what sort is, set this parameter to true.

Let's take a peek at elevateArtists.xml:

```
<elevate>
  <query text="corgan">
    <doc id="Artist:11650" /><!--the Smashing Pumpkins-->
    <doc id="Artist:510" /><!-- Green Day -->
    <doc id="Artist:35656" exclude="true" /><!-- Starchildren -->
  </query>
  <!-- others queries... -->
</elevate>
```

In this elevation file, we've specified that when a user searches for corgan, the Smashing Pumpkins then Green Day should appear in the top two positions in the search results (assuming typical sort of a descending score) and that the artist Starchildren is to be excluded. Note that query elevation kicks in when the configured query text matches the user's query exactly, while taking into consideration configured text analysis. Thus a search for billy corgan would not be affected by this configuration.

This component is quite simple with unsurprising results, so an example of this in action is not given. The only thing notable about the results when searching for corgan with the configuration mentioned above is that the top two results, the Smashing Pumpkins and Green Day, have scores of 1.72 and 0.0 respectively, yet the maxScore value in the result element is 11.3. Normally a default sort results in the first document having the same score as the maximum score, but in this case that happens at the third position, as the first two were inserted by this component. Moreover, normally a result document has a score greater than 0, but in this case one was inserted by this component that never matched the user's query.

The MoreLikeThis component

Have you ever searched for something and found a link that wasn't quite what you were looking for but was reasonably close? If you were using an Internet search engine such as Google, then you may have tried the "more like this…" link next to a search result. Some sites use other language like "find similar…" or "related documents…" As these links suggest, they show you pages similar to another page. Solr supports **more-like-this (MLT)** too.

The MLT capability in Solr can be used in the following three ways:

- **As a search component**: The MLT search component performs MLT analysis on each document returned in a search. This is not usually desired and so it is rarely used.

- **As a dedicated request handler**: The MLT request handler will give MLT results based on a specific indexed document. This is commonly used in reaction to a user clicking a "more like this" link on existing search results. The key input to this option is a reference to the indexed document that you want similar results for.

- **As a request handler with externally supplied text**: The MLT request handler can give MLT results based on text posted to the request handler. For example, if you were to send a text file to the request handler, then it would return the documents in the index that are most similar to it. This is atypical, but an interesting option nonetheless.

The essences of the internal workings of MLT operate like this:

1. Gather all of the terms with frequency information from the input document:
   - If the input document is a reference to a document within the index, then loop over the fields listed in `mlt.fl`, and then the term information needed is readily there for the taking if the field has `termVectors` enabled. Otherwise get the stored text, and re-analyze it to derive the terms (slower).
   - If the input document is posted as text to the request handler, then analyze it to derive the terms. The analysis used is that configured for the first field listed in `mlt.fl`.

2. Filter the terms based on configured thresholds. What remains are only the *interesting terms*.

3. Construct a query with these interesting terms across all of the fields listed in `mlt.fl`.

Configuration parameters

In the following configuration options, the input document is either each search result returned if MLT is used as a component, or it is the first document returned from a query to the MLT request handler, or it is the plain text sent to the request handler. It simply depends on how you use it.

Parameters specific to the MLT search component

Using the MLT search component adorns an existing search with MLT results for each document returned.

- `mlt`: You must set this to `true` to enable MLT when using it as a search component. It defaults to `false`.

- `mlt.count`: The number of MLT results to be returned for each document returned in the main query. It defaults to `5`.

Parameters specific to the MLT request handler

Using the MLT request handler is more like a regular search except that the results are documents similar to the input document. Additionally, any filters (the `fq` parameter) that are specified are also in effect.

- `q`, `start`, `rows`: The MLT request handler uses the same standard parameters for the query start offset, and row count as used for querying. But in this case, `start` and `rows` is for paging into the MLT results instead of the results of the query. The query is typically one that simply references one document such as `id:12345` (if your unique field looks like this). `start` defaults to `0` and `rows` to `10`.

- `mlt.match.offset`: This parameter is the offset into the results of `q` for picking which document is the input document. It defaults to `0` so that the first result from `q` is chosen. As `q` will typically search for one document, this is rarely modified.

- `mlt.match.include`: The input document is normally included in the response if it is in the index (see the `match` element in the output of the example) because this parameter defaults to `true`. Set this to `false` to exclude this if that information isn't needed.

- `mlt.interestingTerms`: If this is set to `list` or `details`, then the so-called *interesting terms* that the MLT uses for the similarity query are returned with the results in an `interestingTerms` element. If you enable `mlt.boost`, then specifying `details` will additionally return the query boost value used for each term. `none` or `blank`, the default, disables this. Aside from diagnostic purposes, it might be useful to display these in the user interface, either listed out or in a tag cloud.

> Use `mlt.interestingTerms` while experimenting with the results to get an insight into why the MLT results matched the documents it did.

- `facet, ...`: The MLT request handler supports faceting the MLT results. See the previous chapter on how to use faceting.

> Additionally, remember to configure the MLT request handler in `solrconfig.xml`. An example of this is shown later in the chapter.

Common MLT parameters

These parameters are common to both the search component and request handler. Some of the thresholds here are for tuning which terms are *interesting* to MLT. In general, expanding thresholds (that is, lowering minimums and increasing maximums) will yield more useful MLT results at the expense of performance. The parameters are explained as follows:

- `mlt.fl`: A comma or space separated list of fields to consider in MLT. The *interesting terms* are searched within these fields only. These field(s) must be indexed. Furthermore, assuming the input document is in the index instead of supplied externally (as is typical), then each field should ideally have `termVectors` set to `true` in the schema (best for query performance although index size is larger). If that isn't done, then the field must be stored so that MLT can re-analyze the text at runtime to derive the term vector information. It isn't necessary to use the same strategy for each field.

- `mlt.qf`: Different field boosts can optionally be specified with this parameter. This uses the same syntax as the `qf` parameter used by the dismax query parser (for example: `field1^2.0 field2^0.5`). The fields referenced should also be listed in `mlt.fl`. If there is a title or similar identifying field, then this field should probably be boosted higher.

- `mlt.mintf`: The minimum number of times (frequency) a term must be used within a document (across those fields in `mlt.fl` anyway) for it to be an *interesting term*. The default is 2. For small documents, such as in the case of our MusicBrainz data set, try lowering this to 1.

- `mlt.mindf`: The minimum number of documents that a term must be used in for it to be an *interesting term*. It defaults to 5, which is fairly reasonable. For very small indexes, as little as 2 is plausible, and maybe larger for large multi-million document indexes with common words.

- `mlt.minwl`: The minimum number of characters in an *interesting term*. It defaults to 0, effectively disabling the threshold. Consider raising this to 2 or 3.

- `mlt.maxwl`: The maximum number of characters in an *interesting term*. It defaults to 0 and disables the threshold. Some really long terms might be flukes in input data and are out of your control, but most likely this threshold can be skipped.

- `mlt.maxqt`: The maximum number of *interesting terms* that will be used in an MLT query. It is limited to 25 by default, which is plenty.

- `mlt.maxntp`: Fields without `termVectors` enabled take longer for MLT to analyze. This parameter sets a threshold to limit the number of terms to consider in a given field to further limit the performance impact. It defaults to 5000.

- `mlt.boost`: This boolean toggles whether or not to boost each *interesting term* used in the MLT query differently, depending on how interesting the MLT module deems it to be. It defaults to `false`, but try setting it to `true` and evaluating the results.

Usage advice

For ideal query performance, ensure that `termVectors` is enabled for the field(s) referenced in `mlt.fl`. In order to further increase performance, use fewer fields, perhaps just one dedicated for use with MLT. Using the `copyField` directive in the schema makes this easy. The disadvantage is that the source fields cannot be boosted differently with `mlt.qf`. However, you might have two fields for MLT as a compromise. Use a typical full complement of text analysis including lowercasing, synonyms, using a stop list (such as `StopFilterFactory`), and aggressive stemming in order to normalize the terms as much as possible. The field needn't be stored if its data is copied from some other field that is stored. During an experimentation period, look for *interesting terms* that are not so interesting for inclusion in the stop word list. Lastly, some of the configuration thresholds which scope the interesting terms can be adjusted based on experimentation.

MLT results example

Firstly, an important disclaimer on this example is in order. *The MusicBrainz data set is not conducive to applying the MLT feature, because it doesn't have any descriptive text.* If there were perhaps an artist description and/or widespread use of user-supplied tags, then there might be sufficient information to make MLT useful. However, to provide an example of the input and output of MLT, we will use MLT with MusicBrainz anyway.

We'll be using the request handler method, the recommended approach. The MLT request handler needs to be configured in solrconfig.xml. The important bit is the reference to the class, the rest of it is our prerogative.

```
<requestHandler name="mlt_tracks" class="solr.MoreLikeThisHandler">
  <lst name="defaults">
    <str name="mlt.fl">t_name</str>
    <str name="mlt.mintf">1</str>
    <str name="mlt.mindf">2</str>
    <str name="mlt.boost">true</str>
  </lst>
</requestHandler>
```

This configuration shows that we're basing the MLT on just track names. Let's now try a query for tracks similar to the song "The End is the Beginning is the End" by The Smashing Pumpkins. The query was performed with echoParams to clearly show the options used:

```
<?xml version="1.0" encoding="UTF-8"?>
<response>
<lst name="responseHeader">
  <int name="status">0</int>
  <int name="QTime">2</int>
  <lst name="params">
    <str name="mlt.mintf">1</str>
    <str name="mlt.mindf">2</str>
    <str name="mlt.boost">true</str>
    <str name="mlt.fl">t_name</str>
    <str name="rows">5</str>
    <str name="mlt.interestingTerms">details</str>
    <str name="indent">on</str>
    <str name="echoParams">all</str>
    <str name="fl">t_a_name,t_name,score</str>
    <str name="q">id:"Track:1810669"</str>
    <str name="qt">mlt_tracks</str>
  </lst>
```

```
</lst>
<result name="match" numFound="1" start="0"
    maxScore="16.06509">
  <doc>
    <float name="score">16.06509</float>
    <str name="t_a_name">The Smashing Pumpkins</str>
    <str name="t_name">The End Is the Beginning Is the End</str>
  </doc>
</result>
<result name="response" numFound="853390" start="0"
    maxScore="6.352738">
  <doc>
    <float name="score">6.352738</float>
    <str name="t_a_name">In Grey</str>
    <str name="t_name">End Is the Beginning</str>
  </doc>
  <doc>
    <float name="score">5.6811075</float>
    <str name="t_a_name">Royal Anguish</str>
    <str name="t_name">The End Is the Beginning</str>
  </doc>
  <doc>
    <float name="score">5.6811075</float>
    <str name="t_a_name">Mangala Vallis</str>
    <str name="t_name">Is the End the Beginning</str>
  </doc>
  <doc>
    <float name="score">5.6811075</float>
    <str name="t_a_name">Ape Face</str>
    <str name="t_name">The End Is the Beginning</str>
  </doc>
  <doc>
    <float name="score">5.052292</float>
    <str name="t_a_name">The Smashing Pumpkins</str>
    <str name="t_name">The End Is the Beginning Is the End</str>
  </doc>
</result>
<lst name="interestingTerms">
  <float name="t_name:end">1.0</float>
  <float name="t_name:is">0.7420872</float>
  <float name="t_name:the">0.6686879</float>
  <float name="t_name:beginning">0.6207893</float>
</lst>
</response>
```

The `<result name="match">` element is there due to `mlt.match.include` defaulting to `true`. The `<result name="response" ...>` element has the main MLT search results. The fact that so many documents were found is not material to any MLT response; all it takes is one interesting term in common. The *interesting terms* were deliberately requested so that we can get an insight on the basis of the similarity. The fact that `is` and `the` were included shows that we don't have a stop list for this field—an obvious thing we'd need to fix. Nearly any stop list is going to have such words.

> For further diagnostic information on the score computation, set `debugQuery` to `true`. This is a highly advanced method but exposes information invaluable to understand the scores. Doing so in our example shows that the main reason the top hit was on top was not only because it contained all of the interesting terms as did the others in the top 5, but also because it is the shortest in length (a high `fieldNorm`). The #5 result had "Beginning" twice, which resulted in a high term frequency (`termFreq`), but it wasn't enough to bring it to the top.

The Stats component

The Stats component computes some mathematical statistics of specified numeric fields in the index. The main requirement is that the field be indexed. The following statistics are computed over the non-null values (except `missing` which counts the nulls):

- `min`: The smallest value.
- `max`: The largest value.
- `sum`: The sum.
- `count`: The quantity of non-null values accumulated in these statistics.
- `missing`: The quantity of records skipped due to missing values.
- `sumOfSquares`: The sum of the square of each value. This is probably the least useful and is used internally to compute `stddev` efficiently.
- `mean`: The average value.
- `stddev`: The standard deviation of the values.

Configuring the stats component

This component performs a simple task and so as expected, it is also simple to configure.

- `stats`: Set this to `true` in order to enable the component. It defaults to `false`.

- `stats.field`: Set this to the name of the field to perform statistics on. It is required. This parameter can be set multiple times in order to perform statistics on more than one field.

- `stats.facet`: Optionally, set this to the name of the field in which you want to facet the statistics over. Instead of the results having just one set of stats (assuming one `stats.field`), there will be a set for each value in this field, and those statistics will be based on that corresponding subset of data. This parameter can be specified multiple times to compute the statistics over multiple fields' values. In addition, you can use the field-specific parameter name syntax for cases when you are computing stats on different fields and you want to use a different facet field for each statistic field. For example, you can specify `f.t_duration.stats.facet=tracktype` assuming a hypothetical field `tracktype` to categorize the `t_duration` statistics on. The field should be indexed and not tokenized.

 Due to bug SOLR-1782, a `stats.facet` field should *not* be multi-valued, and it should be limited to a string. If you don't heed this advice then the results are in question and you may get an error!

Statistics on track durations

Let's look at some statistics for the duration of tracks in MusicBrainz at:

```
http://localhost:8983/solr/mbtracks/select/?rows=0&indent=on&qt=
mb_tracks&stats=true&stats.field=t_duration
```

And here are the results:

```
<?xml version="1.0" encoding="UTF-8"?>
<response>
<lst name="responseHeader">
  <int name="status">0</int>
  <int name="QTime">5202</int>
</lst>
<result name="response" numFound="6977765" start="0"/>
<lst name="stats">
  <lst name="stats_fields">
    <lst name="t_duration">
```

```
      <double name="min">0.0</double>
      <double name="max">36059.0</double>
      <double name="sum">1.543289275E9</double>
      <long name="count">6977765</long>
      <long name="missing">0</long>
      <double name="sumOfSquares">5.21546498201E11</double>
      <double name="mean">221.1724348699046</double>
      <double name="stddev">160.70724790290328</double>
    </lst>
  </lst>
 </lst>
</response>
```

This query shows that on average, a song is `221` seconds (or 3 minutes 41 seconds) in length. An example using `stats.facet` would produce a much longer result, which won't be given here in order to leave space for other components. However, there is an example at `http://wiki.apache.org/solr/StatsComponent`.

The Clustering component

The Clustering component is a Solr *contrib module* that provides an extension point to integrate a clustering engine. **Clustering** is a technology that groups documents into *similar* clusters, using sophisticated statistical techniques. Each cluster is identified by a few words that were used to distinguish the documents in that cluster from the other clusters. As with the `MoreLikeThis` component which also uses statistical techniques, the quality of the results is hit or miss.

> The primary means of navigation / discovery of your data should generally be search and faceting. For so-called *un-structured text* use cases, there are, by definition, few attributes to facet on. Clustering search results and presenting tag-clouds (a visualization of faceting on words) are generally exploratory navigation methods of last-resort in the absence of more effective document metadata.

Presently, there are two **search-result clustering** algorithms available as part of the Carrot2 open source project that this module has adapters for. Solr ships with the needed third-party libraries—JAR files. The clustering component has an extension point to support **document clustering** with anticipation of a solution coming from the Apache Mahout open source project, but it has yet to materialize. Document clustering is different than search-result clustering as in that it is calculated on the entire corpus in advance of searches.

To get started with exploring this feature, I'll direct you to Solr's wiki: `http://wiki.apache.org/solr/ClusteringComponent`. There is "quick start" set of instructions in which you'll be clustering Solr's example documents in under five minutes. It should be easy to copy the necessary configuration to your Solr instance and modify it to refer to your document's fields. As you dive into the technology, Carrot2's powerful GUI workbench should be of great help in tuning it to get more effective results. For a public demonstration of Carrot2's clustering, go here: `http://search.carrot2.org/stable/search`

Result grouping/Field collapsing

Result Grouping and **Field Collapsing** are two names that suggest different ways of looking at the same Solr feature. Result grouping, the preferred name, is the ability to group the search results by a field value or some other criteria. This is very useful in using Solr for reporting but also for presenting top search results from multiple document categories. Field collapsing, the original name, is having the ability to collapse (that is remove / withhold) search result documents that have the same field value as a previous document. A common use-case is to mimic how Google only shows one result for a website. The feature is roughly similar to a SQL `group by` query; but the SQL incarnation returns aggregate summary rows for each group whereas in Solr you get back a configurable number of the top rows for each group.

 This important feature was officially first released in Solr 3.3. Solr 3.4 added post-group faceting and Solr 3.5, not yet released as I write this, will have distributed-search support. Expect to see other various improvements soon.

For an example of this feature in MusicBrainz, consider attempting to provide a search for tracks where the tracks collapse to the artist. If a search matches multiple tracks produced by the same artist, then only the highest scoring track will be returned for that artist. That particular document in the results can be said to have "rolled-up" or "collapsed" those that were removed.

A track's artist ID is stored in `t_a_id` with field type `long`. The grouping capability in Solr 3 is limited to grouping on `string` fields; doing otherwise yields an error. I added a string variant of this field named `t_a_id_str` with a `copyField` to copy the value from `t_a_id`. Here's the URL for a search for `Cherub Rock` using the `mb_tracks` request handler collapsing on `t_a_id_str`:

```
http://localhost:8983/solr/mbtracks/select?qt=mb_tracks
&q=Cherub+Rock&fl=score,id,t_a_id,t_a_name,t_name,t_r_name
&rows=2&group=true&group.field=t_a_id_str&group.ngroups=true
```

We only asked for two rows, for brevity. Here are the results:

```
<response>
<lst name="responseHeader">
  <int name="status">0</int>
  <int name="QTime">299</int>
</lst>
<lst name="grouped">
  <lst name="t_a_id_str">
    <int name="matches">87</int>
    <int name="ngroups">18</int>
    <arr name="groups">
      <lst>
        <str name="groupValue">11650</str>
        <result name="doclist" numFound="69" start="0"
            maxScore="14.219993">
          <doc>
            <float name="score">14.219993</float>
            <str name="id">Track:414903</str>
            <long name="t_a_id">11650</long>
            <str name="t_a_name">The Smashing Pumpkins</str>
            <str name="t_name">Cherub Rock</str>
            <str name="t_r_name">Cherub Rock</str>
          </doc>
        </result>
      </lst>
      <lst>
        <str name="groupValue">33677</str>
        <result name="doclist" numFound="1" start="0"
            maxScore="13.9314">
          <doc>
            <float name="score">13.9314</float>
            <str name="id">Track:6855353</str>
            <long name="t_a_id">33677</long>
            <str name="t_a_name">Razed in Black</str>
            <str name="t_name">Cherub Rock</str>
            <str name="t_r_name">Cherub Rock: A Gothic-Industrial
                Tribute to the Smashing Pumpkins</str>
          </doc>
        </result>
      </lst>
    </arr>
  </lst>
</lst>
</response>
```

I've highlighted the beginning part of the grouping, which reflects that a grouped response has a fairly different response structure than a regular one. The `matches` number is 87 which is equivalent to `numFound` attribute when there is no grouping—the number of matching documents. `ngroups` is 18, which is the number of groups found. Each group begins by showing the group's value and then a document list structure that looks just like normal search results. Instead of this grouped response, you'll see a parameter soon that will use the normal response format but it lacks information like how many documents are in the group.

Configuring result grouping

Result grouping is actually not a Solr component but it *feels* like one because it modifies the response and it has its own set of parameters that start with a common prefix. Due to the ways it must interact with the search, it is implemented internally as an adjunct to the Query component.

Grouping is either by field value, as we have explained thus far, or by documents that match a given query. This is analogous to how the facet component features field value faceting (`facet.field`) and facet queries (`facet.query`), but for grouping. You can set the corresponding grouping parameters any number of times, but you must set at least one of them or you'll get an error. Each grouping list is independent.

The following are a list of the query parameters to configure result grouping:

- `group:` This must be set to `true` to enable result grouping.
- `group.field`: The name of the field to group results on. The field requirements are the same as sorting—one indexed token. Additionally, the field can only be a string; however, Solr 4 lifts that restriction. This parameter can be set multiple times, which adds separate group lists to the response.

 Grouping on multiple fields as one grouping is not supported. You can achieve this by creating a combined field in the index and grouping on that.

- `group.query:` A Solr query that will group all documents that match it into a single group. This parameter can be set multiple times, which adds separate group lists to the response. This parameter is analogous to `facet.query` but for grouping.

- group.truncate: (new in Solr 3.4) A boolean option that, when enabled, will make the Facet and Stats components only use the first document in each group, ignoring all other documents. This feature is also known as *post group faceting*. It's disabled by default but it's likely you should enable it.

 Multi-select faceting (tagging and excluding filters) doesn't work with group.truncate—see SOLR-2780. It might be fixed by Solr 3.5.

- rows and start and sort: These parameters page across the groups and sort the groups. So, rows means the number of groups to return, not the number of documents, which might be more depending on group.limit. If group.format is changed to simple, then rows and start (but not sort) retains the original document based meaning.

- group.limit: The number of documents to return within each group. By default, this is set to 1—typical usage for a field collapsing scenario.

- group.offset: The offset into the result documents of each group to page into. Defaults to 0.

- group.sort: The sort order for the documents within each group. If not specified, it sorts by how the groups are sorted.

- group.ngroups: A boolean that, when enabled, will return the number of matching groups in the response. It's disabled by default for performance reasons.

- group.format: The response format: grouped (the default) or simple (that is flat). The simple format appears like a flattened version of grouped, as it is a single list of documents. It does not contain information on how many documents in total matched each group because each group is not delineated. The start and rows parameters now operate on the resulting flat document list instead of the groups.

- group.main: A boolean option that, when true, will make the response formatted like a normal non-grouped search, taking the documents from the first group only. It forces group.format to simple, and therefore the start and rows parameters work normally.

- group.cache.percent: The grouping cache size, expressed in terms of the percentage of the number of documents in the index (0-100). It defaults to 0. A plain keyword search or match-all-docs query performs best *without* the cache, whereas other queries perform better. If you wish to use caching, a suggested number is 20. The cache is an intermediate transient one used in the course of the grouping query execution.

There are some features that have already been implemented in the Solr 4 codebase that are unlikely to happen in Solr 3, like grouping by function query, and grouping on all field types (not just string). Remember that result grouping is fairly new, with improvements to it happening at a quick pace. Support for distributed-search (see *Chapter 10, Scaling Solr*) is coming in Solr 3.5, for example, but it doesn't support `group.truncate`. For the latest information, see Solr's Wiki: `http://wiki.apache.org/solr/FieldCollapsing`

The TermVector component

This component is used to expose the raw **term vector** information for fields that have this option enabled in the schema—`termVectors` set to `true`. It is `false` by default. The term vector is per field and per document. It lists each indexed term in order with the offsets into the original text, term frequency, and document frequency. It's not that useful so I'll refer you to the wiki for further information:

`http://wiki.apache.org/solr/TermVectorComponent`

Summary

Consider what you've seen with Solr search components: highlighting search results, suggesting search spelling corrections, query autocomplete, editorially modifying query results for particular user queries, suggesting documents "more like this", calculating mathematical statistics of indexed numbers, grouping/collapsing search results. By now it should be clear why the text search capability of your database is inadequate for all but basic needs. Even Lucene-based solutions don't necessarily have the extensive feature-set that you've seen here. You may have once thought that searching was a relatively basic thing, but Solr search components really demonstrate how much more there is to it.

The chapters thus far have aimed to show you the majority of the features in Solr and to serve as a reference guide for them. The remaining chapters don't follow this pattern. In the next chapter, you're going to learn about various deployment concerns, such as logging, testing, security, and backups.

8
Deployment

Now that you have identified the information you want to make searchable, built the Solr schema to support your expected queries, and made the tweaks to the configuration you need, you're ready to deploy your Solr based search platform into production. While the process of deployment may seem simple after all of the effort you've gone through in development, it brings its own set of challenges. In this chapter, we'll look at the issues that come up when going from "Solr runs on my desktop" to "Solr is ready for the enterprise".

We'll see the following topics in this chapter:

- Implementation methodology
- Install Solr into a Servlet container
- Logging
- A SearchHandler per search interface
- Solr cores
- Monitoring Solr
- Securing Solr

Deployment methodology for Solr

There are a number of questions that you need to ask yourself in order to inform the development of a smooth deployment strategy for Solr. The deployment process should ideally be fully scripted and integrated into the existing **Configuration Management (CM)** process of your application.

Configuration Management is the task of tracking and controlling changes in the software. CM attempts to make the changes knowable that occur in software as it evolves to mitigate mistakes caused due to those changes.

Questions to ask

The list of questions that you'll want to answer to work in conjunction with your operations team include:

- How similar is my deployment environment to my development and test environments? Can I project that if one Solr instance was enough to meet my load requirements in test then it is also applicable to the load expected in production based on having similar physical hardware?

- Do I need multiple Solr servers to meet the projected load? If so, then what approach am I to use? Replication? Distributed Search? We cover this topic in *Chapter 10, Scaling Solr*.

- Do I have an existing build tool such as Ant/MSBuild/Capistrano with which to integrate the deployment process into? Does my organization use a deployment tool such as Puppet or Chef that I can leverage?

- How will I import the initial data into Solr? Is this a one time only process that might take hours or days to perform and needs to be scheduled ahead of time? Is there a nightly process in the application that will perform this step? Can I trigger the load process from the deploy script?

- Have I changed the source code required to build Solr to meet my own needs? Do I need to version it in my own source control repository? Can I package my modifications to Solr as discrete components instead of changing the source of Solr and rebuilding?

- Do I have full access to index data in the production environment, or do I have to coordinate with an Operations Team who are responsible for controlling access to production? If Operations is performing the indexing tasks, are the steps required properly documented and automated?

- Do I need to define acceptance tests for ensuring Solr is returning the appropriate results for a specific search before moving to production?

- What are the defined performance targets, such as requests per second, time to index data, time to perform query that Solr needs to meet? Are these documented as a Service Level Agreement (SLA)?

- Into what kind of servlet container (Tomcat, Jetty, and so on) will Solr be deployed? Does how I secure Solr change depending on the servlet container?

- What is my monitoring strategy for making sure Solr is performing properly? This isn't just about Solr's response time or error monitoring but critically includes the user queries. The single best tool for improving your search relevance is to look at your user queries. A reasonable user query that returns zero results directly points to how to improve your relevancy.

- Do I need to store index data directories separately from application code directories, for instance on a separate hard drive? If I have small enough indexes to fit in RAM, can I use a memory-based filesystem?

- What is my backup strategy for my indexes, if any? If the indexes can be rebuilt quickly from another data source, then backups may not be needed. But if the indexes are the "Gold Master", such as from crawling the Web for data that can't be re-crawled, or the lead time to rebuild an index is too great, then frequent backups are crucial.

- Are any scripted administration tasks required, for example performing index optimizations, old backups removal, deletion of stale data, or rebuilding spell check dictionaries?

- Am I better off with an externally hosted Solr capability? There are a number of companies that have launched SaaS offerings for Solr, from Acquia offering hosted Solr search specifically for Drupal based sites to WebSolr and SolrHQ providing generic Solr hosting.

Installing Solr into a Servlet container

Solr is deployed as a simple **WAR (Web application archive)** file that packages up servlets, JSP pages, code libraries, and all of the other bits that are required to run Solr. Therefore, Solr can be deployed into any Java EE Servlet Container that meets the Servlet 2.4 specification, such as Apache Tomcat, Websphere, JRun, and GlassFish, as well as Jetty, which ships with Solr to run the example app.

Differences between Servlet containers

The key thing to resolve when working with Solr and the various Servlet containers is that technically you are supposed to compile a single WAR file and deploy that into the Servlet container. It is the container's responsibility to figure out how to unpack the components that make up the WAR file and deploy them properly. For example, with Jetty you place the WAR file in the `/webapps` directory, but when you start Jetty, it unpacks the WAR file in the `/work` directory as a subdirectory, with a somewhat cryptic name that looks something like `Jetty_0_0_0_0_8983_solr.war__solr__k1kf17`. In contrast, with Apache Tomcat, you place the `solr.war` file into the `/webapp` directory. When you either start up Tomcat, or Tomcat notices the new `.war` file, it unpacks it into the `/webapp` directory. Therefore, you will have the original `/webapp/solr.war` and the newly unpacked (exploded) `/webapp/solr` version. The Servlet specification carefully defines what makes up a WAR file. However, it does not define exactly how to unpack and deploy the WAR files, so your specific steps will depend on the Servlet container you are using. For information specific to various servlet containers, see Solr's wiki:
`http://wiki.apache.org/solr/SolrInstall`

 If you are not strongly predisposed to choosing a particular Servlet container, then consider Jetty, which is a remarkably lightweight, stable, and fast Servlet container. While written by the Jetty project, they have provided a reasonably unbiased summary of the various reasons to choose Jetty at `http://www.webtide.com/choose/jetty.jsp`

Defining solr.home property

Probably the biggest thing that trips up folks deploying into different containers is specifying the `solr.home` property. Solr stores all of its configuration information outside of the deployed `webapp`, separating the **data** part from the **code** part for running Solr. In the example app, while Solr is deployed and running from a subdirectory in `/work`, the `solr.home` directory is pointing to the top level `/solr` directory, where all of the data and configuration information is kept. You can think of `solr.home` as being analogous to where the data and configuration is stored for a relational database like MySQL. You don't package your MySQL database as part of the WAR file, and nor do you package your Lucene indexes.

By default, Solr expects the `solr.home` directory to be a subdirectory called `/solr` in the current working directory as defined by the Servlet container. With both Jetty and Tomcat you can override that by passing in a JVM argument that is somewhat confusingly namespaced under the `solr` namespace as `solr.solr.home`:

    -Dsolr.solr.home=/Users/epugh/solrbook/solr

Alternatively, you may find it easier to specify the `solr.home` property by appending it to the `JAVA_OPTS` system variable. On Unix systems you would do:

```
>>export JAVA_OPTS=\"$JAVA_OPTS -Dsolr.solr.home=/Users/epugh/
  solrbook/solr"
```

Or lastly, you may choose to use JNDI with Tomcat to specify the `solr.home` property as well as where the `solr.war` file is located. **JNDI (Java Naming and Directory Interface)** is a very powerful, if somewhat difficult to use, directory service that allows Java clients such as Tomcat to look up data and objects by name.

By configuring the stanza appropriately, I was able to load up the solr.war (cit) file and home directory from the example configuration shipped with Jetty using Tomcat instead. The following stanza went in the `/apache-tomcat-6-0.18/conf/ Catalina/localhost` directory that I downloaded from `http://tomcat.apache. org`, in a file called `solr.xml`:

```
<Context docBase="/Users/epugh/solr_src/example/webapps/solr.war"
  debug="0" crossContext="true" >
<Environment name="solr/home" type="java.lang.String"
        value="/Users/epugh/solr_src/example/solr" override="true" />
</Context>
```

I had to create the `./Catalina/localhost` subdirectories manually.

Note the somewhat confusing JNDI name for `solr.home` is `solr/home`. This is because JNDI is a tree structure, with the home variable being specified as a node of the Solr branch of the tree. By specifying multiple different context stanzas, you can deploy multiple separate Solr instances in a single Tomcat instance.

Logging

Solr's logging facility provides a wealth of information, from basic performance statistics, to what queries are being run, to any exceptions encountered by Solr. The log files should be one of the first places to look when you want to investigate any issues with your Solr deployment. There are two types of logs:

- The HTTP server request style logs, which record the individual web requests made to Solr.
- The Solr application logging that uses SLF4J (Simple Logging Framework for Java, a logging façade),which uses the built-in Java JDK logging facility to log the internal operations of Solr.

HTTP server request access logs

The HTTP server request logs record the requests that come in and are defined by the Servlet container in which Solr is deployed. For example, the default configuration for managing the server logs in Jetty is defined in `jetty.xml`:

```
<Ref id="RequestLog">
  <Set name="requestLog">
    <New id="RequestLogImpl" class="org.mortbay.jetty.NCSARequestLog">
    <Arg><SystemProperty name="jetty.logs"
     default="./logs"/>/yyyy_mm_dd.request.log</Arg>
  <Set name="retainDays">90</Set>
  <Set name="append">true</Set>
  <Set name="extended">false</Set>
  <Set name="LogTimeZone">GMT</Set>
    </New>
  </Set>
</Ref>
```

The log directory is created in the subdirectory of the Jetty directory. If you have multiple drives and want to store your data separately from your application directory, then you can specify a different directory. Depending on how much traffic you get, you should adjust the number of days to preserve the log files.

I recommend you keep the log files for as long as possible by archiving them. The search request data in these files is some of the best data available to help you improve the relevancy of your search results. By using web analytics tools such as a venerable commercial package WebTrends or the open source AWStats package to parse your request logs, you can quickly visualize how often different queries are run, and what search terms are frequently being used. This leads to a better understanding of what your users are searching for.

Tailing the HTTP logs is one of the best ways to keep an eye on a deployed Solr. You'll see each request as it comes in and can gain a feel for what types of transactions are being performed, whether it is frequent indexing of new data, or different types of searches being performed. A pause in the logging will quickly highlight Garbage Collection issues!

The request time data will let you quickly see performance issues. Here is a sample of some requests being logged. You can see the first request is a POST to the `/solr/update` URL from a browser running locally (`127.0.0.1`) with the date. The request was successful, with a 200 HTTP status code being recorded. The POST took 149 milliseconds. The second line shows a request for the admin page being made, which also was successful and took a slow 3,816 milliseconds, primarily because in Jetty, the JSP page is compiled the first time it is requested.

The last line shows a search for `dell` being made to the `/solr/select` URL. You can see that up to 10 results were requested and that it was successfully executed in 378 milliseconds.

On a faster machine with more memory and a properly "warmed" Solr cache, you can expect a few 10s of millisecond result time. Unfortunately, you don't get to see the number of results returned, as this log only records the request.

```
127.0.0.1 - - [25/02/2009:22:57:14 +0000] "POST /solr/update HTTP/1.1"
200 149
127.0.0.1 - - [25/02/2009:22:57:33 +0000] "GET /solr/admin/ HTTP/1.1"
200 3816
127.0.0.1 - - [25/02/2009:22:57:33 +0000] "GET /solr/admin/
           solr-admin.css
       HTTP/1.1" 200 3846
127.0.0.1 - - [25/02/2009:22:57:33 +0000] "GET /solr/admin/favicon.ico
       HTTP/1.1" 200 1146
127.0.0.1 - - [25/02/2009:22:57:33 +0000] "GET /solr/admin/
           solr_small.png
       HTTP/1.1" 200 7926
127.0.0.1 - - [25/02/2009:22:57:33 +0000] "GET /solr/admin/favicon.ico
       HTTP/1.1" 200 1146
127.0.0.1 - - [25/02/2009:22:57:36 +0000] "GET /solr/select/?q=dell%0D
%0A&version=2.2&start=0&rows=10&indent=on
       HTTP/1.1" 200 378
```

While you may not see things quite the same way Neo did in the movie *The Matrix*, you will get a good gut feeling about how Solr is performing!

 AWStats is a full-featured open source request log file analyzer under the GPL license and available from `http://awstats.sourceforge.net`.

Solr application logging

Logging events is a crucial part of any enterprise system. Veteran Java programmers know that the history of Java and logging is complicated, resulting in a fragmented landscape. As of Version 1.4, Solr standardized on using the **Simple Logging Facade for Java (SLF4J)** package, which logs to another target logging package selected at runtime instead of at compile time. The default distribution of Solr targets Java's built-in logging (aka JDK logging), but now alternative more powerful packages like Log4j or Logback are easily supported.

Configuring logging output

By default, Solr's JDK logging configuration sends its logging messages to the standard error stream:

```
2009-02-26 13:00:51.415::INFO: Logging to STDERR via org.mortbay.log.
StdErrLog
```

Obviously, in a production environment, Solr will be running as a service, which won't be continuously monitoring the standard error stream. You will want the messages to be recorded to a log file instead. In order to set up basic logging to a file, create a logging.properties file at the root of Solr with the following contents:

```
# Default global logging level:
.level = INFO

# Write to a file:
handlers = java.util.logging.ConsoleHandler, java.util.logging.
FileHandler

# Write log messages in human readable format:
java.util.logging.FileHandler.formatter = java.util.logging.
SimpleFormatter
java.util.logging.ConsoleHandler.formatter = java.util.logging.
SimpleFormatter

# Log to the logs subdirectory, with log files named solrxxx.log
java.util.logging.FileHandler.pattern = ./logs/solr_log-%g.log
java.util.logging.FileHandler.append = true
java.util.logging.FileHandler.count = 10
java.util.logging.FileHandler.limit = 10000000 #Roughly 10MB
```

When you start Solr, you need to pass the following code snippet in the location of the logging.properties file:

```
>>java -Djava.util.logging.config.file=logging.properties -jar
  start.jar
```

By specifying two log handlers, you can send output to the console as well as log files. The FileHandler logging is configured to create up to 10 separate logs, each with 10 MB of information. The log files are appended, so that you can restart Solr and not lose previous logging information. Note, if you are running Solr as a service, it is probably going to redirect the STDERR output from the ConsoleHandler to a log file as well. In that case, you will want to remove the java.util. ConsoleHandler from the list of handlers. Another option is to reduce how much is considered as output by specifying java.util.logging.ConsoleHandler.level = WARNING.

Logging using Log4j

Most Java developers prefer Log4j over JDK logging. You might choose to configure Solr to use it instead, for any number of reasons:

- You're using a Servlet container that itself uses Log4j, such as JBoss. This would result in a more simplified and integrated approach.

- You wish to take advantage of the numerous Log4j **appenders** available, which can log to just about anything, including Windows Event Logs, SNMP, syslog, and so on.

- To use a Log4j compatible logging viewer such as:
    - **Chainsaw**—http://logging.apache.org/chainsaw/
    - **Vigilog**—http://vigilog.sourceforge.net/

- Familiarity—Log4j has been around since 1999 and is very popular.

The latest supported Log4j JAR file is in the 1.2 series and can be downloaded here at http://logging.apache.org/log4j/1.2/. Avoid **1.3** and **3.0**, which are defunct releases that don't have wide adoption.

In order to change Solr to use Log4j, just remove the slf4j-jdk14-1.5.5.jar from the webapp/WEB-INF/lib directory and replace it with slf4j-log4j12-1.5.5.jar. Of course, you must also place Log4j's JAR file in that directory. You can find the various SLF4J distributions at http://www.slf4j.org/dist/. Make sure that you download the distribution that matches the version of SLF4J packaged with Solr or upgrade Solr's versions. Otherwise you may end up with JAR compatibility issues. As Erik Hatcher in a post to the solr-dev mailing list memorably called it: *JARmageddon*.

More information on configuring Log4j is available at http://logging.apache.org/log4j/.

Jetty startup integration

Regardless of which logging solution you go with, you don't want to make the startup arguments for Solr more complex. You can leverage Jetty's configuration to specify these system properties during startup. Edit jetty.xml and add the following stanza to the outermost <Configure id="Server" class="org.mortbay.jetty.Server"/> element:

```
<Call class="java.lang.System" name="setProperty">
<Arg>log4j.properties</Arg>
<Arg>file:/Users/epugh/log4j.properties</Arg>
</Call>
```

Managing log levels at runtime

Sometimes you need more information than you are typically logging to debug a specific issue, so Solr provides an admin interface at `http://localhost:8983/solr/admin/logging` to change the logging verbosity of the components in Solr. Unfortunately, it only works with JDK logging.

While you can't change the overall setup of your logging strategy, such as the appenders or file rollover strategies at runtime, you can change the level of detail to log without restarting Solr. If you change a component like `org.apache.solr.core.SolrCore` to FINE level of logging, then make a search request to see more detailed information. One thing to remember is that these customizations are NOT persisted through restarts of Solr. If you find that you are reapplying log configuration changes after every restart, then you should change your default logging setup to specify custom logging detail levels.

Even if you adjust the logging levels here to something more detailed, you still probably won't see the messages in the console. By default, the `ConsoleHandler` has an INFO level threshold. You can lower it with this in your logging.properties: `java.util.logging.ConsoleHandler.level = FINE`

One of the challenges with logging is that you need to log enough details to troubleshoot issues, but not so much that your log files become ridiculously large and you can't winnow through the information to find what you are looking for.

Tools have arisen to manage those log files and make actionable decisions on the information stored within. Splunk is one commercial product, another is Loggly, a cloud based logging tool that is based on Solr!

More information is available at `http://www.splunk.com/` and `http://www.loggly.com`.

A SearchHandler per search interface?

Two questions to answer early on when configuring Solr and thinking about who the consumers of the search services are:

- Are you providing generic search services that may be consumed by a variety of end user clients?
- Are you providing search to specific end user applications?

If you are providing generic search functionality to an unknown set of clients, then you may have just a single request handler handling search requests at /solr/ select, which provides full access to the index. However, it is likely that Solr is powering interfaces for one or more applications that you know are going to make certain specific kinds of searches.

For example, say you have an e-commerce site that supports searching for products. In that case, you may want to only display products that are available for purchase. A specifically named request handler that always returns the stock products (using appends, as fq can be specified multiple times) and limits the rows to 50 (using invariants) would be appropriate:

```
<requestHandler name="/products" class="solr.SearchHandler" >
  <lst name="invariants">
    <int name="rows">50</int>
  </lst>
  <lst name="appends">
    <str name="fq">inStock:true</str>
  </lst>
</requestHandler>
```

However, the administrators of the same site would want to be able to find all products, regardless of if they are in stock or not. They would be using a different search interface and so you would provide a different request handler that returns all of the information available about your products:

```
<requestHandler name="/allproducts" class="solr.SearchHandler" />
```

Later on, if your site needs to change, or if the internal searching site changes, particularly with respect to tuning search relevancy, you can easily modify the appropriate request handler without impacting other applications interacting with Solr.

You can always add new request handlers to meet new needs by requiring the qt request parameter to be passed in the query like this: / solr/select?qt=allproducts. However, this doesn't look quite as clean as having specific URLs like /solr/allproducts. A fully named request handler can also have access to them controlled by use of Servlet *security* (see the *Securing Solr from prying eyes* section later in this chapter).

Leveraging Solr cores

Recall from *Chapter 2, Schema and Text Analysis* that you can either put different types of data into a single index or use separate indexes. Up to this point, the only way you would know how to use separate indexes is to actually run multiple instances of Solr. However, adding another complete instance of Solr for each type of data you want to index is a rather cumbersome process!

Solr cores allow multiple separate indexes to exist within a single Solr server instance as well as bringing features like hot core reloading and swapping that make administration easier.

Each Solr core consists of its own configuration files and data. Performing searches and indexing in a multicore setup is almost the same as using Solr without cores. You just add the name of the core to the individual URLs. Instead of doing a search through the URL:

```
http://localhost:8983/solr/select?q=dave%20matthews
```

In a multicore environment, you would search a core named mbartists via:

```
http://localhost:8983/solr/mbartists/select?q=dave%20matthews
```

Other than the introduction of the core name in the URL, you still perform all of your management tasks, searches, and updates in the same way as you always did in a single core setup.

Configuring solr.xml

When Solr starts up, it checks for the presence of a `solr.xml` file in the `solr.home` directory. If one exists, then it loads up all the cores defined in `solr.xml`. We've used multiple cores in the sample Solr setup shipped with this book to manage the various indexes used in the examples.

You can see the multicore configuration at `./examples/cores/solr.xml`:

```xml
<solr persistent="false" sharedLib="lib">
  <coresadminPath="/admin/cores" shareSchema="true">
    <core name="mbtracks" instanceDir="mbtype"
      dataDir="../../cores_data/mbtracks" />
    <core name="mbartists" instanceDir="mbtype"
      dataDir="../../cores_data/mbartists" />
    <core name="mbreleases" instanceDir="mbtype"
      dataDir="../../cores_data/mbreleases" />
    <core name="crawler" instanceDir="crawler"
      dataDir="../../cores_data/crawler" />
    <core name="karaoke" instanceDir="karaoke"
      dataDir="../../cores_data/karaoke" />
  </cores>
</solr>
```

Notice that three of the cores: `mbtracks`, `mbartists`, and `mbreleases` all share the same `instanceDir of mbtype`? This allows you to make configuration changes in one location and affect all three cores.

Some of the key multicore configuration values are:

- `persistent="false"` specifies that any changes we make at runtime to the cores, like renaming them, are not persisted. If you want to persist changes to the cores between restarts, then set `persistent="true"`. Note, this means the `solr.xml` file is regenerated without any original comments and requires the user running Solr to have write access to the filesystem.

- `sharedLib="lib"` specifies the path to the `lib` directory containing shared JAR files for all the cores. On the other hand, if you have a core with its own specific JAR files, then you would place them in the `core/lib` directory. For example, the karaoke core uses Solr Cell (see *Chapter 3, Indexing Data*) for indexing rich content, so the JARs for parsing and extracting data from rich documents are located in `./examples/cores/karaoke/lib/`.

- `adminPath` specifies the URL path at which the cores can be managed at runtime. There's no need to change it from `"/admin/cores"`. See below for details on the various operations you perform to cores.

- `shareSchema` allows you to use a single in-memory representation of the schema for all the cores that use the same `instanceDir`. This can cut down on your memory use and startup time, especially in situations where you have many cores, like if you are streaming in data and generating cores on the fly. If you are interested in using many cores, you should keep an eye on SOLR-1293 which is the umbrella JIRA issue for Solr that fully supports lots of cores. I have seen Solr run with dozens of cores with no issues beyond increased startup time.

- `defaultCoreName`, if present defines the core to use if you don't include the core name in the URL, that is `/solr/select?q=*:*`. This makes it easier to upgrade from a single core Solr to a multicore setup without changing client URLs.

Each core is configured via a fairly obvious set of properties:

- `name` specifies the name of the core, and therefore what to put in the URL to access the core.

- `instanceDir` specifies the path to the directory that contains the `conf` directory for the core, and `data` directory too, by default. A relative path is relative to `solr.home`. In a basic single-core setup, this is typically set to the same place as `solr.home`. In the preceding example we have three cores using the same configuration directory, and two that have their own specific configuration directories.

- `dataDir` specifies where to store the indexes and any other supporting data, like spell check dictionaries. If you don't define it, then by default each core stores its information in the `<instanceDir>/data` directory.

- `properties="test.properties"` allows you to specify a properties file made up of name value pairs to load for the core. This is either an absolute path or relative to the `instanceDir`.

Property substitution

Property substitution allows you to externalize configuration values, which can be very useful for customizing your Solr install with environmental specific values. For example, in production you might want to store your indexes on a separate solid state drive, then you would specify it as property: `dataDir="${ssd.dir}"`. You can also supply a default value to use if the property hasn't been set as well: `dataDir="${ssd.dir:/tmp/solr_data}"`. This property substitution works in `solr.xml`, `solrconfig.xml`, `schema.xml`, and DIH configuration files.

You can supply the property value in a number of ways:

- You can pass in the property as a Java system property: `-Dssd.dir=/Volumes/ssd`.

- You can specify the property in `solr.xml:<property name="ssd.dir" value="/Volumes/ssd"/>`. You can provide properties at two scoping levels, within a core by defining it inside the `<core/>` element, and then at the container level by defining inside the `<solr/>` element. If you define it at both the container level and the core level, then the core level will take precedence. This is a very powerful tool for defining global values and then letting you override them on a core by core basis!

- Classic properties file. As listed in the various core attributes above, you can specify in your core definition the full path to a properties file to load. You may have a pattern that your properties file will always be in `/etc/solr/solr.properties` on your filesystem, and you just drop in a new Solr install and it picks up whatever environmental values, like database parameters for DIH or replication values, that may be needed.

The `examples/cores/solr.xml` file displayed above may look rather verbose because of the `dataDir` parameter being essentially copied over and over. We could have used property substitution at the `solrconfig.xml` level to specify the data directory like this: `<dataDir>${solr.data.dir}/${solr.core.name}</dataDir>`

I like to manage my environment settings by checking them into source, so I'll have `development.properties`, `test.properties`, `staging.properties`, `production.properties`. I add to my environment variables (or `JAVA_OPTS`) `solr.environment=staging`, and then load the correct properties file based on that variable: `<core name="mycore" properties="${solr.environment}.properties"/>`.

Include fragments of XML with XInclude

XInclude stands for **XML Inclusions** and is a W3C standard for merging a chunk of XML into another document. Solr has support for using XInclude tags in `solrconfig.xml` to incorporate a chunk of xml at load time.

In `./examples/cores/karaoke/conf/solrconfig.xml` I have externalized the `<query/>` configuration into three flavors: a default query cache setup, a no caching setup, and a big query cache setup:

```
<xi:includehref="cores/karaoke/conf/${karaoke.xinclude.query}"
  parse="xml" xmlns:xi="http://www.w3.org/2001/XInclude">
  <xi:fallback>
    <xi:include href="cores/karaoke/conf/solrconfig-query-default.
        xml"/>
  </xi:fallback>
</xi:include>
```

The `${karaoke.xinclude.query}` property is defined in the core definition:

```
<core name="karaoke" instanceDir="karaoke"
  dataDir="../../cores_data/karaoke">
<property name="karaoke.xinclude.query"
  value="solrconfig-query-nocache.xml"/>
</core>
```

If the XML file defined by the `href` attribute isn't found, then the `xi:fallback` included file is returned. The fallback metaphor is primarily if you are including XML files that are loaded via HTTP and might not be available due to network issues.

Managing cores

While there isn't a nice GUI for managing Solr cores the way there is for some other options, the URLs you use to issue commands to Solr cores are very straightforward, and they can easily be integrated into other management applications. The response by default is XML, but you can also return results in JSON by appending `wt=json` to the command. If you specify `persistent="true"` in `solr.xml`, then these changes will be preserved through a reboot by overwriting `solr.xml` to reflect the changes.

We'll cover a couple of the common commands using the example Solr setup in `./examples`. The individual URLs listed below are stored in plain text files in `./examples/8/` to make it easier to follow along in your own browser:

- STATUS: Getting the status of the current cores is done through `http://localhost:8983/solr/admin/cores?action=STATUS`. You can select the status of a specific core, such as `mbartists` through `http://localhost:8983/solr/admin/cores?action=STATUS&core=mbartists`. The status command provides a nice summary of the various cores, and it is an easy way to monitor statistics showing the growth of your various cores.

- CREATE: You can generate a new core called `karaoke_test` based on the `karaoke` core, on the fly, using the CREATE command through `http://localhost:8983/solr/admin/cores?action=CREATE&name=karaoke_test&instanceDir=karaoke&config=solrconfig.xml&schema=schema.xml&dataDir=./examples/cores_data/karaoke_test`. If you create a new core that has the same name as an old core, then the existing core serves up requests until the new one is generated, and then the new one takes over.

- RENAME: Renaming a core can be useful when you have fixed names of cores in your client, and you want to make a core fit that name. To rename the `mbartists` core to the more explicit core name `music_brainz_artists`, use the URL `http://localhost:8983/solr/admin/cores?action=RENAME&core=mbartists&other=music_brainz_artists`. This naming change only happens in memory, as it doesn't update the filesystem paths for the index and configuration directories and doesn't make much sense unless you persist on the name change to `solr.xml`.

- SWAP: Swapping two cores is one of the key benefits of using Solr cores. Swapping allows you to have an offline "on deck" core that is fully populated with updated data. In a single fast atomic operation, you can swap out the current live core that is servicing requests with your freshly populated "on deck" core. As it's an atomic operation, there isn't any chance of mixed data being sent to the client. As an example, we can swap the `mbtracks` core with the `mbreleases` core through `http://localhost:8983/solr/admin/cores?action=SWAP&core=mbreleases&other=mbtracks`. You can verify the swap occurred by going to the `mbtracks` admin page and verifying that Solr Home is displayed as `cores/mbreleases/`.

- RELOAD: As you make minor changes to a core's configuration through solrconfig.xml, schema.xml, and supporting files you don't want to be stopping and starting Solr constantly. In an environment with even a couple of cores, it can take some tens of seconds to restart all the cores during which Solr is unavailable. By using the reload command, you can trigger just a reload of a specific core without impacting the others. An example of this is if you use synonyms.txt for query time synonym expansion. If you modify it you can just reload the affected core! A simple example for mbartists is http://localhost:8983/solr/admin/cores?action=RELOAD&core=mbartists.

- UNLOAD: Just like you would expect, the unload action allows you to remove an existing core from Solr. Currently running queries are completed, but no new queries are allowed. A simple example for mbartists is http://localhost:8983/solr/admin/cores?action=UNLOAD&core=mbartists.

- MERGEINDEXES: (for advanced users) The merge command allows you to merge one or more indexes into yet another core. This can be very useful if you've split data across multiple cores and now want to bring them together without re-indexing the source data all over again. You need to issue commits to the individual indexes that are sources for data. After merging, issue another commit to make the searchers aware of the new data. This all happens at the Lucene index level on the filesystem, so functions such as deduplication that work through request handlers are never invoked.

The full set of commands using curl is listed in ./8/MERGE_COMMAND.txt.

Why use multicore?

Solr's support of multiple cores in a single instance enables you to serve multiple indexes of data in a single Solr instance. Multiple cores also address some key needs for maintaining Solr in a production environment:

- **Rebuilding an index:** While Solr has a lot of features to handle such as doing sparse updates to an index with minimal impact on performance, occasionally you need to bulk update significant amounts of your data. This invariably leads to performance issues, as your searchers are constantly being reopened. By supporting the ability to populate a separate index in a bulk fashion, you can optimize the offline index for updating content. Once the offline index has been fully populated, you can use the SWAP command to take the offline index and make it the live index.

- **Testing configuration changes**: Configuration changes can have very differing impacts depending on the type of data you have. If your production Solr has massive amounts of data, moving that to a test or development environment may not be possible. By using the CREATE and the MERGE commands, you can make a copy of a core and test it in relative isolation from the core being used by your end users. Use the RELOAD command to restart your test core to validate your changes. Once you are happy with your changes, you can either SWAP the cores or just reapply your changes to your live core and RELOAD it.

- **Merging separate indexes together:** You may find that over time you have more separate indexes than you need, and you want to merge them together. You can use the MERGEINDEXES command to merge two cores together into a third core. However, note that you need to do a commit on both cores and ensure that no new data is indexed while the merge is happening.

- **Renaming cores at runtime**: You can build multiple versions of the same basic core and control which one is accessed by your clients by using the RENAME command to rename a core to match the URL the clients are connecting to.

Should I use multiple cores?

Multi core support was first added in Solr 1.3, matured further in Solr 1.4, and now is almost required in Solr 3.x. We strongly encourage you to start with the multiple core approach, even if your solr.xml only has a single core listed! While slightly more complex then just having a single index, using multi core allows you to take advantage of all the administrative goodness of cores. We expect the concept of a single core will be deprecated in the future as multiple cores are the key to Solr's support for massively distributed indexes and/or huge numbers of individual indexes.

You can learn more about Solr core related features at http://wiki.apache.org/solr/CoreAdmin.

Monitoring Solr performance

Ensuring that Solr is meeting the SLA expectations of the enterprise is the goal of monitoring. Solr provides both XML and JMX hooks to allow you to integrate Solr into your enterprise monitoring platform.

Don't have your own monitoring platform? There are two offerings, available from New Relic (`http://newrelic.com`) and Sematext (`http://sematext.com/spm/`) that provide a comprehensive monitoring solution. Both are cloud based which communicate via a small agent installed into Solr and provide a wealth of statistics and analysis about the JVM, as well as Solr specific metrics such as request response time and throughput, cache hit rate, and indexing performance.

Stats.jsp

From the admin interface, when you click on the **Statistics** link you receive a web page of information about a specific index. However, what isn't immediately obvious is that this information is actually being served up to the browser as XML with an embedded link to an XSL style sheet that transforms it in the browser into HTML. This means that if you perform a GET request on `stats.jsp` you get back XML:

```
>>curl http://localhost:8983/solr/mbartists/admin/stats.jsp
```

Open the downloaded file and you will see all the data as XML. Below is an excerpt of the statistics available for the cache that stores individual documents and the standard request handler with the metrics you might want to monitor highlighted.

```
<entry>
    <name>documentCache</name>
    <class>org.apache.solr.search.LRUCache</class>
    <version>1.0</version>
    <description>LRU Cache(maxSize=512, initialSize=512)</description>
    <stats>
        <stat name="lookups">3251</stat>
        <stat name="hits">3101</stat>
        <stat name="hitratio">0.95</stat>
        <stat name="inserts">160</stat>
        <stat name="evictions">0</stat>
        <stat name="size">160</stat>
        <stat name="warmupTime">0</stat>
        <stat name="cumulative_lookups">3251</stat>
        <stat name="cumulative_hits">3101</stat>
        <stat name="cumulative_hitratio">0.95</stat>
        <stat name="cumulative_inserts">150</stat>
        <stat name="cumulative_evictions">0</stat>
    </stats>
</entry>
<entry>
```

```
<name>standard</name>
<class>org.apache.solr.handler.component.SearchHandler</class>
<version>$Revision: 1052938 $</version>
<description>Search using components:
   org.apache.solr.handler.component.QueryComponent,
   org.apache.solr.handler.component.FacetComponent</description>
<stats>
    <stat name="handlerStart">1298759020886</stat>
    <stat name="requests">359</stat>
    <stat name="errors">0</stat>
    <stat name="timeouts">0</stat>
    <stat name="totalTime">9122</stat>
    <stat name="avgTimePerRequest">25.409472</stat>
    <stat name="avgRequestsPerSecond">0.446995</stat>
</stats>
</entry>
```

While integrating into each monitoring system will be different, as an example you can look at `./examples/8/check_solr.rb` for a simple Ruby script that queries a core and checks if the average hit ratio and the average time per request are above certain thresholds:

```
>> ./check_solr.rb -w 13 -c 20 -imbtracks
CRITICAL - Average Time per request more than 20 milliseconds old:
39.5
```

JMX

Java Management Extensions (JMX) is a Java standard API for monitoring and managing applications and network services. Originally meant to help with server administration, it was added to J2SE Version 5. JMX enabled applications and services expose information and available operations for resources such as **MBeans (Managed Bean)**. MBeans can be managed remotely by a wide variety of management consoles such as the JConsole GUI that comes with Java and the web-based JMX Console that comes with the JBoss application server.

As of Version 1.4, Solr exposes information about its components through MBeans. However, actual management operations, such as re-indexing information, are not exposed through JMX. You can leverage JMX to monitor the status of Solr, such as finding out how many documents have been indexed, and in large enterprise environments the JMX standard simplifies integrating monitoring tasks into existing monitoring platforms.

The information exposed via JMX Mbeans is now exposed as XML as well: `http://localhost:8983/solr/mbartists/admin/mbeans/`. This is an easier way to quickly query for JMX information.

Starting Solr with JMX

In `solrconfig.xml`, the stanza `<jmx/>` needs to be uncommented to enable JMX support. In order to actually start up with JMX, you need to provide some extra parameters to support remote connections, including the port to be connected to:

```
>>java -Dcom.sun.management.jmxremote -Dcom.sun.management.jmxremote.
port=3000 -Dcom.sun.management.jmxremote.ssl=false -Dcom.sun.
management.jmxremote.authenticate=false -jar start.jar
```

However, this configuration is totally insecure. In a production environment, you would want to require usernames and passwords for access. For more information, please refer to the JMX documentation at `http://java.sun.com/j2se/1.5.0/docs/guide/management/agent.html#remote`.

J2SE ships with JConsole, a GUI client for connecting to JMX servers. In order to start it, run the following command:

```
>> [JDK_HOME]/bin/jconsole
```

In order to connect to Solr, choose the **Remote** tab, and enter **localhost** for the **Host or IP** and **3000** for the **Port**. As we have started without requiring authentication, you do not need to enter a username and password:

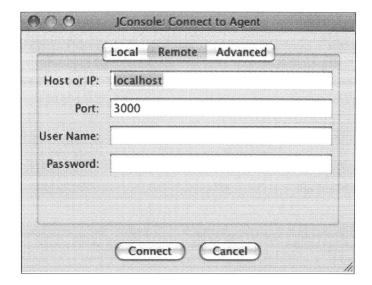

For Solr, the key tabs to use in JConsole are **Memory** and **MBeans**. **Memory** provides a visual charting of the consumption of memory and can help you monitor low memory situations and when to start optimizing your indexes (as discussed in *Chapter 9, Integrating Solr*).

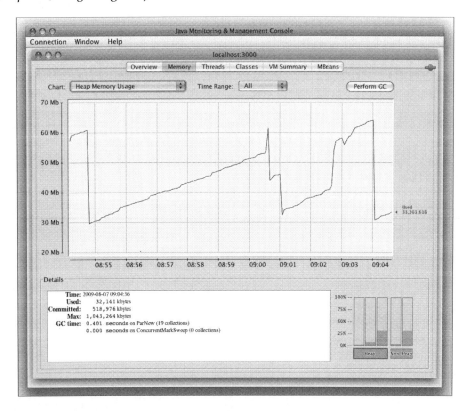

You can also monitor the various components of Solr by choosing the **MBeans** tab. In order to find out how many documents you've indexed, you would look at the **SolrIndexSearch** Mbean. Select **solr** from the tree listing on the left, and drill down to the `searcher` folder and select the `org.apache.solr.search.SolrIndexSearcher` component. You can see in the following screenshot that there are currently 15 documents indexed and the most ever was 25 documents. While you can pull this type of information out of the admin statistics web page, the JMX standard provides a much simpler method that can be easily integrated into other tools.

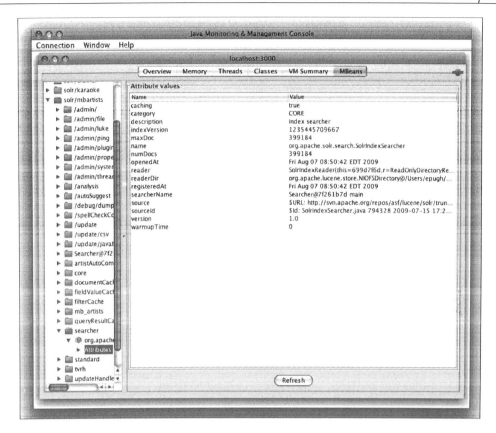

In order to save yourself typing in the extra startup parameters, see the previous *Jetty Startup Integration* section for how to add these JMX startup parameters like `-Dcom.sun.management.jmxremote` to your Jetty configuration.

Take a walk on the wild side! Use JRuby to extract JMX information

While JConsole is useful as a GUI application, it is hard to integrate into a larger environment. However, by leveraging the standard nature of JMX, we can easily script access to Solr components to use in our own monitoring systems. This makes it easy to expose extra information to our users such as "15 documents are available for searching". There are a number of scripting packages for Java that you might look at, including Jython, Groovy, and BeanShell; however, in this example we are going to use JRuby.

JRuby is an implementation of the Ruby language running on the Java Virtual Machine that blends the library support of Java with the simplicity of the Ruby language in a winning combination. More information is available at http://jruby.org.

JRuby is very simple to install on Windows and Unix using your operating system's package manager.

Once you have JRuby installed, you need to install the jmx4r gem that provides the simple interface to JMX. The Ruby standard is to package functionality in **gems**, which are similar to traditional Java JAR files.

```
>>jruby -S gem install jmx4r
```

Assuming you have started Solr with JMX enabled on port 3000, you are now ready to interactively query Solr for status through JMX using the **JRuby Interactive Browser (JIRB)** tool. JIRB allows you to type in Ruby code and interactively manipulate your environment.

Start JIRB from the command line by running the following command:

```
>>jirb
```

Enter the following commands at the interpreter prompts:

```
require 'rubygems'
require 'jmx4r'
JMX::MBean.establish_connection :port => 3000
```

You now have an interactive connection to the running Solr through JMX. In order to find out how many queries have been issued, you just request the searcher MBean by name solr:type=searcher,id=org.apache.solr.search.SolrIndexSearcher:

```
searcher = JMX::MBean.find_by_name
        "solr:type=searcher,id=org.apache.solr.search.SolrIndexSearcher"
```

You may need to use JConsole to figure out the name of the MBean that you want. Simply select the **Info** tab for a specific MBean, and use the MBean name attribute. Once you have the MBean, you can view all available attributes in a hash data structure by typing the following snippet of code:

```
irb(main):013:0>searcher.attributes
=> {"source_id"=>"sourceId", "category"=>"category",
"description"=>"description", "source"=>"source", "name"=>"name",
"version"=>"version", "searcher_name"=>"searcherName",
"caching"=>"caching", "num_docs"=>"numDocs", "max_doc"=>"maxDoc",
"reader"=>"reader", "reader_dir"=>"readerDir", "index_
version"=>"indexVersion", "opened_at"=>"openedAt", "registered_
at"=>"registeredAt", "warmup_time"=>"warmupTime"}
```

The attribute `searcher.num_docs` will return the current number of indexed documents in Solr.

Returning to our previous example of finding out how many documents are in the index, you just need to issue the following:

```
>>jirb
require 'rubygems'
require 'jmx4r'
JMX::MBean.find_by_name
    ("solr:type=searcher,id=org.apache.solr.search.
SolrIndexSearcher").num_docs => "15"
```

You can now integrate this Ruby script into some sort of regular process that saves the number of documents in your database, so you can display that information to your users.

You also can now start getting information about other parts of the system, like how many search queries have been issued per second, and how long they are averaging, by looking at the search handler MBean:

```
search_handler = JMX::MBean.find_by_name
    "solr:type=standard,id=org.apache.solr.handler.component.
    SearchHandler"
search_handler.avg_requests_per_second
=> .0043345
search_handler.avg_time_per_request
=> 45.0
```

In order to see all the available Solr Mbean's and their JMX names, just issue:

```
puts JMX::MBean.find_all_by_name("solr:*").map{ |mbean|
  mbean.object_name}
```

Ruby is a wonderful language for scripting utility tasks that interact with Solr and other systems.

Jmx4r is hosted at `http://github.com/jmesnil/jmx4r/` and has a comprehensive suite of tests and example code. It's a good library to look at for tips on using JRuby.

Securing Solr from prying eyes

Solr, by default, comes completely open. Anyone can make search requests, anyone can upload documents, anyone can access the administration interface, and anyone can delete data. However, it isn't difficult to lock down Solr to use in any kind of environment. We can do this by making use of the standard practices, which you would apply to any kind of web application or server software.

Limiting server access

The single biggest thing you can do to secure Solr is to lock down who has access to the server. Using standard firewall techniques, you can control what IP addresses are allowed to connect to the Solr through the 8983 port.

Unless you have very unusual needs, you won't expose Solr to the Internet directly; instead users will access Solr through some sort of web application, that in turn forwards requests to Solr, collects the results, and displays them to your users. By limiting the IP addresses that can connect to Solr to just those belonging to your web farm, you've ensured that random Internet users and internal users don't mess with Solr.

 If you lock down access via IP addresses, then don't forget that if you have external processes uploading content, you need to make sure those IP addresses are added.

Using IP addresses to control access is crude and basic; it doesn't help if someone is connecting to Solr from one of the valid IP addresses. Fortunately, Solr is just a WAR file deployed in a Servlet container, so you can use all of the capabilities of Servlet containers to control access. In order to limit access to /solr/update* and /solr/admin/* in Jetty by requiring BASIC authentication from your users, you merely edit the web.xml in your Solr WAR adding the following stanza at the bottom:

```
<security-constraint>
  <web-resource-collection>
    <web-resource-name>Solr Admin</web-resource-name>
    <url-pattern>/admin/*</url-pattern>
  </web-resource-collection>
  <auth-constraint>
    <role-name>admin</role-name>
  </auth-constraint>
</security-constraint>
<security-constraint>
  <web-resource-collection>
```

```
    <web-resource-name>Solr Update</web-resource-name>
    <url-pattern>/update*</url-pattern>
  </web-resource-collection>
  <auth-constraint>
    <role-name>admin</role-name>
    <role-name>content_updater</role-name>
  </auth-constraint>
</security-constraint>

<login-config>
  <auth-method>BASIC</auth-method>
  <realm-name>Test Realm</realm-name>
</login-config>
```

This specifies that access to the `/update*` URLs is limited to anyone in the roles of `admin` or `content_updater`, although only admin users can access the `/admin/*` URLs. The `realm-name` is what ties the security constraints to the users configured in Jetty.

Customizing web.xml in Jetty

Sometimes cracking open a WAR file just to customize the `web.xml` can be a pain. But if you are a Jetty user, then you can put the changes into the `./etc/webdefault.xml` file and Jetty will apply the changes to any WAR file deployed. This is a nice trick if you have just a single webapp in the Jetty container. See `./examples/solr/etc/webdefault.xml` and `./examples/solr/etc/jetty.xml` for an example.

Edit the `jetty.xml` file and uncomment the `<Set name="UserRealms"/>` stanza so that it looks like the following:

```
<Set name="UserRealms">
  <Array type="org.mortbay.jetty.security.UserRealm">
    <Item>
      <New class="org.mortbay.jetty.security.HashUserRealm">
        <Set name="name">Solr Realm</Set>
        <Set name="config">
          <SystemProperty name="jetty.home" default="."/>/etc/
          realm.properties
        </Set>
      </New>
    </Item>
  </Array>
</Set>
```

The `./etc/realm.properties` file contains a list of users with their password and roles to which they belong. We've specified that the user named `administrator` has the roles of `content_updater` and `admin`, and therefore can access any `/update` and `/admin` URLs. However, the user `eric` can only access the `/update` URLs:

```
administrator: $ecretpa$$word,content_updater,admin
eric: mypa$$word, content_updater
guest: guest,read-only
```

Adding authentication introduces an extra roadblock for automated scripts that need to interact with Solr to upload information. However, if you use BASIC authentication, then you can easily pass the username and password as part of the URL request. The only downside is that the password is being transmitted in cleartext, and you should wrap the entire request in SSL for maximum security:

```
http://USERNAME:PASSWORD@localhost:8080/solr/update
```

> Normally you wouldn't want to store passwords in plain text on the server in a file such as `realm.properties` that isn't encrypted. More information is available at `http://docs.codehaus.org/display/JETTY/Realms`.

Securing public searches

Although typically you access Solr through an intermediate web application, you may want to expose Solr directly to the Internet, albeit in a limited way. One scenario for this is exposing a search in an RSS/Atom feed made possible with Solr's XSLT support (see *Chapter 4, Searching* for more on XSLT). Another is using **JavaScript**, **AJAX**, and **JSONP** callbacks from the browser to directly connect to Solr and issue searches. We discuss this more in the next chapter. There may be other scenarios where firewall rules and/or passwords might still be used to expose parts of Solr, such as for modifying the index, but some search requests must be exposed to direct Internet access. In this case, you need to configure the exposed request handlers with `invariants` and/or `appends` clauses as applicable. For a limited example of this, see the *A SearchHandler per search interface?* section earlier in this chapter.

If there are certain records that need to be excluded from public access, then you'll need to specify an appropriate `fq` (filter query). If there are certain fields on documents that need to be kept private, then this can be problematic to completely secure, especially if you are working with sensitive data. It's simple enough to specify `fl` (field list) through `invariants`, but there are a good number of other parameters that might expose the data (for example, highlighting, maybe faceting) in ways you didn't realize.

```
<lst name="invariants">
  <int name="fl">public_id,public_description</int>
  <str name="fq">public:true</int>
</lst>
```

Therefore, if you are working with sensitive data then exposing Solr in this way is not recommended.

Controlling JMX access

If you have started Solr with JMX enabled, then you should also have a JMX username and password configured. While today the JMX interface only exposes summary information about the Solr components and memory consumption, in future versions actual management options like triggering optimizing indexes will most likely be exposed through JMX. So, putting JMX access under lock and key is a good idea.

Securing index data

One of the weaknesses of Solr due to the lack of a built-in security model is that there aren't well defined approaches for controlling which users can manipulate the indexes by adding, updating, and deleting documents, and who can search which documents. Nevertheless, there are some approaches for controlling access to documents being searched.

Controlling document access

You can start off with some of the ideas talked about in the *A SearchHandler per search interface?* section to control search access to your index. However, if you need to control access to documents within your index and must control it based on the user accessing the content, then one approach is to leverage the faceted search capabilities of Solr. You may want to look back at *Chapter 5, Search Relevancy* to refresh your memory on faceting. For example, you may have a variety of documents that have differing visibility depending on if someone is a member of the public or an internal publicist. The public can only see a subset of the data, but a publicist can see more information, including information that isn't ready for public viewing. When indexing documents, you should store in a separate multiValued field the roles that a user must belong to in order to gain access to the document:

```
<field name="roles" type="text" indexed="true" stored="true"
  multiValued="true" />
```

A document that was for everyone would be indexed with the role values Public and Publicist. Another document that was for internal use would just have the Publicist role. Then, at query time, you could append extra request parameters to limit what is returned depending on the roles that someone belonged to by treating the roles as a facet:

```
/solr/select/?q=music&start=0&facet=on&facet.
field=roles&fq=role%3Apublic
```

In the preceding example, we are querying for `music` that is accessible by anyone with the role `public`. Obviously, this requires significant logic to be implemented on the client side interfacing with Solr, and is not as robust a solution as we may wish.

Other things to look at

Remote streaming is the ability to give Solr the URL to a remote resource or local file and have Solr download the contents as a stream of data. This can be very useful when indexing large documents as it reduces the amount of data that your updating process needs to move around. However, it means that if you have the `/debug/dump` request handler enabled, then the contents of any file can be exposed. Here is an example of displaying to anyone my `~/.ssh/authorized_keys` file:

```
http://localhost:8983/solr/debug/dump?stream.file=/Users/epugh/.ssh/
authorized_keys
```

If you have this turned on, then make sure that you are monitoring the log files, and also that access to Solr is tightly controlled. *The example application has this function turned on by default.*

In addition, in a production environment, you want to comment out the `/debug/dump` request handler, unless you are actively debugging an issue.

Just as you need to be wary of a SQL injection attack for a relational database, there is a similar concern for Solr. Solr should not be exposed to untrusted clients if you are concerned about the risk of a denial of service attack. This is also a concern if you are lax in how your application acts as a broker to Solr. It's fairly easy to bring down Solr by, say asking it to sort by every field in the schema, which would result in sudden exorbitant memory usage. There are other similar attacks if an attacker can submit an arbitrary function query as part of their query.

Summary

We briefly covered a wide variety of the issues that surround taking a Solr configuration that works in a development environment and getting it ready for the rigors of a production environment. Solr's modular nature and stripped down focus on search allows it to be compatible with a broad variety of deployment platforms. Solr offers a wealth of monitoring options, from log files, to HTTP request logs, to JMX options. Nonetheless, for a really robust solution, you must define what the key performance metrics are that concern you, and then implement automated solutions for tracking them.

Now that we have set up our Solr server, we need to take advantage of it to build better applications. In the next chapter, we'll look at how to easily integrate Solr search through various client libraries.

9
Integrating Solr

As the saying goes, if a tree falls in the woods and no one hears it, did it make a sound? Similarly, if you have a wonderful search engine, but your users can't access it, do you really have a wonderful search engine? Fortunately, Solr is very easy to integrate into a wide variety of client environments via its modern easy-to-use REST-like interface and multiple data formats. In this chapter, we will:

- Quickly prototype a search UI using "Solritas" (the `/browse` UI).
- Look at accessing Solr results through various language-based clients, including Java, Ruby, and PHP.
- Learn how you can call Solr from from a web browser via AJAX.
- Briefly cover building your own Google-like search engine by crawling the `MusicBrainz.org` site with the Nutch web crawler.
- Translate search results into the OpenSearch XML standard via XSLT.
- Review ManifoldCF, a framework for synching content from external repositories that respects external document access rules.

There are so many possible topics we could have covered in this chapter and only so much space available. For information on accessing Solr from .NET, Python, and many other client environments, see: `http://wiki.apache.org/solr/IntegratingSolr`. That page also contains information on integrating Solr with other frameworks and applications, such as Django. There is a similar page that we started on the wiki called the "Solr Ecosystem": `http://wiki.apache.org/solr/SolrEcosystem`. It is larger in scope than the "Integrating Solr" page, referencing document processing pipelines, crawlers, and more.

In a hurry?

This chapter covers a wide variety of integrations with Solr. If you are in a hurry, jump to the next section *Inventory of examples* to find source code that you can immediately start using. Then read the sections that apply to the environment you are working in.

We will be using our MusicBrainz dataset to power these examples. You can download the full sample code for these integrations from our website http://www. SolrEnterpriseSearchServer.com. This includes a prebuilt Solr and scripts to load *mbtracks* with seven million records and *mbartists* with 400,000 records. When you have downloaded the zipped file, you should follow the setup instructions in the README.txt file.

Working with included examples

We have included a wide variety of sample integrations that you can run as you work through this chapter. The examples stored in ./examples/9/ of the downloadable ZIP file are as self-contained as we could make them, are detailed in this chapter, and you shouldn't run into any problems making them work. Check the support section of the book website for any errata.

Inventory of examples

This is a quick summary of the various examples of using Solr, available unless otherwise noted in ./examples/9/.

- **ajaxsolr** is an example of building a fully featured Solr Search UI using just JavaScript.
- **php** is a barebones example of PHP integration with Solr.
- **solr-php-client** is a richer example of integrating Solr results into a PHP based application.
- **Solritas,** a web search UI using template files in the /cores/mbtypes/conf/velocity directory.
- **jquery_autocomplete** is an example of using the jQuery Autocomplete library to provide search suggestions based on Solr searches.
- **myfaves** is a Ruby on Rails application using the Ruby Solr client library Sunspot to search for music artists.
- **nutch** is a simple example of the Nutch web crawler integrated with Solr.
- **crawler** is a more complex example of doing web crawling and indexing into Solr using the SolrJ Java client and Heritrix crawler.

Solritas, the integrated search UI

The contrib module `velocity`, nicknamed Solritas, is a simple template engine that lets you build user interfaces directly in Solr using `Apache Velocity`, a very simple macro language to generate the HTML. It's similar to JSPs, ASPs, PHPs, and so on, but simpler with a syntax consisting of just a handful of commands. It is very simple to pick up as you can see in the following snippet of code for rendering two lines of HTML displaying the ID and name of an artist pulled from the first Solr document in a list of results:

```
#set($doc = $response.results.get(0))
#set($id = $doc.getFieldValue("id"))
<div>ID: $id</div>
<div> Name: #field('a_name')</div>
```

When a Velocity template is invoked, Solritas places some objects, indicated with a $ character, into a rendering context that you can use, like `$response` and `$request`. In the preceding example you can see the first result in the response is assigned to the `$doc` object variable using the `#set` command. Java methods like `getFieldValue()` are easily called in Velocity, allowing you to access the full power of Java within a scripting environment that is evaluated at runtime. Velocity also supports building your own functions, like the `#field()` function for displaying a field from a document.

You can try out an interface optimized for searching for MusicBrainz artists by browsing to `http://localhost:8983/solr/mbartists/browse/`. This web interface supports faceted browsing, auto-completion of queries, boosting of artists based on recency of release, More Like This based on artist name, and even "Did You Mean" spell checking!

When the browser invokes the URL, Solr hands the request off to a request handler with the name `/browse` which is a search request handler that works like any other. The point where the request takes a different turn is in rendering the response, which in Solr is configured with the `wt` parameter. Short for "writer type", the choices are better known as **response writers**. Instead of letting it default to `xml`, it's set to `velocity`. The Velocity response writer uses the `v.layout` and `v.template` and parameters to determine which template file to use for the overall page layout as well as what template for the specific page to render. The templates are located in the `conf/velocity/` directory relative to the Solr core, and they end in `.vm`. To use another directory, set the `v.base_dir` parameter. Note that the use of parameters to choose the template allows you to override it in the URL if desired.

```
<?xml version="1.0"?>
<requestHandler name="/browse" class="solr.SearchHandler">
<lst name="defaults">
<str name="wt">velocity</str>
<str name="v.template">browse</str>
<str name="v.layout">layout</str>
<str name="title">MusicBrainz</str>

<str name="defType">edismax</str>
<str name="mm">1</str>
<str name="q.alt">*:*</str>
<str name="rows">10</str>
<str name="fl">*,score</str>
<str name="qf">a_name^1.5 a_member_name^1.0</str>
<str name="pf">a_name^1.5 a_member_name^1.0</str>

<str name="mlt.qf">a_name^1.5 a_member_name^1.0</str>
<str name="mlt.fl">a_name,a_member_name</str>
<int name="mlt.count">3</int>
<int name="mlt.mintf">1</int>
<int name="mlt.mindf">2</int>
<str name="mlt.boost">true</str>

<str name="facet">on</str>
<str name="facet.field">a_type</str>
<str name="facet.field">type</str>
<str name="facet.mincount">1</str>
<str name="facet.range">a_release_date_latest</str>
<str name="f.a_release_date_latest.facet.range.start">NOW/YEAR-
10YEARS</str>
<str name="f.a_release_date_latest.facet.range.end">NOW</str>
<str name="f.a_release_date_latest.facet.range.gap">+1YEAR</str>
<str name="f.a_release_date_latest.facet.range.other">before</str>
<str name="f.a_release_date_latest.facet.range.other">after</str>

<str name="spellcheck">on</str>
<str name="spellcheck.dictionary">a_spell</str>
<str name="spellcheck.collate">true</str>

<str name="hl">on</str>
<str name="hl.fl">a_name a_member_name</str>
<str name="f.a_name.hl.fragsize">0</str>
<str name="f.a_name.hl.alternateField">a_name</str>
</lst>
```

```
<arr name="last-components">
<str>spellcheck</str>
</arr>
</requestHandler>
```

Pros and Cons of Solritas

As great as it is to impress your boss by quickly building a remarkably full featured search interface using Solritas, there are some cons to keep in mind:

- While many of the various Velocity files are fairly agnostic about the structure of the data being rendered, there are enough places where you have to both configure some parameters in `solrconfig.xml` and hardcode them in the Velocity template and that means you'll have to customize the templates to fit your schema. This can be a bit of a gotcha!

- Using Velocity to render UI for a high volume website isn't a good idea as you are putting the entire search and render load on the same server, and Solr isn't optimized for serving up assets such as CSS or JavaScript files.

- Building a web application based only on a collection of page templates, no matter if the technology is Velocity, JSPs, ASPs, or PHPs, gets harder to maintain and comprehend as it grows in complexity. Arguably, the `/browse` out-of-the-box interface has reached that complexity point since there is no strong MVC model to follow.

- Integrating a Velocity driven UI in a larger system isn't simple since you can't easily add your own Java-based logic without modifying Solr itself.

However, some aspects of what I really love about Solritas are:

- The ability to quickly prototype an interface. I find that most end users don't know what fields they want searchable until they have something they can play with. Quickly prototyping a search interface for the business stakeholders is powerful.

- If you need to need to emit a small chunk of HTML to integrate Solr into another application, or even other text formats such as JSON or custom XML, then this can be a simple yet powerful integration method. This query: `http://localhost:8983/solr/mbartists/select?limit=1&q=corgan&qt=mb_artists&wt=velocity&v.template=fragment` returns a small fragment of HTML rendered by the completely standalone Velocity template `fragment.vm`:

- Velocity is great for quickly building small tools for internal users to perform tasks like debugging why certain search results come back. These aren't meant for mass consumption, so the fact they run on the search server is fine. The example UI has nice **toggle explain** and **toggle all fields** options that let you see the detailed scoring which is nice for debugging:

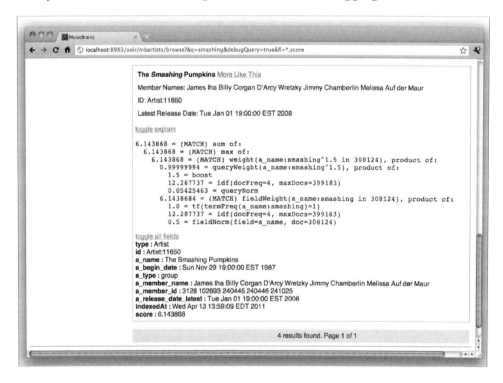

To learn more about building your own Velocity based interface, look at the example code in `/cores/mbtype/conf/velocity`. The example application that ships with Solr also has some good examples of exposing Solr features such as spatial search using Velocity. You can get more information about the list of tools and objects added to the rendering context from the wiki at `http://wiki.apache.org/solr/VelocityResponseWriter`. More information about Velocity is available from `http://velocity.apache.org/`.

SolrJ: Simple Java interface

SolrJ is the simple Java client interface to Solr that insulates you from the dirty details of parsing and sending messages back and forth between your application and Solr, and by default communicates using a fast binary format instead of XML. You work in the familiar world of objects like **SolrQuery**, **QueryResponse**, and **SolrDocument**. SolrJ is a core part of the Solr project, and typically, though not always, it is updated as soon as new features are added to Solr on the server side.

We'll demonstrate using SolrJ to index web pages downloaded from `MusicBrainz.org` and stored in a binary format called **ARC** using the crawler **Heritrix**. If you want to run Heritrix yourself, proceed to the next section. If you want to use the already downloaded ARC files in `./examples/9/crawler/heritrix-3.0.0/jobs` with the SolrJ client, then skip down to the section *SolrJ-based client for Indexing HTML*.

Using Heritrix to download artist pages

Heritrix is an extremely full featured and extensible web crawler used by the **InternetArchive** for archiving the contents of the Internet. The InternetArchive is a non-profit organization established to preserve websites by taking regular snapshots of them. You may be more familiar with the site under the name *The Wayback Machine*. By looking back at the original indexed version of the Solr homepage taken on January 19th, 2007 at `http://web.archive.org/web/*/http://lucene.apache.org/solr`, we learn that Solr had just graduated from the Apache Incubator program!

Going into the full details of using Heritrix is outside the scope of this book. However, you can play with a version configured for crawling only artist pages on `MusicBrainz.org` in `./examples/9/crawler/heritrix-2.0.2/`. Start Heritrix by running:

```
>> ./bin/heritrix -a admin:admin
```

And then browsing to the secure web interface at `https://localhost:8443/` and logging in using the username and password you specified through the `-a` parameter. You will see a web console with a single **Engine** configured. Click on it to see the profiles configured for it. You should see a **musicbrainz-only-artists** profile; click on **Copy**, and choose the default option of generating a new ready-to-run job.

You will now have a new job configured with a name similar to **musicbrainz-only-artists-20090501142451**. Click on **Launch** to start the crawler covering the `MusicBrainz.org` site. You will see the console interface of the crawler and can monitor the progress of downloading content:

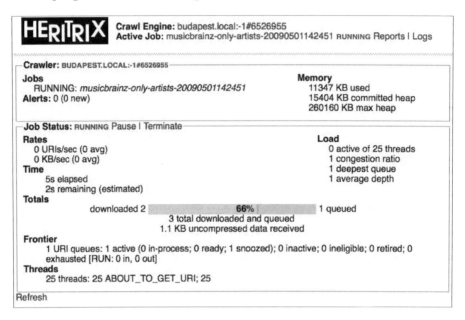

The crawler can take a while to complete a crawl, as it is designed to not overload the sites being crawled and we only have 25 threads configured. `MusicBrainz.org` has roughly 119,000 distinct pages, and in my testing, running Heritrix for 10 hours only downloaded 6,600 pages. The pages being crawled are stored in the compact text format called an ARC file that contains multiple web resources individually compressed using `.gzip`. There are various options for checkpointing the resulting ARC files as they are generated so that you can start using them while it continues to crawl. Learn more about checkpointing and more advanced features at Heritrix's site at `http://crawler.archive.org/`. The resulting ARC file is stored in the `./crawler/heritrix-2.0.2/jobs/[THE_NAME_OF_YOUR_JOB]/arcs/` directory. For the rest of this example, we will work with the already generated ARC files in `./crawler/heritrix-2.0.2/jobs/completed-musicbrainz-only-artists-20090707185058/arcs` that contains 1,532 downloaded pages.

You can view the meta information of the resources in an ARC file such as the timestamp, mime type, and URL by running the `arcreader` command line client (the first response is listed below):

```
>> ./bin/arcreader jobs/completed-musicbrainz-only-
artists-20090707185058/arcs/IAH-20090707185106-00000-budapest.local.arc

20090430202747 72.29.166.157 http://musicbrainz.org/show/
artist/?artistid=217990 text/html - - 3700547 28627 IAH-20090707185106
-00000-budapest.local
```

SolrJ-based client for Indexing HTML

Solr does provide some basic support for working with HTML documents that can that makes indexing simpler. For example, if you look at `./examples/cores/crawler/conf/schema.xml`, you can see that the schema has been optimized for storing HTML documents. There are two new field types defined: `html-text` and `html-shingle`. Both field types leverage the `HTMLStripStandardTokenizerFactory` tokenizer to strip out the various HTML related tags and just preserve the textual content of the web page during indexing for searching against. However, `html-shingle` is designed specifically for multiword phrase searches by using a technique called **shingling** that results in faster phrase queries at the expense of more disk use and indexing time. The `html-text` field is indexed in a more straightforward manner. We delve more into shingling in *Chapter 10, Scaling Solr*.

The fields we are storing are:

```
<fields>
<field name="url" type="string" />
<field name="mimeType" type="string" />
<field name="host" type="string" />
<field name="path" type="string" />
<field name="docText" type="html-text"/>
<field name="docTextShingle" type="html-shingle" stored="false" />
</fields>

<copyField source="docText" dest="docTextShingle" />

<uniqueKey>url</uniqueKey>
<defaultSearchField>docText</defaultSearchField>
```

With the `url` being the unique key and the `docText` being the default field for searches, `Host` and `path` fields give us something with which to facet our results.

There is a very simple Java application in `./examples/9/crawler/` `SolrJforMusicBrainz` that deletes any existing records, parses the individual records from the ARC files, and inserts them into Solr if they have the MIME type of `text/html`. `SolrJforMusicBrainz` is built using the **Maven** project management/ build tool. Maven is an Apache project at `http://maven.apache.org/` that brings a specific approach to structuring Java projects and introduced the concept of public repositories for storing JAR dependencies.

 Solr uses Ant as the official supported build, but it includes a Maven build option as well. For each Solr release, the build artifacts get published to Maven's central repository.

In order to compile the application yourself, assuming you have installed Maven 3, execute the following command from the `./SolrJforMusicBrainz` directory:

```
>>mvn package
```

You will download all of the JAR dependencies for both Solr and Heritrix, resulting in a roughly 12 megabyte executable JAR file in `./SolrJforMusicBrainz/target/` `SolrJForMusicBrainz-1.1.jar`.

In order to index the web pages stored in the ARC format, execute the JAR file, passing in parameters that specify the directory in which the ARC files are located, whether you are using a remote or local Solr connection, and the specific connection information. In order to connect to your already running Solr, run:

```
>>java -jar target/SolrJForMusicBrainz-1.1.jar ../heritrix-2.0.2/jobs/
completed-musicbrainz-only-artists-20090707185058/arcs/ REMOTE http://
localhost:8983/solr/crawler
```

You should see a long list of URLs being indexed, along with how many milliseconds it took to process all of the documents:

```
http://musicbrainz.org/show/artist/?artistid=317388
http://musicbrainz.org/show/artist/?artistid=593877
http://musicbrainz.org/show/artist/?artistid=419076
Execution time was 12454 ms for 210 documents
```

In order to index the ARC files into an embedded Solr, run:

```
>>java -jar target/SolrJForMusicBrainz-1.1.jar ../heritrix-2.0.2/
jobs/completed-musicbrainz-only-artists-20090707185058/arcs/ EMBEDDED
../../../cores
```

You will see similar output as before, but interleaved with the logging messages generated by the embedded Solr instance as well:

```
http://musicbrainz.org/show/artist/?artistid=334589
May 4, 2009 9:06:45 PM org.apache.solr.update.processor.
LogUpdateProcessor finish
INFO: {add=[http://musicbrainz.org/show/artist/?artistid=334589]} 0 17
May 4, 2009 9:06:45 PM org.apache.solr.core.SolrCore execute
INFO: [crawler] webapp=null path=/update params={} status=0 QTime=17
```

SolrJ client API

SolrJ has a very straightforward object model for representing interaction with Solr. You can play with the basic methods for interacting with Solr by running the `BrainzSolrClient` class in your IDE. `BrainzSolrClient` merely provides some settings to pass into an instance of `Indexer`, the main class that parses ARC records and indexes them into Solr. Regardless of whether you choose the remote or the embedded approach for interacting with Solr, you use the same interface defined in `org.apache.solr.client.solrj.SolrServer`.

Starting a connection to a remote Solr is very simple, with the only parameter being the URL to the Solr instance. Note the inclusion of the *crawler* core in the URL:

```
public org.apache.solr.client.solrj.SolrServer startRemoteSolr()
        throws MalformedURLException,
    SolrServerException {
    CommonsHttpSolrServer solr = new
        CommonsHttpSolrServer("http://localhost:8983/solr/crawler");
    solr.setRequestWriter(new BinaryRequestWriter());
    return solr;
}
```

Solr supports the ability to specify requests and responses in a Java binary format called `javabin` that is much smaller and faster than XML. `javabin` avoids doing XML parsing, and the data being transmitted over the wire is in a much smaller more compact format. Setting the request writer to use the **BinaryRequestWriter** turns this on. By default, the SolrJ client performs updates using the `javabin` format.

You need to make sure that both your SolrJ client and Solr server are using the same version when using the `javabin` format. If your server is Solr 1.4 and your client is Solr 3.1 then you will get a runtime error. You may be okay with a minor version change like 3.1 to 3.2.

Embedding Solr

One of the interesting aspects of SolrJ is that because Solr and SolrJ are both written in Java, you can instantiate Solr and interact with it directly instead of starting up Solr as a separate process. While this speeds up indexing by removing the cost of transporting data over the wire, it does tie you to running your client on the same local box as Solr so that it can access the Solr configuration files and Lucene indexes directly. It's typically simpler and almost as fast to use Solr's **remote streaming** feature (the `stream.file` parameter) to maximize indexing performance with CSV uploads and rich document extraction. The following is an example of using an `EmbeddedSolrServer` class and SolrJ to interface with Solr.

Starting up an embedded Solr is a bit more complex, as you are starting Solr with a specific core instead of running it in a separate servlet container:

```
public SolrServer startEmbeddedSolr() throws IOException,
        ParserConfigurationException, SAXException,
        SolrServerException {
    File root = new File("../../../cores");
container = new CoreContainer();

    SolrConfig config = new SolrConfig(root + "/crawler",
            "solrconfig.xml",null);
    CoreDescriptor descriptor = new CoreDescriptor(container,
                "crawler",root + "/solr");
    SolrCore core = new SolrCore("crawler", root +
            "/../cores_data/crawler", config,  null, descriptor);

container.register(core, false);
    EmbeddedSolrServer solr = new EmbeddedSolrServer(container,
                "crawler");
    return solr;
    }
```

The `SolrConfig` and `CoreDescriptor` classes wrap the information about `solrconfig.xml` and your specific named core. Both of these are used to define the `SolrCore`, which is then registered in a `CoreContainer`. Both `EmbeddedSolrServer` and `CommonsHttpSolrServer` implement the same `SolrServer` interface, so you can specify at runtime the connectivity method to use.

Searching with SolrJ

Performing a query is very straightforward:

```
SolrQuery solrQuery = new SolrQuery("Smashing Pumpkins");
QueryResponse response = solr.query(solrQuery);
```

You can customize the query, for instance, by adding faceting to find out the most popular hosts and paths indexed by the crawler using the methods provided by SolrJ client:

```
SolrQuery solrQuery = new SolrQuery("*:*");
solrQuery.setRows(0);
solrQuery.setFacet(true);
solrQuery.addFacetField("host");
solrQuery.addFacetField("path");
solrQuery.setFacetLimit(10);
solrQuery.setFacetMinCount(2);
QueryResponse response = solr.query(solrQuery);
```

The result in XML makes it easy to display results faceted by host and path:

```
<result name="response" numFound="1446" start="0"/>
<lst name="facet_fields"
<lst name="host">
<int name="musicbrainz.org">1432</int>
<int name="blog.musicbrainz.org">3</int>
<int name="stats.musicbrainz.org">3</int>
<int name="musicbrainz.uservoice.com">2</int>
<int name="www.musicbrainz.org">2</int>
</lst>
<lst name="path">
<int name="/showartist.html">473</int>
<int name="/browseartists.html">381</int>
<int name="/show/artist/">209</int>
<int name="/show/user/">65</int>
<int name="/mod/search/pre/editor-open.html">64</int>
<int name="/browselabels.html">29</int>
</lst>
</lst>
```

As part of the indexing process, we want to clear out the existing index. So we use the `deleteByQuery`, and specify the entire index. Obviously, this can be very dangerous, and if you have a really large Solr index it will take a while to actually commit that change to the file system. Note, in real life you would want to use the multiple core feature of Solr to build a new index in the background and just swap it with the live one when indexing was completed!

```
solr.deleteByQuery( "*:*" ); // delete everything!
solr.commit();
```

Any type of query that you would want to do with Solr is available through the SolrJ client. SolrJ also makes deleting documents simple by providing two easy methods: `deleteByQuery()` and `deleteById()`. `deleteById()` takes in a value for the defined `uniqueKey` field (in this case, the URL). Removing the **Contact Us** page is as simple as running:

```
solr.deleteById("http://musicbrainz.org/doc/ContactUs");
```

Indexing

In the following example, you can see the heart of the loop for parsing through the list of ARC files and extracting and indexing the information. As previously mentioned, we only want HTML pages to be indexed, so we check for a MIME type of `text/html`. Every 100 documents that are added to Solr triggers a commit to be issued to Solr. At the end of the loop, a single optimize request is issued:

```
File arcFiles[] = arcDir.listFiles(new ArcFilenameFilter());
int hits = 1;
for (File arcFile : arcFiles) {
System.out.println("Reading " + arcFile.getName());
    ArchiveReader r = ArchiveReaderFactory.get(arcFile);
r.setDigest(true);

for (ArchiveRecord rec : r) {
if (rec != null) {
            ArchiveRecordHeader meta = rec.getHeader();
if (meta.getMimetype().trim().startsWith("text/html")) {
                ByteArrayOutputStream baos = new
                    ByteArrayOutputStream();
rec.dump(baos)
if (indexIntoSolr) {
                    SolrInputDocument doc = new SolrInputDocument();

doc.addField("url", meta.getUrl(), 1.0f);
```

```
doc.addField("mimeType", meta.getMimetype(),
                        1.0f);
doc.addField("docText", baos.toString());
 // should parse out HTML body and specify character encoding
                    URL url = new URL(meta.getUrl());
doc.addField("host", url.getHost());
doc.addField("path", url.getPath());
solr.add(doc);
                        }

hits++;
                }
            }
rec.close();


        }
}
solr.commit();
solr.optimize();
```

In order to optimize the performance, we could potentially batch send documents to Solr by building a `Collection` of `SolrInputDocuments`, and then add them all at once:

```
Collection<SolrInputDocument> docs = new
            ArrayList<SolrInputDocument>();
// Loop through Archive Records and add documents via docs.add( doc );
server.add( docs );
```

This requires more memory on the client side and it's hard to know how many documents to batch. Instead, SolrJ includes a streaming multi-threaded subclass of `CommonsHttpSolrServer` called `StreamingUpdateSolrServer`. It opens a configurable number of HTTP connections on-demand with a document queue buffer in front of each. `add()` now becomes an asynchronous operation. That means it returns immediately if the buffers have capacity, and an indexing error would not be thrown since it is triggered in another thread. To handle errors, you need to subclass `StreamingUpdateSolrServer` and override `handleError()`. You can see the performance gain by running the following command:

```
>>java -jar target/SolrJForMusicBrainz-1.1.jar ../heritrix-2.0.2/jobs/
completed-musicbrainz-only-artists-20090707185058/arcs/ STREAMING http://
localhost:8983/solr/crawler
```

On my machine I saw a 40 percent gain in performance by streaming the documents using three threads processing a queue of 20 documents.

 If indexing speed is of critical importance to you, consider updating to Solr 4, the current trunk branch, which hasn't been released yet. There are some incredible indexing performance improvements already completed there that you can achieve if you have many CPUs, plenty of RAM, and a fast disk.

Indexing POJOs

POJOs (Plain Old Java Objects) typically follow the JavaBean naming pattern for properties that each have a getter and setter method. Moreover, in many use cases, you want to index information that is exposed as Java objects, such as a product versus document oriented data such as the ARC records in the previous example. Often these objects are backed by a relational database of some type, and you manage them through object relational mapping tools such as Hibernate, JPA, or JDO. Working with objects can provide much richer types of manipulations than working with documents and allows you to leverage the power of strong typing to validate your code.

Annotations provide a richer means of supplying extra information to tools and libraries beyond what is in the Java code itself. For example, the classic JavaDoc tag `@throws SolrServerException` on the method `startEmbeddedSolr()` can be thought of as a type of annotation that has meaning to the JavaDoc tools. However, unlike JavaDoc tags, annotations can be read from source files, class files, and reflectively at runtime. Solr leverages annotations to markup a POJO with information that SolrJ needs to know how to properly index it.

`./SolrJForMusicBrainz/src/main/java/solrbook/RecordItem.java` is an example of a JavaBean that imports the Solr Field class and allows each property to be annotated. In the following example, `RecordItem` has the properties `id` and `html` mapped to the differently named Solr fields `url` and `docText` while `host` and `path` map to the identically named Solr fields `host` and `path`:

```java
import org.apache.solr.client.solrj.beans.Field;

public class RecordItem {

@Field("url")
    String id;

    @Field
    String mimeType;

@Field("docText")
    String html;
```

```
@Field
String host;

@Field
String path;
```

Indexing the `RecordItem` POJOs is very similar to using the `SolrDocument` directly:

```
RecordItem item = new RecordItem();

item.setId(meta.getUrl());
item.setMimeType(meta.getMimetype());
item.setHtml(baos.toString());
URL url = new URL(meta.getUrl());
item.setHost(url.getHost());
item.setPath(url.getPath());
solr.addBean(item);
```

You can also index a collection of beans through `solr.addBeans(collection)`. Performing a query that returns results as POJOs is very similar to returning normal results. You build your `SolrQuery` object the exact same way as you normally would, and perform a search returning a `QueryResponse` object. However, instead of calling `getResults()` and parsing a `SolrDocumentList` object, you would ask for the results as POJOs:

```
public List<RecordItem> performBeanSearch(String query) throws
        SolrServerException {
    SolrQuery solrQuery = new SolrQuery(query);
    QueryResponse response = solr.query(solrQuery);
    List<RecordItem> beans = response.getBeans(RecordItem.class);
System.out.println("Search for '" + query + "': found " +
        beans.size() + " beans.");
    return beans;
}
>> Perform Search for '*:*': found 10 beans.
```

You can then go and process the search results, for example rendering them in HTML with a JSP.

When should I use embedded Solr?

There has been extensive discussion on the Solr mailing lists on whether removing the HTTP layer and using a local embedded Solr is really faster than using the `CommonsHttpSolrServer`. Originally, the conversion of Java `SolrDocument` objects into XML documents and sending them over the wire to the Solr server was considered fairly slow, and therefore embedded Solr offered big performance advantages. However, as of Solr 1.4, the binary `javabin` format is used to transfer messages, which is more compact and requires less processing than XML. The common thinking is that storing a document in Solr is typically a much smaller portion of the time spent on indexing compared to the actual parsing of the original source document to extract its fields. Additionally, by putting both your data importing process and your Solr process on the same computer, you are limiting yourself to only the CPUs available on that computer. If your importing process requires significant processing, then by using the HTTP interface you can have multiple processes spread out on multiple computers munging your source data.

There are several use cases where using embedded Solr is really attractive:

- Indexing locally available content directly into Solr
- Standalone desktop Java applications where you are embedding Solr to supply search
- Upgrading from an existing Lucene search solution to a Solr based search

In-process indexing

If you expect to index large amounts of content from a single file system, which is mounted on the same server as Solr, and indexed in a fairly straightforward manner as quickly as possible, then embedded Solr can be very useful. This is especially true if you don't want to go through the hassle of firing up a separate process or have concerns about having a servlet container, such as Jetty, running.

Consider writing a custom DIH DataSource instead

Instead of using SolrJ for fast importing, consider using Solr's **DataImportHandler** (DIH) framework. Like embedded Solr, it will result in in-process indexing, and it has the added performance boost option of parallelized/multi-threaded indexing. Look at the `org.apache.solr.handler.dataimport.DataSource` interface and existing implementations like **JdbcDataSource**. Using the DIH gives you supporting infrastructure like starting and stopping imports, a debugging interface, chained transformations, and the ability to integrate with data available from other DIH data-sources.

A good example of an open source project that took the approach of using embedded Solr is **Solrmarc**. Solrmarc (hosted at `http://code.google.com/p/solrmarc/`) is a project to parse MARC records, a standardized machine format for storing bibliographic information. Solrmarc uses an embedded Solr just to index the content. After it is optimized, the index is moved to a Solr server to perform search queries.

Standalone desktop applications

In my mind, the most compelling reason for using the embedded Solr approach is when you have a rich client application developed using technologies such as **Swing** or **JavaFX** which is running in a much more constrained client environment. Adding search functionality using the Lucene libraries directly is a more complicated lower-level API and it doesn't have any of the value-add that Solr offers, like faceting. By using embedded Solr you can leverage the much higher level API's of Solr for search, and you don't need to worry about the environment your client application exists in blocking access to ports or exposing the contents of a search index through HTTP. It also means that you don't need to manage spawning another Java process to run a Servlet container, leading to fewer dependencies. Additionally, you still get to leverage skills in working with the typically server based Solr on a client application—a win-win situation for most Java developers!

Upgrading from legacy Lucene

A common situation is when you have an existing Java-based web application that was architected prior to Solr becoming the well-known and stable product that it is today. Many web applications leverage Lucene as the search engine with a custom layer to make it work with a specific Java web framework such as Struts. As these applications grow older, and Solr has progressed, revamping them to keep up with the features that Solr offers has become increasingly difficult. However, these applications have many ties into their homemade Lucene based search engines. Performing the incremental step of migrating from directly interfacing with Lucene to directly interfacing with Solr through embedded Solr can reduce risk. Risk is minimized by limiting the impact of the change to the rest of the application by isolating change to the specific set of Java classes that previously interfaced directly with Lucene. Moreover, this does not require a separate Solr server process to be deployed. A future incremental step would be to leverage the scalability aspects of Solr by moving away from the embedded Solr to interfacing with a separate Solr server.

Using JavaScript with Solr

During the Web 1.0 epoch, JavaScript was primarily used to provide basic client-side interactivity such as a roll-over effect for buttons in the browser for what were essentially static pages generated by the server. However, in today's Web 2.0 environment, AJAX has led to JavaScript being used to build much richer web applications that blur the line between client-side and server-side functionality. Solr's support for the **JavaScript Object Notation** format (**JSON**) for transferring search results between the server and the web browser client makes it simple to consume Solr information by modern Web 2.0 applications. JSON is a human-readable format for representing JavaScript objects, which is rapidly becoming a defacto standard for transmitting language independent data with parsers available to many languages, including Java, C#, Ruby, and Python, as well as being syntactically valid JavaScript code! The `eval()` function will return a valid JavaScript object that you can then manipulate:

```
var json_text = ["Smashing Pumpkins","Dave Matthews Band","The
    Cure"];
var bands = eval('(' + json_text + ')');
alert("Band Count: " + bands.length()); // alert "Band Count: 3"
```

While JSON is very simple to use in concept, it does come with its own set of quirks related to security and browser compatibility. Anytime you are performing an `eval()` you are risking crashing the browser. To learn more about the JSON format, the various client libraries that are available, and how it is and is not like XML, visit the homepage at `http://www.json.org`.

As you may recall from *Chapter 4*'s discussion of query parameters, you change the format of the response from Solr from the default XML to JSON by specifying the JSON writer type as a parameter in the URL via `wt=json`. Here is the result with `indent=on`:

```
{
  "responseHeader":{
  "status":0,
  "QTime":1,
  "params":{
    "q":"hills rolling",
    "wt":"json",
    "indent":"on"}},
  "response":{"numFound":44,"start":0,"docs":[
    {
    "a_name":"Hills Rolling",
    "a_release_date_latest":"2006-11-30T05:00:00Z",
    "a_type":"2",
```

```
    "id":"Artist:510031",
    "type":"Artist"}
...
    ]
}}
```

There is another parameter affecting the JSON, Ruby, and Python formats for field value faceting: `json.nl`. Yes, it's not just for JSON, and it technically affects output of Solr's so-called **NamedList** internal data but only in rare circumstances. The default choice, `flat`, is inconvenient to work with despite its succinctness, so other options are available. Note that the `map` choice does not retain the ordering once it is materialized in memory. Here is a table showing the affects of each choice on faceting on the MusicBrainz artist type:

`flat`	`"a_type":["person",126,"group",71,"0",0]`
`map`	`"a_type":{"person":126,"group":71,"0":0}`
`arrarr`	`"a_type":[["person",126],["group",71],["0",0]]`
`arrmap`	`"a_type":[{"person":126},{"group":71},{"0":0}]`

You may find that you run into difficulties while parsing JSON in various client libraries, as some are stricter about the format than others. Solr does output very clean JSON, such as quoting all keys and using double quotes and offers some formatting options for customizing handling of lists of data. If you run into difficulties, a very useful website for validating your JSON formatting is `http://www.jsonlint.com/`. This can be invaluable for finding issues like an errant trailing comma.

Wait, what about security?

If requests to Solr come from a web browser, then you **must** consider security. You may recall from *Chapter 8, Deployment* that one of the best ways to secure Solr is to limit what IP addresses can access your Solr install through firewall rules. Obviously, if users on the Internet are accessing Solr through JavaScript, then you can't do this. However, if you look back at *Chapter 8, Deployment*, there is information on how to expose a read-only request handler that can be safely exposed to the Internet without exposing the complete admin interface. Also make sure that any filters that MUST be applied to your data, such as a filter query enforcing only active products are shown is applied as an `appends` parameter in your request handler. Additionally, you might proxy Solr requests to ensure the parameters meet a whitelist, to include their values. This can be where you apply various business rules such as preventing a malicious user from passing parameters such as `rows=1000000`!

Building a Solr powered artists autocomplete widget with jQuery and JSONP

It's well established now in the search industry that some form of query auto-completion remarkably improves the effectiveness of a search application. There are several fundamentally different types of autocompletion—be sure to read about them in *Chapter 7, Search Components*. Here is a screenshot of Google showing completions based on search queries it has seen before:

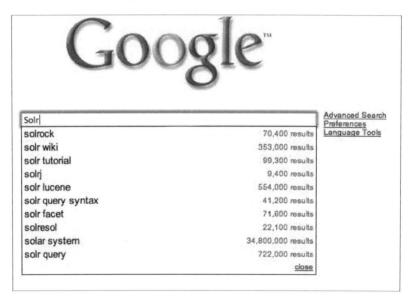

Building an autocomplete text box powered by Solr is very simple by leveraging the JSON output format and the very popular **jQuery** JavaScript library's **Autocomplete** widget.

jQuery is a fast and concise JavaScript library that simplifies HTML document traversing, event handling, animating, and AJAX interactions for rapid web development. It has gone through explosive usage growth in 2008 and is one of the most popular AJAX frameworks. **jQueryUI** is a sub project that provides widgets such as Autocomplete. You can learn more about jQuery at http://www.jquery.com and http://www.jqueryui.com.

A working example using search-result based completions (versus query
log completion or term completion) is available at /examples/9/jquery_
autocomplete/index.html that demonstrates suggesting an artist as you type in his
or her name. You can read the doc and see a live demo of various auto-completions
online at http://jqueryui.com/demos/autocomplete/.

There are three major sections to the HTML page:

- the JavaScript script import statements at the top
- the jQuery JavaScript that actually handles the events around the text being
  input
- a very basic HTML page for the form at the bottom

We start with a very simple HTML form that has a single text input box with the
id="artist" attribute:

```
<div class="ui-widget">
  <label for="artist">Artist: </label>
  <input id="artist" />
</div>
```

We then add a function that runs, after the page has loaded, to turn our basic input
field into a text field with suggestions:

```
$( "#artist" ).autocomplete({
  source: function( request, response ) {
    $.ajax({
      url: "http://localhost:8983/solr/mbartists/select/?wt=json&json.
wrf=?",
      dataType: "jsonp",
      data: {
        q: request.term,
        rows: 10,
        fq: "type:Artist",
        qt: "artistAutoComplete"
      },
      success: function( data ) {
        response( $.map(data.response.docs,function(doc) {
          return {
            label: doc.a_name,
            value: doc.a_name,
          }
        }));
```

```
        }
      });
    },
    minLength: 2,
    select: function( event, ui ) {
      log( ui.item ?
        "Selected: " + ui.item.label :
        "Nothing selected, input was " + this.value);
    },
    open: function() {
      $( this ).removeClass( "ui-corner-all" ).addClass
                                      ( "ui-corner-top" );
    },
    close: function() {
      $( this ).removeClass( "ui-corner-top" ).addClass
                                      ( "ui-corner-all" );
    }
  });
```

The `$("#artist").autocomplete()` function takes in the URL of our data source, in our case Solr, and an array of options and custom functions and ties it to the input form element. The `source: function( request, response )` function supplies the list of suggestions to display via a `$.ajax` callback. The `dataType: "jsonp"` option informs jQuery that we want to retrieve our data using **JSONP**. JSONP stands for **JSON with Padding**, an admittedly not very intuitive name! It means that when you call the server for JSON data, jQuery will dynamically create a JavaScript callback function wrapping the JSON data structure that is evaluated by the browser to actually do something with your JSON objects ("the padding"). This allows you to work around web browser cross-domain scripting issues of running Solr on a different URL and/or port from the originating web page. jQuery takes care of all of the low level plumbing to create the callback function, which is supplied to Solr through the `json.wrf=?` URL parameter. If you look at the Solr logs, you will see the name of a function passed in: `json.wrf=jQue ry15104412757297977805_1309313922023`.

Notice the `data` structure:

```
data: {
  q: request.term,
  rows: 10,
  fq: "type:Artist",
  qt: "artistAutoComplete"
},
```

These items are tacked onto the URL, which is passed to Solr.

Following the best practices, we have created a specific request handler called `artistAutoComplete`, which uses the dismax query parser to search over all of the fields in which an artist's name might show up: `a_name`, `a_alias`, and `a_member_name`, so arguably this is more of an instant search versus word autocompletion! The handler is specified via `qt=artistAutoComplete` parameter.

The `response()` function is called to convert the JSON result data from Solr into the format Autocomplete requires. It consists of a `map()` function that takes the returned JSON data structure for the documents returned and calls an anonymous function for each document. The anonymous function parses out the value to use as the label and value, in our case just the artist name.

Once the user has selected a suggestion, the `select()` function is called, and the name of the selected artist is appended to the `<div id="log">` div.

You now have a nice Solr powered text autocomplete field so that when you enter `Rolling`, you get a list of all of the artists including the Stones:

Artist Autocomplete Demo

Artist: rolling

> **The Rolling Stones**
> Hills Rolling
> Rolling Stock
> AC-DC & Rolling Stones
> Rolling Boil Blues Band
> The Rolling Scabs
> The Rolling Blackouts
> The Rolling Creekdippers
> Boy & His Rolling Kids
> Rolling Thunder Band

Result:
Selecte

One thing that we haven't covered is the pretty common use case for an Autocomplete widget that populates a text field with data that links back to a specific row in a table in a database. For example, in order to store a list of artists, I would want the Autocomplete widget to simplify the process of looking up the artists, but would need to store the list of selected artists in a database. You can still leverage Solr's superior search ability, but tie the resulting list of artists to the original database record through a primary key ID, which is indexed as part of the Solr document.

If you try to lookup the primary key of an artist using the name of the artist, then you may run into problems such as having multiple artists with the same name or unusual characters that don't translate cleanly from Solr to the web interface to your database record.

Instead, a hidden field stores the primary key of the artist and is used in your server-side processing in place of the text typed into the search box:

```
<input type="hidden" id="artist_id"/>
<input id="artist" />
```

We use the change() function to ensure freeform text that doesn't result in a match is ignored by clearing out the artist_id form field and returning false from the function:

```
change: function( event, ui ) {
if (!ui.item){
log("term " + $( this ).val() + " was not found, clearing");
    $( this ).val( "" );
return false;
  }
else {
log("hidden field artist_id:" + ui.item.id);
    $( "#artist_id").val( ui.item.id);
return true;
  }
}
```

Look at /examples/9/jquery_autocomplete/index_with_id.html for a complete example. Change the field artist_id from input type="hidden" to type="text" so that you can see the ID changing more easily as you select different artists. Make sure you click away from the suggestion box to see the change occur!

Where should I get my results to display as suggestions?

There are many approaches for supplying the list of suggestions for autocomplete, and even the nomenclature of **autosuggest, autocomplete,** or **suggest as you type** have loosely defined meanings. If the user is looking for a specific document by name or other identifier, then simple search-results based autocompletion as we've done here is very effective. This is sometimes called "Search as Navigation" because you can skip the search results page. We demo it in `./jquery_autocomplete/index.html`. For broader searching, query log or search-term based completion is typically used. `./jquery_autocomplete/index_terms.html` provides an example of using terms as the source data for autocompletion. For more detail, flip back to the information in *Chapter 7, Search Components* on query completion.

AJAX Solr

AJAX Solr is an excellent Solr search UI framework or building AJAX based search interfaces. It is an off-shoot of an older project call **SolrJS** which is now defunct. AJAX Solr adds some interesting visualizations of result data, including widgets for displaying tag clouds of facets, plotting country code-based data on a map of the world using the Google Chart API, and filtering results by date fields. When it comes to integrating Solr into your web application, if you are comfortable with JavaScript, then this can be a very effective way to add a really nice AJAX view of your search results without changing the underlying web application. If you're working with an older web framework that is brittle and hard to change, such as IBM's Lotus Notes and Domino framework, then this keeps the integration from touching the actual business objects, and keeps the modifications in the client layer via HTML and JavaScript.

The AJAX Solr project homepage is at `http://evolvingweb.github.com/ajax-solr/` and provides a great demo of searching Reuters business news wire results:

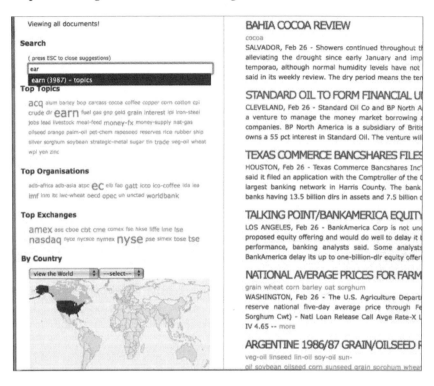

A slightly tweaked copy of the demo is at `/examples/9/ajaxsolr/reuters.html`.

AJAX Solr provides rich UI functionality through widgets—small blocks of JavaScript that render a specific UI component. It comes with widgets like autocompletion of field values, a tag cloud, a facet view, a country code, and calendar based date ranges, as well as displaying the results with paging. They all inherit from an `AbstractWidget` and follow pretty much the same pattern. They are configured in the file `reuters/js/reuters.js` by passing in a set of options. Here is an example of configuring the autocomplete widget to populate the search box with autocomplete suggestions drawn from the topics, organizations, and exchanges fields:

```
Manager.addWidget(new AjaxSolr.AutocompleteWidget({
id: 'text',
target: '#search',
field: 'allText',
fields: [ 'topics', 'organisations', 'exchanges' ]
}));
```

A central `AjaxSolr.Manager` object coordinates the event handling between the various widgets, makes the queries to Solr, and messages the widgets. Shown above is the call to add the widget to the `AjaxSolr.Manager` object. Working with AJAX Solr and creating new widgets for your specific display purposes comes easily to anyone who comes from an object-oriented background.

> The various widgets that come with AJAX Solr serve more as a foundation and source of ideas rather than as a finished set of widgets. You'll find yourself customizing them extensively to meet your specific display needs.

We've developed a MusicBrainz based example at `./examples/9/ajaxsolr/mbtracks.html` for browsing track data. It is based on the Reuters example with a custom widget for term autocompletion using the `facet.prefix` technique. We did *not* configure Solr to load these facets via Solr's `firstSearcher` event in `solrconfig.xml` because this is the only demo that uses it and it takes up to 30 seconds to load given the large index. Therefore, be patient waiting for the first completion results.

Using XSLT to expose Solr via OpenSearch

A relatively unknown, but powerful way to integrate with Solr is via its support for **XSLT**, eXtensible Stylesheet Language Transformations. XSLT is a specification for transforming XML documents into other XML formats, which includes HTML. There are various implementations of this specification and Java includes one. Solr provides a query response writer that executes a provided XSLT stylesheet, to transform Solr's XML search results into some other format. Solr comes with a couple of examples in `./conf/xslt/`. Here is an example of transforming search results into an RSS feed:

```
http://localhost:8983/solr/mbartists/select/?q=marley&wt=xslt&tr=example_rss.xsl
```

The `wt` parameter triggers the use of XSLT, and the `tr` parameter supplies the name of the stylesheet to be used.

There are some caveats to keep in mind for XSLT support. Compiling XSLT transformations is an extra step, and while Solr will cache the last transformation for a period of time, configured in the `queryResponseWriter` via the `xsltCacheLifetimeSeconds` parameter, it only caches a single XSLT transformation. So if you use more than one XSLT stylesheet then you are likely to find Solr constantly recompiling it. Additionally, because Solr has to have the entire XML document in memory first to render the XSL stylesheet, you may run into memory issues if you are returning large numbers of results.

Need a debugger for Solr queries?

Want to understand how Solr determined the score for the documents you returned? You can use the `example.xsl` to quickly transform your results to HTML and expose the query debugging information in an easy to read format. Just make sure you specify the score field to be returned so you get the toggle for the scoring info: `http://localhost:8983/solr/mbartists/select/?q=smashing&wt=xslt&tr=example.xsl&fl=*,score&debugQuery=true`

OpenSearch based Browse plugin

In this section we will show how to use XSLT to support OpenSearch. OpenSearch is a collection of simple formats/standards for search engine interoperability. About half of the standard governs an XML document that describes the web interface of a search engine to invoke searches on it, including various metadata. The other half defines a set of XML elements for formatting search results, typically Atom/RSS. This standard enables you to build a single interface that works with multiple different search engines. OpenSearch was originally developed by A9, a subsidiary of Amazon, and has seen some adoption in the market, especially by the browsers to power their toolbar search boxes. You can find more information at `http://www.opensearch.org/`.

Installing the Search MBArtists plugin

This example builds on the Velocity based UI for the *mbartists* core described earlier, and works best with Firefox. Open the browse interface for the *mbartists* core and you will be able to add a custom **Search MBArtists** plugin to the search bar:

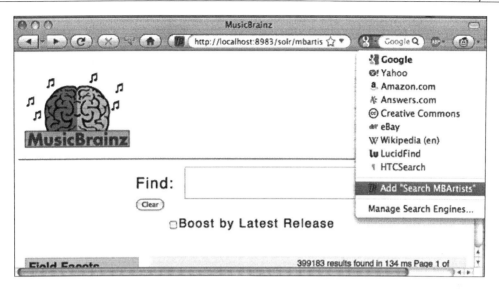

This was prompted by providing a link to an OpenSearch descriptor file in the `cores/mbtypes/conf/velocity/head.vm` file:

```
<link rel="search" href="#{url_for_solr}/admin/file?file=/velocity/
opensearch_description.xml&contentType=text/xml"
type="application/opensearchdescription+xml"
title="Search MBArtists">
</link>
```

Browsers that understand this link will allow the user to add the described search engine. The `opensearch_description.xml` file is just a static XML file that describes how to make both regular queries to Solr as well as autosuggest queries. OpenSearch returns results in either RSS or Atom formats. If you look at `./xslt/opensearch_atom.xsl` you can see the transformation that is applied to a standard XML return document. Opening the link `http://localhost:8983/solr/mbartists/browse?q=wailer&wt=xslt&tr=opensearch_atom.xsl` in Firefox or Safari will return an RSS feed of the various artists named *Wailer*. Open the results in Chrome and you can see the results in the Atom standard XML syntax:

```
<id>tag:localhost:wailers</id>
<opensearch:totalResults>5</opensearch:totalResults>
<opensearch:startIndex>0</opensearch:startIndex>
<opensearch:itemsPerPage>20</opensearch:itemsPerPage>
<opensearch:Query role="request" searchTerms="wailers" startPage="1"/>
&amp;wt=xslt&amp;tr=opensearch_atom.xsl&amp;start=4&amp;rows=20"/>
<link rel="search" type="application/opensearchdescription+xml"
href="opensearch_description.xml"/>
<entry>
```

```
<title>Tubby Wailer</title>
<link href="select?q=id:&quot;Artist:184526&quot;"/>
<id>tag:localhost:Artist:184526</id>
<summary/>
<updated>2011-04-13T17:58:31Z</updated>
</entry>
```

Type into Firefox's search bar, and not only will you be able to perform searches that open up in the browse interface, but you can also get autocompletion of your queries!

 While OpenSearch is somewhat interesting for exposing your website search functionality through browsers, it's even more exciting if you are setting up federated search or trying to plug Solr into another system and need a common lingua franca that won't change and isn't Solr specific.

Accessing Solr from PHP applications

There are a number of ways to access Solr from PHP, and none of them seem to have taken hold of the market as the single best approach. So keep an eye on the wiki page at `http://wiki.apache.org/solr/SolPHP` for new developments.

Adding the URL parameter `wt=php` produces simple PHP output in a typical array data structure:

```
array(
  'responseHeader'=>array(
  'status'=>0,
  'QTime'=>0,
  'params'=>array(
    'wt'=>'php',
    'indent'=>'on',
    'rows'=>'1',
    'start'=>'0',
    'q'=>'Pete Moutso')),
  'response'=>array('numFound'=>523,'start'=>0,'docs'=>array(
array(
    'a_name'=>'Pete Moutso',
    'a_type'=>'1',
    'id'=>'Artist:371203',
    'type'=>'Artist'))
  ))
```

The same response using the Serialized PHP output specified by `wt=phps` URL parameter is a much less human-readable format that is more compact to transfer over the wire:

```
a:2:{s:14:"responseHeader";a:3:{s:6:"status";i:0;s:5:"QTime";i:1;s:6:"
params";a:5:{s:2:"wt";s:4:"phps";s:6:"indent";s:2:"on";s:4:"rows";s:1:
"1";s:5:"start";s:1:"0";s:1:"q";s:11:"Pete Moutso";}}s:8:"response";a
:3:{s:8:"numFound";i:523;s:5:"start";i:0;s:4:"docs";a:1:{i:0;a:4:{s:6:
"a_name";s:11:"Pete Moutso";s:6:"a_type";s:1:"1";s:2:"id";s:13:"Artist
:371203";s:4:"type";s:6:"Artist";}}}}
```

Think twice before using the php writer types

Un-serializing potentially untrusted data can increase security vulnerability. Additionally, the future of these writer types is in some doubt as PHP client abstraction projects such **solr-php-client** and **Solarium** both use JSON in preference to the php writer types.

solr-php-client

Showing a lot of progress towards becoming the dominant solution for PHP integration is the `solr-php-client`, available from `http://code.google.com/p/solr-php-client/`. Interestingly enough, this project leverages the JSON writer type to communicate with Solr instead of the PHP writer type, showing the prevalence of JSON for facilitating inter-application communication in a language agnostic manner. The developers chose JSON over XML because they found that JSON parsed much quicker than XML in most PHP environments. Moreover, using the native PHP format requires using the `eval()` function, which has a performance penalty and opens the door for code injection attacks.

`solr-php-client` can both create documents in Solr as well as perform queries for data. In `/examples/9/solr-php-client/demo.php`, there is a demo of creating a new artist document in Solr for the singer Susan Boyle, and then performing some queries. Installing the demo in your specific local environment is left as an exercise for the reader. On a Macintosh, you should place the `solr-php-client` directory in `/Library/WebServer/Documents/`.

An array data structure of key value pairs that match your schema can be easily created and then used to create an array of `Apache_Solr_Document` objects to be sent to Solr. Notice that we are using the artist ID value `-1`. Solr doesn't care what the ID field contains, just that it is present. Using `-1` ensures that we can find Susan Boyle by ID later!

```
$artists = array(
  'susan_boyle' => array(
    'id' => 'Artist:-1',
    'type' => 'Artist',
    'a_name' => 'Susan Boyle',
    'a_type' => 'person',
    'a_member_name' => array('Susan Boyle')
  )
);
```

The value for a_member_name is an array, because a_member_name is a multi-valued field.

Sending the documents to Solr and triggering the commit and optimize operations is as simple as:

```
$solr->addDocuments( $documents );
$solr->commit();
$solr->optimize();
```

If you are not running Solr on the default port, then you will need to tweak the `Apache_Solr_Service` configuration:

```
$solr = new Apache_Solr_Service( 'localhost', '8983',
  '/solr/mbartists' );
```

Queries can be issued using one line of code. The variables `$query`, `$offset`, and `$limit` contain what you would expect them to.

```
$response = $solr->search( $query, $offset, $limit );
```

Displaying the results is very straightforward as well. Here we are looking for Susan Boyle based on her ID of -1, highlighting the result using a `blue` font:

```
foreach ( $response->response->docs as $doc ) {

  $output = "$doc->a_name ($doc->id) <br />";

  // highlight Susan Boyle if we find her.
  if ($doc->id == 'Artist:-1') {
    $output = "<em><font color=blue>" . $output . "</font></em>";
  }

  echo $output;
}
```

Successfully running the demo creates Susan Boyle and issues a number of queries, producing a page similar to the one below. Notice that if you know the ID of the artist, it's almost like using Solr as a relational database to select a single specific row of data. Instead of `select * from artist where id=-1` we did `q=id:"Artist:-1"`, but the result is the same!

Solarium may be what you want!

Solarium (`http://www.solarium-project.org/`) attempts to improve on other PHP client libraries by not just abstracting away the HTTP communication layer but also more fully modeling the concepts expressed by Solr. It has objects that allow you to easily build complex filter queries and faceting logic.

Drupal options

Drupal is a very successful open source **Content Management System (CMS)** that has been used for building everything from the `WhiteHouse.gov` site to political campaigns and university websites. Drupal's built-in search has always been considered adequate, but not great, so the option of using Solr to power search has been very popular.

Apache Solr Search integration module

The Apache Solr Search integration module, hosted at `http://drupal.org/project/apachesolr`, builds on top of the core search services provided by Drupal, but provides extra features such as faceted search and better performance by offloading servicing search requests to another server. The module has had significant adoption and is the basis of some other Drupal search related modules.

In order to see the Apache Solr module in action, just visit the `Drupal.org` and perform a search to see the faceted results.

Hosted Solr by Acquia

Acquia is a company providing commercially supported Drupal distributions, and also offers hosted Solr search, for Drupal sites that want better search than the built-in MySQL based search. Acquia's adoption of Solr as a better solution for Drupal than Drupal's own search shows the rapid maturing of the Solr community and platform.

Acquia maintains "in the cloud" (Amazon EC2), a large infrastructure of Solr servers saving individual Drupal administrators from the overhead of maintaining their own Solr server. A module provided by Acquia is installed into your Drupal and monitors for content changes. Every five or ten minutes, the module sends content that either hasn't been indexed, or needs to be re-indexed, up to the indexing servers in the Acquia network. When a user performs a search on the site, the query is sent up to the Acquia network, where the search is performed, and then Drupal is just responsible for displaying the results. Acquia's hosted search option supports all of the usual Solr goodies including faceting. Drupal has always been very database intensive, with only moderately complex pages performing 300 individual SQL queries to render! Moving the load of performing searches off one's Drupal server into the cloud drastically reduces the load of indexing and performing searches on Drupal.

Acquia has developed some slick integration beyond the standard Solr features based on their tight integration into the Drupal framework, which include:

- The **Content Construction Kit (CCK)** allows you to define custom fields for your nodes through a web browser. For example, you can add a select field onto a blog node such as oranges/apples/peaches. Solr understands those CCK data model mappings and actually provides a facet of oranges/apples/peaches for it.

- Turn on a single module and instantly receive content recommendations giving you **more like this** functionality based on results provided by Solr. Any Drupal content can have recommendations links displayed with it.

- Multi-site search is a strength of Drupal and provides the support of running multiple sites on a single codebase, such as `drupal.org`, `groups.drupal.org`, and `api.drupal.org`. Currently, part of the Apache Solr module is the ability to track where a document came from when indexed, and as a result, add the various sites as new filters in the search interface.

Acquia's hosted search product is a great example of **Platform as a Service (PaaS)**, and hosted Solr search is a very common integration approach for many organizations that don't wish to manage their own Java infrastructure or need to customize the behavior of Solr drastically. For a list of all the companies offering hosted Solr search please visit `http://wiki.apache.org/solr/SolrHostingProviders`.

Ruby on Rails integrations

There has been a lot of churn in the Ruby on Rails world for adding Solr support, with a number of competing libraries attempting to support Solr in the most Rails-native way. Rails brought to the forefront the idea of **Convention over Configuration**, the principle that sane defaults and simple rules should suffice in most situations versus complex configuration expressed in long XML files. The various libraries for integrating Solr in Ruby on Rails applications establish conventions in how they interact with Solr. However, often there are a lot of conventions to learn, such as suffixing String object field names with _s to match up with the dynamic field definition for String in Solr's `schema.xml`.

The Ruby query response writer

The Ruby hash structure looks very similar to the JSON data structure with some tweaks to fit Ruby, such as translating nulls to nils, using single quotes for escaping content, and the Ruby => operator to separate key-value pairs in maps. Adding a `wt=ruby` parameter to a standard search request returns results that can be `eval()` into a Ruby hash structure like this:

```
{
  'responseHeader'=>{
  'status'=>0,
  'QTime'=>1,
  'params'=>{
    'wt'=>'ruby',
    'indent'=>'on',
    'rows'=>'1',
    'start'=>'0',
    'q'=>'Pete Moutso'}},
```

```
'response'=>{'numFound'=>523,'start'=>0,'docs'=>[
  {
  'a_name'=>'Pete Moutso',
  'a_type'=>'1',
  'id'=>'Artist:371203',
  'type'=>'Artist'}]
}}
```

 Note: Evaluating these results has the same security implications that using the JSON and PHP writers have!

sunspot_rails gem

The **sunspot_rails** gem hooks into the lifecycle of ActiveRecord model objects and transparently indexes them in Solr as they are created, updated, and deleted. This allows you to do queries that are backed by Solr searches, but still work with your normal ActiveRecord objects. Let's go ahead and build a small Rails application that we'll call **MyFaves** that both allows you to store your favorite MusicBrainz artists in a relational model and allows you to search for them using Solr.

Sunspot comes bundled with a full install of Solr as part of the gem, which you can easily start by running `rake sunspot:solr:start`, running Solr on port 8982. This is great for quickly doing development since you don't need to download and set up your own Solr. Typically, you are starting with a relational database already stuffed with content that you want to make searchable. However, in our case we already have a fully populated index of artist information, so we are actually going to take the basic artist information out of the *mbartists* index of Solr and populate our local `myfaves` database used by the Rails application. We'll then fire up the version of Solr shipped with Sunspot, and see how `sunspot_rails` manages the lifecycle of ActiveRecord objects to keep Solr's indexed content in sync with the content stored in the relational database. Don't worry, we'll take it step by step! The completed application is in `/examples/9/myfaves` for you to refer to.

Setting up MyFaves project

This example assumes you have Rails 3.x already installed. We'll start with the standard plumbing to get a Rails application set up with our basic data model:

```
>>rails new myfaves
>>cd myfaves
>>./script/generate scaffold artist name:string group_type:string
   release_date:datetime image_url:string
>>rake db:migrate
```

This generates a basic application backed by a **SQLite** database. Now we need to specify that our application depends on Sunspot. Edit the file Gemfile and add:

```
gem 'sunspot_rails', '~> 1.2.1'
```

Next, update your dependencies and generate the config/sunspot.yml configuration file:

```
>>bundle install
>>rails generate sunspot_rails:install
```

We'll also be working with roughly 399,000 artists, so obviously we'll need some page pagination to manage that list, otherwise pulling up the artists /index listing page will timeout. We'll use the popular will_paginate gem to manage pagination. Add the will_paginate gem declaration to your Gemfile and re-run bundle install:

```
gem "will_paginate", "~> 3.0.pre4"
```

Edit the ./app/controllers/artists_controller.rb file, and replace in the index method the call to @artists = Artist.all with:

```
@artists = Artist.paginate :page => params[:page], :order =>
   'created_at DESC'
```

Also add to ./app/views/artists/index.html.erb a call to the view helper to generate the page links:

```
<%= will_paginate @artists %>
```

Start the application using ./script/rails start, and visit the page http://localhost:3000/artists/. You should see an empty listing page for all of the artists. Now that we know the basics are working, let's go ahead and actually leverage Solr.

Populating MyFaves relational database from Solr

Step one will be to import data into our relational database from the mbartists Solr index. Add the following code to ./app/models/artist.rb:

```
class Artist < ActiveRecord::Base
  searchable do
    text :name, :default_boost => 2
    string :group_type
    time :release_date
  end
end
```

The searchable block maps the attributes of the Artist ActiveRecord object to the artist fields in Solr's schema.xml. Since Sunspot is designed to store any kind of data in Solr that is stored in your database, it needs a way of distinguishing among various types of data model objects. For example, if we wanted to store information about our User model object in Solr in addition to the Artist object then we need to provide a field in the schema to distinguish the Solr document for the *artist* with the primary key of 5 from the Solr document for the *user* with the primary key of 5. Fortunately, the *mbartists* schema has a field named type that stores the value Artist, which maps directly to our ActiveRecord class name of Artist.

There is a simple script called populate.rb at the root of /examples/9/myfaves that you can run that will copy the artist data from the existing Solr mbartists index into the MyFaves database:

>>./populate.rb

populate.rb is a great example of the types of scripts you may need to develop to transfer data into and out of Solr. Most scripts typically work with some sort of batch size of records that are pulled from one system and then inserted into Solr. The larger the batch size, the more efficient the pulling and processing of data typically is at the cost of more memory being consumed, and the slower the commit and optimize operations are. When you run the populate.rb script, play with the batch size parameter to get a sense of resource consumption in your environment. Try a batch size of 10 versus 10000 to see the changes. The parameters for populate.rb are available at the top of the script:

```
MBARTISTS_SOLR_URL = 'http://localhost:8983/solr/mbartists'
BATCH_SIZE = 1500
MAX_RECORDS = 100000
```

There are roughly 399,000 artists in the `mbartists` index, so if you are impatient, then you can set `MAX_RECORDS` to a more reasonable number to complete running the script faster.

The connection to Solr is handled by the **RSolr** library. A request to Solr is simply a hash of parameters that is passed as part of the GET request. We use the `*:*`query to find all of the artists in the index and then iterate through the results using the `start` parameter:

```
rsolr = RSolr.connect :url => MBARTISTS_SOLR_URL
response = rsolr.select({
:q => '*:*',
:rows=> BATCH_SIZE,
:start => offset,
:fl => ['*','score']
})
```

In order to create our new Artist model objects, we just iterate through the results of `response['response']['docs']`, parsing each document in order to preserve our unique identifiers between Solr and the database and creating new ActiveRecord objects. In our MusicBrainz Solr schema, the ID field functions as the primary key and looks like `Artist:11650` for The Smashing Pumpkins. In the database, in order to sync the two, we need to insert the Artist with the ID of `11650`. We wrap the insert statement `a.save!` in a `begin/rescue/end` structure so that if we've already inserted an artist with a primary key, then the script continues. This allows us to run the populate script multiple times without erroring out:

```
response['response']['docs'].each do |doc|
   id = doc["id"]
   id = id[7..(id.length)]
   a = Artist.new(
   :id => id,
   :name => doc["a_name"],
   :group_type => doc["a_type"],
   :release_date => doc["a_release_date_latest"]

   begin
     a.save!
   rescue ActiveRecord::StatementInvalid => err
     raise err unless err.to_s.include?("PRIMARY KEY must be unique") #
sink duplicates
   end
end
```

We've successfully migrated the data we need for our MyFaves application out of Solr and we're ready to use the version of Solr that's bundled with Sunspot.

Solr configuration information is listed in `./myfaves/config/sunspot.yml`. Sunspot establishes the convention that development is on port 8982, unit tests that use Solr connect on port 8981, and then production connects on the traditional 8983 port:

```
development:
  solr:
    hostname: localhost
    port: 8982
```

Start the included Solr by running `rake sunspot:solr:start`. To shutdown Solr run the corresponding Rake command: `sunspot:solr:stop`. On the initial startup rake will create a new top level `./solr` directory and populate the `conf` directory with default configuration files for Solr (including `schema.xml`, `stopwords.txt`, and so on) pulled from the Sunspot gem.

Build Solr indexes from a relational database

Now we are ready to trigger a full index of the data from the relational database into Solr. `sunspot` provides a very convenient rake task for this with a variety of parameters that you can learn about by running `rake -D sunspot:reindex`.

```
>>rake sunspot:solr:start
>>rake sunspot:reindex
```

Browse to `http://localhost:8982/solr/admin/schema.jsp` to see the list of dynamic fields generated by following **Convention over Configuration** pattern of Rails applied to Solr. Some of the conventions that are established by Sunspot and expressed by Solr in `./solr/conf/schema.xml` are:

- Primary key field for model object in Solr is always called `id`.

- Type field that stores the disambiguating class name of the model object is called `type`.

- Heavy use of the dynamic field support in Solr. The data type of ActiveRecord model objects is based on the database column type. Therefore, when `sunspot_rails` indexes a model object, it sends a document to Solr with the various suffixes to leverage the dynamic column creation. In `./solr/conf/schema.xml`, the only fields defined outside of the management fields are dynamic fields:

```
<dynamicField name="*_text" type="text" indexed="true"
stored="false"/>
```

- The default search field is called `text`. However, you need to define what fields are copied into the text field. Sunspot's DSL is oriented towards naming each model field you'd like to search from Ruby.

The document that gets sent to Solr for our Artist records creates the dynamic fields such as `name_text`, `group_type_s` and `release_date_d`, for a text, string, and date field respectively. You can see the list of dynamic fields generated through the schema browser at `http://localhost:8982/solr/admin/schema.jsp`.

Now we are ready to perform some searches. Sunspot adds some new methods to our ActiveRecord model objects such as `search()` that lets us load ActiveRecord model objects by sending a query to Solr. Here we find the group *Smash Mouth* by searching for matches to the word `smashing`:

```
% ./script/rails console
Loading development environment (Rails 3.0.9)
>>search= Artist.search{keywords "smashing"}
=><Sunspot::Search:{:fq=>["type:Artist"], :q=>"smashing",
:fl=>"* score", :qf=>"name_text^2", :defType=>"dismax", :start=>0,
:rows=>30}>
>>search.results.first
=>[#<Artist id: 93855, name: "Smashing Atoms", group_type: nil,
release_date: nil, image_url: nil, created_at: "2011-07-21 05:15:21",
updated_at: "2011-07-21 05:15:21">]
```

The raw results from Solr are stored in the variable `search.hits`. The variable `search.results` returns the ActiveRecord objects from the database.

Let's also verify that Sunspot is managing the full lifecycle of our objects. Assuming *Susan Boyle* isn't yet entered as an artist, let's go ahead and create her:

```
>>Artist.search{keywords  'Susan Boyle', :fields => [:name]}.hits
=>[]
>>susan = Artist.create(:name => "Susan Boyle", :group_type =>'1',
    :release_date => Date.new)
=> #<Artist id: 548200, name: "Susan Boyle", group_type: 1,
    release_date: "-4712-01-01 05:00:00", created_at: "2011-07-22
21:05:53"", updated_at: "2011-07-22 21:05:53"">
```

Check the log output from your Solr running on port 8982, and you should also have seen an update query triggered by the insert of the new Susan Boyle record:

```
INFO: [] webapp=/solr path=/update params={} status=0 QTime=24
```

Now, if we delete Susan's record from our database:

```
>>susan.destroy
=> #<Artist id: 548200, name: "Susan Boyle", group_type: 1,
   release_date: "-4712-01-01 05:00:00", created_at: "2009-04-21
   13:11:09", updated_at: "2009-04-21 13:11:09">
```

Then there should be another corresponding update issued to Solr to remove the document:

```
INFO: [] webapp=/solr path=/update params={} status=0 QTime=57
```

You can verify this by doing a search for Susan Boyle directly, which should return no rows at `http://localhost:8982/solr/select/?q=Susan+Boyle`.

Complete MyFaves website

Now, let's go ahead and put in the rest of the logic for using our Solr-ized model objects to simplify finding our favorite artists. We'll store the list of favorite artists in the browser's session space for convenience. If you are following along with your own generated version of MyFaves application, then the remaining files you'll want to copy over from `/examples/9/myfaves` are as follows:

- `./app/controller/myfaves_controller.rb` contains the controller logic for picking your favorite artists.

- `./app/views/myfaves/` contains the display files for picking and showing the artists.

- `./app/views/layouts/myfaves.html.erb` is the layout for the MyFaves views. We use the Autocomplete widget again, so this layout embeds the appropriate JavaScript and CSS files.

- `./public/stylesheets/jquery.autocomplete.css` and `./public/stylesheets/indicator.gif` are stored locally in order to fix pathing issues with the `indicator.gif` showing up when the autocompletion search is running.

The only other edits you should need to make are:

- Edit `./config/routes.rb` by adding `resources :myfaves` and `root :to => "myfaves#index"`.

- Delete `./public/index.html` to use the new `root` route you just defined.

- Copy the index method out of `./app/controllers/artists_controllers.rb` because we want the index method to respond with both HTML and JSON response types.

- Run `rake db:sessions:create` to generate a sessions table, then `rake db:migrate` to update the database with the new sessions table. Edit `./config/initializers/session_store.rb` and change to using the `:active_record_store` for preserving session state.

You should now be able to run `./script/rails start` and browse to `http://localhost:3000/`. You will be prompted to enter search by entering the artist's name. If you don't receive any results, then make sure you have started Solr using `rake sunspot:solr:start`. Also, if you have only loaded a subset of the full 399,000 artists, then your choices may be limited. You can load all of the artists through the `populate.rb` script and then run `rake sunspot:reindex`, although it will take a long time to complete. Something good to do just before you head out for lunch or home for the evening!

If you look at `./app/views/myfaves/index.rhtml`, then you can see the jQuery autocomplete call is a bit different:

```
$("#artist_name").autocomplete( '/artists.json?callback=?', {
```

The URL we are hitting is `/artists.json`, with the `.json` suffix telling Rails that we want JSON data back instead of normal HTML. If we ended the URL with `.xml`, then we would have received XML formatted data about the artists. We provide a slightly different parameter to Rails to specify the JSONP callback to use. Unlike the previous example, where we used `json.wrf`, which is Solr's parameter name for the callback method to call, we use the more standard parameter name `callback`. We changed the `ArtistController index` method to handle the `autocomplete` widgets data needs through JSONP. If there is a `q` parameter, then we know the request was from the `autocomplete` widget, and we ask Solr for the `@artists` to respond with. Later on, we render `@artists` into JSON objects, returning only the `name` and `id` attributes to keep the payload small. We also specify that the JSONP callback method is what was passed when using the `callback` parameter:

```
def index
if params[:q]
   @artists = Artist.search{ keywords params[:q] }.results
else
   @artists = Artist.paginate :page => params[:page], :order =>
       'created_at DESC'
end

respond_to do |format|
format.html # index.html.erb
format.xml { render :xml => @artists }
```

```
    format.json { render :json => @artists.to_json(:only => [:name,
            :id]), :callback => params[:callback] }
  end
end
```

At the end of all of this, you should have a nice autocomplete interface for quickly picking artists.

When you are selecting Sunspot as your integration method, you are implicitly agreeing to the various conventions established for indexing data into Solr. If you are used to working with Solr directly you may find understanding the Sunspot DSL for querying a bit of an obstacle. But if your background is in Rails, or you are building very complex queries, then learning the DSL will pay off in productivity and ability to maintain complex expressive queries.

Which Rails/Ruby library should I use?

The two most common high level libraries for interacting with Solr are **acts_as_solr** and **Sunspot**. However, in the last couple of years, Sunspot has become the more popular choice, and comes in a version designed to work explicitly with Rails called `sunspot_rails` that allows Rails `ActiveRecord` database objects to be transparently backed by a Solr index for full text search.

For lower-level client interface to Solr from Ruby environments, there are two libraries duking it out to be the client of choice: **solr-ruby**, a client library developed by the Apache Solr project and **rsolr**, which is a reimplementation of a Ruby centric client library. Both of these solutions are solid and act as great low level API libraries. However, `rsolr` has gained more attention, has better documentation, and some nice features such as a direct embedded Solr connection through JRuby. `rsolr` also has support for using `curb` (Ruby bindings to `curl`, a very fast HTTP library) instead of the standard `Net::HTTP` library for the HTTP transport layer.

In order to perform a select using `solr-ruby`, you would issue:

```
response = solr.query('washington', {
:start=>0,
:rows=>10
})
```

In order to perform a select using `rsolr`, you would issue:

```
response = solr.select({
:q=>'washington',
:start=>0,
:rows=>10
})
```

So you can see that doing a basic search is pretty much the same in either library. Differences crop up more as you dig into the details on parsing and indexing records. You can learn more about `solr-ruby` on the Solr Wiki at `http://wiki.apache.org/solr/solr-ruby` and learn more about `rsolr` at `http://github.com/mwmitchell/rsolr/tree`.

 Think about if you really need another layer of abstraction between you and Solr. Making a call to Solr using `wt=ruby` and evaluating the results may be the simplest solution.

Nutch for crawling web pages

A very common source of data to to be searchable is content in web pages, either from the Internet or inside the firewall. The long-time popular solution for crawling and searching web pages is **Nutch**, a former Lucene sub-project. Nutch is focused on performing Internet scale web crawling similar to Google with components such as a web crawler, a link graphing database, and parsers for HTML and other common formats found on the Internet. Nutch is designed to scale horizontally over multiple machines during crawling using the bigdata platform **Hadoop** to manage the work.

Nutch has gone through varying levels of activity and community involvement and recently reached version 1.3. Previously Nutch used its own custom search interface based on Lucene, but it now leverages Solr for search. This allows Nutch to focus on web crawling, while Solr works as a generic search tool with features such as query spellcheck and faceting that Nutch previously couldn't match. Nutch natively understands web relevancy concepts such as the value of links towards calculating a page rank score, and how to factor in what an HTML `<title/>` tag is, when building the scoring model to return results.

Nutch works off of a seed list of URLs that are used as the source of web pages to crawl. The `./examples/9/nutch/` directory contains a configured copy of Nutch for crawling through a list of Wikipedia pages for the 300 most popular artists according to MusicBrainz's count of track lookups. Look at the script `seed_urls.rb` to see the logic used for extracting the URL seed list. To crawl the Internet using a subset of the seed list and index into Solr run from the `./examples/9/nutch/runtime/local` directory:

```
>> ./bin/nutch crawl urls -solr http://localhost:8983/solr/nutch/
-depth 1 -topN 5
```

Browse to `http://localhost:8983/solr/nutch/select?q=*:*&wt=json&indent=true&fl=url,title` and you will see the five wiki pages indexed by Nutch into Solr.

The `depth` parameter tells Nutch how deep to crawl, with a depth of 1 being just to index each webpage listed in the `./urls/Wikipedia_seed_urls.txt` file. The `topN` parameter controls how many documents at each level to crawl, with 5 meaning that only five artist pages in total are crawled. Once you are satisfied that Nutch is working the way you want, trigger the crawl again with a larger `topN` parameter, at least 300 to index each of the wiki pages listed in the `wikipedia_seed_urls.txt` file.

The schema file (at `./cores/nutch/conf/schema.xml`) that Nutch uses is very self explanatory. The biggest change you might make is to set `stored="false"` on the `content` field to reduce the index size if you are doing really big crawls.

For more information about the plugins that extend Nutch, and how to configure Nutch for more sophisticated crawling patterns, look at the documentation at `http://nutch.apache.org`.

Maintaining document security with ManifoldCF

A frequent requirement for search engines is to maintain document level security. While a public search engine may expose all documents to all users, many intranet oriented search engines maintain information that that is accessible to only a subset of users. Historically, the solution to maintaining document level security has been a roll-your-own with the most common approaches being:

1. Implement a post processing filter on the document result set that removes documents that don't match a specific user access controls. This approach is nice because you can just wrap your calls to Solr with your own proprietary security model, and doesn't require any changes to your indexing logic. However, this can lead to smaller then normal results since you may return 10 results, but only one or two may match the user access criteria! Working around this by returning much larger result sets, say 50 or 100, or making multiple calls to Solr to ensure you always return a minimum of 10 results is awkward at best. Also, the filtering process can often be very expensive to perform.

2. You may be able to perform deeper integration with Solr by writing your own query parser that taps into Solr's filter queries and avoid the post processing step.

3. The other approach is to enrich your indexed document with information about who can access which documents. This access information is exposed by using filter queries to control who can access which documents. For example, to allow only documents marked as accessible to the marketing department, or unclassified, you would append: `fq=group_label:marketing_department OR -group_label:[* TO *]` to your query.

Apache **ManifoldCF (CF meaning Connector Framework)** provides a framework for extracting content from multiple repositories, enriching it with document level security information, and outputting the resulting document into Solr based on the security model found in Microsoft's Active Directory platform. Working with ManifoldCF requires understanding the interaction between extracting content from repositories via a **Repository Connector**, outputting the documents and security tokens via an **Output Connector** into Solr, listing a specific user's access tokens from an **Authority Connector**, and finally performing a search that filters the document results based on the list of tokens. ManifoldCF takes care of ensuring that as content and security classifications for content are updated in the underlying repositories it is synched to Solr, either on a scheduled basis or a constantly monitoring basis.

Connectors

ManifoldCF provides **connectors** that index into Solr content from a number of enterprise content repositories including SharePoint, Documentum, Meridio, LiveLink, and FileNet. Competing with DataImportHandler and Nutch, ManifoldCF also crawls web pages, RSS feeds, JDBC databases, and remote Windows shares and local file systems, while adding the document level security tokens where applicable. The most compelling use case for ManifoldCF is leveraging ActiveDirectory to provide access tokens for content indexed in Microsoft SharePoint repositories, followed by just gaining access to content in the other enterprise content repositories.

Putting ManifoldCF to use

While the sweet spot for using ManifoldCF is with an Authority like ActiveDirectory, we're going to reuse our `MusicBrainz.org` data and come up with a simple scenario for playing with ManifoldCF and Solr. We will use our own `MusicBrainzConnector` class to read in data from a simple CSV file that contains a MusicBrainz ID for an artist, the artist's name, and a list of music genre tags for the artist:

```
4967c0a1-b9f3-465e-8440-4598fd9fc33c,Enya,folk,pop,irish
```

The data will be streamed through Manifold and out to our `/manifoldcf` Solr core with the list of genres used as the access tokens. To simulate an Authority service that translates a username to a list of access tokens, we will use our own `GenreAuthority`. `GenreAuthority` will take the first character of the supplied username, and return a list of genres that start with the same character. So a call to ManifoldCF for the username `paul@example.com` would return the access tokens *pop* and *punk*. A search for "Chris" would match on "Chris Isaak" since he is tagged with *pop*, but "Chris Cagle" would be filtered out since he plays only *American* and *country* music.

Browse the source for both `MusicBrainzConnector` and `GenreAuthority` in `./examples/9/manifoldcf/connectors/` to get a better sense of how specific connectors work with the greater ManifoldCF framework.

To get started we need to add some new dynamic fields to our schema in `cores/manifoldcf/conf/schema.xml`:

```
<dynamicField name="allow_token_*" type="string" indexed="true"
stored="true" multiValued="true"/>
<dynamicField name="deny_token_*" type="string" indexed="true"
stored="true" multiValued="true"/>
```

These rules will allow the Solr output connector to store access tokens in the fields such as `allow_token_document` and `deny_token_document`.

Now we can start up ManifoldCF. The version distributed with this book is a stripped down version, with just the specific connectors required for this demo! In a separate window from the `./examples/9/manifoldcf/example` directory run:

```
>>java -jar start.jar
```

ManifoldCF ships with Jetty as a servlet container, hence the very similar start command to the one Solr uses!

Browse to `http://localhost:8345/mcf-crawler-ui/` to access the ManifoldCF user interface which exposes the following main functions:

- **List Output Connections**: Provides a list of all the recipients of extracted content. This is configured to store content in the `manifoldcf` Solr core.
- **List Authority Connections**: Authority Connectors translate user credentials to a list of security tokens. You can test that our GenreAuthority is functioning by calling the API at `http://localhost:8345/mcf-authority-service/UserACLs?username=paul@example.com` and verifying you receive a list of genre access tokens starting with the letter p.

- **List Repository Connections**: The only repository of content we have is the CSV file of author/genre information. Other repositories, like RSS feeds or SharePoint sites would be listed here. When you create a repository you associate a connector and the Authority you are going to use, in our case the GenreAuthority.

- **List All Jobs**: This lists all the combinations of input repository and output Solrs.

- **Status and Job Management**: This very useful screen allows you to stop, start, abort, and pause the jobs you have scheduled, as well as provide a basic summary of the number of documents that have been found in the repository as well as those processed into Solr.

Go ahead and choose the **Status** and **Job Management** screen and trigger the indexing job. Click **Refresh** a couple of times, and you will see the artist content being indexed into Solr. To see the various genres being used as access tokens browse:

```
http://localhost:8983/solr/manifoldcf/
select?q=*:*&facet=true&facet.field=allow_token_document&rows=0
```

Now that you have data in Solr, this is only half the challenge. At the time of writing, neither ManifoldCF nor Solr have a component that hooked ManifoldCF based permissions directly into Solr. However, based on code from the upcoming *ManifoldCF in Action* book (http://code.google.com/p/manifoldcfinaction/), you can easily add a Search Component to your request handler. Add to solrconfig.xml:

```
<requestHandler name="standard" class="solr.SearchHandler"
                default="true">
  <arr name="components">
    <str>manifoldcf</str>
  </arr>
</requestHandler>

<searchComponent name="manifoldcf" class="org.apache.manifoldcf.
               examples.ManifoldCFSecurityFilter">
  <str name="AUTHENTICATED_USER_NAME">username</str>
</searchComponent>
```

You are now ready to perform your first query! Do a search for *Chris*, specifying your `username` as `paul@example.com` and you should see only *pop* and *punk* music artists being returned!

```
http://localhost:8983/solr/manifoldcf/
select?q=Chris&username=paul@example.com
```

Change the `username` parameter to `courtney@example.com` and Chris Cagle, *country* singer should be returned! As documents are added/removed from the CSV file, ManifoldCF will notice the changes and reindex the updated content.

Summary

As you've seen, Solr offers a plethora of integration options, from its ability to customize its output using the various query response writers, to clients for specific languages, to frameworks that enable powerful front ends for both indexing content as well as providing a jump start in developing the search user interface. The simplicity of using HTTP GET to request actions to be performed by Solr and responding with simple documents makes it very straightforward to integrate Solr based search into your applications regardless of what your preferred development environment is.

If you are looking to explore more integration options with your favorite language, framework, or other software, then visit: `http://wiki.apache.org/solr/IntegratingSolr` and `http://wiki.apache.org/solr/SolrEcosystem`.

In the next chapter, we are going to look at how to scale Solr to meet growing demand by covering approaches for scaling an individual Solr server as well as scaling out by leveraging multiple Solr servers working cooperatively.

10
Scaling Solr

You've deployed Solr, and the world is beating a path to your door, leading to a sharp increase in the number of queries being issued, and meanwhile you've indexed tenfold the amount of information you originally expected. You discover that Solr is taking longer to respond to queries and index new content. When this happens, it's time to start looking at what configuration changes you can make to Solr to support more load. We'll look at a series of changes/optimizations that you can make, starting with the simplest changes that give the most bang for your buck to more complex changes that require thorough analysis of the impact of the system changes.

In this chapter, we will cover the following topics:

- Tuning complex systems
- Testing Solr Performance with SolrMeter
- Optimizing a single Solr server (Scale up)
- Moving to multiple Solr servers (Scale horizontally)
- Combining replication and sharding (Scale deep)

In a hurry?

If you flipped to this chapter because you need to scale Solr, look at the section *Solr caching* as well as how to use replication to share load over multiple Solr servers described in *Moving to multiple Solr servers (Scale horizontally)*.

Tuning complex systems

Tuning any complex system, whether it's a database, a message queuing system, or the deep dark internals of an operating system, is something of a black art. Researchers and vendors have spent decades figuring out how to measure the performance of systems and coming up with approaches for maximizing the performance of those systems. For some systems that have been around for decades, such as databases, you can just search online for *Tuning Tips for X Database* and find explicit rules that suggest what you need to do to gain performance. However, even with those well-researched systems, it still can be a matter of trial and error.

In order to measure the impact of your changes, you should look at a couple of metrics and optimize for these three parameters:

- **Transactions Per Second (TPS)**: In the Solr world, how many search queries and document updates are you able to perform per second? You can get a sense of that by using the **Statistics** page at `http://localhost:8983/solr/mbtracks/admin/stats.jsp` and looking at the `avgTimePerRequest` and `avgRequestsPerSecond` parameters for your request handlers.

- **CPU usage**: To quickly gain a sense of CPU usage of Solr using JConsole. You can also use OS specific tools such as **PerfMon** (Windows) and **top** (Unix) to monitor your Java processes, which can be helpful if you have a number of services running on the same box that are competing for resources (not recommended for maximum scaling!)

- **Memory usage**: When tuning for memory management, you are looking to ensure that the amount of memory allocated to Solr doesn't constantly grow. While it's okay for the memory consumption to go up a bit, letting it grow unconstrained eventually means you will receive out-of-memory errors! Balance increases in memory consumption with significant increases in TPS. You can use JConsole to keep an eye on memory usage.

In order to get a sense of what the **Steady State** is for your application, you can gather the statistics by using the SolrMeter product to put your Solr under load. We'll discuss in the next section how to build a load testing script with SolrMeter that accurately mirrors your real world interactions with Solr. This effort will give you a tool that can be run repeatedly and allows more of an apple-to-apple comparison of the impact of changes to your configuration.

Solr's architecture has benefited from its heritage as the search engine developed in-house from 2004 to 2006 that powers CNET.com, a site that is ranked 86th for traffic by Alexa.com today. Solr, out of the box, is already very performant, with extensive effort spent by the community to ensure that there are minimal bottlenecks. But the tuning of Solr hasn't matured to where there are hard and fast rules for optimization that you should follow by rote step to increase scalability. Most tuning will trade off increases in search performance at the expense of disk index size, indexing speed, and/or memory requirements (and vice versa). The three system changes to perform in increasing complexity are:

- **Scale up**: Optimize a single instance of Solr. Look at caching and memory configuration. Run Solr on a dedicated server (no virtualization) with very fast CPUs and SSD drives if you can afford it. In the scale up approach, you are trying to maximize what you can get from a single server.

- **Scale horizontally**: Look at moving to multiple Solr servers. If your queries run quickly with an acceptable avgTimePerRequest, but have too many incoming requests, then replicate your complete index across multiple Solr servers in a master/slave configuration. If your queries take too long to complete due to complexity or size of the index, then use sharding to share the load of processing a single query across multiple sharded Solr servers. Note: most, but not every feature of Solr is available in a distributed query, check http://wiki.apache.org/solr/DistributedSearch for compatibility. Both these approaches can be considered scaling out techniques.

- **Scale deep**: If you need both sharding for query performance and multiple replicated indexes to support the query load, then move to each shard being a master server with multiple slave servers. This is the scale deep approach and is the most complex architecture to implement.

There is some great research being performed on measuring the limits of scaling Solr by a consortium of libraries called the *HathiTrust*. You can follow their research (and others working in this space) by following links from http://wiki.apache.org/solr/SolrPerformanceData.

Testing Solr performance with SolrMeter

One of the biggest challenges when doing performance testing is to know when you've accomplished your goals. SolrMeter, available from `http://code.google.com/p/solrmeter/`, makes it very easy to test your Solr configuration. When performance testing Solr, you typically are tweaking configuration values such as cache sizes and query parameters in response to two ongoing activities: the pace of documents being indexed into Solr, and the pace of queries being issued to Solr. SolrMeter makes it very easy to control the pace of these two activities through a simple GUI tool. SolrMeter brings together both basic load testing functionality with some visualization and analytics of your Solr instance. A typical example is looking at your cache rates. While you can use the Solr Admin **statistics** page to pull back these results, you are only seeing a snapshot in time. In the following screenshot, you can see a visualization of the **queryResultCache** over time. The middle four slopes were created because I began the **Update Console** at second 75 indexing new data. You can easily see the impact of commits on the caches. This type of visualization can help you go beyond just using the default caching configurations.

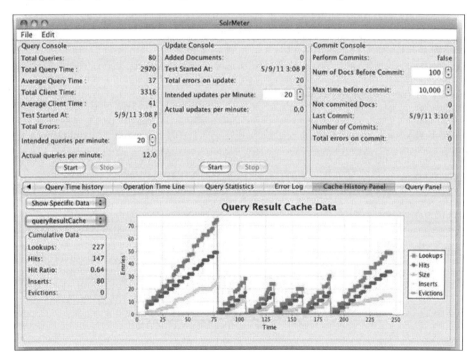

Start SolrMeter with the embedded configuration for the mbartists core by running from the ./examples/10/solrmeter directory:

```
>>java -Dsolrmeter.configurationFile=./mbartists.smc.xml-jar
solrmeter-0.2.0-jar-with-dependencies_3_1_4_0.jar
```

mbartists.smc.xml specifies to SolrMeter which data files to use to power the queries to be made and the data to be indexed. SolrMeter takes in separate data files to randomly build combinations of queries with filters, faceting, and updates applied: queries.txt, filterQueries.txt, fields.txt, and updates.txt. If you are already using Solr and logging the queries then you should instead provide an externalQueries.txt file that has the full set of query parameters:

```
q="Maxtor Corp"+OR+Belkin&rows=5&fq=inStock:true&facet=true&facet.
field=price
```

Just extract the entire line after the ? character logged by the GET requests in the Solr log. That is great for repeating the same set of queries so you are doing A/B testing as you tweak the various settings. SolrMeter also supports exporting the query time and a histogram of query time in CSV format to make your own graphs.

You can also use SolrMeter to place a "base" load on a Solr, and then use other testing tools that offer more scripting or analytics options to ensure that what works just fine when Solr isn't under load continues to meet expectations when Solr is under load. For example, you might want to set up 60 updates per minute and 300 queries per minute as a base load. Using SolrMeter you can quickly set this scenario up, and then use another tool like JMeter that drives your front-end search user interface to ensure your application meets your expected SLA when Solr is under load. Or you can easily change settings such as cache configurations or faceting settings and see the impact of these changes on performance.

 I like to build my list of queries for load testing by extracting a day's worth of queries from your existing search engine log or HTTP web server log files. This gives me a realistic set of data so I am tuning to what my users actually search for, not what I think they search for!

Optimizing a single Solr server (Scale up)

There are a large number of different options that Solr gives you for enhancing performance of a specific Solr instance, and for most of these options, deciding to modify them depends on the specific performance result you are trying to tune for. This section is structured from most generally useful to more specific optimizations.

Configuring JVM settings to improve memory usage

Solr runs inside a **Java Virtual Machine** (**JVM**), an environment that abstracts your Java-based application from the underlying operating system. JVM performance improves with every release, so use the latest version (*except the recently released Java 7 that has issues that causes Solr to fail! Wait till a .1 release comes out!*). There are many different parameters that you can tune the JVM for. However, most of them are "black magic", and changing them from the defaults can quickly cause problems if you don't know what you're doing. Additionally, the folks who write JVMs spend a lot of time coming up with sophisticated algorithms that mean the JVM will usually tune itself better than you can. However, there is a fairly simple configuration change that most Java server applications benefit from (not just Solr), which is to set the initial and maximum heap memory allocated to the JVM to the same value and specify that you are running a server application, so the JVM can tune its optimization strategy for a long running process:

```
java-Xms1024M -Xmx1024M -server -jar start.jar
```

Of course, the question now is how much memory should be allocated to the Java heap. If you specify too little then you run the risk of getting an OutOfMemoryException. If you specify the largest practical value, which is the actual memory you have, less some for the operating system and other processes, this is a sub-optimal configuration too. Operating systems make use of available memory as caches for disk access, and Solr searches benefit substantially from this, while indexing does not. I recommend measuring how much heap you need by picking some highish value, then run a full battery of queries against Solr so all its caches get filled, then use JConsole to perform a full garbage collection. At that point you can see how much memory it's using. With that figure, estimate some breathing room of perhaps 20%. You can modify this process to incorporate concurrent indexing as applicable. The ultimate figure is of course highly dependent on the size of your Solr caches and other aspects of the Solr configuration; therefore, tuning the heap size should be one of the later steps.

Look back at the discussion about JMX in *Chapter, Deployment* for more details on using JConsole.

MMapDirectoryFactory to leverage additional virtual memory

If you have plenty of virtual memory relative to your index size, then using memory-mapped IO via **MMapDirectoryFactory** should be faster than **StandardDirectoryFactory** for interacting with the file system on 64-bit JVMs. This is set via the `<directoryFactory />` tag in `solrconfig.xml`, and is chosen by default on 64-bit Solaris and Linux JVMs. The memory used is outside of the Java heap so you do not need to modify any JVM startup options. Be sure to test your system thoroughly to validate the performance improvement and make sure RAM requirements are satisfied.

Enabling downstream HTTP caching

Solr has great support for using HTTP caching headers to enable downstream HTTP software to cache results. Web browsers, intermediate proxy servers, and web servers can decide if they need to re-query for updated results by using various rules. For example, often applications allow a user to take a query and make it an **Alert** that will e-mail them results if there is a match. This leads to the same search running over and over, even if the results are almost always the same. Placing an intermediate caching server, such as Squid, in front of Solr should reduce the load on Solr and potentially reduce Solr's internal "query cache" requirements, thus freeing up more RAM. When a request uses certain caching headers, Solr can then indicate whether the content has changed by either sending back an HTTP 200 status code if it has, or a **304 Not Modified** code when the content hasn't changed since the last time the request asked for it.

In order to specify that you want Solr to do HTTP caching, you need to configure the `<httpCaching/>` stanza in `solrconfig.xml`. By default, Solr is configured to never return 304 codes, instead always returning a 200 response (a normal non-cached response) with the full body of the results. In `./examples/core/mbtype/solrconfig.xml` uncomment the "production" `httpCaching` stanza and restart Solr:

```
<httpCachinglastModifiedFrom="openTime"
    etagSeed="Solr" never304="false">
  <cacheControl>max-age=43200, must-revalidate</cacheControl>
</httpCaching>
```

We have specified that sending back 304 messages is okay and specified in the `cacheControl` that the max time to store responses is 43,200 seconds, which is half a day. We've also specified through `must-revalidate` that any *shared cache*, such as a Squid proxy, needs to check back with Solr to see if anything has changed, even if the `max-age` hasn't expired, which acts as an extra check.

 During development you may want to set `never304="true"` to ensure that you are always looking at the results of fresh queries and aren't misled by looking at cached results, unless you are using eTags and the browser properly honors them.

By running `curl` with the `mbartists` core, we can see additional cache related information in the header, as well as the full XML response from Solr (not listed). For your typing convenience, these curl commands are available in `./examples/10/http_cache_commands.txt`.

```
>>curl -v "http://localhost:8983/solr/mbartists/
  select/?q=Smashing+Pumpkins"
< HTTP/1.1 200 OK
< Cache-Control: max-age=43200, must-revalidate
< Expires: Sat, 07 May 2011 02:13:01 GMT
< Last-Modified: Fri, 06 May 2011 14:12:18 GMT
<ETag: "ZTMyMzQwMzhmNDgwMDAwMFNvbHJNdXNpcY0JyYWlueg=="
```

So let's look at what we get back if we take advantage of the **Last-Modified** header information by specifying that we have downloaded the content after the last modified time:

```
>>curl -v -z "Fri, 06 May 2011 14:12:18 GMT"
  http://localhost:8983/solr/mbartists/select/?q=Smashing+Pumpkins
* About to connect() to localhost port 8983 (#0)
*   Trying ::1... connected
* Connected to localhost (::1) port 8983 (#0)
> GET /solr/mbartists/select/?q=Smashing+Pumpkins HTTP/1.1
> User-Agent: curl/7.16.3 (powerpc-apple-darwin9.0) libcurl/7.16.3
OpenSSL/0.9.7l zlib/1.2.3
> Host: localhost:8983
> Accept: */*
>If-Modified-Since: Fri, 06 May 2011 14:12:18 GMT
>
< HTTP/1.1 304 Not Modified
< Cache-Control: max-age=43200
< Expires: Tue, 03 May 2011 09:38:47 GMT
< Last-Modified: Mon, 02 May 2011 21:36:22 GMT
<ETag: "ODMyMzQwMzhmNDgwMDAwMFNvbHI="
< Server: Jetty(6.1.3)
```

Specifying an `If-Modified-Since` time just one second after the `Last-Modified` time means that Solr gives us back a `304 Not Modified` code and doesn't have to return all of the XML data over the wire, which is much faster and reduces the load on the server. When you ran the `curl` command you didn't receive any of the XML result data back in your console!

Entity tags are a newer method for uniquely identifying responses that are more robust and flexible than using the `Last-Modified` date. An `ETag` is a string that identifies a specific version of a component. In the case of Solr, they are generated by combining the current version of the index with the `etagSeed` value. Every time the index is modified, the current ETag value will change. If we add the fake artist "The Eric Band" to the `mbartists` index, and then run our previous query, we'll see that the ETag has changed because the version of the Solr index has changed:

```
>>curl 'http://localhost:8983/solr/mbartists/update?commit=true' -H
  "Content-Type: text/xml" --data-binary '<add><doc><field name=
  "a_name">The Eric Band</field><field name="id">Fake:99999
  </field><field name="type">Artist</field></doc></add>'

>>curl -v -z "Tue, 03 May 2011 09:36:36 GMT GMT"
  http://localhost:8983/solr/mbartists/select/?q=Smashing+Pumpkins
>
< HTTP/1.1 304 Not Modified
< Cache-Control: max-age=43200
<Expires: Sat, 07 May 2011 02:17:02 GMT
<Last-Modified: Fri, 06 May 2011 14:16:55 GMTGMT
<ETag: "NTMyMzQwMzhmNDgwMDAwMFNvbHJNdXNpY0JyYW1ueg=="
< Server: Jetty(6.1.3)
```

To take advantage of the HTTP protocol level caching supplied by Solr you need to make sure your client respects the caching directives returned by Solr. Two very popular caches that understand ETags are Varnish (`http://www.varnish-cache.org`) and Squid (`http://www.squid-cache.org`).

> Remember, the fastest query response possible from Solr's perspective is the query that it doesn't have to make!

Solr caching

Caching is a key part of what makes Solr fast and scalable, and the proper configuration of caches is a common topic on the solr-user mailing list! Solr uses multiple **Least Recently Used** in-memory caches. The caches are associated with individual **Index Searchers**, which represent a snapshot view of the data. Following a commit, new index searchers are opened and then **auto-warmed**. **Auto-warming** is when the cached queries of the former searcher are rerun to populate the new searcher. Following auto-warming, predefined searches are run as configured in solrconfig.xml. Put some representative queries in the newSearcher and firstSearcher listeners, particularly for queries that need sorting on fields. Once complete, the new searcher will begin servicing new incoming requests.

 Each auto-warming query and predefined search increases the commit time so make sure those searches are actually increasing the cache hit ratio and don't over do it!

There are a number of different caches configured in solrconfig.xml:

- **filterCache**: Stores unordered lists of documents that match a query. This is primarily used for storing filter queries (the fq parameter) for re-use, but it's also used in faceting under certain circumstances. It is arguably the most important cache. The filter cache can optionally be used for queries (the q parameter) that are not score-sorted if useFilterForSortedQuery is enabled in solrconfig.xml. However, unless testing reveals performance gains, it is best left disabled—the default setting.

- **queryResultCache**: Stores ordered lists of documents. The order is defined by any sorting parameters passed. This cache should be large enough to store the results of the most common searches, which you can identify by looking at your server logs. This cache doesn't use much memory, as only the ID of the documents is stored in the cache. The queryResultWindowSize setting allows you to preload document IDs into the cache if you expect users to request documents that bound the ordered list. So, if a user asks for products 20 through 29, then there is a good chance they will next look for 30 through 39. If the queryResultWindowSize is 50, then the documents bounding the initial request from 0 to 50 will be returned and cached. When the user asks for 30 through 39, they will have their data cached and won't have to access the Lucene indexes!

- **documentCache**: Caches field values that have been defined in schema. xml as being stored, so that Solr doesn't have to go back to the filesystem to retrieve the stored values. Fields are stored by default.

The documented wisdom on sizing this cache is to be larger than the max results * max concurrent queries being executed by Solr to prevent documents from being re-fetched during a query. As this cache contains the fields being stored, it can grow large very quickly.

These caches are all configured the same way:

- **class:** Defines whether to use **LRUCache** or **FastLRUCache**. The current wisdom is that for caches that don't have a high hit ratio, therefore have more churn. You should use LRUCache because the cache is evicting content frequently. If you have a high hit ratio, then the benefits of FastLRUCache kick in because it doesn't require a separate thread for managing the removal of unused items. You want a high hit ratio to maximize the FastLRUCache because storing data is slower as the calling thread is responsible for making sure that the cache hasn't grown too large.

- **size:** Defines the maximum items that the cache can support and is mostly dependent on how much RAM is available to the JVM.

- **autowarmCount:** Specifies how many items should be copied from an old search to a new one during the auto-warming process. Set the number too high and you slow down commits; set it too low and the new searches following those commits won't gain the benefits of the previously cached data. Look at the warmupTime statistic for your searches to balance these needs. There are some other options too, such as initialSize, acceptableSize, minSize, showItems, and cleanupThread specific to FastLRUCache, but specifying these are uncommon. There is a wealth of specific information available on the Wiki at http://wiki.apache.org/solr/SolrCaching that covers this constantly evolving topic.

Tuning caches

Using the statistics admin page, you can get a sense of how large you need to make your caches. If the hit ratio for your caches is low, then it may be that they aren't caching enough to be useful. However, if you find that the caches have a significant number of evictions, then that implies they are filling up too quickly and need to be made larger. Caches can be increased in size as long as Solr has sufficient RAM to operate in.

 If your hit ratio for a cache is very low, then you should evaluate reducing its size, perhaps turning it off altogether by commenting out the cache configuration sections in solrconfig.xml. This will reduce memory needs that aren't being used effectively and may also help improve performance by removing the overhead of managing the caches.

Indexing performance

There are several aspects of Solr tuning that increase indexing performance. We'll start with optimizing the schema, then look at sending data to Solr in bulk, and then finish with Lucene's merge factor and optimization. But first, one of the easiest things you can do is increase the buffer size Solr uses to accumulate data before flushing it to disk. In `solrconfig.xml` in the `<mainIndex>` element there is a `<maxRamBufferSizeMB>` element set to 32 by default -- a relatively low number. If you will be loading a lot of data at once, then increase this value. It is hard-limited to 2048 which almost nobody should choose. Many experts seem to find that a number in the vicinity of 128 to be good for many apps. In chose 64 in our MusicBrainz configuration.

Designing the schema

Good schema design is probably one of the most important things you can do to enhance the scalability of Solr. You should refer to *Chapter 2, Schema and Text Analysis*, for a refresher on many of the design questions that are inextricably tied to scalability. The biggest schema issue to look at for maximizing scalability is: Are you storing the minimum information you need to meet the needs of your users? There are a number of attributes in your schema field definitions, which inform us about what is being indexed:

- `omitTermFreqAndPositions`: This feature allows you to skip indexing term related data such as the frequency and payload for non-textual fields. If your schema version is at least 1.2, then this will be set appropriately already. The version is specified in `schema.xml` in the XML stanza:

  ```
  <schema name="example" version="1.4">
  ```

- `indexed`: You may find that you have indexed data that you don't ever search against. By specifying that they are NOT indexed, you can reduce the size of your index and the overall number of terms.

- `stored`: Storing field values in the index simplifies and speeds search results because results need not be cross-referenced and retrieved from original sources. It is also required for features such as highlighting. But storing field values will obviously increase the index size and indexing time. A quick way to see what fields are stored is to do a simple search with `fl=*` as a parameter; the fields in the result are the stored fields. You should only store fields that you actually display in your search results or need for debugging purposes. It is likely that your index has some data repeated but indexed differently for specialized indexing purposes like faceting or sorting—only one of those, if any, needs to be stored.

Another thing to look at is: If you need to store lots of data in a document, are you appropriately loading it? If you don't always read all the fields, then enabling lazy field loading in `solrconfig.xml` via `<enableLazyFieldLoading>true </enableLazyFieldLoading>` can be very helpful.

> If you need faster indexing, reduce the text analysis you perform in `schema.xml` to only what you need. For example, if you are certain the input is plain ASCII text then don't bother mapping accented characters to ASCII equivalents.

Sending data to Solr in bulk

Indexing documents into Solr is often a major bottleneck due to the volume of data that needs to be indexed initially compared to the pace of ongoing updates. The best way to speed up indexing is to index documents in batches. Solr supports sending multiple documents in a single add operation, and this will lead to a drastic speedup in performance.

However, as the size of your individual documents increase, performance may start to decrease. A reasonable rule of thumb is doing document add operations in batches of 10 for large documents, and 100 for small documents.

To see the impact of batching I indexed some data using the scripts in `examples/10/batch/simple_test.rb` and documented the time it took.

Scenario	Script	Time
Single process adding documents one at a time	simple_test.rb	24m13.391s
Single process adding documents in batches of 100	simple_test.rb	5m43.492s
Single process adding documents in batches of 500	simple_test.rb	5m51.322s
One thread adding documents in batches of 500	threaded_test.rb	5m25.986s
Four threads adding documents in batches of 100	threaded_test.rb	5m29.357s
Four threads adding documents in batches of 500	threaded_test.rb	5m12.694s

SolrJ can load data the fastest

The fastest client approach to load data into Solr is SolrJ's
StreamingUpdateSolrServer Java class. It places documents to be
added onto queues that separate background threads stream to Solr on
independent connections. Solr receives the documents from different
connections in different threads and can load data faster. Due to the
asynchronous nature of its use, StreamingUpdateSolrServer must
be extended to implement a callback to respond to errors. Look back at
Chapter 9's crawler example to learn more.

The preceding table shows that sending the documents in batches certainly helps the
performance, but only up to a point. With a single process the cost of parsing and
shoveling 500 documents over the wire versus 100 documents started to show up.
The other interesting data point is that *in this benchmark*, running multiple threads
did not offer appreciable greater performance over a single process. This is because
the processing logic in threaded_test.rb for building the XML documents was so
slight on the client side that having multiple threads didn't help. However, if your
indexing script is doing more complex business logic, such as multiple SQL calls
(often an issue with the DIH), extracting text from rich documents, or calling external
services for operations like entity extraction, in order to build the correct document
to be submitted to Solr then using a multi threaded process, or multiple separate
processes, will increase index throughput.

Don't overlap commits

During indexing you may find that you are starting to see this error message:

```
<h2>HTTP ERROR: 503</h2><pre>Error opening new searcher. exceeded
limit of maxWarmingSearchers=2, try again later.</pre>
```

Every time a commit happens, a new searcher is created, which invokes the searcher
warm up process for populating the cache, which can take a while. While you can
bump up the maxWarmingSearchers parameter in solrconfig.xml, you are likely
to still hit the new limit if you have multiple process doing commits because each
additional warming searcher slows things down for the rest. In order to deal with
this, reduce how often commits are happening. You can also reduce the amount
of time auto-warming takes by reducing the autowarmCount and removing the
newSearch query. Of course, this will lead to slower initial queries as well. If you are
bulk loading data, then you don't need real-time display of the changes and can just
do a single commit at the end. Alternatively, to prevent overlapping commits from
happening by each thread, you should use the **autoCommit** feature to let Solr decide
when to commit.

Disabling unique key checking

By default, if you specify a **uniqueKey** for your schema, when indexing content, Solr checks the uniqueness of the document being indexed so that you don't end up with multiple documents sharing the same primary key. If you know you have unique keys and don't have those documents in the index when doing a bulk load of data, then you can disable this check. For an update request in any format supported by Solr, add overwrite=false as a request parameter in the URL.

Index optimization factors

There are some other factors that can impact how often you want commit and optimize operations to occur. If you are using Solr's support for scaling horizontally through replication of indexes, then each time a commit or optimize occurs you are causing the transfer of updated indexes to all the slave servers. This is okay if your commits are small and you are just generating small segment files that are quickly transferred. But when you perform an optimization you cause the entire index to be replicated. If you have a multi gigabyte index, you may decide that optimizing the index is not something you want to do on a frequent basis because each time you optimize you cause the entire index to be replicated.

Optimizing your index is no longer quite as important as it used to be. Optimizing the index saves all the individual segment files into a single segment and removes deleted documents, which reduces the size and number of binary files that Lucene has to operate over. However, the automatic merging of segments by Lucene, specified by the `mergeFactor` setting puts an upper limit on how many segment files will be generated and keeps your index in a near optimal state.

If your index is so large that optimizations are taking longer than desired or using more disk space during optimization than you can spare, but you still want to take advantage of removing deleted documents from your indexes then consider adding the `maxSegments` parameter to the optimize command. In the Update-XML format, this would be the `maxSegments` attribute on the `optimize` element, and in the URL it would be a correspondingly named parameter. By default this parameter is 1 since an optimize results in a single Lucene "segment". By setting it larger than 1 but less than the `mergeFactor`, you permit partial optimization to no more than the specified number of segments. Of course, the index won't be fully optimized and therefore searches will be slower.

```
curl 'http://localhost:8983/solr/mbtracks/update?optimize=
    true&maxSegments=16'
```

You may find it is better to frequently compress down to 32 or 16 segments during periods of load, and then infrequently compress all the way down to 1 segment.

 Since a "segment" may be made up of a varying number of files per segment, an easy way to see the number of current segments is in the admin statistic page: `SolrIndexReader{this=64a7c45e,r=ReadOn lyDirectoryReader@64a7c45e,refCnt=1,`**`segments=10`**`}`

 Think about if you can have two strategies for indexing your content. One that is used during bulk loads that focuses on minimizing commits/optimizes and indexes your data as quickly as possible, and then a second strategy used during day-to-day routine operations that potentially indexes documents more slowly, but commits and optimizes more frequently to reduce the impact on any search activity being performed.

Another setting that causes a fair amount of debate is the `mergeFactor` setting, which controls how many segments Lucene should build before merging them together on disk.

 The rule of thumb is that the more static your content is, the lower the merge factor you want. If your content is changing frequently, or if you have a lot of content to index, then a higher merge factor is better.

So, if you are doing sporadic index updates, then a merge factor of 2 is great, because you will have fewer segments, which leads to faster searching. However, if you expect to have large indexes (> 10 GB), then having a higher merge factor like 25 will help with the indexing time.

 Check out the great blog post by *Lucene in Action* author Mike McCandless that has a visualization of what happens during segment merging. This really helped me understand the behavior of Solr during commits: `http://blog.mikemccandless.com/2011/02/visualizing-lucenes-segment-merges.html`

Enhancing faceting performance

There are a few items to look at when ensuring that faceting performs well. First of all, faceting and filtering (the `fq` parameter) go hand-in-hand, thus monitor the filter cache to ensure that it is adequately sized. The filter cache is used for faceting itself as well. In particular, any `facet.query` or `facet.date` based facets will store an entry for each facet count returned. You should ensure that the resulting facets are as reusable as possible from query to query. For example, it's probably not a good idea to have direct user input to be involved in either a `facet.query` or in `fq` because of the variability. As for dates, try to use fixed intervals that don't change often or round NOW relative dates to a chunkier interval (for example, NOW/DAY instead of just NOW). For text faceting (example `facet.field`), the `filterCache` is not used unless you explicitly set `facet.method` to enum. You should do this when the total number of distinct values in the field is somewhat small, say less than 50. Finally, you should add representative faceting queries to `firstSearcher` in `solrconfig.xml` so that when Solr executes its first user query, the relevant caches are already warmed up.

Using term vectors

A **term vector** is a list of terms resulting from the text analysis of a field's value. It optionally contains the term frequency, document frequency, and numerical offset into the text. Without them, the same information can be derived at runtime but that's slower. While disabled by default, enabling term vectors for a field in `schema.xml` enhances:

- MoreLikeThis queries, assuming that the field is referenced in `mlt.fl` and the input document is a reference to an existing document (that is not externally passed in).
- Highlighting search results with the FastVectorHighlighter
- Enabling term vectors for a field increases the index size and indexing time, and isn't required to perform MoreLikeThis queries or highlighting search results; however typically, if you are using these features, then the enhanced performance gained is worth the longer indexing time and greater index size.

Improving phrase search performance

For indexes reaching a million documents or more, phrase searches can be slow. If you are using the automatic phrase boosting features of the dismax query parser (excellent for relevancy) then more phrase queries are occurring than you may be aware of. What slows down phrase searches are the presence of terms in the phrase that show up in a lot of documents. In order to ameliorate this problem, the particularly common and uninteresting words like "the" can be filtered out through a stop filter. But this thwarts searches for a phrase like "to be or not to be" and prevents disambiguation in other cases where these words, despite being common, are significant. Besides, as the size of the index grows, this is just a band-aid for performance as there are plenty of other words that shouldn't be considered for filtering out yet are common.

Shingling (sometimes called word-grams) is a clever solution to this problem, which combines pairs of consecutive terms into one so-called shingle. The original terms still get indexed, but only the shingles are used in phrase queries. Shingles naturally have a very low frequency relative to single words. Consider the text "The quick brown fox jumped over the lazy dog". Use of shingling in a typical configuration would yield the indexed terms (shingles) "the quick", "quick brown", "brown fox", "fox jumped", "jumped over", "over the", "the lazy", and "lazy dog" in addition to all of the original nine terms. Since so many more terms are indexed, naturally there is a commensurate increase in indexing time and resulting size. **Common-grams** is a more selective variation of shingling that only shingles when one of the consecutive words is in a configured list. Given the sentence above using an English stop word list, the indexed terms would be "the quick", "over the", "the lazy", and the original nine terms.

As a side benefit, these techniques also improve search relevancy since the TF and IDF factors are using coarser units (the shingles) than individual terms.

In our MusicBrainz data set, there are nearly seven million tracks, and that is a lot! These track names are ripe for either shingling or common-grams. Despite the high document count, the documents are small and so the actual index is only a couple gigabytes. Either approach is quite plausibly appropriate given different trade-offs. Here is a variation of the MusicBrainz title field called `title_commonGrams`.

Notice that the filter's class name varies from index to query time, which is very unusual.

```
<fieldType name="title_commonGrams" class="solr.TextField"
  positionIncrementGap="100"">
  <analyzer type="index">
    <tokenizer class="solr.StandardTokenizerFactory"/>
    <filter class="solr.LowerCaseFilterFactory"/>
    <filter class="solr.EnglishMinimalStemFilterFactory"/>
    <filter class="solr.CommonGramsFilterFactory"
            words="commongrams.txt" ignoreCase="true"/>"/>
  </analyzer>
  <analyzer type="query">
    <tokenizer class="solr.StandardTokenizerFactory"/>
    <filter class="solr.LowerCaseFilterFactory"/>
    <filter class="solr.EnglishMinimalStemFilterFactory"/>
    <filter class="solr.CommonGramsQueryFilterFactory"
            words="commongrams.txt" ignoreCase="true""/>
  </analyzer>
</fieldType>
```

To come up with a list of common words for common-grams, use stop words and add some of the **Top Terms** list in Solr's schema browser as a guide for the field in question. You could try a more sophisticated methodology, but this is a start.

Shingle filters go in the same position, but they are configured a little differently:

```
<!-- index time …-->
<filter class="solr.ShingleFilterFactory"
  maxShingleSize="2" outputUnigrams="true"/>
<!-- query time -->
<filter class="solr.ShingleFilterFactory"
  maxShingleSize="2" outputUnigrams="false"
  outputUnigramsIfNoShingles="true"/>
```

You might choose to save additional index space and search performance by adding a stop filter after shingling or common-grams for typical stop-words so long as they don't need to be searchable by themselves. This wasn't done here since it's not a good decision for short fields.

Evaluating the search performance improvement of shingling proved to be tricky for the limited time I gave to it. Some rough (non-scientific) testing showed that a search for *Hand in my Pocket* against the shingled field versus the non-shingled field was two to three times faster. I've seen very compelling search performance numbers using common-grams from others online but I didn't evaluate it.

Shingling and common-grams increase phrase search performance at the expense of indexing speed and disk use. In the following table I present the relative cost of these two techniques on the track name field in MusicBrainz compared to the cost of doing typical text analysis. These percentages may look high and might scare you away but remember that these are based purely on one aspect (the index portion) of one field. The overall index time and disk use didn't change dramatically, not even with shingling. You should try it on your data to see the effects.

	Indexing time increase %	Disk space increase %
Common-Grams	220%	25%
Shingling	450%	110%

Use of either is recommended for most applications

Given that shingling takes over five times as long and uses twice as much disk space, it makes more sense on small to medium scale indexes where phrase boosting is used to improve relevancy. Common-grams is a relative bargain for all other applications.

Moving to multiple Solr servers (Scale horizontally)

Once you've optimized Solr running on a single server, and reached the point of diminishing returns for optimizing further, the next step is to split the querying load over multiple slave instances of Solr. The ability to scale horizontally is a hallmark of modern scalable Internet systems, and Solr shares this.

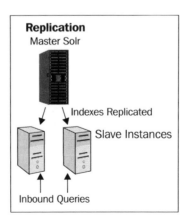

Replication

Introduced in Solr 1.4 is an HTTP-based replication strategy that is tightly integrated into Solr. Configuration is done through the already familiar `solrconfig.xml`, and replication encompasses transferring both data as well as configuration files such as `solrconfig.xml` and works across both Unix and Windows environments. The admin interface provides monitoring and control of replication—for example, to force the start of replication or aborting a stalled replication. Replication works by taking advantage of the fact that changes to indexes are appended to the end of the index data structure. This means that when you modify a single document as part of a 3 GB index, you are not changing the 3 GB segment file, but instead recording that change to a much smaller segment file, measured in megabytes or less! The master Solr server exposes an overall **index version** that is incremented each time a change is made, and exposes all the segment files to the slaves. The individual slave Solr instances periodically poll the master to compare their list of segments with what the master Solr offers, and then download via HTTP the segments that they are missing. Once the files are downloaded the slaves internally perform a commit operation that adds the new segments to their index and exposes the new data to users querying them.

Prior to Solr 1.4, replication was performed using Unix shell scripts that transferred data between servers through **rsync**, scheduled using **cron**. This replication was based on the fact that by using rsync, you could replicate only Lucene segments that had been updated from the master to the slave servers. The script-based solution has worked well for many deployments, but suffers from being relatively complex, requiring external shell scripts, cron jobs, and rsync daemons in order to be setup. You can get a sense of the complexity by looking at the Wiki page `http://wiki.apache.org/solr/CollectionDistribution` and looking at the various rsync and snapshot related scripts in `./examples/cores/crawler/bin` directory.

Starting multiple Solr servers

We'll test running multiple separate Solr servers by firing up multiple copies of our example Solr using separate ports and data directories. A very typical replication pattern is one master and two slaves. Go ahead and start our normal Solr using `run.sh`. To start the slaves we have two startup scripts in `./examples/10/` directory: `run_8984.sh` and `run_8985.sh` that startup copies of our normal Solr on ports 8984 and 8985 in separate terminal windows. You should now have three terminal windows running three separate Solr instances on separate ports.

If you look at the scripts you'll see we are passing in a different port number for Jetty, a different data directory (named with the port number to make it easier to distinguish) to store the slave indexes in, and enabling the instance to function as a slave:

```
-Dsolr.slave.enable=true -Dsolr.data.dir=../../cores_data/data8984
-Djetty.port=8984
```

- `-Dsolr.master.enable=true` specifies that a Solr server is running as a **master** server. The master server is responsible for pushing out indexes to all of the slave servers. You will store documents in the master server, and perform queries against the pool of slave servers.

- `-Dsolr.slave.enable=true` specifies that a Solr server is running as a **slave** server. Slave servers periodically poll the master server for updated indexes, or you can manually trigger updates by calling a URL or using the Admin interface. A pool of slave servers, managed by a load balancer of some type service the search requests made by end users.

- `-Djetty.port=8984` will start up Solr on port 8984 instead of the usual port 8983. You'll need to do this if you have multiple Servlet engines on the same physical server.

- `-Dsolr.data.dir=./solr/data8984` specifies a different data directory from the default one, configured in `solrconfig.xml`. You typically wouldn't want two Solr servers on the same physical server attempting to share the same data directory. I like to put the port number in the directory name to help distinguish between running Solr servers, assuming different servlet engines are used.

You actually can have multiple Solr servers share an index, just make sure only one Solr makes changes to the index. When changes are made, make sure you tell the others to reopen their view of the index by performing a commit operation, despite the fact that they have not made any changes! This can be really useful when your indexes are huge and you don't want to make copies of them, but have plenty of RAM and CPU available.

Configuring replication

Configuring replication is very easy. We have already configured the replication handler for the various cores through the following stanza in `./examples/cores/mbtypes/solrconfig.xml`:

```
<requestHandler name="/replication" class="solr.ReplicationHandler" >
<lst name="master">
  <str name="enable">${solr.master.enable:false}</str>
  <str name="replicateAfter">startup</str>
  <str name="replicateAfter">commit</str>
  <str name="confFiles">stopwords.txt</str>
</lst>
<lst name="slave">
  <str name="enable">${solr.slave.enable:false}</str>
  <str name="masterUrl">
  http://localhost:8983/solr/${solr.core.name}/replication
  </str>
  <str name="pollInterval">00:00:60</str>
</lst>
</requestHandler>
```

Notice the use of `${}` values for doing configuration of `solrconfig.xml` at runtime? This allows us to configure a single request handler for replication, and pass `-Dsolr.master.enable=true` and `-Dsolr.slave.enable=true` to control which list of parameters are used and dynamically build the URL to poll for changes. The master server has been set to trigger replication on startup and when commits are performed. Configuration files can also be replicated to the slave servers through the list of `confFiles`. Replicating configuration files is useful when you modify them during runtime and don't want to go through a full redeployment process of Solr. Just update the configuration file on the master Solr, and they will be pushed down to the slave servers the next time the index is changed as well. You can force this by modifying a document and issuing a commit that changes the index version, the actual replication ONLY happens when the index changes. The slave server is smart enough to pick up the fact that a configuration file was updated and reload the core. If you have a differing configuration file for master and slaves then you can have a dedicated configuration file replicated to the slave via: `<str name="confFiles">solrconfig_slave.xml:solrconfig.xml</str>`.

The pollInterval controls how often the slave checks the master for updated segments. If the master index is constantly changing, but you don't need to have those changes immediately reflected in the slaves, then a longer poll interval, such as 15 minutes, will reduce the overall amount of data that needs to be transferred over the network. Also, this highlights that in a replicated environment, optimizations are expensive not because of the time it takes to perform the operation, but because of the network download time. When you optimize a 3 GB index down to 1 segment then the entire 3 GB index will need to be downloaded by each of the slaves, which can quickly bottleneck your average 100 BASE-TX Ethernet network.

For updated information on setting up replication view the wiki at http://wiki. apache.org/solr/SolrReplication.

Load balancing searches across slaves

Go ahead and fire up three separate instances of Solr. Two of the servers will serve up results for search queries, while one server will function as the master copy of the index. Make sure to keep track of the various ports!

Indexing into the master server

In a new terminal session, we're going to take a CSV file of the MusicBrainz album release data to use as our sample data. The CSV file is stored in a ZIP format in ./ examples/10/mb_releases.csv.zip. Unzip the file so you have the full dataset with over 600K releases running:

```
>>unzip mb_releases.csv.zip
```

You can index the CSV data file using curl. Make sure you supply the correct path for the stream.file parameter:

```
>>curl http://localhost:8983/solr/mbreleases/update/csv -F
  f.r_attributes.split=true -F f.r_event_country.split=true -F
  f.r_event_date.split=true -F f.r_attributes.separator=' ' -F
  f.r_event_country.separator=' ' -F f.r_event_date.separator=' ' -F
  commit=true -F stream.file=/Users/epugh/Downloads/solrbook/examples/10/
  mb_releases.csv
```

You can monitor the progress of streaming the release data by using the statistics page at http://localhost:8983/solr/mbreleases/admin/stats.jsp#update and looking at the docPending value. Refresh the page, and it will count up to the total 603,090 documents.

Configuring slaves

Once the indexing is done, check the number of documents indexed; it should be 603,090. Each slave has been configured via the `pollInterval` value to check the master Solr for updated segments every 60 seconds. The master Solr is defined by the `masterUrl` parameter.:

```
<lst name="slave">
  <str name="enable">${solr.slave.enable:false}</str>
  <str name="masterUrl">http://localhost:8983/solr/${solr.core.name}
    /replication</str>
  <str name="pollInterval">00:00:60</str>
</lst>
```

To start up another slave Solr run:

```
>> cd ~/examples
>>java -Xms512M -Xmx1024M -Dfile.encoding=UTF8 -Dsolr.solr.home=cores
-Dsolr.slave.enable=true -Dsolr.data.dir=../../cores_data/data8984
-Djetty.port=8984 -Djetty.home=solr -Djetty.logs=solr/logs -jar solr/
start.jar
```

You can keep starting more slave servers by passing in a separate port and data directories that will each start polling the same master Solr.

You can trigger a replication by using the Replication admin page for each slave. The page will reload showing you how much of the data has been replicated from your master server to the slave server. In the following screenshot, you can see that **71** of **128** megabytes of data have been replicated:

Current Replication Status	Start Time: Thu Jun 18 16:48:52 EDT 2009
	Files Downloaded: 32 / 35
	Downloaded: 71.92 MB / 128.94 MB [55.0%]
	Downloading File: _0.fdt, Downloaded: 24 MB / 80.99 MB [29.0%]
	Time Elapsed: 14s, Estimated Time Remaining: 11s, Speed: 5.14 MB/s
Controls	Disable Poll
	Replicate Now
	Abort

Typically, you would want to use a proper DNS name for the `masterUrl`, such as `master.solrsearch.mycompany.com`, so you don't have to edit each slave server. Alternatively, you can specify the `masterUrl` as part of the URL and manually trigger an update:

```
>>curl http://slave12.solrsearch.mycompany.com/solr/mbreleases/
  replication?
command=fetchindex&masterUrl=http://master.solrsearch.mycompany.com/
  solr/mbreleases/replication
```

Configuring load balancing

We now have three Solr's running, one master and two slaves in separate terminals. We don't have a single URL that we can provide to clients, which leverages the pool of slave Solr servers. For the purposes of this example, we are going to use a simple Java load balancer called **Distributor** to provide a proxy in front of our two slaves that sends traffic in a very simple round robin fashion.

HAProxy

For production use, I like **HAProxy**, a simple and powerful HTTP proxy server to do a round robin load balancing between the pool of slaves. This allows us to have a single IP address, and have requests redirected to one of the pool of servers, without requiring configuration changes on the client side. A sample `haproxy.cfg` is available in `./examples/10/amazon/` that listen to port 80, and then redirect requests to each of the slave servers, equally weighted between them. Going into the full configuration of HAProxy is out of the scope of this book; for more information visit `http://haproxy.1wt.eu/`.

Assuming you have your pool of slaves running on ports 8984 and 8985 then you can fire up the distributor from `./examples/10/distributor/`:

```
>>java -jar distributor-0.7.jar distributor.conf
```

`distributor.conf` is configured to listen to traffic on port 8000 and send traffic to the set of slaves:

```
<target_group>
    <target hostname="localhost" port="8985"/>
    <target hostname="localhost" port="8984"/>
</target_group>
```

Distributor runs a test against each target server in the `target_group` to check if it is available or not by checking a URL's response for various conditions. Solr includes a request handler called **PingRequestHandler** at `/admin/ping` designed for this purpose.

```
<test_parameters
    service_type="http"
    frequency="60000"
    timeout="5000">
    <get path="/solr/mbreleases/admin/ping">
        <response_code value="200"/>
    </get>
</test_parameters>
```

You can manually control the response of the ping request handler by enabling the `<healthcheck type="file">server-enabled</healthcheck>` XML element in `solrconfig.xml`. Adding the `healthcheck` adds an **Enable/Disable** link to the admin web page, and a file named `server-enabled` is created/deleted in the data directory. If you click on **Disable**, then `/admin/ping` will always return false.

You should now be able to hit port 8000, `http://localhost:8000/solr`, and be transparently forwarded to one of the slave servers. Go ahead and issue some queries and you will see them logged by whichever slave server you are directed to. If you then stop Solr on one slave server and do another search request, you will be transparently forwarded to the other slave server! The admin page for each slave will reflect the actual address and port the slave is running on.

> There is a SolrJ client side interface that does load balancing as well. `LBHttpSolrServer` requires the client to know the addresses of all of the slave servers and isn't as robust as a proxy, though it does simplify the architecture. More information is on the Wiki at `http://wiki.apache.org/solr/LBHttpSolrServer`.

Sharding indexes

Sharding is the process of breaking a single logical index in a horizontal fashion across records versus breaking it up vertically by entities. It is a common database scaling strategy when you have too much data for a single database server to handle. In Solr terms, sharding is breaking up a single Solr core across multiple Solr servers, each with identical schemas, as compared to breaking up a single Solr core over multiple cores with differing schemas on a single server through a multi core setup. Solr has the ability to take a single query and run it over multiple Solr shards, and then aggregate the results together into a single result set that is returned to the client. You should use sharding if your queries start to take too long to execute on a single server that isn't otherwise heavily taxed. You typically only need sharding when you have millions of documents to be searched and complex queries that require significant amounts of CPU and memory to process.

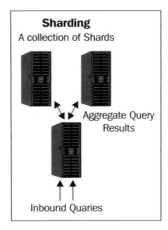

Sharding
A collection of Shards

Aggregate Query
Results

Inbound Quaries

If running a single query is fast enough, and you need to handle more users, then use the whole index replication approach instead!

Sharding isn't a completely transparent operation the way replicating whole indexes is from an external perspective. The key constraint is when indexing documents you want to evenly balance the distribution of documents across the shards so each shard is more or less evenly sized to maintain relevancy. Solr doesn't have any logic for evenly distributing indexed data over shards. When querying for data, you supply a `shards` parameter that lists which Solr shards to aggregate results from. This means a lot of knowledge of the structure of the Solr architecture is required on the client side. Lastly, every document needs a unique key (ID), because you are breaking up the index based on documents, and these documents are distinguished from each other by their document ID.

Assigning documents to shards

There are a number of approaches you can take for splitting your documents across servers. Assuming your servers share the same performance characteristics, such as if you are sharding across multiple EC2 servers, then you want to break your data up more or less equally across the servers. We could distribute our *mbreleases* data based on the release names. All release names that start between *A* and *M* would go to one shard, the remaining *N* through *Z* would be sent to the other shard. However, the chance of an even distribution of release names isn't very likely! A better approach to evenly distribute documents is to perform a hash on the unique ID and take the mod of that value to determine which shard it should be distributed to like in this chunk of Ruby code:

```
SHARDS = ['http://ec2-174-129-178-110
          .compute-1.amazonaws.com:8983/solr/mbreleases',
          'http://ec2-75-101-213-59
          .compute-1.amazonaws.com:8983/solr/mbreleases']
unique_id = document[:id]
ifunique_id.hash % SHARDS.size == local_thread_id
  # index to shard
end
```

As long as the number of shards doesn't change, every time you index the same document, it will end up on the same shard! With reasonably balanced document distribution, the individual shards calculation of what documents are relevant should be good enough. If you have many more documents on one server versus another, then the one with fewer documents will seem as relevant as the one with many documents, as relevancy is calculated on a per-server basis.

You can test out the script `shard_indexer.rb` in `./examples/10/amazon/` to index the `mb_releases.csv` across as many shards as you want by using the hashing strategy. Just add each shard URL to the SHARDS array defined at the top of `shard_indexer.rb`:

```
>>rubyshard_indexer.rb ../mbreleases.csv
```

 You might want to change this algorithm if you have a pool of servers supporting your shards that are of varying capacities and if relevance isn't a key issue for you. For your higher capacity servers, you might want to direct more documents to be indexed on those shards. You can do this by using the existing logic, and then by just listing your higher capacity servers in the SHARDS array multiple times.

Searching across shards (distributed search)

The ability to search across shards as if they were a single logical data set is known as **distributed search**, and it's built into the search request handler and most search components. It is activated simply by issuing an otherwise normal search request with the `shards` request parameter, which is a comma-delimited list of URL-like references to Solr instances to search across. Here is an example searching two shards:

```
http://[SHARD_1]:8983/solr/select?shards=ec2-174-129-178-110.compute-1.
amazonaws.com:8983/solr/mbreleases,ec2-75-101-213-59.compute-1.amazonaws.
com:8983/solr/mbreleases&indent=true&q=r_a_name:Joplin
```

You can issue the search request to one of the shards or to another Solr instance that is configured like them. The data in the Solr instance receiving the request is not searched unless it is referenced in the shards parameter. Under the hood, a distributed search results in one or more requests to each shard depending on the components used. These internal sharded requests will go to the default request handler, which is not necessarily the original one. This can be overridden with the `shards.qt` parameter if needed. The data from each shard is merged appropriately and the final results are returned normally. Here are the results of the previous example search with nothing unusual about it:

```
<response>
<lst name="responseHeader">
  <int name="status">0</int>
  <int name="QTime">697</int>
  <lst name="params">
    <str name="indent">true</str>
```

```
<str name="q">r_a_name:Joplin</str>
<str name="shards">
  ec2-174-129-178-110.compute-1.amazonaws.com
    :8983/solr/mbreleases,ec2-75-101-213-59.compute-
    1.amazonaws.com:8983/solr/mbreleases
</str>
</lst>
</lst>
<result name="response" numFound="15" start="0"/>
</response>
```

> The URLs listed in the shards parameter do not include the leading transport protocol, just the host with the port and path to the Solr core. You will get no results if you specify http:// in the shard URLs. You can pass as many shards as you want up to the length a GET URI is allowed, which is at least 4,000 characters. A common technique to shorten the URL and simplify configuration is to use a separate request handler with the shards parameter defined in the request handler. This relieves the end users from needing to know which shards to query. You can also POST the parameters in the body of the request to get around the URI limit.

You can verify that the results are distributed and then combined by issuing the same search for r_a_name:Joplin to each individual shard and then adding up the numFound values.

There are a few key points to keep in mind when using shards to support distributed search:

- Most components support a distributed search, but not all. Distributed Range Faceting is only supported in the future Solr 4 release, although there is a patch for 3.x -- SOLR-1709. Result Grouping / Field Collapsing will support it in Solr 3.5. The More Like This feature doesn't support it either but there is a patch -- SOLR-788. The Query Elevation component has no support for it. Check the wiki page at http://wiki.apache.org/solr/DistributedSearch for an up to date list.

- Each document must have a unique ID. This is how Solr figures out how to merge the documents back together.

- Each shard should be roughly equal in size and distribution of documents for ideal performance and relevancy scores.

- If one of the shards fails to respond, then a connection error is thrown. You can pass a `timeAllowed` parameter that will return the results from the shard after a set amount of time; however, if the shard is not accessible it will still fail and make the whole query fail.

- If multiple shards return documents with the same ID, then the first document is selected and the rest are discarded. This can happen if you have issues in cleanly distributing your documents over your shards.

Combining replication and sharding (Scale deep)

Once you've scaled horizontally by either replicating indexes across multiple servers or sharding a single index, and then discover that you still have performance issues it's time to combine both approaches to provide a deep structure of Solr servers to meet your demands. This is conceptually quite simple, and getting it set up to test is fairly straightforward. The challenge typically is keeping all of the moving pieces up-to-date, and making sure that you are keeping your search indexes up-to-date. These operational challenges require a mature set of processes and sophisticated monitoring tools to ensure that all shards and slaves are up-to-date and are operational.

In order to tie the two approaches together, you continue to use sharding to spread out the load across multiple servers. Without sharding, it doesn't matter how large your pool of slave servers is because you need more CPU power than what just one slave server has to handle an individual query. Once you have sharded across the spectrum of shard servers, you treat each one as a Master Shard server, configured in the same way as we did in the previous replication section. This develops a tree of a master shard server with a pool of slave servers. Then, to issue a query, you have multiple small pools of one slave server per shard that you issue queries against, managed at the application level. You can even have dedicated Solr for doing the distributed search, one that doesn't have data.

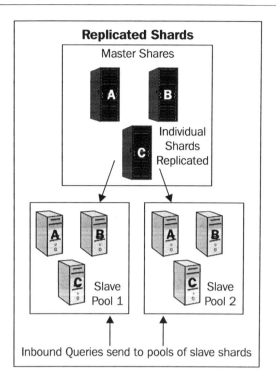

Data updates are handled by updating the top Master Shard servers and then replicated down to the individual slaves, grouped together into small groups of distributed sharded servers.

Obviously, this is a fairly complex setup and requires a fairly sophisticated load balancer to frontend this whole collection, but it does allow Solr to handle extremely large data sets.

Near real time search

Real time search is defined as the ability to search for content immediately after adding/updating it—perhaps within a second or so. This means that if an end-user is performing some sort of add/update action on content, then the system is able to process it fast enough so that if they then search for that content as fast as they can, they will always be able to search for it. **Near real time search** (often abbreviated as NRT) allows for a larger time window—most would say less than 30 seconds. This time window is also known as the **index latency**. Many users want real time search, but unless you have a trivially small amount of data, that simply isn't possible yet. You'll have to settle for near real time search or worse. Reducing the index latency is an ongoing effort with the biggest leap forward expected in Solr 4.0.

Here are a series of tips, in no particular order, to consider in your quest for the holy grail of real time search with Solr. You won't get there but you'll get close, especially if you have time to dedicate to this challenge.

- Follow any previous guidance on performance tuning, especially:
  - Carefully tailor the schema to the essentials.
  - Load data efficiently in bulk in multiple threads.

- Use SSDs if you can afford it. Definitely avoid virtualization.

- Manage the commit rate so that it's fast enough to satisfy the desired latency but never so frequent that Solr's warming from the previous commit isn't yet complete. Using `autoCommit` and/or `commitWithin` helps.

- Minimize warming. Reduce the `autowarmCount` of your caches and reduce the amount of work your queries do in the `newSearcher` listener. Keep those queries to their essentials—a query that uses sorting, faceting, and function queries on applicable fields.

- Set `maxWarmingSearchers` to 1; experiment with setting `useColdSearcher` to `true`.

- Spread the documents over more shards so that the shards are smaller, which will query faster. In striving for NRT search, many configuration choices slow down searches and so smaller shards help balance those effects.

- Consider reducing the ratio of Solr shards on a machine per number of CPU cores so that more machine resources are available for the frequent commit rate and warming activity.

- Do *not* use replication to split an indexing master and searching slave; you want the indexing and searching to be on the same index. It's okay to use replication for backup/availability purposes though.

- If you only need NRT search for added documents instead of updated ones, then you can index all new documents into a small shard that will perform well due to having a small number of documents. Occasionally, you'll need to coordinate a merge into another larger shard via the `mergeIndexes` core command.

Where next for scaling Solr?

While Solr offers some impressive scaling techniques through replication and sharding of data, it assumes that you know a priori what your scaling needs are. The distributed search of Solr doesn't adapt to real time changes in indexing or query load and doesn't provide any fail-over support. **SolrCloud** is an ongoing effort to build a fault tolerant, centrally managed support for clusters of Solr instances and is part of the trunk development path (Solr 4.0). SolrCloud introduces the idea that a logical **collection** of documents (otherwise known as an index) is distributed across a number of **slices**. Each slice is made up of **shards**, which are the physical pieces of the collection. In order to support fault tolerance, there may be multiple **replicas** of a shard distributed across different physical **nodes**. To keep all this data straight, Solr embeds Apache ZooKeeper as the centralized service for managing all configuration information for the cluster of Solr instances, including mapping which shards are available on which set of nodes of the cluster. At the time of writing, you still need to manage creating the various shards and replica copies yourself during index time. However, compared to the current sharding approach where you have to supply via the `shards` parameter the addresses of all the shards to search over, with SolrCloud you can just add a `distrib=true` parameter to your query to let Solr figure out what the relevant shards are to query:

```
http://localhost:8983/solr/mbreleases/select?q=*:*&distrib=true
```

Of course, you can still search a specific set of shards with failover replicas delimited using the | character:

```
http://localhost:8983/solr/mbreleases/select?q=*:*&shards
=localhost:8983/solr|localhost:8900/solr,localhost:7574/
solr|localhost:7500/solr
```

In this case we queried for all the documents in the collection *mbreleases*, made up of two shards, each shard consisting of two replicas, each in their own individual Solr server.

The first release will be in Solr 4.0; however, it is already in a useable state for many use cases and it is well worth investigation. SOLR-1873 is the JIRA issue for tracking the progress of this development. See the wiki page here for more information: `http://wiki.apache.org/solr/SolrCloud`.

Summary

Solr offers many knobs and levers for increasing performance; the biggest challenge can be figuring out which knobs and levers to use! Make sure you budget time to try a number of approaches, and take a stepwise approach to trying different approaches out. From turning the simpler knobs for enhancing the performance of a single server, to pulling the big levers of scaling horizontally through replication and sharding, performance and scalability with appropriate hardware are issues that can be solved fairly easily. Moreover, for those projects where truly massive search infrastructure is required, the ability to shard over multiple servers and then delegate to multiple slaves provides an almost linear scalability capacity.

Search Quick Reference

This appendix is a convenient reference for common search related request parameters. It is assumed you already read the related material in the book and are just looking for something to jog your memory.

The content is on the following two pages. You can find an electronic PDF version of this appendix here: http://www.solrenterprisesearchserver.com. Having it printed is especially convenient.

Quick reference

A ⁺ means the parameter can appear a variable number of times.

Core search (*Chapter 4, Searching*)

qt	The **query type**. A named request handler.
q	The **query string**. Usually, as entered by an end user.
defType=lucene	The query parser for q. Recommended: dismax (or edismax).
fq ⁺	A **filter query**. (p. 120)
start=0	The index into the search results to start returning documents.
rows=10	The number of search result documents to return.
fl=*	The **field list** to retrieve, comma separated. To get scores: *,score
sort=score desc	The sort order. A comma separated list with asc or desc. (p. 142)
wt=xml	The **writer type**, that is response format. One of xml, json, python, php, phps, ruby, javabin, csv, xslt (p. 121), velocity (p. 282).

Others: version=2.2, omitHeader=off, timeAllowed=-1

Diagnostic related (*Chapter 4, Searching*)

indent=off, debugQuery=off, explainOther (a query for one doc), debug. explain.structured=off, echoParams=explicit (none|explicit|all), echoHandler=off

Tip: Use wt=xslt&tr=example.xsl&debugQuery=true&fl=*,score

Lucene query parser (*Chapter 4, Searching*)

df	The **default field** to search.
q.op=OR	The default **query operator**. One of AND, OR.

Dismax query parser (*Chapter 4, Searching* and *Chapter 5, Search Relevancy*)

q.alt	An alternate query to run when q is absent. Recommend: *:* (all docs)
qf	The **query fields**, including optional boosts. Ex: id^5.0 name^2.0 body
mm=100%	The **min-should-match** specification. To change to all-optional, use 0%
qs=0	The **query slop** for phrases *explicitly* in the query string.
pf	The **phrase fields** for automatic phrase boosting. Same qf syntax.
ps=0	The **phrase slop** for pf.
tie=0	The score tie-breaker. Recommend: 0.1
bq ⁺	A **boost query**. The boost is added.

bf [+]	A **boost** function. The boost is added.
boost [+]	A boost function. The boost is multiplied. *edismax only*

Other edismax additions: `pf2`, `pf3`, `stopwords=on`, `lowercaseOperators=on`

Lucene Query Syntax (*Chapter 4, Searching*)

Boolean operators: `AND`, `OR`, `NOT`, `&&`, `||`. Leading + or -.

Ex: `{!lucene df=title q.op=$myop}` `"phrase query slop"~2 w?ldcard*`
`fuzzzy~0.7 -( updatedAt:[* TO NOW/DAY-2YEAR] +boostMe^5 )`

Faceting (*Chapter 6, Faceting*)

Example of a field specific parameter: `f.myfieldname.facet.mincount=1`

Field value faceting: `facet=off`, `facet.field` [+], `facet.sort=count` (count | lex),
`facet.limit=100`, `facet.offset=0`, `facet.mincount=0`, `facet.missing=off`,
`facet.prefix`, `facet.method` (enum | fc)

Range faceting: `facet=off`, `facet.range` [+] (field name), `facet.range.start`,
`facet.range.end`, `facet.range.gap` (ex: +1DAY), `facet.range.hardend=off`,
`facet.range.other=off`, `facet.range.include=lower` [+] (lower, upper, edge,
outer, all)

Facet queries: `facet=off`, `facet.query` [+]

Exclude a filter: `fq={!tag=r_type}r_type:Album&facet.field={!ex=r_type}`
`r_type`

Highlighting (*Chapter 7, Search Components*, p. 202)

Common parameters: `hl=off`, `hl.fl`, `hl.requireFieldMatch=off`,
`hl.usePhraseHighlighter=off` (**recommend** on), `hl.highlightMultiTerm=off`,
`hl.snippets=1`, `hl.fragsize=100`, `hl.mergeContiguous=off`

Spell checking (*Chapter 7, Search Components*, p. 215)

Parameters: `spellcheck=off`, `spellcheck.dictionary=default`, `spellcheck.q`
(alternative to q), `spellcheck.count=1`, `spellcheck.onlyMorePopular=off`,
`spellcheck.extendedResults=off`, `spellcheck.collate=off`, `spellcheck.`
`maxCollations=1`, `spellcheck.maxCollationTries=0`, `spellcheck.`
`maxCollationEvaluations=10000`, `spellcheck.collateExtendedResults=off`

Miscellaneous non-search

Commit: `/update?commit=true` (`optimize=true` **to optimize**)

Delete: `/update?stream.body=<delete><query>*:*</query></delete>`

Reload config: `/admin/cores?action=RELOAD&core=mycorename`

Index

Symbols

&& operator 126
|| operator 126

A

<add> tag 20
abort command 99
Acquia 312
acts_as_solr 322
additive boosting 157
aggregate index 32
AJAX 272
AJAX Solr 278, 303-305
alphabetic range bucketing 181
analyzers 52
AND or && operator 126
Apache Solr 3.1 Cookbook 27
appends parameter 118, 297
ARC 283
arcreader command 285
arr element 22, 114
artist 31
artists.xml 78
asc 142
ASCIIFoldingFilterFactory token filter
    56, 72
a_type 141
audio formats
  MIDI 100
  MP3 100
  Wave audio 100
autoCommit 83, 342
autocomplete widgets 298, 321
autoGeneratePhraseQueries Boolean

attribute 53
automatic phrase boosting
  about 153
  configuring 153, 154
  partial phrase boosting 154, 155
  phrase slop configuration 154
Auto-warming 338
avgRequestsPerSecond parameter 330
avgTimePerRequest 330, 331

B

baseUrl 97
bbox query parsers 144, 145
BeanShell 267
bf param 157
Billy Corgan 129
BinContentStreamDataSource 90
BinFileDataSource 90
bonafide tokenizer 52
book supplement
  about 12
  code supplement 12
boolean operators
  about 126
  AND 126
  NOT 126
  OR 126
Boolean parameters 119
Boolean query 152
bool element 115
boost attribute 80
boost.[fieldname], Solr Cell parameters 104
boost functions 156
boosting 133, 148
boost parameter 156, 157

boost(q,boost) 163
boost query 155
boost query parser 158
bq query 155
browse interface
  about 24
  URL 24
bucketFirstLetter 181
buildOnCommit 214
buildOnOptimize 214
built-in field types, schema.xml file
  about 42
  geospatial 43
  numbers and dates 42

C

<charFilter> element 55
<copyField> elements 26
cacheControl 336
CachedSqlEntityProcessor 92
CapitalizationFilterFactory token filter 72
captureAttr, Solr Cell parameters 102
capture, Solr Cell parameters 102
catenateAll 60
catenateNumbers 60
catenateWords 60
Caverphone 66
cbrt(x), mathematical primitives 161
CCK 312
ceil(x), mathematical primitives 161
CF 325
Chainsaw
  URL 253
change() function 302
characterEncoding, FileBasedSpellChecker
      options 213
character filters
  about 52, 55
  HTMLStripCharFilterFactory 56
  MappingCharFilterFactory 56
  PatternReplaceCharFilterFactory 56
ClassicFilterFactory token filter 72
ClassicTokenizerFactory tokenizer 57, 58
ClassNotFoundException error 88
client directory, Solr 12
ClientUtils.escapeQueryChars() method 135

ClobTransformer 93
clustering
  about 238
  document clustering 238
  search-result clustering 238
CMS 311
CNET 7
CollationKeyFilterFactory 71
column attribute 92
combined index
  about 32
  advantages 33
combined schema 46
commands, DIH
  importing 98
commands, Solr
  CREATE 260
  MERGE 261
  RELOAD 261
  RENAME 260
  STATUS 260
  SWAP 260
  UNLOAD 261
commit, Solr
  about 82
  autoCommit 83
  commitWithin 83
  significance 82
commitWithin 83
common-grams 65, 154, 346
CommonGramsFilterFactory 65
comparatorClass 219
compilation 155
complex systems
  CPU usage 330
  memory usage 330
  system changes 331
  TPS 330
  tuning 330, 331
compressed, field options 44
conf directory 63, 97
Configuration Management (CM) 245
configuration options, CSV
  about 86
  encapsulator 86
  escape 86
  fieldnames 86

header 86
keepEmpty 86
map 87
overwrite 86
separator 86
skip 86
skipLines 86
split 87
trim 86
configuration parameters, MLT
  about 231
  parameters, specific to MLT request handler
    231
  parameters, specific to MLT search
    component 231
Connector Framework. *See* **CF**
connectors 325
ConsoleHandler 252
Content Construction Kit. *See* **CCK**
content field 324
Content Management System. *See* **CMS**
ContentStreamDataSource 91
content_updater 271
Continuous Integration (CI) server 164
contrib modules
  about 10, 13
  DataImportHandler (DIH) 10
  JAR files 13
  Solr Cell 10
Convention over Configuration 313
coordination factor 153
coord, scoring factors 148
copyField directive
  about 48
  uses 48
copyField, schema.xml file 48
core instance directory 14
correctlySpelled 219
crawler 278
crawling 97
CREATE command 260
cron 349
CSV
  about 77
  configuration options 86
CSV data
  sending, to Solr 84, 85

cURL 77, 337
Cygwin
  URL 77

D

<dataSource/> 90
<directoryFactory /> tag 335
<doc> tag 20
<document/> element 91
d parameter 145
database technology
  comparing 10
data formats, for indexing data
  about 76
  CSV 77
  Java-Bin 77
  Rich documents 77
  Solr's Update-JSON 77
  Solr's Update-XML 76
DataImportHandler (DIH)
  about 10, 13, 76, 77, 87, 294
  alternatives 88
  capabilities 87
  commands, importing 98
  development console 89
  DIH configuration file, writing 90
  example DIH configurations 94
  JAR files 88
  reference documentation, URL 88
  setup 88
  sub-entities 96
DataImportHandler transformer 56
data part 248
data, schema design
  denormalizing 37
data source types, DIH
  BinContentStreamDataSource 90
  BinFileDataSource 90
  ContentStreamDataSource 90
  FieldReaderDataSource 90
  FieldStreamDataSource 90
  FileDataSource 90
  JdbcDataSource 90
  URLDataSource 90
date element 115
date faceting 182

DateField 42
DateFormatTransformer 93
DateMath syntax 132, 133
DebugComponent 197, 199
debug queries. *See* queries, troubleshooting
debugQuery parameter 121, 124, 156, 197
decompounding 61
defaultField 49, 103
defaultOperator attribute 49, 124
defaults 118
defaultSearchField element 49, 124
defType=dismax 135
defType parameter 119, 151
delete tag 81
delta import 98, 99
deltaImportQuery attributes 99
denormalization
  about 37
  one-to-many associated data 38
  one-to-one associated data 37
deployment process, Solr
  questions 246, 247
desc 142
development console, DIH 89
diagnostic related parameters
  about 121
  debugQuery 122
  echoHandler 122
  echoParams 122
  explainOther 122
  indent 121
dictionary 207
  building, from source 214
dictionary attribute 62
Did you mean. *See* spell checking
DIH configuration file
  about 94
  commands, importing 98
  data sources 90
  delta import 99
  entity processors 91
  fields 92
  importing, from databases 94, 95
  multiple rich document files, importing 97, 98
  transformers 93
  writing 90

XML, importing from file with XSLT 96
directory structure, Solr
  about 12
  client 12
  contrib 13
  dist 13
  docs 13
  example 14
DirectSolrSpellChecker 214
DisjunctionMaxQuery query type 135, 152
dismax parser 119, 122
dismax query parser
  about 9, 48, 67, 129, 135, 136, 151
  additive boosting 157
  automatic phrase boosting 153
  automatic phrase boosting, configuring 153
  bf + 367
  boost + 367
  boost functions 156
  boost queries 155
  bq + 366
  default search 140
  DisjunctionMaxQuery 152
  features 136
  limited query syntax 137, 138
  min-should-match 138
  mm=100% 366
  multiple fields, searching 137
  multiplicative boosting 157
  pf 366
  ps=0 366
  q.alt 366
  qf 366
  qs=0 366
  queries, boosting 155
  tie=0 366
dist, directory structure 13
distrib=true parameter 363
distributed search 34, 182, 358
Distributor 354
div(x,y), mathematical primitives 161
doc element 116
docs, directory structure 13
document access
  controlling 273
document clustering 238
document frequency values 33

document, Lucene 8
document oriented data model 10
document security
  maintaining, ManifoldCF used 324
documents indexing, with Solr cell
  about 100
  karaoke lyrics, extracting 104, 105
  metadata, extracting from files 100, 101
  richer documents, indexing 106, 107
  Solr Cell parameters 102, 103
  Solr, configuring 101, 102
  text, extracting from files 100, 101
documents, Solr's Update-XML format
  deleting 80
double element 114
DoubleMetaphone 66
DoubleMetaphoneFilterFactory analysis
    filter
  about 67
  inject, options 67
  maxCodeLength, options 67
  options 67
Drupal options, PHP applications
  about 311
  Apache Solr Search integration module 312
  Hosted Solr 312, 313
dynamicField 45

E

<em></em> HTML markup 206
element 204
element 92
echoHandler parameter 122
echoParams 122, 187, 234
EdgeNGram analyzer 70
EdgeNGramFilterFactory 70
EdgeNGramTokenizerFactory 70, 220
edismax query parser
  about 119, 128, 151
  default search 135
edit distance 131
elevateArtists.xml 229
e(), mathematical primitives 161
Embedded Solr 76
embedded Solr, using
  in-process indexing 294, 295

  legacy Lucene, upcoming 295
  standalone desktop applications 295
  use cases 294
encoder attribute 67
encodeURIComponent() 117
endOffset 219
EnglishMinimalStemFilterFactory stemmer
    62
EnglishPossessiveFilterFactory token filter
    72
entities returned from search, schema
    design
  determining 36
entity processors, DIH
  about 91
  CachedSqlEntityProcessor 92
  FileListEntityProcessor 92
  LineEntityProcessor 92
  MailEntityProcessor 92
  PlainTextEntityProcessor 92
  SqlEntityProcessor 91
  TikaEntityProcessor 92
  XPathEntityProcessor 92
Entity tags 337
enum method 181
ETag
  about 337
  Squid 337
  Varnish 337
ETL (Extract Transform and Load) 95
eval() function 296-310
event 31
example, directory structure
  about 14
  child directories 14
examples, Solr
  ajaxsolr 278
  crawler 278
  jquery_autocomplete 278
  myfaves 278
  nutch 278
  php 278
  Solritas 278
  solr-php-client 278
existence (and non-existence) queries 134
explainOther parameter 122
explicit mapping 63

exp(x), mathematical primitives 161
eXtensible Stylesheet Language Transformations. *See* XSLT
ExternalFileField 170
extractFormat, Solr Cell parameters 104
ExtractingRequestHandler 75, 100
extractOnly, Solr Cell parameters 104

F

element 26, 41, 44
element 206
facet 232
FacetComponent 197, 199
facet count 176
facet.date 345
faceted navigation 7, 173, 194
facet.field parameter 179
facet_fields 178
faceting 367
  about 7, 173
  example 174, 175
  facet.missingparameter 176
  field requirements 178
  filters, excluding 190-194
  hierarchical faceting 194, 195
  multi-select faceting 190
  MusicBrainz schema changes 176, 177
  release types example 174, 175
  types 178, 179
faceting, types
  field values 178
  queries 179
  ranges 179
facet.limit parameter 180
facet.method paramter 180
facet.mincount parameter 180
facet.missing facet 189
facet.missing parameter 180
facet navigation. *See* also faceting
facet.offset parameter 180
facet.prefix 220
facet.prefix parameter 195
facet queries
  about 179, 187
  configuring 187
  facet.query parameter 187

facet.query parameter 187, 345
facet.range.end parameter 186
facet range filter queries 189
facet.range.gap parameter 186
facet.range.hardend parameter 186
facet.range.include parameter 186
facet.range.other parameter 186
facet.range parameter 185
facet_ranges 179
facet.range.start parameter 185
facet.sort parameter 179
facet value 176
fallback 259
FastLRUCache 339
fast vector highlighter (FVH)
  about 205
  parameters 206
  with, multi-colored highlighting 205
field attributes, schema.xml file
  default 44
  name 44
  required 45
  type 44
Field collapsing 239, 241
field element 92
field, IndexBasedSpellChecker options 212
fieldNorm, scoring factors 148
field options, schema.xml file
  about 43
  compressed 44
  indexed 43
  multiValued 44
  omitNorms 43
  positionIncrementGap 44
  sortMissingFirst 43
  sortMissingLast 43
  stored 44
  termVectors 44
field qualifier, query syntax 128
FieldReaderDataSource 90
field references, function query 159
field requirements, faceting 178
field , schema.xml file
  attributes 44
  dynamic field 45
fields, DIH 92
fields, Lucene 8

FieldStreamDataSource 90
field types, schema.xml file
about 41
class attribute 41
field value cache 221
field value filter queries 189
field values
about 178
alphabetic range bucketing 181
faceting 179
FileBasedSpellChecker options
characterEncoding 213
sourceLocation 213
FileDataSource 90
FileHandler logging 252
FileListEntityProcessor 92
filter
adding 141
filter cache 141, 187, 338
filtering 141
filter query
about 141
building, from facet 188
facet range filter queries 189
field value filter queries 189
filters
excluding, in faceting 190, 191
first-components 119
firstSearcher warming query 225
float element 114
floor(x), mathematical primitives 161
fl parameter 121
fmap.content=text parameter 104
fmap.[tikaFieldName], Solr Cell parameters
103
forceElevation 229
formulas, function query boosting
inverse reciprocals 165, 166
linear 168
logarithm 164, 165
reciprocal 167
fq parameter 120, 141, 338
Frange (function range) query parser 159
full import 98
FULL INTERFACE link 112
func query parser 146, 159
function query

about 158
document based on numeric fields,
boosting 168, 169
field references 159
function query boosting 164
function references 160
incorporating, in Solr 158, 159
recent releases, boosting 170
function query boosting
about 164
examples 164
formulas 164
function reference, function query
about 160
argument 160
geometric/trigonometric functions 161
mathematical functions 161
mathematical primitives 161
miscellaneous functions 162
ord and rord 162
fuzzy queries 131, 207
fuzzy searching 66

G

gazetteer 143
gems 268
generateNumberParts 59
generateWordParts 59
generic XML data structure
about 114
appends 118
components 119
defaults 118
first-components 119
invariants 118
last-components 119
XML elements 114
geodist() 145, 163
geofilt 144
Geohashes 144
GeoHashField 144
geometric/trigonometric functions, function
reference
acos(x) 161
asin(x) 161
atan2(y,x) 161

atan(x) 161
cosh(x) 161
cos(x) 161
deg(x) 161
hypot(x,y) 161
pi() 161
rad(x) 161
sinh(x) 161
sin(x) 161
tan(x) 161

Geonames
  URL 143
geospatial, built-in field types 43
geospatial distance
  calculating 163
geospatial search
  about 143
  locations, indexing 143, 144
  search results, filtering by distance 144, 145
  search results, sorting by distance 145, 146
geospatial support 143
getFieldValue() method 279
Grapher 164
Groovy 267
group.cache.percent, query parameter 242
group.field, query parameter 241
group.format, query parameter 242
grouping
  Field collapsing 239, 241
  Result Grouping 239, 241
group.limit, query parameter 242
group.main, query parameter 242
group.ngroups, query parameter 242
group.offset, query parameter 242
group, query parameter 241
group.query, query parameter 241
group.sort, query parameter 242
guided navigation. *See* **also faceting 173**

H

<highlighting/> element 202
Hadoop 323
HAProxy 354
HathiTrust 331
Haversine formula
  using 145

Heritrix
  about 283
  using, for artist pages, downloading 283, 284
hierarchical faceting 194, 195
highlight component
  about 200
  configuration options 202
  configuring 202
  example 200, 202
  fast vector highlighter 205
  hl.fl 200
  regex fragmenter 205
highlighter search component
  parameters 202
highlighting 367
highlighting configuration 202
highlight matches 54
hl.alternateField, highlighter search component
  about 204
  hl.maxAlternateFieldLength 204
hl.encoder, highlighter search component 204
hl.fl, highlighter search component 200-202
hl.formatter, highlighter search component
  about 204
  hl.simple.post 204
  hl.simple.pre 204
hl.fragListBuilder 206
hl.fragmenter, highlighter search component 204
hl.fragmentsBuilder
  about 206
  hl.multiValuedSeparatorChar 207
  hl.tag.post 206
  hl.tag.pre 206
hl.fragsize, highlighter search component 203
hl, highlighter search component 202
hl.maxAnalyzedChars, highlighter search component 203
hl.mergeContiguous, highlighter search component 203
hl.phraseLimit 207
hl.requireFieldMatch, highlighter search component 203

hl.snippets, highlighter search component 203
hl.useFastVectorHighligher 206
hl.usePhraseHighlighter, highlighter search component
  about 203
  hl.highlightMultiTerm 203
home directory, Solr 14
horizon 165
Hosted Solr 312
href attribute 259
HTML indexing
  SolrJ based client, using 285
HTMLStripCharFilterFactory 56, 93
HTMLStripTransformer 93
HTMLStripWhitespaceTokenizerFactory 56
HTTP caching 335-337
HTTP POST
  sending 77
HTTP POSTing options 77
HTTP server request style logs
  about 250
  tailing 250
HTTP Solr interaction 76

I

ICUTokenizer 59
IDF 33
idf, scoring factors 148
id tag 81
ignoreCase Boolean option 62
indent parameter 121
index and file based spellcheckers, options
  accuracy 211
  buildOnCommit 211
  buildOnOptimize 211
  classname 211
  distanceMeasure 211
  fieldType 212
  name 211
  spellcheckIndexDir 211
IndexBasedSpellChecker
  about 212
  field 212
  sourceLocation 212
  thresholdTokenFrequency 212

Index box 54
index data
  securing 273
indexed 43, 340
indexes, sharding
  about 356, 357
  distributed search 358
  documents, assigning 357, 358
  shards, searching across 358
indexing
  about 290-292
  POJOs 292, 293
indexing performance, enhancing
  factors, committing 343, 344
  factors, optimizing 343, 344
  strategies 341
  unique document checking, disabling 343
indexing ways, Solr 78
Index Searchers 338
index-time boosting 81, 149
index version 349
Information Retrieval (IR) principles 8
int element 114
internal workings, MLT 230
InternetArchive 283
IntField 42
invariants 118
inverse reciprocals, function query boosting example formulas
  about 165-169
  graph 166
inverted index, Lucene 8

J

JAR files, contrib modules
  analysis-extras 13
  clustering 13
  dataimporthandler 13
  extraction 13
  uima 13
JAR files, DIH
  about 88
  adding, to Solr configurations 88
JARmageddon 253
Java
  downloading 11

Java-Bin 77
Java Development Kit (JDK) 12
JavaFX 295
Java Management Extensions. *See* JMX
Java replication
  versus script 349
JavaScript 272
  Solr, using with 296, 297
JavaScript Object Notation. *See* JSON
JavaScript, using with Solr
  about 296
  AJAX Solr 303-305
  security, checking 297
  Solr powered artists autocomplete widget,
    building 298-303
Java servlet engine 116
java.util.ConsoleHandler 252
java.util.UUID 49
Java Virtual Machine. *See* JVM
JConsole 12, 267
JdbcDataSource 294 90
JDK logging 251
Jetty servlet engine 15
Jetty startup integration 253
JIRA software 27
JMX
  about 264
  Solr, starting with 265-267
Jmx4r
  about 269
  URL 269
jmx4r gem
  installing 268
JMX access
  controlling 273
JMX information
  extracting, JRuby used 267-269
JMX Mbeans
  about 265
  URL 265
JNDI (Java Naming and Directory Interface)
  249
join capability 10
join support 37
jquery_autocomplete 278
jQueryUI 298
JRuby

about 268
URL 268
used, for extracting JMX information
  267-269
JRuby Interactive Browser (JIRB) tool 268
JSON 7
JSONP 272, 300
JVM
  about 334
  configuration 334
JVM settings configuration, for memory us-
  age improvement 334
Jython 267

K

karaoke lyrics
  extracting 104, 105
KeepWordFilterFactory token filter 72
KeywordMarkerFilter 62
KeywordTokenizerFactory tokenizer 57,
  132, 220
KStemFilterFactory stemmer 61

L

language detection 59
last-components 119, 228
last_modified 101, 106
Last-Modified header 336
LatLonType field 144, 163
LBHttpSolrServer 355
Least Recently Used 338
LengthFilterFactory token filter 72
LetterTokenizerFactory tokenizer 58
Levenshtein Distance algorithm 131
limited query syntax 137, 138
LimitTokenCountFilterFactory token filter
  72
linear, function query boosting example
  formulas 168
linear(x,m,c), mathematical functions 162
LineEntityProcessor 92
literal() function 160
ln(x), mathematical primitives 161
local-params 111, 122, 123, 160
Log4j
  URL 253

used, for Solr application logging 253
Log4j appenders 253
Log4j compatible logging viewer
  Chainsaw 253
  Familiarity 253
  using 253
  Vigilog 253
Log4j JAR file 253
logarithm, function query boosting example
       formulas
  about 164, 165
  graph 164, 165
Loggly
  about 254
  URL 254
logs
  about 249
  HTTP server request style logs 249
  Solr application logging 249
  types 249
LogTransformer 93
LogUpdateProcessorFactory 109
log(x), mathematical primitives 161
long element 114
LowerCaseFilterFactory token filter 72
LowerCaseTokenizerFactory tokenizer 58
lowernames parameters 103
LRUCache 339
Lucene
  about 8
  DisjunctionMaxQuery 152
  document 8
  features 8
  fields 8
  inverted index 8
  overview 8
  scoring 148
  stemming 8
  terms 8
  text analysis 8
  text analyzer 8
Lucene In Action book 27
lucene native syntax 119
lucene query parser. *See* **also query syntax**
  about 124, 158
  df 124, 366
  q.op 124, 366

Lucene query syntax
  about 367
  URL 48
Lucid Imagination 11
LucidWorks 11

M

MailEntityProcessor 92
Managed Bean. *See* **MBeans**
ManifoldCF
  connectors 325
  document security, maintaining 324
  using 325-328
map() function 301
MappingCharFilterFactory, character filters
  about 56
  mapping-FoldToASCII.txt 56
  mapping-ISOLatin1Accent.txt 56
map(x,min,max,target,def?), mathematical
       functions 161
master server 350
mathematical functions, function reference
  linear(x,m,c) 162
  map(x,min,max,target,def?) 161
  max(x,c) 161
  recip(x,m,a,c) 162
  scale(x,minTarget,maxTarget) 161
mathematical primitives, function reference
  cbrt(x) 161
  ceil(x) 161
  div(x,y) 161
  e() 161
  exp(x) 161
  floor(x) 161
  ln(x) 161
  log(x) 161
  pow(x,y) 161
  product(x,y,z,...) 161
  rint(x) 161
  sqrt(x) 161
  sub(x,y) 161
  sum(x,y,z,...) 161
Maven project 286
maxBlockChars 56
maxBooleanClauses threshold 33
maxChars 48

maxCollationTries 218
maxScore 21, 115
maxSegments parameter 343
maxShingleSize 155
maxTokenCount attribute 72
maxWarmingSearchers parameter 342
max(x,c), mathematical functions 161
mbartists 116, 136, 256
mbartists index 337
mb_artists request handler 200, 228
mbartists Solr index 316
MBeans 264
MERGE command 261
mergeFactor setting 344
mergeIndexes core command 363
Microsoft Office 100
min-should-match
  about 138
  basic mm specification formats 138, 139
  multiple rules 139
  rules 138, 139
  search terms, selecting 140
miscellaneous functions, function reference
  about 162
  boost(q,boost) 163
  ms(date1?,date2?) 163
  query(q,def?) 163
  strdist(x,y,alg) 163
MLT
  about 230, 231
  configuration parameters 231
  internal workings 230
  results example 234
  used, as dedicated request handler 230
  used, as request handler with externally
    supplied text 230
  used, as search component 230
  using ways 230
mlt.boost 233
mlt.count 231
mlt.fl 232
mlt.interestingTerms 232
mlt.match.include 231
mlt.match.offset 231
mlt.maxntp 233
mlt.maxqt 233
mlt.maxwl 233

mlt.mindf 233
mlt.mintf 233
mlt.minwl 233
MLT parameters
  facet 232
  mlt 231
  mlt.boost 233
  mlt.count 231
  mlt.fl 232
  mlt.interestingTerms 232
  mlt.match.include 231
  mlt.match.offset 231
  mlt.maxntp 233
  mlt.maxqt 233
  mlt.maxwl 233
  mlt.mindf 233
  mlt.mintf 233
  mlt.minwl 233
  mlt.qf 232
  q 231
  rows 231
  start 231
mlt.qf 232
MLT results example 234, 236
MMapDirectoryFactory 335
MongoDB 10
more like this functionality 312
ms(date1?,date2?), miscellaneous functions
    163
ms() value 160
mul() function query 156
multicore
  about 261
  benefits 261, 262
  configuration changes, testing 262
  cores, renaming at runtime 262
  index, rebuilding 261
  separate indexes, merging 262
multicore configuration values
  adminPath 257
  defaultCoreName 257
  persistent= 257
  sharedLib= 257
  shareSchema 257
multipartUploadLimitInKB setting 78
multiple rich document files
  importing 97

multiple Solr servers
  indexes, sharding 356
  load balancing searches, across slaves 352
  master server, indexing into 352
  moving to 348-356
  replication 349
  replication, configuring 351
  script versus Java replication 349
  starting 350
multiplicative boosting 157
multi-select faceting 190-194, 242
multiValued field 38, 44, 48, 273
multi-word synonyms 64
MusicBrainzConnector class 325
MusicBrainz database schema 30
MusicBrainz field definitions 46, 47
MusicBrainz.org 30, 35
MusicBrainz schema changes, faceting 176
MusicBrainz terminology 40
MyFaves 278, 314

N

name attribute 92, 176
NamedList 297
name field 33
navigation menu, Solr
  ANALYSIS 17
  CONFIG 17
  DISTRIBUTION 17
  FULL INTERFACE 18
  INFO 17
  JAVA PROPERTIES 18
  LOGGING 18
  PING 18
  REPLICATION 17
  SCHEMA 17
  SCHEMA BROWSER 17
  STATISTICS 17
  THREAD DUMP 18
near query 129
near real time search 83, 362
nested queries 127
Net::HTTP library 322
Netflix 7
newSearcher 143, 159
newSearch query 342

N-gram analysis
  about 69
  analyzer configuration 69
  maxGramSize 69
  minGramSize 69
  N-gram costs 70
N-gram costs 70
NGramFilterFactory 69
nodes 363
NOT operator 126
NumberFormatTransformer 93
numbers and dates, built-in field types
  BCDIntField 42
  ExternalFileField 42
  IntField 42
  SortableIntField 42
  TrieIntField 42
numeric and date ranges
  faceting 182
numFound 115, 219
Nutch 278
  about 323, 324
  depth parameter 324
  topN parameter 324

O

omitNorms 41, 43
omitTermFreqAndPositions 340
one-to-many associated data, schema design
  denormalizing 38
  issues, with denormalizing 38
OpenSearch
  based Browse plugin 306
  Solr exposing, XSLT used 305, 306
OpenSearch based Browse plugin
  Search MBArtists plugin, installing 306,
    307, 308
optimize command 83
optional clauses, query expression
  about 125
  Pumpkins 125
optional phrase 153
ord 162
ord() value 160
org.apache.solr.schema.BoolField class 41

org.apache.solr.search.SolrIndexSearcher
component 266
OR or | | operator 126
OutOfMemoryException 334
Output Connector 325
output related parameters
about 121
fl 121
sort 121
version 121
wt 121
overwrite attribute 80

P

PaaS 313
parameters 116
parameters, FVH
hl.fragListBuilder 206
hl.fragmentsBuilder 206
hl.phraseLimit 207
hl.useFastVectorHighligher 206
parameters, highlighter search component
hl 202
hl.alternateField 204
hl.encoder 204
hl.fl 202
hl.formatter 204
hl.fragmenter 204
hl.fragsize 203
hl.maxAnalyzedChars 203
hl.mergeContiguous 203
hl.requireFieldMatch 203
hl.snippets 203
hl.usePhraseHighlighter 203
parameters, QueryElevation component
config-file 228
forceElevation 229
queryFieldType 228
parameters, spellcheck requests
q 215
spellcheck 215
spellcheck.collate 216
spellcheck.count 215
spellcheck.dictionary 215
spellcheck.extendedResults 216
spellcheck.onlyMorePopular 215

spellcheck.q 215
parametric search. See also faceting 173
parsedquery 124
partial phrase boosting 154, 155
PathHierarchyTokenizerFactory
tokenizer 58
PatternReplaceCharFilterFactory 56
PatternReplaceFilterFactory token
filter 68, 71, 73
PatternTokenizerFactory tokenizer 58
PerfMon 330
pf parameter 153
phoneme 66
phonetic encoding algorithms
about 66
Caverphone 66
DoubleMetaphone 66
Metaphone 66
RefinedSoundex 66
Soundex 66
phonetic sounds-like analysis 66
about 66
configuration 66
php 278
PHP applications
Drupal, options 311
Solr, accessing from 309
solr-php-client 310
php writer types
using 309
phrase queries, query syntax 129
phrase search performance
shingling 346
phrase slop
about 154
configuring 154
PlainTextEntityProcessor 92
Platform as a Service. See PaaS
POJOs (Plain Old Java Objects) 292
PortableUniqueIdentifier. See PUID
PorterStemFilterFactory stemmer 61
positionIncrementGap, field options 44
PostgreSQL database 30
post group faceting 242
postImportDeleteQuery attribute 99
post.jar Java program
about 77

invoking 18
post.sh shell script 19
pow(x,y), mathematical primitives 161
precision 61
preImportDeleteQuery attribute 99
preserveOriginal 60
primary key. *See* unique key
product(x,y,z,...), mathematical primitives 161
properties, Solr cores
  dataDir 258
  name 257
  properties= 258
property substitution 258
protected attribute 62
pt parameter 145
public searches
  securing 272
PUID 31, 168

Q

qf parameter 137
q.op parameter 124
q parameter
  about 119, 215, 231, 338
  processing 213
qt=artistAutoComplete parameter 301
QTime 115
qt parameter 120, 136
queries 179
queries, troubleshooting 149
queryAnalyzerFieldType 213
query autocomplete
  about 219
  facet / field value completion 220
  instant-search 219
  query log completion 219
  query term completion 220
Query box 54
query complete / suggest 219
QueryComponent 197-199
QueryElevation component
  about 227
  configuration parameters 228
  configuring 228
query expression

about 125
clauses 125
queryFieldType 228
query() function 143
querying 112
queryNorm part 157
query parameters
  about 119
  Boolean parameters 119
  diagnostic related parameters 121
  output related parameters 121
  result pagination related parameters 120
  search criteria related parameters 119
query parameters, Result Grouping
  group 241
  group.cache.percent 242
  group.field 241
  group.format 242
  group.limit 242
  group.main 242
  group.ngroups 242
  group.offset 242
  group.query 241
  group.sort 242
  group.truncate 242
  rows 242
  sort 242
  start 242
query parser 122
query(q,def?) 163
query response writer 121
queryResultWindowSize setting 338
query spellchecking 66
query syntax
  about 81, 123
  boolean operators 126
  boosting 133
  clauses 125
  documents, matching 125
  existence (and non-existence) queries 134
  field qualifier 128
  nested queries 127
  phrase queries 129
  range queries 131, 132
  special characters 134
  sub-queries 127
  term proximity 129

wildcard queries 129, 130
query tag 81
query term completion
  via, facet.prefix 221-223
  via, Suggester 223-225
  via, Terms component 226
query-time boosting
  about 81, 149
quick search
  performing 112

R

<requestHandler/> element 21, 26, 198
<response/> element 20, 115
<result/> element 21
range faceting
  about 182
  example 184, 185
range facet parameters
  about 185
  facet.range 185
  facet.range.end 186
  facet.range.gap 186
  facet.range.hardend 186
  facet.range.include 186
  facet.range.other 186
  facet.range.start 185
range queries, query syntax
  about 131, 132
  date math 133
  DateMath syntax 132
ranges 179
r_attributes field 176
RDBMS 10
README.txt files 27
realm.properties 272
recall 61
reciprocal 167, 170
recip(x,m,a,c), mathematical functions 162
RefinedSoundex 66
regex 57
regex fragmenter
  about 205
  options 205
regex fragmenter, options
  hl.increment 205

hl.regex.maxAnalyzedChars 205
hl.regex.pattern 205
hl.regex.slop 205
RegexTransformer 93
regular expression 57, 124
release 31
RELOAD command 261
reload-config command 99
remote streaming
  about 76-79, 274
  local file, accessing 79
**RemoveDuplicatesTokenFilterFactory token
    filter 72**
RENAME command 260
replace attribute 73
replicas 363
replication and sharding
  combining 360-363
Repository Connector 325
request handler
  about 116, 117
  configuring 117, 118
request handler configuration
  creating 117
request handlers
  defType=lucene 366
  fl=* 366
  fq + 366
  q 366
  qt 366
  rows=10 366
  sort=score desc 366
  start=0 366
  wt=xml 366
request parameters
  facet.field 179
  facet.limit 180
  facet.method 180
  facet.mincount 180
  facet.missing 180
  facet.offset 180
  facet.sort 179
request processors
  updating 109
resource.name, Solr Cell parameters 102
response() function 301
response writers 279

REST
  URL 77
Result Grouping
  about 38, 239, 241
  configuring 241
  query parameters 241
result pagination related parameters
  about 120
  rows 120
  start 120
results element 116
ReversedWildcardFilterFactory 68, 129
Rich documents 77
richer documents
  indexing 106, 107
rint(x), mathematical primitives 161
r_official field 155, 176
rollback 84
root entity 91
rord 162
rows parameter 120, 231, 242
rsolr 12, 322
RSolr library 317
rsync 349
r_type 73, 142, 155, 176, 191
Ruby on Rails integration
  about 313
  Rails/Ruby library, selecting 322
  Ruby query response writer 313, 314
  sunspot_rails gem 314
RunUpdateProcessorFactory 109

S

<script/> element 93
<solr_home>/lib directory 88
**scale(x,minTarget,maxTarget), mathematical
    functions 161**
schema
  <copyField> elements 26
  <fields> element 26
  <types> element 26
  <requestHandler> elements 26
  about 26
  designing 340
**schema configuration, SpellCheck compo-
    nent 208, 209**

schema design
  about 35
  data, denormalizing 37
  entities returned from search, determining
    36
  inclusion of fields used in search results,
    omitting 39, 40
  indexed 340
  omitTermFreqAndPositions 340
  Solr powered search, determining 36
schema.xml file
  <fields/> element 41
  <types/> element 41
  about 40, 41
  built-in field types 42
  copyField 48
  defaultSearchField 49
  field definitions 44
  field options 43
  field types 41
  MusicBrainz field definitions 46
  solrQueryParser 49
  unique key 49
schema.xml snippet 32
score desc. score 121, 142
score, Lucene 8
score pseudo-field 71
scoring
  about 148
  factors 148
  index-time boosting 149
  query-time boosting 149
  troubleshooting 149-151
scoring factors
  co-ordination factor 148
  Field length 148
  inverse document frequency 148
  term frequency 148
**SCOWL (Spell Checker Oriented Word
    Lists) 207**
script
  versus Java replication 349
ScriptTransformer 93, 94, 109
search() 319
Search Component
  about 197, 199
  Clustering component 197, 238

highlight component 200
highlighting 197
MLT component 230
More-like-this 197
QueryElevation component 197, 227
Result grouping 197
SpellCheck component 197, 207
Stats 197
Stats component 236
Suggester 197
Terms 197
TermVector component 187, 243
search components 119
search criteria related parameters
about 119
defType 119
fq 120
g 119
qt 120
SearchHandler 254
searching
about 112
working 116
Search MBArtists plugin 306
search-result clustering 238
security, Solr
about 270
document access, controlling 273
index data, securing 273
JMX access, controlling 273
public searches, securing 272
server access, limiting 270, 271
segments 83
select() function 301
separate indices
about 34
limitations 34
server access
limiting 270-272
Servlet 2.4 specifications
Apache Tomcat 247
GlassFish 247
JRun 247
Websphere 247
Servlet containers
differences 248
solr.home property, defining 248

Solr, installing in 247
sfield parameter 145, 163
sharding
about 356
and replication, combining 360-363
index latency 362
near real time search 362
real time search 362
shards parameter 363
shards.qt parameter 199, 358
shingling 154, 285, 346
SignatureUpdateProcessorFactory 109
Simple Logging Facade for Java (SLF4J)
    package 251
SimplePostTool 18
simple query
running 20-22
single combined index
using, issues 33
single combined indexschema
schema.xml snippet, sample 32
single Solr server optimization
about 334
downstream HTTP caching, enabling 335
faceting performance, enhancing 345
indexing, speeding up 341, 342
JVM settings configuration, for memory
    improvement 334
phrase search performance, improving 346,
    347, 348
schema, designing 340
Solr caching 338
statistics admin page, using 339
term vectors, using 345
slaves
load balancing searches 352
master slaves, indexing 352
slaves, configuring 353
slave server 350
SLF4J distributions
URL 253
slices 363
slop. *See* **phrase slop**
slop factor 129
Smashing Pumpkins example 31
diagrammatic representation 31
SnowballPorterFilterFactory stemmer 61

Solarium 309, 311
Solr
  about 7, 9, 277
  accessing, from PHP applications 309
  book supplement 12
  browse interface 24
  client API 287
  commands 260
  commit 82
  communicating with 76
  complex systems, tuning 330
  configuration files 25
  configuring 101, 102
  contrib modules 10
  CSV data, sending to 84, 85
  database technology, comparing with 10
  Data Import Handler framework 87
  deployment process 245
  diagrammatic representation 29
  directory structure 12
  downloading 11
  examples 278
  features 7, 9
  filter cache 141
  filtering 141
  function query, incorporating 158, 159
  generic search functionality, providing 255
  generic XML data structure 114
  home directory 14
  indexing ways 78
  installing, in Servlet container 247
  JavaScript, using 296, 297
  logging facility 249
  logs 249
  optimize 83
  query parameters 119
  request handler 117
  result grouping feature 38
  rollback 84
  running 15
  sample data, loading 18-20
  scaling, future 363
  schema 26
  schema design 35
  search components 119
  searching 111
  securing 270

simple query, running 20-22
solr.home property 248
sorting 142
starting, with JMX 265-267
statistics admin page 23
working with 29
XML response format 115
Solr 3.3
  URL 100
Solr 4
  about 37
  join support 37
SOLR-1226 97
Solr admin
  Assistance area 18
Solr admin site
  example 17
  navigation menu 17
  URL 16
Solr application logging
  about 251
  Jetty startup integration 253
  Log4j, used 253
  logging output, configuring 252
  log levels, managing at runtime 254
solr.body feature 78
Solr caching 338
  autowarmCount 339
  class 339
  configuring 339
  documentCache 338
  FastLRUCache, using 339
  filterCache 338
  queryResultCache 338
  size 339
Solr Cell
  about 10, 100
  documents, indexing with 100
  URL 100
SolrCell 13
Solr Cell contrib module 77
Solr Cell parameters
  about 102, 103
  boost.[fieldname] 104
  capture 102
  captureAttr 102
  defaultField 103

extractFormat 104
extractOnly 104
fmap.[tikaFieldName] 103
literal.[fieldname] 103
lowernames 103
resource.name 102
stream.type 102
uprefix 103
xpath 103
SolrCloud 363
solrconfig.xml
<requestHandler/> 198
about 49, 78, 98, 157, 349
Solr core directory
about 14
conf 14
conf/schema.xml 14
conf/solrconfig.xml 14
conf/velocity 15
conf/xslt 14
data 15
lib 15
Solr cores
about 14, 32
features, reference link 262
leveraging 256
managing 259, 260
mbartists 256, 257
mbreleases 257
mbtracks 257
multicore 261
multicore configuration 256
multicore configuration values 257
multicore, using 261
properties 257
property substitution 258
solr.xml, configuring 256, 257
XML fragments. including with XInclude 259
Solr Distributed-search 199
Solr Ecosystem 277
Solr filter query 144
Solr, filters
StandardFilterFactory 72
Solr function queries 156
solr.highlight.DefaultEncoder class 204
solr.home property 248, 249

Solr index 34
Solr integration API 76
Solr, interacting with
convenient client API 76
data formats 76, 77
Direct HTTP 76
HTTP POSTing options 77
remote streaming 76, 79
Solritas
about 9, 24, 279-280
cons 281
pros 281-283
SolrJ
about 76, 283
embedded Solr, using 294
Heritrix, using for artist pages download 283-285
QueryResponse 283
SolrDocument 283
SolrQuery 283
SolrJ API 76
SolrJ client API
about 77, 287
embedding 288
indexing 290
searching 289, 290
Solrmarc 295
SolrMeter
using, for Solr performance testing 332, 333
Solr performance
JMX 264
monitoring 262
Stats.jsp 263, 264
testing, SolrMeter used 332, 333
solr-php-client 278, 309, 310
Solr powered search, schema design
determining 36
Solr queries
debugger 306
solrQueryParser 49
Solr resources
Apache Solr 3.1 Cookbook 27
mailing lists 27
README.txt files 27
Solr's issue tracker 27
Solr's Wiki 27
solr-ruby 12, 322

Solr's issue tracker 27
Solr's Update-JSON 77
Solr's Update-XML format
  about 76, 80
  documents, deleting 81
  using 80
  XML-based commands, sending 80
solr.TextField 51
Solr tools
  fuzzy searching 66
  phonetic sounds-like 66
  query spellchecking 66
solr.UUIDField class 49
Solr Wiki
  solr-ruby 323
  URL 27, 239
Solr Wiki page
  URL 51
solr.xml 98
  configuring 256
SortableIntField 42
sorting
  about 71, 142, 159
  limitations 71
sortMissingFirst 42, 43, 142
sortMissingLast 42, 43, 142
sort parameter 121, 143
sort, query parameter 242
Soundex 66
sourceLocation, FileBasedSpellChecker options 213
sourceLocation, IndexBasedSpellChecker options 212
spatial search 143
special characters, query syntax 134, 135
spellcheck.build 214
spellcheck.collate, spellcheck requests parameters
  about 216
  spellcheck.collateExtendedResults 216
  spellcheck.maxCollationEvaluations 216
  spellcheck.maxCollations 216
  spellcheck.maxCollationTries 216
SpellCheck component
  about 207
  dictionary, building from source 214
  example usage, for misspelled query 217,

218
  indexed content 207
  q parameter, processing 213
  schema configuration 208, 209
  solrconfig.xml, configuring in 209
  spellcheck.q parameter, processing 213
  spellcheck requests, issuing 215
  text file of words 207
spellcheck.count, spellcheck requests parameters 215
spellcheck.dictionary, spellcheck requests parameters 215
spellcheckers
  accuracy 211
  a_spell 209
  buildOnCommit 211
  buildOnOptimize 211
  classname 211
  configuring 211
  distanceMeasure 211
  fieldType 212
  file 210
  FileBasedSpellChecker options 213
  IndexBasedSpellChecker options 212
  jarowinkler 210, 211
  name 211
  spellcheckIndexDir 211
spellcheck.extendedResults, spellcheck requests parameters 216
spellcheckIndexDir 214
spell checking 197, 367
spellcheck.onlyMorePopular, spellcheck requests parameters 215
spellcheck.q parameter
  about 212, 215
  processing 213
spellcheck.reload command 211, 214
spellcheck requests
  issuing 215
  parameters 215
spellcheck, spellcheck requests parameters 215
spelled words 207
Splunk
  URL 254
SQL AS mkeyword 92
SqlEntityProcessor 91, 99

SQL file 30
SQLite database 315
sqrt(x), mathematical primitives 161
Squid 337
standard component list 199
StandardDirectoryFactory 335
StandardTokenizerFactory tokenizer 57
startEmbeddedSolr() method 292
start parameter 115, 120, 231, 242
statistics admin page
  URL 23
Statistics page
  using 330
Stats component
  about 236
  configuring 237
  statistics 236
  statistics, on track durations 237
  stats 237
  stats.facet 237
  stats.field 237
stats.jsp 263, 264
status command 115, 260
Steady State 330
StemmerOverrideFilter 62
stemmers 61
stemmers, for English language
  EnglishMinimalStemFilterFactory 62
  KStemFilterFactory 61
  PorterStemFilterFactory 61
  SnowballPorterFilterFactory 61
stemming
  about 61, 62
  augmenting 62
  correcting 62
stemming algorithm 61
stemming, Lucene 8
StopFilterFactory 55, 65
stop words
  filtering 65
store 144
strdist(x,y,alg) 163
stream.body parameter 78
stream.file parameter 78, 352
stream.type parameter 101, 102
stream.url parameter 78
str element 114

string distance
  calculating 163
string field type 71, 132, 195
sub-entities, DIH 96
sub-queries
  about 127
  example 127
  prohibited clauses, limitations 128
sub-query syntax 123
substring indexing 67
sub(x,y), mathematical primitives 161
Suggester 220, 223
sum(x,y,z,...), mathematical primitives 161
sunspot:solr:stop command 318
Sunspot 322
sunspot_rails gem 314
  about 314
  edits, making 320, 321
  MyFaves project, setting up 315
  MyFaves relational database, populating
    316, 317, 318
  MyFaves website, finishing 320
  Solr indexes, building from relational data-
    base 318, 319
SWAP command 260
SweetSpotSimilarity 151
Swing 295
synonym
  about 63
  index-time, versus query-time 64, 65
  sample analyzer configuration line 63
  with index-time 64
SynonymFilter 64
system changes, complex systems
  scale deep 331
  scale horizontally 331
  scale up 331

T

<title/> tag 323
<tokenizer> element 57
element 26, 41
tailing
  HTTP server request style logs 250
taxonomy 194
TemplateTransformer 93

term 50
term position 55
term proximity 129
term query parser 135, 189
terms, Lucene 8
TermVector component 243, 345
termVectors, field options 44, 233
text analysis 13
  about 50
  character filters 55
  configuration 51, 52
  experimenting with 54, 55
  phonetic sounds-like analysis 66
  stemming 61, 62
  stop words 65
  substring indexing 67
  synonyms 63
  text, sorting 71
  token filters 72
  tokenization 57
  uses 50
  wildcards 67
  WordDelimiterFilter 59
text analysis, Lucene 8
text analyzer, Lucene 8
text and metadata
  extracting, from files 100, 101
text_en_splitting field type 54, 60
  configuration 51, 52
text indexing technology 67
Text Search
  URL 11
text sorting 71
tf, scoring factors 148
threads attribute 91
thresholdTokenFrequency, IndexBased-
    SpellChecker options 212
tie parameter 152
Tika 100
TikaEntityProcessor 13, 92, 98
Tika project
  URL 101
tika-test sub-entity 97
timeAllowed parameter 360
title_commonGrams 346
toggle all fields option 282
token filters

about 52, 72
ASCIIFoldingFilterFactory 72
CapitalizationFilterFactory 72
ClassicFilterFactory 72
EnglishPossessiveFilterFactory 72
KeepWordFilterFactory 72
LengthFilterFactory 72
LimitTokenCountFilterFactory 72
LowerCaseFilterFactory 72
PatternReplaceFilterFactory 73
RemoveDuplicatesTokenFilterFactory 72
TrimFilterFactory 72
WordDelimeterFilterFactory 72
tokenization
  about 57
  language detection 59
tokenizer
  about 51, 52, 57
  ClassicTokenizerFactory 57
  KeywordTokenizerFactory 57
  LetterTokenizerFactory 58
  LowerCaseTokenizerFactory 58
  PathHierarchyTokenizerFactory 58
  PatternTokenizerFactory 58
  StandardTokenizerFactory 57
  UAX29URLEmailTokenizer 57
  WhitespaceTokenizerFactory 57
  WikipediaTokenizerFactory 58
tokenizerFactory attribute 63
tokens 8, 57
topN parameter 324
top (Unix) 330
TPS
  about 330
  optimizing 330
track_PUID 33
tracks 31
Transactions Per Second. See TPS
transformers attribute 93
transformers, DIH
  about 93
  ClobTransformer 93
  DateFormatTransformer 93
  HTMLStripTransformer 93
  LogTransformer 93
  NumberFormatTransformer 93
  RegexTransformer 93

ScriptTransformer 93
TemplateTransformer 93
TrieDateField 160
TrieIntField 42
TrimFilterFactory token filter 72
TRM 168
troubleshooting
  queries 149-151
  scoring 149-151
tr parameter 305
type attribute 52

U

<uniqueKey> 49
/update request handler 23
UAX29URLEmailTokenizer tokenizer 57
UIMAUpdateProcessorFactory 109
unique key 49, 106, 343
Unix mkfifo command 85
UNLOAD command 261
update.chain parameter 109
UpdateProcessorFactory 109
UpdateRequestProcessor 75, 94, 134
update request processor chain
  updating 109
uprefix, Solr Cell parameters 103
URL
  parsing 116, 117
URLDataSource 90
username parameter 328
useSolrAddSchema 97
UX Design Pattern Library 173

V

val_ pseudo-field hack 158
Varnish 337
v.base_dir parameter 279
Velocity
  URL 24
version parameter 121
Vigilog
  URL 253

W

warmupTime statistic 339

WAR (Web application archive) file 247
Web Hook
  URL 91
web.xml
  customizing, in Jetty 271
  editing 270
weightBuckets 224
WhitespaceTokenizerFactory
    tokenizer 57, 59
Wiki 27, 239, 339
WikipediaTokenizerFactory tokenizer 58
wildcard queries, query syntax
  about 129, 130
  fuzzy queries 131
wildcards
  about 67
  ReversedWildcardFilter 68
will_paginate gem 315
wolframapha
  URL 164
WordDelimeterFilterFactory 52, 55, 57, 59
word-grams. *See* **shingling**
WordNet 63
writer type 121
wt parameter 121, 279, 305
wt=phps URL parameter 309
wt=ruby parameter 313

X

XInclude 34, 259
XML 7. *See* **also Solr's Update-XML format**
  importing, from file with XSLT 96
XML-based commands
  sending 80
XML elements
  1st 114
  arr 114
  bool 115
  date 115
  double 114
  float 114
  int 114
  long 114
  str 114
XML files, posted to Solr monitor.xml 19
XML Inclusions. *See* **XInclude**

XML response format
  <lst name= 115
  about 115
  maxScore 115
  numFound 115
  QTime 115
  start 115
  status 115
  URL, parsing 116, 117
XPathEntityProcessor 92
xpath, Solr Cell parameters 103
XSLT
  used, for Solr exposure via OpenSearch 305
xsltCacheLifetimeSeconds parameter 306
XSLT file 97

Z

Zappos 7

Thank you for buying
Apache Solr 3 Enterprise Search Server

About Packt Publishing

Packt, pronounced 'packed', published its first book "*Mastering phpMyAdmin for Effective MySQL Management*" in April 2004 and subsequently continued to specialize in publishing highly focused books on specific technologies and solutions.

Our books and publications share the experiences of your fellow IT professionals in adapting and customizing today's systems, applications, and frameworks. Our solution based books give you the knowledge and power to customize the software and technologies you're using to get the job done. Packt books are more specific and less general than the IT books you have seen in the past. Our unique business model allows us to bring you more focused information, giving you more of what you need to know, and less of what you don't.

Packt is a modern, yet unique publishing company, which focuses on producing quality, cutting-edge books for communities of developers, administrators, and newbies alike. For more information, please visit our website: www.packtpub.com.

About Packt Open Source

In 2010, Packt launched two new brands, Packt Open Source and Packt Enterprise, in order to continue its focus on specialization. This book is part of the Packt Open Source brand, home to books published on software built around Open Source licences, and offering information to anybody from advanced developers to budding web designers. The Open Source brand also runs Packt's Open Source Royalty Scheme, by which Packt gives a royalty to each Open Source project about whose software a book is sold.

Writing for Packt

We welcome all inquiries from people who are interested in authoring. Book proposals should be sent to author@packtpub.com. If your book idea is still at an early stage and you would like to discuss it first before writing a formal book proposal, contact us; one of our commissioning editors will get in touch with you.

We're not just looking for published authors; if you have strong technical skills but no writing experience, our experienced editors can help you develop a writing career, or simply get some additional reward for your expertise.

Apache Axis2
Web Services
2nd Edition

Create secure, reliable, and easy-to-use web services using Apache Axis2

Deepal Jayasinghe
Afkham Azeez   [PACKT] open source *

Apache Axis2 Web Services, 2nd Edition

ISBN: 978-1-84951-156-8   Paperback: 308 pages

Create secure, reliable, and easy-to-use web services using Apache Axis2

1. Extensive and detailed coverage of the enterprise ready Apache Axis2 Web Services / SOAP / WSDL engine

2. Attain a more flexible and extensible framework with the world class Axis2 architecture

3. Learn all about AXIOM - the complete XML processing framework, which you also can use outside Axis2

Quick answers to common problems

Apache Solr 3.1
Cookbook

Over 100 recipes to discover new ways to work with Apache's Enterprise Search Server

Rafał Kuć   [ ] open source *

Apache Solr 3.1 Cookbook

ISBN: 978-1-84951-218-3   Paperback: 300 pages

Over 100 recipes to discover new ways to work with Apache's Enterprise Search Server

1. Improve the way in which you work with Apache Solr to make your search engine quicker and more effective

2. Deal with performance, setup, and configuration problems in no time

3. Discover little-known Solr functionalities and create your own modules to customize Solr to your company's needs

4. Part of Packt's Cookbook series; each chapter covers a different aspect of working with Solr

Please check **www.PacktPub.com** for information on our titles

Apache Maven 3 Cookbook

ISBN: 978-1-84951-244-2   Paperback: 224 pages

Over 50 recipes towards optimal Java Software Engineering with Maven 3

1. Grasp the fundamentals and extend Apache Maven 3 to meet your needs

2. Implement engineering practices in your application development process with Apache Maven

3. Collaboration techniques for Agile teams with Apache Maven

4. Use Apache Maven with Java, Enterprise Frameworks, and various other cutting-edge technologies

Apache Wicket Cookbook

ISBN: 978-1-84951-160-5   Paperback: 312 pages

Master Wicket by example by implementing real-life solutions to every day tasks

1. The Apache Wicket Cookbook covers the full spectrum of features offered by the Wicket web framework

2. Implement advanced user interactions by following the live examples given in this Cookbook

3. Create reusable components and speed up your web application development

Please check **www.PacktPub.com** for information on our titles

Made in the USA
Lexington, KY
14 May 2013